# THE
# SEVENTEENTH
# CENTURY

# THE
# SEVENTEENTH
# CENTURY

*Studies in the History of*
*English Thought and Literature*
*from Bacon to Pope*

BY

RICHARD FOSTER JONES

*and Others Writing*
*in His Honor*

Stanford University Press
Stanford, California
London: Oxford University Press

This volume was conceived by friends of Richard Foster Jones during the 1948 meeting of the Modern Language Association, and was presented to him in 1951, on the occasion of his sixty-fifth birthday. The academic affiliations of the contributors are given as they were at that time.

## CONTENTS

v

# RICHARD FOSTER JONES

## Marjorie Nicolson

S CHOLARS are seldom pioneers. For the most part we build upon the work of our predecessors, "line upon line, here a little and there a little," emending, disputing, occasionally adding our cubit to the stature of knowledge. In methodology, too, most of us are derivative, following patterns laid down by teachers or scholars under whose influence we have fallen. But fortunately for the advancement of learning, once in a while a pathfinder appears to blaze out new trails, to lead us along different paths to new countries of the mind. Richard Foster Jones has been one of the most important pioneers of my generation.

Modern graduate students, reading "The Background of *The Battle of the Books*" condensed in this volume, may wonder why we have republished it thirty years after it was written. It may well seem obvious to them, in part because they are familiar with the fuller development in Mr. Jones's *Ancients and Moderns*, in part because many of their undergraduate teachers, whether they read the early monograph or not, are familiar with its conclusions. The more obvious it seems today, the greater the tribute to R. F. Jones. It was radical three decades ago.

The long essay appeared in *Washington University Studies* in April 1920, preceding by a few weeks or months J. B. Bury's *Idea of Progress*. In an attempt to think myself back to an era in scholarship before these works came as an illumination, I went to *The Cambridge History of English Literature* and reread the volumes on the seventeenth and eighteenth centuries (for the first time, I am sure, since I read them in preparation for Doctors' orals!). I turned first to George Atherton Aitken's chapter

I

on Swift in order to determine the "accepted attitude" toward Swift's mock-epic in 1913, when Volume IX of the *History* appeared. The "Battle of the Books," I found, was a quarrel about ancient and modern learning, in which Sir William Temple played a part. After a brief statement to that effect, Mr. Aitken added: "The controversy has now lost its interest." A few lines farther on, I read: "Among Swift's satires, the fragmentary *Battle of the Books* is relatively so little remembered that its main features may be here recalled." There follows a two-page outline of the parody. Mr. Aitken naturally missed the real meaning and emphasis of Swift's work, "so little remembered" in 1913. In the same volume J. W. Adamson treated Swift briefly and Temple more fully in his chapter on "Education." He discussed the English "Battle of the Books" in relation to the French "Querelle," but it is clear that in his mind both the English and the French battles were originally and primarily literary quarrels. "The contrast between the two ages," said Mr. Adamson, "was limited first to letters, and it was this particular field which subsequently displayed the English 'squabble,' as Swift called it." Although Mr. Adamson twice mentioned Sprat's *History of the Royal Society* elsewhere, he made no connection between its publication and the battle in which Temple found himself overcome by the opposition. His major emphasis was upon the "Phalaris controversy," and his conclusion not fundamentally different from that of Mr. Aitken: "This particular 'squabble' is now even more outworn than the greater issue of which it is a part."

Mr. Jones first made clear to my generation that the English "Battle" was no pale reflection of the French "Querelle," that it was, indeed, a peculiarly English Battle, the background of which must be sought in science and philosophy rather than in belles-lettres. We had been only vaguely aware, I think, how much less *belles-lettristic* than his French contemporary was the seventeenth-century Englishman, living in the "Century of Revolutions" as well as the "Century of Genius," forced to concern himself with literature less as literature than as religious, political, philosophical, scientific propaganda. In 1920 few of us had considered the significance of the fact that, in an age of academies, the French established a French Academy, the English a Royal Society, which, though they had common origins, had already begun to go their separate ways, the one to concern itself largely with establishment of standards in literature, the other with the advancement of philosophical and scientific learning. Indeed, most literary students in 1920 knew little or nothing about the Royal Society, which seemed an organization completely separate from the literary life of the time. *The Cambridge History of English Literature* did not entirely neglect the history of science. The names of Galileo and Kepler, Harvey and Gilbert, Descartes and Newton were mentioned occasionally, though usually in sections on education and learning rather than in chapters on men of letters. In the penultimate chapter of the eighth volume, I found a brief statement of the foundation of the Royal Society, in which the author, A. E. Shipley, F.R.S., was clearly reading the accounts of the early Society from the perspective of his own membership in an organization that has developed a specifically scientific emphasis in modern times. From Mr. Shipley's account, the reader would infer that the only man of letters connected with the Royal Society was Abraham Cowley. It was R. F. Jones who began to make literary students aware of the important impact of the Society upon letters in general and the Battle of the Books in particular, who showed us that the English Battle was only one skirmish in a long warfare between "ancient" and "modern" which, even in the seventeenth century, was settling into the feud between "science" and "the humanities" so familiar today.

During my rereading of the *Cambridge History*, I had in mind Mr. Jones's later articles on science and prose style as well as his treatment of the Battle of the Books, though here comparison was less justifiable, since the articles on prose style began to appear a decade after the early "Background," nearly twenty years after the publication of the *History*. I found a good deal of interest in "style" among the contributors to the *Cambridge History*, though it was often confined to analysis of the style of an individual writer, and the word was usually used in connection with poetry rather than with prose. Although the historians occasionally commented on the change that came over prose style during the seventeenth century, few of them attempted to account for the change. Harold Routh went further than most of his fellow critics when he wrote in his chapter on Addison and Steele: "Men had confined their literary interests to the library and, as a consequence, their style was either ponderous or precious. The Royal Society had already started a movement against redundance of phrase, but it may well be doubted whether the protests of Spratt [*sic*], Evelyn, and South would have had lasting effect without the influence of the coffee houses."

It is customary today to consider R. F. Jones's work under the general methodology we call "the history of ideas." In the sense in which we apply that term to such a book as *The Great Chain of Being*, it is not entirely appropriate to the approach Jones developed for himself. There is little question that his influence has merged with that of A. O. Lovejoy in developing the methodology we know today, though if there was any influence of Lovejoy on Jones, it came late rather than early in Jones's scholarly career. In 1920 Professor Lovejoy had published none of the books and articles through which his name became so familiar to students of literature. The early papers, in which we now find germs of the later idea, were scattered in journals seldom seen by literary students, who in 1920 did not comb bibliography in allied fields as assiduously as they do today. Jones's emphasis in his early work and in his first articles on prose style was more specific in its approach than the more general "history of ideas": during the first two decades of his scholarly career, he was concerned with one particular aspect of intellectual history—the scientific background of seventeenth-century literature.

I do not know how he happened upon this field, so novel at the time. The Columbia records of his generation were sparser than they are today, and nothing I can discover in the files sheds light on possible "influences." His doctoral dissertation on Lewis Theobald, published in 1918, was still in the conventional mold, yet by 1920 he had developed an entirely new approach. Carson Duncan's *New Science and English Literature* had been published as early as 1913, but, privately printed and not frequently available in libraries, it had met with no such reception as its originality deserved. It is probable that Mr. Jones discovered it, as did I, after its usefulness to him was past. Dorothy Stimson's *Gradual Acceptance of the Copernican Theory*, published in 1917—another important "pioneer" work of the same general period, as important in its way as Jones's "Background" study in its—was complementary rather than similar in its approach. Morris Croll published his important and influential essays on seventeenth-century prose style before Richard Jones's first article on the subject appeared, but Mr. Croll dealt almost entirely with classical rhetorical models and rhetorical practices, Mr. Jones with the impact of science. If R. F. Jones had an "onlie begetter," I suspect it may have been J. E. Spingarn, whose introduction to his *Critical Essays of the Seventeenth Century* is the most illuminating study of the period published during the first quarter of our century. Each time I reread that introduction I am impressed by its "modernity." When I remember that it had been in print for five years before the corresponding volume of *The Cambridge History of English Literature* appeared, I wonder more than ever at the conventional and antiquated position of many contributors to that volume. Because of his self-imposed limits, Spingarn did not discuss the Battle of the Books in detail, but he was aware that it was more than a literary quarrel. He was familiar with Hakewill; he had much to say of the *virtuosi*; he was well informed about Sprat's *History* and recognized some interplay of science and literature in connection with the Royal Society. His long section on "The Trend Toward Simplicity" went further than any other work of the first quarter-century in its analysis of the complex causes that produced "simplicity" in other aspects of life as well as style. But while Spingarn may well have been an influence, it was, I imagine, the temper of the times rather than any particular author that led R. F. Jones to blaze the trail that led to new countries of scholarship he made peculiarly his own.

The first World War made men more conscious than laymen had been since the mid-Victorian period of the impact of science upon their own lives, leading them to more sympathetic understanding of the problems of men in the first great scientific era, who experienced the clash of pessimism and optimism. It is not surprising that the 1920's saw the inception of new and important works in the history of science, in which the roots were traced more fully and the word "science" interpreted more broadly than before. The first volume of Lynn Thorndike's monumental *History of Magic and Experimental Science* appeared in 1923, the first volume of George Sarton's *History of Science* in 1927, Dampier-Whetham's *History of Science and Its Relations with Philosophy and Religion* in 1929. J. H. Randall's *Making of the Modern Mind*, the first version of which appeared early in the 'twenties, paid more attention to the development of science than had preceding books of the kind—if indeed there were preceding books of that particular kind. As I look back to publications that made science "come home to men's business and bosoms" in the 1920's, three stand out vividly: Alfred North Whitehead's *Science and the Modern World*, which has not been surpassed, I think, in the twenty-five years since it was published; I. A. Richards' *Science and Poetry*, which inaugurated a controversy that is still being carried on by literary critics; and— perhaps most influential of all, so far as lay imagination was concerned—Bertrand Russell's *A Free Man's Worship*. Each of these, in different ways, led imagination back from the twentieth to the seventeenth century, when the basic preconceptions of that modern world were being established. In each of them some members of my generation found the seeds of a despair more profound than anything we have heard from the apostles of pessimism in our present Atomic Age. We were living, we were told, in an alien universe, a universe from which magic, myth, religion, and purpose had been banished. From such books as these (not to mention Bernard Shaw's *Back to Methuselah!*) our contemporary Joseph Wood Krutch drew the disillusion he expressed in *The Modern Temper*, widely read and hotly debated when it was published in 1929.

In spite of the increasing interest in science in general during the 1920's, however, literary scholarship was not really widely affected by the new temper until the next decade, and such studies as Mr. Jones's and Miss Stimson's remained almost unique. In the 1930's the new method began to come into its own, developing with such rapidity after 1935 that it is now one of the most popular "modern" approaches to literature. The best evidence that "literary-scientific relations" has become a respectable field for research and criticism may be seen in the fact that in 1939 the Modern Language Association of America—well known for caution in such matters—recognized as a discussion group "General Topics VII," a study of the reflections of natural science in literature. At every subsequent meeting of the group, an able and active bibliography committee supplied the members with mimeographed sheets of studies in the field. During the decade of the 'forties, 1,300 items appeared on those lists, nearly all of them books and articles published since 1930. In 1949, Fred Dudley, with the assistance of three other editors, prepared a more formal bibliography: "The Relations of Literature and Science: A Selected Bibliography 1930–1949," consisting of 647 entries selected from the more random 1,300 titles. We had sown the wind and are reaping the whirlwind.

Unlike some scholarly adventurers who have merely pointed a way, R. F. Jones has gone on to explore and map the countries he discovered. If there were limitations in his early works—he would be the first to acknowledge them—he himself has corrected them. His *Ancients and Moderns*, published sixteen years after the "Background," will remain a definitive work, proving beyond the possibility of doubt the thesis he proposed in his early study: the great importance of the new science in the English quarrel between ancient and modern. Each year, as Master's essays and doctoral dissertations pass through my hands, and as I read the scholarly periodicals, I find fresh evidence of the extent to which this work has become an "authority," accepted so widely that students and scholars draw from it as a matter of course, many of them neglecting to say (as does Miriam Starkman in her recent study of Swift's *Tale*): "The reader will readily see my great indebtedness to Richard Foster Jones." *Ancients and Moderns* is filled with learning, but it is equally rich in wisdom. Like all Jones's work, impartial and objective in its reporting and weighing of historical facts, it nevertheless exhibits the author's sincere love of "the humanities," shown again and again in his affectionate treatment of old defenses of the humanities that he rightly feels the world should not willingly let die.

As he expanded his early study of the Battle of the Books, so he has developed his first essays on prose style, correcting what may well have seemed an overemphasis on science in general and the Royal Society in particular. The purpose of the first article, "Science and English Prose Style in the Third Quarter of the Seventeenth Century," was "to show that the attacks on the old, as well as the formulation of a new style find consistent expression in those associated with the new science." But even in that essay, in which science seemed to him "the most important influence instrumental in changing the luxuriant prose of the Commonwealth into that of a diametrically opposite nature in the Restoration," Mr. Jones was fully aware that "style" is not simple but extraordinarily complex, as complex indeed as human personality, and that no easy answer will serve to explain the abrupt change in the seventeenth century. Shortly after the publication of Jones's first two articles other scholars—notably Francis Johnson—showed that the supposedly "new" self-consciousness of scientific writers concerning prose style was not new with Bacon and his contemporaries. Morris Croll's brilliant articles on seventeenth-century rhetoric, neglected during the 1920's, began to come into their own in the 1930's, serving in their way, too, to correct an overemphasis upon any one aspect of the complicated change in a complex century. W. Fraser Mitchell's *English Pulpit Eloquence from Andrewes to Tillotson* appeared in 1932. In their various ways these authors showed what Mr. Jones himself was quite willing to grant—that there were other causes than science for the "Attack on Pulpit Eloquence." In those days, before Professor Haller had shown that there were almost as many "varieties" of Puritanism as Professor Lovejoy's "varieties of Romanticism," it was easier than now to generalize about the part played by something we broadly and vaguely called "Puritanism." Mr. Jones's attempt to determine more fully the extent to which "Puritanism" was or was not responsible for the change in prose style led him to one of the latest of his published works: "The Moral Sense of Simplicity."

In the earlier articles Jones had studied the opposition between what Bacon called "manner" and "matter." In this study he concerned himself with another opposition apparent among

the religious and theological writers of the sixteenth and seventeenth centuries: that between "eloquentia" and "doctrina." The
published study, lengthy though it is, is but a small part of the
great task that Mr. Jones set himself, a task involving the reading
of hundreds, perhaps thousands, of sermons and other minor
writing published in that most prolific age of ephemeral literature. We are eagerly awaiting his forthcoming work in which,
I believe, all the strands will be woven together into an intricate
yet revealing pattern, in which we shall see, morely clearly than
ever before, the parts played by both theology and science in
bringing about the most spectacular change that has occurred in
the history of English prose. As *Ancients and Moderns* marked
the climax of his work on the Battle of the Books, this volume
will, I am sure, be the crown and summit of all the work on prose
style.

No tribute to Richard Foster Jones would be complete that
did not include Lucile Jones. Years ago, in speaking lightly of
the limitations of my own sex in the realm of scholarship, I said
that our trouble is that women have no wives! I was undoubtedly thinking of the Joneses, whom I first met in 1927, when the
three of us happened to occupy adjoining seats in Row F in the
British Museum Reading Room. Long before I knew who they
were, I envied the husband-and-wife team, working so smoothly
and efficiently together, as I have envied them ever since at the
Huntington and other great libraries. R. F. Jones has been fortunate in many things but in nothing more than in his wife, who
—in the finest sense of a word that we are unfortunately losing
from our modern vocabulary—has been the truest of "help-
mates." This volume is dedicated by their friends and fellow
workers to Richard and Lucile Jones:

> Never must you be divided, in our ranks you
> move together,
> Pioneers, O Pioneers!

# THE BACKGROUND OF
## *THE BATTLE OF THE BOOKS**

Richard Foster Jones

ITHERTO, scholars have held that the controversy over the relative merits of the ancients and the moderns, which inspired Swift's satire, was imported from France and was concerned chiefly with oratory and poetry. The present study upholds the thesis that the controversy for the most part sprang from native sources and was philosophic and scientific rather than literary and artistic in nature. Only those stages of the conflict are considered in which at least one definite protagonist on either side appears. These are three in number: the controversy over the theory of the decay of nature with Godfrey Goodman and George Hakewill as opposing heroes; the controversy over the Royal Society with Henry Stubbe opposed by Thomas Sprat and Joseph Glanvill; and the quarrel over ancient and modern learning in which Temple and Boyle faced Wotton and Bentley. Besides introducing other figures of less importance, I shall treat the literary aspect of the conflict, though definite champions of the moderns in literature are not so apparent.

The man largely responsible for creating the war was Sir Francis Bacon, and his spirit directed the campaign through the whole of the seventeenth century. Opposing the authority of the ancients in science and attacking the blind followers of Aristotle and the corrupters of his philosophy, Bacon proposed

* Reprinted from *Washington University Studies*, VII, Humanistic Series II (1920), by permission of the publishers. Parts I, II, and III abridged by the author; Part IV reprinted with minor adaptations.

his method as a means whereby man could rise far above the ancients in knowledge and well-being. His method involved a natural history, composed of data gathered over a wide field by means of direct observation and experiment; the application of an inductive method of reasoning to these data; and insistence upon a doubting attitude of mind and upon the necessity of experiments until all doubts should be removed. He confidently opposed his method to all the scientific knowledge antiquity could offer, and his unwavering faith was caught up by others and went ringing down the century driving back forever the ghosts of Aristotelian natural philosophy. The method produced the controversy.

I. THE CONTROVERSY OVER THE DECAY OF NATURE

The first definite quarrel between the ancients and the moderns occurred over the theory which asserted that men were living in the old age of the universe in which all nature was decaying. Belief in this theory found innumerable expressions in the latter part of the sixteenth and the first part of the seventeenth century and it continued to be noticed beyond the middle of the eighteenth. Its chief exponent, however, was a clergyman, Godfrey Goodman, who later became Bishop of Gloucester, and who in *The Fall of Man, or the Corruption of Nature Proved by Natural Reason,* 1616, held that corruption was introduced into all nature through the fall of man. The argument which Goodman brought forth to support his thesis was based largely upon two theories. The first asserted that the farther a creature departed from the first mold, the more imperfect it became, just as a stream becomes more defiled the farther it goes from its source. The second argued that since parts of the world, such as plants and animals, passed through various stages to the decay of old age, so the universe must partake of the nature of its parts and experience decrepitude. Again and again he introduces the analogy with man's life, in the progress and decay of which are mirrored the infancy, prime, and decay of nature as a whole. Though relying heavily on reason alone, Goodman cites a number of authorities, especially the Bible and St. Cyprian.

He did not, however, compare specifically the ancients and moderns, beyond claiming that all the learning which the world possessed came from the former.

Modernity found a champion in George Hakewill, a kinsman of Sir Thomas Bodley and Archdeacon of Surrey, whose book, *An Apologie or Declaration of the Power and Providence of God in the Government of the World, Consisting in an Examination and Censure of the Common Errour Touching Nature's Perpetual and Universal Decay*, 1627, reached a third enlarged edition in 1635. Believing that he had embarked upon a wholly uncharted sea, Hakewill sought assistance from his many friends and acquaintances both in and outside the universities, as well as ransacking the learning of antiquity, the Middle Ages, and the Renaissance. He attributed the glorifying of the ancients to the habit which the classical poets had of praising past times at the expense of present times, and especially to their invention of the four ages. He is keenly aware of the depressing influence which belief in the decay of nature exerted upon his contemporaries: "For being once thoroughly persuaded in themselves, that by a fatall kinde of necessitie and course of times, they are cast into those straights, that notwithstanding all their striving and industrie, it is impossible they should rise to the pitch of their noble and renowned Predecessors, they begin to yield to the times and to necessitie, being resolved that their endeavours are all in vaine, and that they strive against the streame." Hakewill stoutly maintains that the moderns are in no respect inferior to the ancients; that there is no such thing as natural superiority or inferiority determined by the time at which men live. Against the idea of the progressive decay of all nature he proposes his idea of "circular progress": "There is (it seems) both in wits and Arts, as in all things besides, a kinde of circular progress: they have their birth, their growth, their flourishing, their failing, their fading, and within a while after their resurrection and reflourishing againe."

Hakewill divides his comprehensive book into four parts, the first of which is introductory and treats of the alleged decay in general. The second deals with the idea that the heavens, elements, and elementary bodies are decaying. The third takes up the question of man in respect to longevity, strength, stature, wit, and arts. The fourth upholds modern improvements in manners, especially as regards virtue, and attempts to prove a "future consumation of the world." Since the controversy between the ancients and the moderns was later restricted largely to man's mental power and accomplishments, we are chiefly concerned with that portion of the book which treats of "Arts and Wits." Hakewill attempts to show the superiority of the moderns in imagination, judgment, and memory, in the discussion of which he cites the importance of printing as an aid to learning. The next four chapters exhibit the question as it was generally presented throughout the century. The field of man's achievements is divided into four large areas which in turn are subdivided. Superiority is accorded the moderns in divinity, law, and medicine, in respect to the last of which Paracelsian chemistry and the increased knowledge of anatomy are emphasized. The moderns are considered superior in history because of the improved knowledge of chronology and geography, are not much inferior in poetry, and equal, if they do not surpass, the Romans in arms, fortifications, and strategy. The moderns excel in grammar, but are surpassed in rhetoric. In logic also they are inferior because of the wrangling of the schoolmen. In arguing modern superiority in mathematics, Hakewill introduced an essay of his friend, Mr. Briggs, professor of geometry at Oxford, in which especial attention is called to Copernicus' theory, Galileo's telescope, and certain mathematical discoveries. After granting superiority to the moderns in metaphysics, he says that physics, or natural history, was enriched by Aristotle but is defective in the historical part. Then follows a passage which is significant in showing the only influence that Bacon seems to have exerted on the book: "And for the speculative, both himself [Aristotle] and his followers seeme to referre it rather to *profession* and disputation, matter of wit and credit, than use and practice. It is therefore a noble and worthy endeavour of my Lord of St. Albanes so to mixe and temper practice and speculation together, that they may march hand in hand, and mutually embrace and assist each other. Speculation by precepts and infallible conclusions preparing a way to *Practice*, and

*Practice* again perfecting *Speculation.*" In agriculture, horsemanship, and heraldry the moderns have improved upon the practice of the ancients, whereas in navigation they have far surpassed the ancients through their possession of the compass. Without claiming superiority for the moderns in painting, he mentions Angelo, Raphael, Vasari, Heliad, and especially Dürer of Nuremberg, and the best he can say for the moderns in architecture is that they sometimes vary from ancient rules with good discretion. The last chapter of the third book is devoted to discoveries and inventions, with most of the emphasis placed upon printing, gunpowder, and the compass, "of which Cardane comparatively speaks in high tearmes—all antiquity can boast of nothing equal to these three. Upon these then will I insist, and with these conclude this comparison of the Arts and Wits." More than one-fourth of this section of the work is devoted to showing the effects of these inventions upon the world and to proving that their invention belonged to the moderns.

Hakewill was little influenced by Bacon. His idea of circular progress had been opposed by Bacon; he ascribed the three inventions mentioned above to modern "wit," though Bacon had attributed them to chance and opportunity; and he noticed only in passing the method which Bacon proposed as capable of raising the moderns above the ancients. Yet his influence upon subsequent phases of the quarrel was second only to Bacon's. Bacon determined the bone of contention; he disclosed the issue that was at stake, but he did not hand on to his disciples any means of upholding the new philosophy, besides faith in the idea and the compelling appeal to reason. Hakewill showed how a tangible basis of comparison might be obtained by observing discoveries and inventions. He established for the whole controversy the method of comparing men and accomplishments in particular fields, thus analyzing the problem and making the issue clear-cut. In this he was followed by Glanvill, who in turn was followed by Wotton. Even though the next phase of the quarrel centered around the Royal Society, Glanvill did not hesitate to bring forward in its support discoveries that had nothing to do with it, except that they were modern.

Like Bacon, Hakewill emphasizes the philosophic and scientific nature of the quarrel. The very nature of his task required Hakewill to consider painting, architecture, oratory, and poetry, but his defense of the moderns in these fields is brief and faint-hearted. In most cases he really concedes ancient superiority. Most of his discussion of poetry is devoted to an attempt to prove Latin verse superior to Greek, a thesis that is pertinent to the question of progressive decay, but not to that of the relative merits of the ancients and the moderns. The inventive part of Sidney's *Arcadia*, he says, is not very much inferior to ancient verse, and Ariosto, Tasso, du Bartas, and Spenser are not much inferior to Virgil. Hakewill is not interested in poetry or the arts; science, philosophy, learning, and, above all, inventions are the matters to be discussed. These represent the point of conflict; the arts are introduced only to preserve the completeness of the design. There was, however, one writer during the period who applied the theory of the decay of nature to poetry. Henry Reynolds, in *Mythomystes* (1633?) laments the senility of the world and tries to show the "depth of the Ancients above our Modern Poets."

## II. THE CONTROVERSY OVER THE ROYAL SOCIETY

In 1660 the Royal Society was founded, though it did not receive its charter from the King until two years later. Since this society was founded squarely upon the philosophy and suggestions of Sir Francis Bacon, an intense debate as to the respective merits of the old science and the new philosophy soon arose. In general, the adherents of the Baconian philosophy were on the defensive, but they conducted a very aggressive defense. Some enthusiastic devotees of the method went so far as to express the opinion that nothing could be accomplished unless all ancient arts were rejected and their nurseries abolished; that everything that wore the face of antiquity should be destroyed, root and branch. But the upholders of the old philosophy were just as intolerant, and so violent were their attacks that when Thomas Sprat published his *History of the Royal Society*, 1667, it was more an apology than a history. Sprat takes up the controversy where Bacon had left it. Of Hakewill he seems ignorant. In his defense of the new philosophy he derives most of his argument from Sir Francis. Like his predecessor, he is willing to let the ancients rule supreme in everything except the method to be used in natural science. He pleads the superiority of a method that is active, not disputative, applied to things, not lost in words, and more interested in conquering nature than in overcoming an opponent.

The first part of Sprat's book gives a short history of learning from the Assyrians and the Egyptians to the Renaissance. The second, which alone justifies the title of the book, tells of the establishment of the Society, describes the method employed, and gives some typical transactions. Much of the book introduces matter irrelevant to the controversy in which we are interested, for not only did upholders of the ancients attack the new enterprise, but conservative elements in general set themselves in opposition to it. Sprat found it necessary to combat the charge that the Society was instigating a material, or mechanical, education in place of a humanistic one; the charge that it sought to supplant divine revelation by emphasizing the law of cause and effect; and the charge of elevating material things above the things of the spirit. He advocates the inclusion of experimental sciences in the school curriculum, and he avoids the difficulties raised by the religious issues by frankly separating material and spiritual things, and by emphasizing the support that reason may lend religion.

In defending the Society against the upholders of antiquity, Sprat insists that the Baconians have no intention of disgracing the merits of the ancients, but only of destroying their authority and of giving them no more than their due. However, he criticizes the ancient philosophers for dogmatizing and for their syllogistic reasoning which depended upon uncertain general axioms. In all this he follows Bacon faithfully, repeating the same objections to the old philosophy and citing the same virtues of the new. The method is Sprat's slogan. It is the method he opposes to antiquity. It is not upon the accomplishments of the moderns, as it was with Hakewill, that he bases their superiority. In his book he gives some typical experiments, not to show the results obtained but to illustrate the method employed. Against antiquity he advances the present method and future results. Like Bacon, he stakes his all upon the results that will be obtained. He "saw the vision of the world and all the wonder that would be." In places the enthusiasm of the faith moves him to eloquence: "The Beautiful Bosom of Nature will be Expos'd to our view: we shall enter into its Garden, and taste of its Fruits, and satisfy ourselves with its plenty: instead of Idle talking, and wandering, under its fruitless shadows; as the Peripatetics did in their first institution, and their successors have done ever since." And the thought of what the modern world might then be enjoying, had men of former ages followed the method, intensifies his resentment against the disputative, notional philosophy of the past.

The quarrel continues scientific and philosophical in nature; no literary element is descernible. Sprat seems to have considered ancient poetry superior to modern, though he proposes that the Society establish an academy to purify the English language, and he maintains that the experimental philosophy will furnish poetry finer ornaments than the fables and outworn fictions of the ancients.

The *History* intensified the controversy over the Royal Society. As the result of a tirade against the body overheard in a conversation, Joseph Glanvill wrote in defense of the Society a book entitled *Plus Ultra* (1668). Glanvill follows Sprat in praising the method. He belabors the "notional" philosophy of the ancients and their admirers and the uselessness and folly of their endless disputations. Against the old philosophy he advances the fruitful method of experimental science, by which things rather than words are studied, and efforts are made to promote the knowledge and happiness of mankind. The method as realized by the Royal Society inspired in him as great a zeal for its defense as in Sprat and much more disrespect for the ancients and their defenders. But Hakewill's influence on the *Plus Ultra* is no less apparent than Sprat's. The field is divided in the same way and into some of the same divisions as in the *Apologie.* Geography and arithmetic, chemistry, natural history, and history are each assigned a chapter in which modern is matched with ancient as had been done more than two score years

before. One chapter is devoted to the three inventions of printing, gunpowder, and the compass, in the discussion of which
Hakewill's account was evidently used. Discoveries, such as that
of the circulation of the blood, are used with telling effect. These
last details show how, under Hakewill's influence, Glanvill was
widening the limits of the controversy as established by Sprat.
The defense of the Royal Society broadens into a defense of
modernity against antiquity. In Glanvill the two streams flowing from Bacon and Hakewill unite, and from him the enlarged
current flows to Wotton and the end of the quarrel.

Sprat and Glanvill did not wait long for an opponent. Henry
Stubbe, a physician of Warwick, overheard an admirer of the
Royal Society denounce the uselessness of ancient medicine and
refer to *Plus Ultra* for proof. Stubbe proceeded to read Glanvill's book, whereupon he wrote *The Plus Ultra reduced to a
Non Plus*, 1670, and a little later, learning of Sprat's *History*
from Glanvill, he replied to it in *Legends no Histories*. Stubbe
tells us that he had been sympathetic to experimental science,
but that the enthusiasm with which the experimental scientists
magnified the new philosophy over all other knowledge and
their irreverent attitude toward the ancients angered him. He
accused the Society of a desire to abolish all ancient learning and
of attempting to supplant a humanistic education based upon the
classics with a material and mechanical education. In his answer
to Glanvill, Stubbe upholds the classical learning of the universities against the practical education advocated by the virtuosi,
defends the disputative philosophy of Aristotle and the Peripatetics, and emphasizes the medical knowledge of Aristotle,
Hippocrates, and Galen. He tries to limit the controversy to the
Royal Society by pointing out that some of the discoverers mentioned by Glanvill were moderns who were not members of the
Royal Society, though elsewhere he accepts the wider issue. In
*A Prefætory Answer to Henry Stubbe*, 1674, Glanvill insists
that the quarrel embraces all moderns, not the Royal Society
only. Beginning with the conflict over the method, with Bacon
versus Aristotle, the conflict has spread so as to embrace all
ancients and moderns.

Still the controversy continues scientific and philosophical.

The absence of a literary and artistic aspect is remarkable, the more so when we note what great antagonism to things ancient or modern was aroused on both sides. The upholders of modernity were satisfied to grant artistic superiority to the ancients, and rest their case upon knowledge, while the supporters of the ancients thought it preposterous to suggest the possibility of doubt regarding the arts. "I am surprised," says Stubbe with a sneer, "that Mr. Glanvill doth not make the Moderns to surpass the Ancients in Architecture, Picture, and several other Arts of ingenuous Luxury," to which Glanvill emphatically replies, "I do not believe the moderns surpass the ancients in Architecture, Picture, or the Arts of ingenuous Luxury."

### III. THE CRITICAL DILEMMA

The controversy between the ancients and moderns, particularly in the latter part of the century, was more intense in France than in England, especially as regards literature, for poetry rather than science or philosophy constituted the basis of contention. In the last two decades of the century, Charles Perrault and Fontenelle, in prose and verse, enthusiastically advanced the cause of the moderns against the ancients. Boileau, Dacier, and others took up arms for the ancients, and the battle raged. It is this battle that has been thought to have inspired the controversy in England during the last decade of the century.

The most important figure in the literary aspect of the problem as presented to the English was Dryden; yet he is so inconsistent that he can hardly be considered a champion of either moderns or ancients. In spite of his obvious inconsistencies, however, his preference for the old English dramatists over ancient, and especially French neo-classical, playwrights is apparent. Not only does he expressly state such an opinion in the dedication to *Examen Poeticum*, but even when criticizing the Elizabethans, he nowhere exalts the ancients above them except in *A Parallel of Poetry and Painting*. Yet his subscription to the rules is almost as apparent. The frequency with which he introduces Aristotle and Horace, as well as his expressed reliance upon them, and his praise of Rymer and French neo-classical critics point only one way. His criticism of the rules is not nearly so much emphasized as his agreement with them. The same inconsistent attitude is found in his contemporaries: admiration of English poets and subscription to the rules they violated. In fact, Rymer in his later criticism is the only critic of any importance who attacks the old poets, or rather who does not give them a large share of praise.

What explains this inconsistency? How does it happen that critics refuse to condemn poets who fall far short of measuring up to the standards applied? Here, I think, lies the crux of the chaotic condition of seventeenth-century criticism in England. I believe the explanation lies in the fact that the English embraced a critical creed, clearly and persuasively developed by the French, which did not justify their literary tastes, a critical creed inconsistent with their artistic feelings. The situation finds succinct expression in Dryden's statement that the French were as much better critics than the English as they were worse poets. Yet French poets followed the critics as the English did not. In *The Impartial Critic*, Dennis makes Beaumont ask whether, if Aristotle were alive, he would condemn Dryden's *Oedipus*, which Freeman had shown to violate the rules. Freeman answers, "He would condemn it, or he would be forc'd to recede from his Principles; but at the same time that he passed sentence on it, he would find it so beautiful that he could not choose but love the criminal; and he certainly would crown the Poet before he would damn the Play." Such was exactly the attitude of many of the critics of this period. They crowned with their praise the very poets they damned with their rules. Rymer, it is true, was consistent in condemning completely what the rules did not justify, but the protest he aroused indicates that he stood alone.

In this state of affairs, it was hardly possible for a controversy over the respective merits of ancient and modern poets to arise. Allegiance to the rules prevented critics from asserting the superiority of their own poets. Another factor involved was their attitude to the English language, considered for the most part a barbarous and unstable medium. The nationalistic spirit, which might be expected to support modernity, is revealed more in claiming superiority to French than to ancient writers. Furthermore, the fact that England, unlike France, did not develop a large body of criticism militated against the introduction of a literary element into the quarrel. There was, however, one definite champion of English poets, Charles Gildon, who in *Miscellaneous Letters and Essays*, 1694, came out unreservedly for English over ancient poets, but he was inspired by Dryden and provoked by Rymer. He owed nothing to the controversy in France.

## IV. THE CONTROVERSY OVER ANCIENT AND MODERN LEARNING

After a life of cautious service to his country, Sir William Temple sought the pleasures of solitude in retirement at Moor Park, where he amused himself in pruning his orchard and cultivating the learning of a gentleman rather than that of a pedant. In the course of his superficial studies he happened upon Thomas Burnet's *Sacred Theorie of the Earth*,[1] in which the controversy over the Royal Society again makes its appearance. Now Temple had from the beginning admired the old and scorned the new philosophy,[2] and two years of his life, 1663–65, had been passed in London when the controversy between the two was raging. Thus when he read Burnet's praise of modern learning he was much incensed, and a perusal of Fontenelle's *Digression sur les anciens et les modernes*, in which modern poetry is preferred to ancient, supplied the last bit of provocation needed to prompt him to write *An Essay upon the Ancient and Modern Learning*, 1690.[3]

[1] The first edition, two volumes, in Latin appeared in 1681; the second edition in English, 1684. In 1689 two more volumes were added. It was probably the second edition that inspired Temple's essay.

[2] In speaking of Temple's life at Cambridge, 1658, Macaulay says: "He made no proficiency either in the old philosophy which still lingered in the schools of Cambridge, or in the new philosophy of which Lord Bacon was the founder. But to the end of his life he continued to speak of the former with ignorant admiration, and of the latter with equally ignorant contempt." *Literary Essays* (Oxford ed., 1913), p. 421.

[3] "For the first [Burnet] could not end his learned treatise without a panegyric of modern learning and knowledge in comparison of the ancient; and the other falls so grossly into the censure of the old poetry, and preference of the new, that I could not read either of these strains without some indigna-

In tracing the origin of the quarrel, scholars have emphasized the reference to Fontenelle, and ignored the significance of the reference to Burnet. The very title of the essay shows that it was inspired by the Englishman, and its content bears mostly upon the material presented by the latter.[4] Fontenelle is concerned with the poetical aspect of the conflict, which Temple dismisses with the remark that the consideration of poetry should be a subject by itself. Furthermore, there are a number of allusions which indicate that Temple had the controversy over the Royal Society in mind when he wrote: "Have the studies, the writings, the productions of Gresham College, or the late academies of Paris, outshined or eclipsed the Lycaeum of Plato, the academy of Aristotle, the stoa of Zeno, the garden of Epicurus?" Then he asks if Harvey has outdone Hippocrates, or Wilkins, Archimedes, the first of whom Glanvill had emphasized in defense of the Royal Society, while the latter had been prominent among the founders of the Society. Elsewhere he depreciates Harvey's discovery of circulation of the blood and Copernicus' astronomical discoveries, which had figured prominently in the defense of the new Society. The quarrel was not imported from France; Temple merely revived an English controversy that had begun to die down after raging furiously for some years. It was the revival of the attack on the new science, and had little to do with the quarrel in France, which was largely literary.

In upholding the ancients, Temple divides the question into two parts, knowledge and genius, and attempts to show that the Greeks and Romans were superior in both. While presenting the claims of the moderns for superiority in knowledge, he mentions the conventional figure of a dwarf sitting on a giant's shoulders,[5] in answer to which he advances the idea that the ancients

---

tion, which no quality among men is so apt to raise in me as sufficiency, the worst composition out of the pride and ignorance of mankind." *The Works of Sir William Temple* (London, 1814), III, 445.

[4] *The Battle of the Books, by Jonathan Swift*, ed. A. Guthkelch (London, 1908), p. 27.

[5] This simile was used in Hakewill's *Apologie*, Burton's *Anatomie of Melancholy*, and Herbert's *Jacula Prudentum*. Newton is said to have used the comparison, and Bentley, in Cumberland's *Memoirs*, is reported to have given it as an explanation why he did not attempt creative work.

also had ancestral giants, upon whose shoulders they sat. This method of approach leads him into a remarkable account of the learning of the Chaldeans, Assyrians, Egyptians, Hindus, and even Chinese,[6] in which fiction figures as prominently as fact. He also lays much stress upon the library of 600,000 volumes which was established at Alexandria and later destroyed. All this evidence is evoked to show that if the moderns possessed advantages in having all the knowledge of the ancients, so the latter had other ancients whose knowledge they possessed. So much of his account, however, possesses the quality of "what may have been" that later Wotton took him to task for shrouding the question in mystery.

In the matter of genius, Temple presents the theory that man is born with a little grain of intellect which cannot be increased by any outside aids. In the case of the moderns, he holds that by reliance on the ancients they have weakened that little intellect they have, whereas the ancients, because of the peculiar condition of their environment, were giants in stature and wit. Hakewill's idea of circular progress finds expression in the statement that "science and arts have run their circles, and had their periods in the several parts of the world," and he treats the various periods of civilization in the same manner as Hakewill, Sprat, and Burnet. He seems to adopt the idea that Hakewill so strenuously attacked: "It were a great mortification to think, that the same fate has happened to us, even in our modern learning; as if the growth of that, as well as of natural bodies, had some short periods, beyond which it could not reach, and after which it must begin to decay. It falls in one country or one age, and rises again in others, but never beyond a certain pitch."

He next takes up the sciences in which he says the moderns pretend to excel. In philosophy, he asserts, Descartes and Hobbes do not equal Plato and Aristotle. In grammar and rhetoric no man disputes the superiority of the ancients; nor in poetry

---

[6] This method of approaching the history of knowledge had become popular. Bacon had suggested it; Hakewill and Sprat had attempted it. Stillingfleet in *Sacræ Origines* dipped into the subject. All the names mentioned in the essay, as well as the idea that Greek learning came from the East, are to be found in Burnet's work.

"that ever I heard of" except Fontenelle.[7] In astronomy and physic, he admits, Copernicus and Harvey alone can vie with the ancients; yet their discoveries "made no change in the conclusions of astronomy, nor in the practice of physic; and so have been of little use to the world, though perhaps of much honour to the authors." The charms of music, as related in the ancient fables, and the powers of magic are next presented as powerful arguments against the moderns. Nor can the latter present anything in architecture to compare with the pyramids of Egypt and the Colossus of Rhodes. He feels compelled, however, to grant importance to the invention of the compass, importance which had been stressed by Hakewill and Glanvill, but he blames the moderns for not having advanced geography any further with the aid of such an instrument. After a passing reference to painting and statuary, he falls into a threnody upon the insignificance of man's knowledge and power. But man's pride and sufficiency, he laments, make up for his ignorance, as is shown in the men of Gresham who pretend to excel the ancients.

After speaking of the pretention that *Gondibert* excelled Homer, and Boileau, Virgil, he refuses to discuss the poetical aspect of the controversy on the ground that poetry should be a subject in itself. The next two or three pages are devoted to prose, in which he says the moderns could not hope to surpass the ancients, if for no other reason than for language, which he proceeds to show is a corruption of the classical languages. Among the "great wits" of the moderns Temple places Sidney, Bacon, and Selden, only one of whom is primarily literary.[8] The long list of ancient prose writers is headed by Æsop and Phalaris, whose works, the author claims, are the best of their kind. He then indulges in a paragraph of extravagant praise for the letters of Phalaris, and lays himself open to the later criticism of Bentley, who proved them spurious. He closes his essay

---

[7] Had there been a literary controversy in England, Temple would certainly have heard of it. Saint-Évremond may have introduced the quarrel into the salons and coffeehouses, but it did not go much farther.

[8] Temple's attitude toward Bacon is peculiar when compared with his attitude toward Baconian philosophers. The heart of the controversy was concerned with Bacon and Aristotle.

with an analysis of the hindrances to learning which he thought responsible for the low condition of knowledge.

Temple's prestige was such that his essay created a considerable stir. It especially disturbed, as we shall see later, the members of the Royal Society, who justly suspected it to be an attempt to revive the old attacks. One product of this interest is to be found in the essays of Sir Thomas Pope Blount,[9] a critic of enough significance to receive a notice in Professor Saintsbury's *History of Literary Criticism.* Blount was a man somewhat of Temple's type, that is, a polite scholar. With a horror of pedantry, he wished to be thought learned, and his animosity toward learning was a natural product of his realization that he lacked it. To justify his lack, he furiously attacks learning on the ground that it hinders the mind, is an enemy to virtue and innocence, is hostile to religion, and, worst of all, does not make good politicians. With all this in mind, we are surprised to find him fighting on the side of the moderns. He really belongs to the ancients. The secret of the matter is, I think, that with a fine scorn for learning, he thought it beneath him to get a little for himself, and adopted the much more expeditious method of stealing it from others, or rather the appearance of it. He traced the controversy back and fell upon Hakewill, in whom he found a mine of most learned ore. Nor did he hesitate to steal from Glanvill, only he could hardly make such a display with thefts from that source as from the other. Therefore, he argues for the moderns without acknowledging any indebtedness.

To begin with, he informs us that there is a universal opinion that the world daily declines. That was Hakewill's introduction, but unfortunately much more true in Hakewill's than in Blount's time. This idea he opposes under the divisions (Hakewill's) of virtue, learning, and longevity. After a few of Hakewill's observations, he makes out the latter's case that the moderns are more virtuous. As regards the proper attitude toward the learning of the ancients he is very liberal. He thinks it wrong to consider them either obsolete or canonical. Quoting the dictum of Bacon (whom, strange to say, he mentions by

[9] *Essays upon Several Subjects,* 1692; Essays IV and V.

name), *Antiquitas Seculi, Juventus Mundi,* he says we should use their discoveries and improve on their mistakes. For this reason he sides with the moderns, who have the advantage a pigmy "hath upon the shoulders of a giant." In defending the moderns' claim to superiority in learning, he dips into Glanvill's *Plus Ultra,* and divides the field into anatomy, geography, and navigation. In each division he follows Glanvill closely, especially in the discussion of anatomy, where he copies one passage verbatim. He concludes his essay with Hakewill's decision that there has been little variation in length of life between ancient and modern times.

Below I have made a comparison of Blount's account of the mariner's compass with those of Hakewill and Glanvill; not, however, merely to show the plagiarism, which is a matter of no moment. Blount is dead and gone, and no one is the worse for it; though his case contains a moral for those today who condemn learning because of a conscious lack of it. I have inserted these extracts to show that the true background of Temple's essay is not to be sought in France but in England, and that all three battles of the century-long war are linked together.

BLOUNT (p. 121)

*Cardan,* a great searcher into the Curiosities of Nature, tells us, That among other late Noble Inventions, that of the *Mariners Compass* is the most worthy of admiration, as being of the greatest Use and Convenience to Mankind. By the help hereof, we are now able to find out a way through the *vast Ocean,* in the greatest Storms and darkest Nights, where is neither Path to follow, nor Inhabitant or Passenger to enquire; It points out the way to the skillful Mariner, when all other helps fail him, and that with greater certainty than the wit of Man can possibly do. By means hereof, are

HAKEWILL, *Apologie* (3d ed., p. 333)

And *Cardan,* a man much versed in the rarities of *Nature* . . . Among other rare inventions, that of the Marriners Compasse is most worthy of admiration. By meanes of it, was *Navigation* perfected, the lives and goods of many thousand have bin, and daily are preserved: It findes out a way thorow the vast Ocean, in the greatest stormes and darkest nights, where is neither path to follow, nor inhabitant or passinger to inquire; It points out the way to the skilful Marriner when all other helpes faile him, and that more certainely though it be without reason, sense, the Commodities of all Countries discover'd, Trade, Traffic, and Human Society maintain'd, their several Forms of Government and Religion observ'd, and the whole World made as it were one *Common-Wealth*, and the most distant Nations, *Fellow Citizens* of the same *Body Politick*. But the best way to make us rightly value the blessing of this invention, is, by considering the many Shifts and Inconveniences the Ancients were put to, for want of it. We may easily Imagine, how Inconvenient the Ancients found it to sail by the guidance of the Stars: For in dark Cloudy weather, when their *Pleiades, Helice,* and *Cynosura* were not to be seen, the Pilot was always at a loss for his Guide, and knew not how to steer his Ship, but lay expos'd to the casual conduct both of Winds and Tides. And for this reason, the Ancients seldom or never durst venture into the main Ocean, but were fain to go creeping along by the Shoar side: . . . Hence therefore it was, That the Commerce and Communications of those days were very inconsiderable; Their famed Travels in Comparison were nothing.

and life, then without the helpe thereof all the Wisards and learned Clearkes in the world, using the united strength of their wits and cunning can possibly doe. By means of it are the commodities of all countries discovered, trade, and trafique, and humane societie maintained, their severall formes of government and religion observed, and the whole world made as it were one *Common-wealth,* and the most distant *Nations, fellow citizens* of the same body politique.

GLANVILL's *Plus Ultra*

How *defective* the *Art* of *Navigation was* in *elder* Times, when they *sailed* by the *observation* of the *Stars,* is *easie* to be *imagin'd;* For in dark weather, when their *Pleiades, Helice,* and *Cynosura* were hidden from them by the *intervening clouds,* the *Mariner* was at a loss for his *Guide,* and exposed to the *casual* conduct of *Winds* and *Tides.* For which reason the *Ancients* seldom or never durst venture into the *Ocean,* but steer'd along within sight of the *safer* Shore. So that the *Commerce,* and *Communications* of *those* days were very *narrow;* Their *famed Travels* in comparison but domestick.

In one product of the controversy, *An Essay Concerning Critical and Curious Learning*, by T. R., 1698, there is a significant passage. Speaking of Wotton's *Reflections*, the author says, "It seems Mr. Wotton was engaged by some Friends, or Patrons, to try what could be said in Defence of Modern Learning, against that of the Ancients. Upon which account he found himself obliged to Consider who had appeared on the other side. And, therefore, least he should be accused of betraying his Cause, proclaims open War against Sir *William Temple* for having written an *Essay* in Honour of the Ancients."[10] Now, what body of men could be so interested in the issue created by Temple's essay but the members of the Royal Society? Fearing another display of antagonism such as had attended the first years of the Society, they sought a defender, and pitched upon Wotton, who from his childhood had been considered a prodigy of learning,[11] and who was at this time, or soon became, a member of the Society. He received the mantle that fell from the shoulders of Sprat and Glanvill.

In 1694 Wotton published his *Reflections upon Ancient and Modern Learning*, the most thorough exposition of the problem that had appeared. Although not possessing the cosmic dimensions of Hakewill's discussion, it marshals more evidence in behalf of modern accomplishments than any previous treatise. The book is divided into twenty-nine chapters, each discussing the claims of the ancients and moderns in a particular subject such as astronomy, grammar, physic, and natural philosophy. In matching men and achievements, Wotton employs the method Glanvill borrowed from Hakewill. The first chapters are devoted to the artistic phase of the quarrel—architecture, statuary, painting, poetry, and eloquence—but the bulk of the work is devoted to a thorough discussion of the philosophical and scientific side of the controversy.

At first glance, it might appear that Wotton reflects the French rather than the English controversy. Ignoring Temple's reference to Burnet, he says that Sir William's essay was written to oppose Fontenelle's *Digression*, and at the end of his Preface claims the position of mediator between Temple and Fontenelle. He mentions Perrault frequently, and his chapter on painting, architecture, and statuary is copied almost entirely from the Frenchman. Perrault and Fontenelle appear at frequent inter-

[10] P. 47.
[11] Under the entry for June 14, 1694, Evelyn writes in his diary, "Mr. Wotton, that extraordinary learn'd young man, preach'd excellently."

vals, especially in the first part of the book. The explanation is not far to seek. When Wotton sat down to compose his book, he conducted a far-reaching investigation, and used what material he could find toward accomplishing his purpose.

His relation with the English controversy is much closer and more direct. At the very first of the book he traces the controversy, not to France, but back to the Royal Society, saying that until the new philosophy had obtained ground in England there were few to dispute the superiority of the ancients. Furthermore, the larger part of his book is based much more closely upon Glanvill's *Plus Ultra* than upon Perrault's *Parallèles*. He had already formulated the design of his work, before the latter reached him, and then he had access only to those sections that treated the artistic side of the conflict.[12] In fact, Wotton thought that Perrault's design was to uphold modern superiority only in the arts, taking it for granted that the ancients would be considered inferior in learning and science.[13] For a consideration of these last, Wotton depended entirely upon Glanvill, and chapters xiv to xxvi were definitely modeled upon the *Plus Ultra*, which, in turn, had been patterned, though not so closely, upon Hakewill's book.

Evidence of Wotton's indebtedness to Glanvill appears throughout the book. In his discussion of anatomy, he speaks of Glanvill, though he is of the opinion that the latter hardly gave the ancients their due,[14] while in the section devoted to chemistry the author draws much of his material from the earlier work.[15] The advantages derived from the modern invention of certain instruments are emphasized in both accounts, and the same instruments are mentioned—microscope, telescope, thermometer, barometer, and air pump.[16] After bringing forth various proofs of the usefulness of the telescope, Wotton says, "This is an effectual Answer to all that Rhapsody which *Stubbe* has collected in his Brutal Answer to Mr. Glanvile's *Plus Ultra*,

[12] *Reflections upon Ancient and Modern Learning* (London, 1694), p. 159.
[13] *Loc. cit.*
[14] Wotton, *op. cit.*, p. 195.
[15] Cf. *Plus Ultra*, pp. 11, 25, with Wotton, *op. cit.*, pp. 160, 169, 188.
[16] *Plus Ultra*, p. 10; Wotton, *op. cit.*, p. 170.

about the Uncertainty of all Observations made by the Telescopes."[17] In the list of discoveries made by aid of the telescope, and in the emphasis placed upon the mariner's compass, as well as in the history of the air and history of plants, Wotton makes diligent use of the *Plus Ultra*, employing the same arguments and citing the same authorities.[18] The discovery of the circulation of the blood, which was one of Glanvill's main arguments for the superiority of the moderns, is given a whole chapter in the *Reflections*, where the former account is only amplified and strengthened. In short, Glanvill's book is the basis of the bulk of Wotton's work. Of course the earlier account is expanded and much additional matter is introduced, but in both form and material the *Plus Ultra* is plainly seen.

Further proof of Wotton's affiliation with the new philosophy appears in his frequent use of material and evidence drawn from the *Philosophical Transactions*,[19] in the introduction of much material furnished him by members of the Royal Society,[20] and in the praise he bestows upon the Baconian philosophers. In defense of modern physics, Wotton affirms "That though the noble Discoveries of these latter Ages might, possibly, be found in *Hippocrates*, *Aristotle*, and *Galen*, yet, since no Interpreters could ever find them there, till they had been discovered anew by Modern Physicians, who followed Nature only as their Guide, these late Discoverers have an equal Right to the Glory due to such Discoveries, as the Ancients could possibly have."[21] Finally, the characterization of the old philosophy that was so bitter in the *Plus Ultra* is found in the *Reflections*, and in the latter also are urged the advantages of the new method.[22]

[17] Wotton, *op. cit.*, p. 175.

[18] *Ibid.*, pp. 176, 241, 247, 257; *Plus Ultra*, pp. 15, 49, 73, and chap. v.

[19] Pp. 143, 146.

[20] John Craige furnished eight pages on geometry and arithmetic, and Edmund Halley the chapter on astronomy and optics. See Wotton, *op. cit.*, p. 160.

[21] P. 297. See also pp. 5, 347.

[22] Cf. Wotton, *op. cit.*, p. 154, and *Plus Ultra*, p. 123. Wotton says he had fresh inducement to undertake his work when he found how Bentley had shown "What admirable use may be made of an accurate search into nature, thereby to lead us directly up to its author, so as to leave the unbelieving world without excuse."

But the one respect in which Wotton is farthest from France is the emphasis placed upon learning rather than upon the arts. In France, the controversy had yielded the superiority of the moderns in science and vehemently presented the question of excellence in oratory and poetry.[23] But Wotton refuses to advocate the superiority of the moderns in those two arts. In the chapter devoted to them he contents himself with showing how, on account of the language, ancient poetry excels modern, and how ancient times encouraged greater eloquence than modern. It had been his intention, likewise, to give the ancients precedence in painting and sculpture, but when Perrault's *Parallèles* came to hand, he copied out some pages dealing with these arts, to which he added the words, "Whether his reasonings are just, I dare not determine."[24] He is just as loath as Glanvill to claim modern superiority in art. He even attacks Fontenelle for claiming that ancient poetry is inferior to modern, on the ground that his unproved assertions afforded justification to Temple's charge of sufficiency.[25] Unlike the French, the English generally conceded the palm to the ancients in poetry and the arts, and debated the question of superiority in science and learning. Wotton says, "The Generality of the Learned have given *the Ancients* the Preference in those Arts and Sciences that have hitherto been considered [painting, sculpture, poetry]; But for the Precedency in those Parts of Learning which still remain to be enquired into, *the Moderns* have put in their Claim, with great Briskness. Among this Sort, I reckon *Mathematical* and *Physical Sciences*, considered in their largest Extent."[26] And again, speaking of the matter of superiority, "Now, as this can only be known by an induction of particulars, so of these particulars there are two sorts: one, of those wherein the greatest part of those learned men who have compared ancient and modern performances, either give up the cause to the ancients quite, or think, at least,

[23] In his *Digression*, Fontenelle dismisses consideration of the sciences, "Pour ce qui est de l'eloquence et de la poésie, qui sont le sujet de la principale contestation entre les anciens et des modernes."

[24] Wotton, *op. cit.*, p. 62.

[25] *Ibid.*, p. 5.

[26] *Ibid.*, p. 77–78.

that the moderns have not gone beyond them. The other of those, where the advocates for the moderns think the case so clear on their side, that they wonder how any man can dispute it with them. Poesie, oratory, architecture, painting, and statuary are of the first sort; natural history, physiology, and mathematics, with all their dependencies are of the second."[27]

I have already mentioned some of the reasons that appeared to me to explain the absence of a literary controversy in England —subservience to the rules and distrust of the language. Wotton also brings forth another cause that seems convincing. In speaking of the sciences as the bone of contention, he says, "These are Things which have no Dependence upon the Opinions of Men for their Truth; they will admit of fixed and undisputed *Mediums* of Comparison and Judgment: So that, though it may be always debated, who have been the best Orators, or who the best Poets; yet it cannot always be a Matter of Controversie, who have been the greatest *Geometers, Arithmeticians, Astronomers, Musicians, Anatomists, Chymists, Botanists,* or the like; because a fair Comparison between the Inventions, Observations, Experiments and Collections of the contending Parties must certainly put an end to the Dispute, and give a more full satisfaction to all sides."[28] The English perceived the futility of comparing objects in which no standard was available, and, with their practical turn of mind, sought out questions that could be solved. Furthermore, though the literary controversy might have no utility, the scientific controversy served the great purpose of protecting a movement that has never ceased to shed its blessings.

With Bacon the method was the controversy. Sprat carried on the campaign where Bacon left it. Glanvill, though passionately pleading the superiority of the new method, showed Hakewill's influence in bringing forward tangible proofs of the superiority of the modern times. Since the Royal Society was then in its infancy and could show few results, Glanvill found it necessary to stress discoveries and inventions that bore no relation to the Society, thus associating the moderns with experimental philosophers. In the same direction Wotton went even

[27] Wotton, *op. cit.*, p. 19. See also p. 5.
[28] *Ibid.*, pp. 77, 78.

further. He laid less emphasis upon the method, but introduced much more extensive evidence in the way of discoveries than his predecessor, likewise confounding the moderns and the virtuosi. Hakewill's method of conducting the war became more and more generally accepted, while Bacon's relation with the controversy that was created by him was fading from the minds of men. Temple, an ancient, thinks Bacon one of the great modern wits; Wotton, a modern, seldom mentions him; and Swift, an ancient, commits the crowning error in letting Aristotle's arrow miss its mark. No longer did Faith need to wage the combat alone, but the concrete results of experimental philosophers, combined with the substantial discoveries of other moderns, could of themselves argue superiority over the ancients.

Wotton's temerity in daring to dispute the opinion of a gentleman provoked Sir William Temple to attempt a reply, which, however, was not published until the next century, several years after his death.[29] This essay definitely fixes the nature of the controversy. "It is by themselves confessed," he says, "that, till the new philosophy had gotten ground in these parts of the world, which is about fifty or sixty years date, there were but few that ever pretended to exceed or equal the ancients." Then came Descartes, and next Gresham College, "the members of which," he says, "began early to debate and pursue this pretence, and were followed by the French Academy, who took up the controversy more at large, and descended to many particulars; Monsieur Fontenelle gave the Academy the preference in poetry and oratory."[30] With great scorn he asks what has been produced

[29] *Some Thoughts upon Reviewing the Essay of Ancient and Modern Learning.*

[30] Temple, *op. cit.*, III, 488. I would conjecture that England exerted more influence on the controversy across the channel, than France on that in England. (For the possible influence of Bacon on Descartes and Pascal, see H. Rigault, *Histoire de la Querelle des Anciens et des Modernes* [Paris, 1856], p. 51.) Sprat says that the Royal Society maintained perpetual intercourse with France, which recognized English leadership in the new philosophy. He also claims that in imitation of the Society, the French Academy at last turned from words to experimental philosophy. (See Sprat, *op. cit.*, pp. 56, 124.) Wotton says, "When afterwards the Philosophers of *England* grew numerous, and united their strength, *France*, also took the hint, and its King set up a Royal Society to

by the great advancers of knowledge and learning in these last fifty years, "which is the date of our modern pretenders." In answer, he sarcastically speaks of their fantastic visions—philosopher's stone, transfusion of blood, flying, and other strange things.[31] In three different places he notes that Wotton concedes to the ancients the victory in poetry, painting, statuary, and architecture—matters that he himself had not touched upon, and that had been surrendered without a struggle—and in one passage he promises to give an account of the sciences in which the moderns boast superiority—invention of instruments, chemistry, anatomy, astronomy, optics, music, physic, natural philosophy, philology, theology.[32] But this part was never finished, which fact probably explains the tardiness of publication. To prove the superiority of the ancients in these subjects would have been beyond the powers of a learned man, and much beyond those of Temple.

The interest in the epistles of Phalaris excited by Temple's extravagant praise moved Dr. Aldrich, Dean of Christ Church, to ask one of his pupils, Robert Boyle, to prepare an edition of the letters. During 1693 and 1694, Boyle, assisted by other members of the college, worked on his edition. In the course of its preparation he engaged a bookseller in London to collate a manuscript in the Royal Library at St. James's Palace, of which Bentley was soon to become the librarian. Negotiations for the use of the manuscript were so badly managed that Bentley, who in the meantime had become librarian, demanded back the manuscript before the collation had been completed. When Boyle's edition appeared, January 1695, the Preface contained a slur at Bentley's "humanity," whereupon the latter immediately wrote Boyle a letter explaining his side of the transaction, to which the

---

Rival ours." (Wotton, *op. cit.*, p. 347.) The above quotation from Temple confirms these statements, and connects Fontenelle with the movement. Although Descartes was the central figure in the scientific controversy in France, it is interesting to note that in the decade following that in which the Royal Society was founded, the quarrel reached its highest pitch. H. Gillot, *La Querelle des anciens et des modernes en France* (Paris, 1914), p. 389. Sprat's *History of the Royal Society* was translated into French and published at Paris in 1670.

[31] Temple, *op. cit.*, III, 516.

[32] *Ibid.*, pp. 497, 504, 513.

editor responded in no satisfactory way.[33] Here matters rested until the appearance of the second edition of Wotton's *Reflections*, 1697. It seems that while Wotton was preparing the first edition of his work, Bentley had told him that the letters were spurious and that he would prove them so at some future date. When the time came to issue the second edition, Wotton held Bentley to his promise, with the result that this edition contained an appendix by the great classical scholar, in which the letters themselves were proved spurious and Boyle's edition full of errors. Immediately the members of Christ Church combined their forces, and the next year, under the name of Boyle, issued an *Examination* of the "immortal dissertation," which was as witty as it was faulty, and as malicious as it was untruthful.

In this phase of the controversy two puzzling questions have arisen: Why was Bentley associated with the defenders of the moderns, and why was the hostility of the Christ Church group so venomous toward him and Wotton? The answer to the questions, I think, lies in the peculiar nature of the quarrel. However great Bentley's admiration for classical literature may have been, he was not deterred on that account from assisting Wotton, for the conflict had nothing to do with pure literature. Wotton was an ardent admirer of classical poetry even in preference to modern. Furthermore, in defending the Royal Society, Wotton met with the sympathy of Bentley, for the latter was associated with the Society in several ways. He was a friend of some of the members, especially Wotton and Newton.[34] By some of the virtuosi he had been chosen to deliver the Boyle sermons, in which he used to good effect the discoveries of Newton. Later we find him establishing a biological laboratory at Cambridge. Furthermore, his own work, I think, shows the influence of the new science. That "induction of particulars," by which Wotton says he wrote his *Reflections*,[35] is prominent in all of Bentley's work, while the scientific spirit of his research reflects that of the experimental philosophers. Finally, those who were enemies to the

[33] For a clear account of the Phalaris controversy see Guthkelch's admirable edition of *The Battle of the Books*.

[34] Wotton, *op. cit.*, p. 122 and Preface.

[35] *Ibid.*, pp. 5, 19.

Royal Society were exactly those who were hostile to his own kind of learning. Thus, with his sympathies naturally on the side of the moderns, Bentley's coming to his friend's aid is by no means strange.

Temple says that his reply to Wotton was inspired by solicitude for learning in general, but especially for that in the university. Now, it was the learning of the universities, particularly of Oxford, that in the Royal Society controversy was opposed to the new "mechanical" philosophy of the Society.[36] In Oxford the Aristotelian faction still remained strong. The Dean of Christ Church, Dr. Aldrich himself, was one of the irreconcilables, and he had written a *Logic*, in which, says a writer of the time,[37] "He makes nothing of calling him Coxcomb, Fool, and Blockhead, for dareing to dissent from Aristotle, and for presuming to advance anything New, upon a Subject that great Man had quite exhausted so many Ages before him." So the wits of Christ Church were the inheritors of all the old animosity aroused against the new philosophy, and beheld in Wotton and Bentley the guardians of the institution they detested.

After all, it was a dead controversy that Temple tried to revive.[38] Few there were who cared to argue the superiority of the ancients in science. Because the quarrel no longer possessed any life, its later developments pursued a very different direction. The Wotton-Temple quarrel was quickly swallowed up by the Bentley-Boyle controversy, in which the issue involved had nothing to do with the ancients and moderns, but lay between the careless, inexact scholarship of the old school and the scientific

[36] In speaking of Christ Church about the year 1690, Craik says, "To write graceful Latin verses, to affect a general acquaintance with the classics, was the mark of a cultured gentleman: to be interested in the achievements of the new sciences, to find entertainment in the futilities of the 'Men of Gresham' was the mark of a pedant and dullard." *Life of Jonathan Swift*, 1882, p. 66.

[37] *An Essay Concerning Critical and Curious Learning*, by T. R., Esq., 1698, p. 66. Dyce attributes this to Rymer, but on insufficient evidence, Mr. Spingarn thinks. If Rymer was the author, it is interesting to note that the redoubtable champion of the Greek drama and Aristotelian rules was of the opinion that Wotton and Bentley had much the best of the conflict.

[38] Gildon says that Aristotle has shrunk from a philosopher to a good critic or grammarian. See *Critical Essays of the Eighteenth Century, 1700–1725,* ed. W. H. Durham, p. 15.

method of the new. Moreover, the enemies of the virtuosi no longer made their attacks from the direction of the ancients, but, following the path pursued after the first controversy over the Royal Society, joined with the wits in ridiculing the seemingly trivial experiments and observations of the scientists. Yet Bentley's association with Wotton had far-reaching results. Had Sprat been told that a great scholar of the classics was destined to be the champion of the Society, he would hardly have believed his ears, for his philosophy led to a study of nature, not books. Yet the new method was taken over by Bentley and applied with remarkable results to the very works that had been opposed to it. This natural coalition between modern science and modern literary research caused for the next half-century the scientist and the textual critic to be the double target of Swift, King, Pope, and many others, who conducted an incessant warfare against the "abuses of learning."[39]

The most important literary product of the conflict was, of course, *The Battle of the Books*. There were several forces at work drawing Swift into the combat. First of all, he could not with equanimity see Temple, his friend and benefactor, attacked. Moreover, during his stay at Oxford he had associated with the very men who felt most enmity against the new philosophy. And finally, Swift's own unpleasant experience in getting his degree "gratia speciali," together with his well-known hatred of mathematics, made him an enemy to what he chose to call pedantic learning.

Since Mr. Guthkelch has pointed out the passages in which Swift is indebted to Temple's *Essay* and Wotton's *Reflections*, products of the scientific controversy, it is not necessary to mention all the details of the satire which reflect this controversy. Furthermore, nothing need be said about the episodes in which Bentley appears, for he was concerned in a quarrel independent of the question of ancient or modern superiority. There are, however, in the *Battle* some evidences of the conflict over the new philosophy that have not been noted.

[39] Two productions of this kind may be mentioned: *The Memoirs of Scriblerus*, and the fourth book of *The Dunciad*. For a more extended discussion of the matter see Richard F. Jones, *Lewis Theobald*, chap. iv.

Swift traces the cause of the war to the quarrel over the higher peak of Parnassus. He makes the moderns, who occupy the lower peak, send ambassadors to the ancients asking permission to dig down and level with shovels and mattocks the peak occupied by their rivals. From their refusal, he says, an obstinate war arose, and many controversial books—written in ink manufactured by an engineer—sprang into existence, which finally precipitated the battle. Here, I think, is a reference to the controversy that appeared after the founding of the Royal Society, for such expressions as "shovel," "mattock," and "dig" suggest one of the charges that were made against the new philosophy; namely, that it was material and mechanical, Stubbe going so far as to call it "day-labouring." Also the fable of the bee and spider,[40] in the slur at the latter's knowledge of mathematics, touches upon that point of superiority which the moderns had especially stressed in the persons of such men as Wilkins and Newton. But the clearest references to the controversy are contained in the passage in which the Goddess of Criticism sheds her blessing on Gresham College, and that in which mention is made of a vacant shelf in St. James's Library recently inhabited by a colony of "virtuosoes," the mention of whom prompts Mr. Guthkelch to say, "Presumably the virtuosoes were fighting for the moderns." They constituted, of course, the heart of the conflict. The various allusions to philosophers and scientists, which Swift derived from Temple and Wotton, emphasize the nature of the conflict, but the repeated mention of Harvey and Paracelsus is particularly significant, for from the middle of the century they had been the chief arguments for the moderns. Yet there is one respect in which the *Battle* does not reflect the controversy. In the confusion that is described as reigning in the library, Aristotle is placed next to Descartes, where we would expect Bacon; and later Aristotle's arrow misses Bacon and hits the French philosopher. Though Bacon's intimate relation with the controversy was becoming obscure, the more apparent reason

[40] Bacon had used the same figure; but he made the dogmatical philosophers the spiders who spin out their own webs, and the new philosophers the bees who extract matter from the flowers of the gardens and of the fields. See Bacon, *Advancement of Learning* and *Novum Organum*, ed. J. E. Creighton (in *World's Greatest Literature*, New York), p. 349.

for this seeming inconsistency is the fact that, since Temple had called Bacon a great wit, Swift felt compelled not to show him in an unfavorable light. For this reason, he substituted Descartes, who was Aristotle's enemy in France as Bacon was in England.

Though there was little literary controversy for the satire to reflect, Swift introduces some poets into the arena. *Gondibert* is mentioned, because it had appeared in Temple's essay, and Tasso, Milton, and Blackmore are noticed because they also departed from the ancients in writing Christian epics. Withers was introduced because he was considered a symbol of poetic stupidity; Creech and Ogleby sustain the characters of stupid translators; and Oldham and Afra Behn are presented as writers of Pindarics. But the two poets that are emphasized by the space allotted them are Cowley and Dryden, who, I think, were introduced for reasons other than poetical. As we have seen, Cowley was closely associated with the Royal Society and his ode prefixed to Sprat's *History* openly identified him with the movement. Dryden was no less closely associated with the new philosophy. He was elected a member of the Royal Society in 1662, and later celebrated the virtuosi and their discoveries in his "Epistle to Dr. Walter Charleton," in which the members of the Society are praised for breaking the fetters of Aristotle and following the path pointed out by Bacon.[41] In his *MacFlecknoe* he took Shadwell severely to task for presuming, in the *Virtuoso*, to brand the new learning. Therefore, it is possible that these two poets are introduced on the side of the moderns because of their close association with the moderns in the scientific controversy.[42]

The influence of the French controversy on the satire is, indeed, slight. There is one definite allusion where Homer knocks out Fontenelle's and Perrault's brains, by hurling one Frenchman against the other, but Wotton's frequent references to them can very well account for this notice. The introduction of Boileau on the side of the moderns emphasizes how out of touch with the Continental quarrel Swift was, for Boileau was a

[41] *The Dramatic Works of John Dryden*, ed. Scott-Saintsbury, I, 47.

[42] As we have seen, Gildon advanced Cowley and Dryden against the ancients, but Swift could hardly have had his slight essay in mind, or Gildon would probably have found a place in the *Battle*.

staunch supporter of the ancients.  Swift probably included the
French Horace because in the *Essay* Temple had spoken slightingly of him in comparison with Virgil.  Mr. Guthkelch sees
references to Fontenelle and Perrault in the passage of the *Battle*
that speaks of the moderns claiming to be more ancient than the
ancients, but ever since Bacon the paradox had been popular,
and was, indeed, at the bottom of the Hakewill controversy.  In
Swift's reference to the "modern way of fortification" there
may be an allusion to the fifth dialogue of Perrault's *Parallèles,*
but, though I have no note to that effect, modern superiority in
that field had probably been argued in England.

Macaulay has characterized · the controversy, which he
thought was brought over from France, as childish, idle, and
contemptible.  But in the light of my investigation, it deserves
no such character.  One might as well apply the adjectives to
the Reformation or the French Revolution.  Hakewill's stand
against the corrupting influence of the belief in necessary inferiority was as courageous as it was useful.  Bacon's efforts to
convert the world to the new truth that he had discovered, and
in which he had supreme faith, were neither idle nor contemptible.  The later advocates of his philosophy, in protecting
the struggling truth against the furious attacks of the admirers
of antiquity in a controversy that threatened its existence, were
engaged in no futile enterprise.  Certainly it was no useless controversy that accompanied a new idea thrusting its way to the
light through the tough crust of conservatism.  Bacon, Sprat,
Glanvill, and Wotton engaged in a battle made necessary by the
inevitable conflict between Tradition and Progress.  Whatever
its significance, however, the controversy was more a phenomenon of the scientific movement than of literary history, but the
scientific movement itself was not without influence upon literary ideas.[43]

[43] I wish to acknowledge my obligations to Mr. James McMillan, Librarian
of Washington, for persistent efforts, though often futile, to secure books for me
from other libraries.  To my colleague, Professor W. R. Mackenzie, I am greatly
indebted for many suggestions and criticisms.  Nor would I pass over in silence
the essential aid rendered by my wife, without whom this article would not have
been written.

# SCIENCE AND CRITICISM
# IN THE NEO-CLASSICAL AGE OF
# ENGLISH LITERATURE*

## Richard Foster Jones

BEFORE proceeding to the substance of my argument, it is imperative that I define the first term in my title, for upon my interpretation of it the thesis which I shall present depends. My conception of the history of science in seventeenth-century England differs in many respects from the usual view. The modern historian of science develops his subject in a series of descriptions and evaluations of past discoveries in a more or less chronological order, in which continuity is at best only partially maintained. He may trace the progress of the knowledge of some aspect of nature from its embryonic beginnings to its finished statement. He may, for instance, explain Copernicus' theory of the revolution of the planets round the sun, tell how Kepler determined the elliptical nature of their orbits, show how Galileo advanced the theory by his observation of the satellites of Jupiter, and discuss the laws governing planetary movements as discovered by Newton. He may show how our present knowledge of nature is only the sum of all the increments added at various times in the past to growing conceptions, and describe each increment as it appears. He is primarily interested in positive contributions to knowledge, and in the appearance of those elements that have finally been welded into the elaborate scientific method of today.

* Reprinted, with minor corrections, from *Journal of the History of Ideas*, Vol. I (1940), by permission of the publishers.

There is another way of interpreting scientific history, which considers science primarily as a movement of ideas, which stresses principles giving rise to discoveries more than the discoveries themselves, and seeks to trace these principles as they develop in harmony or conflict with other forces and in relation to contemporary circumstances and needs. In seventeenth-century England the scientific movement comprised a few definite main principles. First was the demand for a sceptical mind, freed from all preconceptions and maintaining a critical attitude toward all ideas presented to it. Second, observation and experimentation were insisted upon as the only trustworthy means of securing sufficient data. And third, the inductive method of reasoning was to be employed on these data. Such were the central or primary ideas in this thought-movement, or, to use an expression borrowed from criticism, the timeless element, for they are as true today—though, perhaps, more generally taken for granted—as they were then. But besides these there was the time element, or those secondary principles which came into being when the primary clashed with their age. To establish experimental science it was necessary to overthrow the principle of authority, especially that of Aristotle and other ancients, who in large part still dominated the human mind. So the anti-authoritarian principle entered the movement. But to undermine the authority of antiquity, it was necessary to attack a prevailing theory of the day, which asserted that modern times represented the old age of the world and the last stages of the decay of nature, in which human powers had degenerated to a level far below those of the ancients, who lived when nature was in its prime. Thus opposition to the theory of nature's decay joins the other principles. Again, the new thinkers, in order to have the opportunity to advance the cause of modern science, found it necessary to insist upon freedom to investigate and to advance their findings against established ideas. So the principle of liberty is insisted upon. And finally, the belief that knowledge could advance if the authority of the ancients were removed, and the realization that some discoveries had already shown the possibility of advancement beyond the ignorance of antiquity, moved the scientists to embrace the idea of progress.

All these values, attitudes, and ideas, together with a few others, combined to form the scientific movement, and they were expressed by an ever increasing chorus of voices throughout the latter half of the seventeenth century, voices not of authentic scientists only, or even chiefly, but of noblemen, state officials, clergymen, and even of the rabble of magicians, astrologers, graceless quacks, and other representatives of the lunatic fringe. Of the four men who probably did more than any others to establish and popularize the idea of the new science, only one, Robert Boyle, was an authentic scientist. John Webster was a Puritan chaplain in the parliamentarian army; Joseph Glanvill was a rector in the Anglican Church; and Thomas Sprat was a noted preacher and later bishop of Rochester. All these men were ardent champions of the great discoveries of the Renaissance, but they were not primarily interested in these discoveries. Their first concern was to promote the idea of science, to support and give impetus to a thought-movement which was sweeping away all obstructions. Toward this end they appreciated scientific discoveries not so much for their intrinsic value as for the support they furnished the movement, either in proving the ideas of the ancients erroneous or in demonstrating the fruitfulness of the experimental and observational method. One other fact must be briefly stated. The scientific movement was organized around Bacon, and its chief embodiment was the Royal Society.[1]

Paralleling the rapid development of the scientific movement was a literary movement, which comprised values and attitudes quite different from those of science. This was a literary criticism, generally called neo-classical, of which the two cardinal principles were the imitation of nature and the moral purpose of art. Since, however, as Pope was to say, nature and Homer were the same, the only way to imitate nature was by following the literary rules and ideas first laid down by Aristotle,

---

[1] This analysis of the scientific movement in seventeenth-century England is based upon the present writer's *Ancients and Moderns: A Study of the Background of the Battle of the Books* (Washington University Studies, New Series; St. Louis, 1936); Bacon's relationship to the movement is discussed in the introduction to an edition of selections from the works of Sir Francis Bacon (New York: Doubleday, Doran & Co., 1937).

Horace, and others, and later elaborated by European critics. Therefore, this criticism maintained that the proper models of writing were to be found only in Greek and Roman literature; that modern writers must follow these models; and that the rules drawn from them by Aristotle and his followers were as the law of the Medes and Persians which altereth not. Here, then, was a critical philosophy which upheld the principal of authority (though many critics tried to equate it with reason or common sense), limited the freedom of the poetic imagination, and rendered impossible any progress beyond the achievements of the past. It also lent its support to the theory of nature's decay, which indeed became one of its major theses. It would be difficult to find a more exact antithesis to the views characteristic of the scientific movement than is found in this criticism. Was it possible for these two thought-movements to proceed side by side without interaction?

# I

To ascertain the answer to this question it is necessary to examine the works of some representative critics of the neoclassical period. The first is Dryden, called by some the father of English criticism and certainly head and shoulders above any English critic of the time. But, if we may employ the words with which he himself described Shakespeare, "he is the very Janus of critics; he wears almost everywhere two faces; and you have scarce begun to admire the one, ere you despise the other." Whenever Dryden passes under the shadow of a French neoclassical critic, he may become as hidebound and narrow as any of his contemporaries. At other times, however, he reveals a critical intelligence of a high order—a sensitivity, insight, and comprehension unique in his own age and not often surpassed since. His mind, if at times too subject to influence, was tentative and sceptical, a characteristic of which he was fully aware, for, in speaking of his translation of Lucretius, he says, "I laid by my natural diffidence and scepticism for a while, to take up the dogmatical way of Lucretius."[2] But if this sceptical, undogmatic

---

[2] *Essays of John Dryden*, ed. W. P. Ker, 1900, I, 260. This work is hereafter referred to under the name of the editor.

attitude of mind was his by nature, it was also, perhaps, fostered and encouraged by his contacts with the scientists of his day. He joined the Royal Society in the year it received its charter from the King, served on two of its committees, and praised and defended it in his poetry.[3] The critical, sceptical attitude which Bacon had enjoined upon his followers, and which the scientists of the Restoration sedulously strove to attain, could hardly have escaped his notice or been without influence upon him. In describing the spirit which informs his first important critical treatise, the *Essay of Dramatic Poesie*, he denies the charge of dogmatism, which had unjustly been brought against him: "my whole discourse was sceptical, according to that way of reasoning which was used by Socrates, Plato, and all the Academics of old, . . . and which is imitated by the modest inquisitions of the Royal Society."[4] Needless to say, the Society to which Dryden belonged, and to the members of which he had frequently listened, must have done more to develop the scepticism he speaks of than the far-off models of antiquity.

Not only is the sceptical attitude of science perceptible in Dryden's criticism; its corollary, the inductive way of reasoning, can frequently be discovered there. The method of reasoning employed by the dogmatic critics of his day was essentially deductive or syllogistic. They reasoned from general principles established largely by authority. Dryden, on the other hand, gathers his data from literature, and from these data draws his conclusions. A few simple examples will suffice. The dogmatic critic reasoned thus: poetry is an imitation of nature (a major premise resting ultimately on the authority of Aristotle); the supernatural is not an imitation of nature; therefore, poetry containing it is not correct poetry. But notice how Dryden opposes this narrow idea: "I will ask any man who loves heroic

[3] In "John Dryden and The Royal Society" (*PMLA*, XLV [1930], 967–76), Mr. Claude Lloyd attempts to show that Dryden possessed no genuine interest in the Royal Society, but he has been convincingly answered by Miss Ella Riske, Professor Louis Bredvold, and Mr. T. B. Stroup. (*Ibid.*, XLVI [1931], 951–61). For a wider discussion of Dryden's scepticism see Bredvold's *The Intellectual Milieu of John Dryden*, and "Dryden, Hobbes, and the Royal Society," *Modern Philology*, XXV (1928), 417–38.

[4] Ker, I, 124.

poetry . . . if the ghost of *Polydorus* in Virgil, the *Enchanted Wood* in Tasso, and the *Bower of Bliss* in Spencer . . . could have been omitted, without taking from their works some of the greatest beauties in them." From these instances Dryden draws the general principle that

an heroic poet is not tied to a bare representation of what is true . . . but . . . he may let himself loose to visionary objects, and to the representation of such things as depending not on sense, and therefore not to be comprehended by knowledge, may give him a freer scope for imagination.[5]

In searching for pertinent data in literature itself, and in drawing from the particular instances found in the three poets mentioned above a principle quite different from that which was founded on authority, Dryden was following, though in a simple and elementary fashion, exactly the same procedure adopted by the experimental scientists who turned their backs on Aristotelian ideas of nature and the syllogistic logic of the Peripatetics, and sought in nature itself the data which by induction would lead to more accurate ideas or principles.

Another example of this inductive method of arriving at conclusions quite at variance with accepted rules is found in his preface to the *Mock Astrologer*, in which he combats the idea that poetic justice is a law of comedy. To support his own view he gathers his instances from Terence, Ben Johnson, and Beaumont and Fletcher.[6] Of course, simple induction is a seemingly obvious procedure, but nevertheless strict neo-classical critics like Thomas Rymer seldom, if ever, employ it to determine their principles, but apply rules secured in other ways to particular poems, generally with disastrous consequences. Moreover, there are passages in Dryden which indicate that he was aware of the nature of the logic he used, for he definitely calls his reasoning induction.[7] In general, we may say that when not in his neo-classical moods, Dryden moves about in literature and collects the data for his opinions; he does not approach it from the outside with a premanufactured yardstick to detect its shortcomings.

Dryden, when in the presence of a French critic, can knuckle

[5] Ker, I, 153.     [6] *Ibid.*, I, 141–42.     [7] *Ibid.*, I, 195; II, 250.

under to authority in the most approved fashion. But when the
influence of the scientific spirit plays upon his mind, he is boldly
defiant. When accused of not respecting the authority of Ben
Jonson, he asks: "Or why should there be any *Ipse dixit* in our
poetry, any more than there is in our philosophy?" (It is necessary to keep in mind that throughout this period the word "philosophy" is consistently used where we should use the term
"science.") And in another passage he declares that there are
no Pillars of poetry, a figure taken from the Pillars of Hercules,
which was used over and over again by the scientists to express
the limits imposed on knowledge by the authority of the ancients.[8]

The idea of progress in scientific knowledge, which stimulated the scientists in their experimenting and observing, creates
in Dryden a similar attitude toward poetry. One of the speakers
in the *Essay of Dramatic Poesie* asks:

> Is it not evident, in these last hundred years (when the study of phi-
> losophy has been the business of all Virtuosi in Christendom), that almost
> a new Nature has been revealed to us?—that more errors of the school
> have been detected, more useful experiments in philosophy have been
> made, more noble secrets in optics, medicine, anatomy, astronomy, dis-
> covered, than in all those doting ages from Aristotle to us?—so true it is,
> that nothing spreads more fast than science, when rightly and generally
> cultivated.

To this another speaker, who wishes to show that modern poetry
may go beyond ancient art, answers: "if natural causes be more
known now than in the time of Aristotle, because more studied, it
follows that poesy and other arts may, with the same pains, arrive
still nearer to perfection."[9] In another passage, Dryden shows us
one way in which he would contribute to the advancement of
poetry, and also the reasons for his hope of success. What he
advocates is the introduction of the supernatural element of
guardian spirits into modern epic poetry, concerning which he
says:

> I am sufficiently sensible of my weakness; and it is not very probable

[8] *Ibid.*, I, 138; II, 149. Cf. Richard F. Jones, *Ancients and Moderns*,
p. 302, note 23.
[9] Ker, I, 36–37, 43–44. In order to show the possibility of progress in
poetry, Dryden denies the theory of the decay of nature. *Ibid.*, II, 25.

that I should succeed in such a project, whereof I have not had the least hint from any of my predecessors, the poets. . . . Yet we see the art of war is improved in sieges, and new instruments of death are invented daily; something new in philosophy and the mechanics is discovered almost every year; and the science of former ages is improved by the succeeding.[10]

The progress which the scientists were achieving inspired in Dryden the desire and hope of a similar advancement in verse. In fact, in one essay he makes this progress the sole aim of his criticism, and to achieve it he is quite willing to remove the bar of ancient authority and supposed perfection:

I hope I shall not be thought arrogant when I enquire into their errors [i.e., the errors of the ancients]. For we live in an age so sceptical, that as it determines little, so it takes nothing from antiquity on trust; and I profess to have no other ambition in this *Essay*, than that poetry may not go backward, when all other arts and sciences are advancing.[11]

It was the scientists who were sceptical and took nothing from antiquity on trust, and it was from them and their discoveries that Dryden took his cue.

There are numerous echoes and suggestions of the scientific movement in Dryden's criticism which hardly merit consideration here. His figures of speech are frequently drawn from the activities of science—mathematical, astronomical, chemical, physical, and medical.[12] He was especially fond of illustrations drawn from the Copernican system, though it is true that he occasionally used the Ptolemaic.[13] Yet this last he is careful to introduce with a "they say." Some of his figures reveal familiarity with the keenest battle of the war which the moderns carried on against the ancients, namely, the onslaught of the chemical doctors, who upheld Baconian principles, upon the Galenists, who subscribed to the methods of the great physician of antiquity.[14] Sometimes one versed in seventeenth-century science detects echoes of it in unsuspected passages, as, for example, when Dryden, in expressing his distrust of the rules, says, "many a fair precept in poetry is, like a seeming demonstration in the

---

[10] Ker, II, 33–34.   [11] *Ibid.*, I, 162–63.
[12] *Ibid.*, I, 63, 155, 252; II, 137.
[13] *Ibid.*, II, 103, 143, 158; and I, 70.   [14] *Ibid.*, II, 158.

mathematics, very specious in the diagram, but failing in the mechanic operation."[15] Can there not be heard in this passage the voice of a Baconian scientist, condemning the theoretical and speculative nature of Peripateticism, and its lack of useful or practical application? Dryden is also one with the scientists in respect to the theory of nature's decay, which in every field underlay the feeling of modern inferiority and increased the power of authority. He maintains that "the course of time rather improves nature than impairs her," and in this simple statement a great deal is contained.

In his sceptical attitude, at times in his method of reasoning, and in his revolt against the domination of the ancients in literature and against the principle of authority in general, Dryden owes a considerable debt to his fellow members of the Royal Society, but in nothing more than in that vision of progress in poetry, which he caught from a similar vision in science, and which is a frequent *motif* in his criticism.

## II

Toward the end of the seventeenth century the scientific movement becomes somewhat weaker,[16] in spite of or perhaps because of Newton's great discoveries, which seemed to have left nothing else to be explained. But in the last decade an event came to pass which again brought its values and attitudes clearly before the public. This was the appearance of Sir William

[15] *Ibid.*, I, 252.

[16] William Wotton expressed fear for the future of science because "the Humour of the Age, as to those things, is visibly altered from what it was Twenty or Thirty Years ago; So that though the ROYAL SOCIETY has weathered the rude Attacks of such sort of Adversaries as STUBBE, who endeavored to have it thought, That Studying of Natural Philosophy and Mathematicks, was a ready Method to introduce Scepticism at least, if not Atheism into the World: Yet the sly Insinuations of the *Men of Wit*, That no great things have ever, or are ever like to be performed by the *Men of Gresham*, and, That every Man whom they call a *Virtuoso* must needs be a *Sir Nicholas Gim-crack*, have so far taken off the Edge of those who have opulent Fortunes, and a Love to Learning, that Physiological Studies begin to be contracted amongst Physicians and Mechanicks." (*Reflections upon Ancient and Modern Learning*, 1694, pp. 356–57.) Much earlier, Sprat had expressed concern over the damage which the satirists might inflict upon science. *History of the Royal Society*, 1667, p. 417.

Temple's essay *Of Ancient and Modern Learning*, 1690. Sir
William was a retired statesman, who in his cautious political
career made no misstep, but who was not so fortunate in his literary activities, for this essay, though it ultimately led to notable
literary results in Swift's *Battle of the Books*, brought only cha-
grin to the author. The essay is a thinly veiled attack on the new
science in general and the Royal Society in particular, in which
the author makes a little learning go a long way, in a graceful
and charming style. The members of the Society became concerned, and engaged a learned young man, William Wotton, to
write a defense of the organization.[17] In it the claims of modern
science against ancient are bravely asserted and the controlling
ideas of the scientific movement are brought again to the front.

[17] See T. R., *An Essay Concerning Critical and Curious Learning*, 1698,
p. 47; William Wotton, *Reflections upon Ancient and Modern Learning*,
3d ed., 1705, pp. 393, 475; Richard F. Jones, "The Background of *The Battle
of the Books*" (*Washington University Studies*, VII, Humanistic Series II, St.
Louis, 1920, pp. 150–55), and *Ancients and Moderns*, p. 278. For specific
references to the Royal Society see Wotton's *Reflections*, 1694, pp. 233, 306–7,
347, 357; and for references to the controversy between the ancients and
moderns, which centered around the Royal Society, see pages 3, 78–80, 156,
170–71, 293, 257. Wotton gives a brief outline of the development of the
scientific movement in the seventeenth century: "Now as this [experimental
and mechanical] Method of Philosophizing laid down above, is right, so it is
easie to prove that it has been carefully followed by Modern Philosophers.
My Lord *Bacon* was the first great Man who took much pains to convince the
World that they had hitherto been in a wrong Path, and that Nature her self,
rather than her Secretaries, was to be addressed to by those who were desirous
to know very much of her Mind. Monsieur *Des Cartes*, who came soon after,
did not perfectly tread in his Steps, since he was for doing most of his Work
in his Closet, concluding too soon, before he had made Experiments enough;
but then to a vast Genius he joined exquisite Skill in Geometry, and working
upon intelligible Principles in an intelligent Manner; though he very often
failed of one Part of his End, namely, a right Explication of the Phænomena
of Nature, yet by marrying Geometry and Physicks together, he put the World
in Hopes of a Masculine Off-spring in process of Time, though the first Productions should prove abortive. This was the State of Natural Philosophy, when
those great Men who after King *Charles* II's Restoration joined in a Body,
called by that Prince himself, the ROYAL SOCIETY, went on with the Design;
they made it their Business to set their Members awork to collect a perfect
History of Nature, in order to establish thereupon a Body of Physicks; what
has been done towards it by the Members of that illustrious Body will be evident by considering that *Boyle, Barrow, Newton, Huygens, Malpighius, Leeu-
wenhoek, Willoughby, Willis* and Abundance more already named amongst the
great Advancers of real Learning, have belonged to it." *Reflections*, 1694,
pp. 306–7.

In the very year in which Wotton published his answer to Temple, 1694, Charles Gildon, a young and enthusiastic critic, produced a collection of short critical essays,[18] which, inspired partly by Dryden's criticism, approach critical problems almost entirely from the point of view of the new science. The first essay replies to Thomas Rymer, a critic who represents the extremes to which the dogmatic rules of neo-classicism and the worship of ancient models went in England.[19] Rymer had applied the rules to Shakespeare, and the result of his appraisal was that the bard of Avon knew no more about human nature than a pug in Barbary. Against this judgment Gildon rises up with considerable warmth. He asks if we are to admire Shakespeare, as Dryden does, or place him below the meanest poets, as Rymer has done—Rymer "whom," he says, "nothing it seems can please, but the Antic Forms and Methods of the *Athenian* Stage, or what comes up, and sticks close to them in our Language." He does not pause for a reply but proceeds immediately to the answer: "I can see no Reason why we shou'd be so very fond of imitating them here, without better proofs than the Critical Historiographer has produc'd." From this negative position he passes to more positive arguments against Rymer.

> 'Tis certain, the *Grecians* had not the advantage of us in *Physics*, or any other part of Philosophy, which with them chiefly consisted in words; they were a Talkative People; and being fond of the Opinion of Learning, more than the thing it self, as the most speedy way to gain that, stop'd their Enquiries on Terms, as is evident from their *Sophistry* and *Dialectic's*.

This characterization of ancient philosophy, or science, could have been taken almost verbatim from Sprat's *History of the Royal Society*. "There can be," Gildon continues, "no dispute among the Learned, but that we excel them in these Points.

---

[18] These are contained in *Miscellaneous Letters and Essays, on several Subjects. Philosophical, Moral, Historical, Critical, Amorous, etc. in Prose and Verse. Directed to John Dryden, Esq; The Honourable Geo. Granvill, Esq; Walter Moile, Esq; Mr. Dennis, Mr. Congreve, and other Eminent Men of the Age. By several Gentlemen and Ladies* (London, 1694). Gildon edited the volume and wrote most of it.

[19] "Some Reflections on Mr. Rymer's Short View of Tragedy, and an Attempt at a Vindication of Shakespeare, in an Essay directed to John Dryden Esq;."

Since the time of *Des Cartes*, when the Dictates of *Greece* began to be laid aside, what a Progress has been made in the discovery of Nature? and what Absurdities laid open in the School Precepts and Terms of *Aristotle?*"[20] Gildon sees in the revolt of modern science against ancient, and in its demonstrated superiority, sufficient reason for questioning the validity of classical rules in literature, and for doubting the superiority of Greek over English drama. From the same source he also draws the hope that as knowledge progresses with the new science, so may literature, if the shackles of authority are removed.

There is one argument advanced by this critic which, I am sure, no student of literature would concede to any scientist; namely, that the investigation of natural causes and effects is more difficult than the writing of plays, which in his eyes required only "a nice observation of Mankind." Nevertheless, he writes that he cannot understand how the Greeks should have so great an advantage over the moderns in drama, as some would allow them, when they are so far behind the moderns in matters of greater difficulty, i.e., science. "But," he says, "it can't be otherways whilst we make that Age and Nation the Standard of Excellence without regard to the difference of Custom, Age, Climate, *etc.*"[21]

In his next essay[22] Gildon is again answering Rymer, and also the French critic Rapin, who wished to prohibit the introduction of love scenes into tragedy because Greek drama does not contain them. He insists, and rightly, that the position of the two critics rests only on authority. "The chief Arguments indeed," he says,

which these Gentlemen bring, are from the Practice of the Ancients, . . . whose Authority they are of opinion shou'd outweigh Reason.

[20] *Miscellaneous Letters and Essays*, pp. 86–87.

[21] *Loc. cit.* Wotton maintains that the superiority of the ancients in poetry and oratory does not argue the inferiority of the moderns in genius, since the latter have surpassed antiquity in science; and he asks, "Does it seem harder to speak and write like *Cicero* or *Virgil*, than to find out the motions of the Heavens, and to calculate the Distances of the Stars?" *Reflections on Ancient and Modern Learning*, 1694, p. 24.

[22] "An Essay at a Vindication of Love in Tragedies, against *Rapin* and Mr. *Rymer*. Directed to Mr. Dennis."

But since the *Ipse dixit* has been so long laid aside in Philosophy, as an enemy to our Enquiries into Nature, I can see no reason why it shou'd be of so much greater force in Poetry; since 'tis perhaps almost as prejudicial to our imitation of Nature in *This*, as to our discovery of it in the Other.

From this analogy Gildon clearly perceived that freedom in art was as essential to the development of poetry as freedom in investigation was essential to the progress of scientific knowledge. He is not arguing only from analogy; he believes that the imposition of authority on literature leads to the same kind of stagnation which it had created in science. He explains rather than modifies his view when he says:

> As far as the Ancients and the Rules *Aristotle* draws from them, agree with the Character you give these, Of being *nothing but good sense and Nature reduc'd to Method*, I shall close with them; but when they either deviate from this, or reach not up to what may be done, I must think it but just to withdraw myself from the subjection of the *Stagyrite*, who has had a Reign long enough o'er the Minds of Mankind, and an Empire that far exceeded the Extent and Continuance of his Royal Pupil *Alexander*.[23]

Our liberal critic is not contending for what might be called a romantic freedom, but for an enlightened and more liberal neoclassicism, one of the fundamental elements of which, the imitation of nature, he upholds. For this reason he attacks the narrow dogmatic rules, for the support of which ancient authority was invoked, and he insists that there are more ways of imitating nature than those specified by these rules. He also further defines his attitude toward antiquity by acknowledging, as the scientists had done in their field, that the Greeks were the inventors of tragedy and comedy, but, like the scientists, he refuses to let that fact bar the development of the drama, and stand as a *non plus ultra* to the progress of poetry.[24]

In his third essay[25] Gildon pursues an argument of a more

---

[23] *Miscellaneous Letters and Essays*, p. 146.     [24] *Ibid.*, pp. 151–52.
[25] "An Essay *at a Vindication of the* Love-Verses of Cowley *and* Waller, *etc. In Answer to the Preface of a Book* Intituled, Letters and Verses Amorous and Gallant. Directed to Mr. Congreve." The author of the "Book" was William Walsh.

novel, if not more significant, nature than any drawn from science. This time he diverts his attack from Rymer to an anonymous author who had maintained that the love poems of the ancients were superior to those of the moderns because, to quote the author's own words,

The occasions upon which the poems are written, are such as happen to every Man almost that is in Love; and the Thoughts such, as are natural for every Man in love to think. The Moderns, on the other hand, have sought out occasions that none meet with but themselves, and fill their Verses with thoughts that are surprising and glittering but not . . . natural to a Man in Love.[26]

This fundamental classical principle of the universal Gildon counters with the idea of a relative aesthetic, an idea which later was incorporated in the conception of historical criticism. To understand his reasoning, however, it is necessary to revert to the clash between the experimental doctors and the Galenists. One of the arguments produced by the physicians of the new science against the authority of the ancients in medicine was that diseases vary according to countries, times, and nations; and, therefore, the remedies that might have been efficacious in antiquity were useless when applied to modern ailments.[27] Thus, they contended, it is necessary to discard the supposedly authoritative principles of ancient medicine, and discover new remedies by observation and experiment. This method of reasoning

[26] See the Preface to *Letters and Poems, Amorous and Gallant*, 1692. In contrast to his staunch championship of the moderns in science, Wotton concedes the superiority of the ancients in poetry and oratory. He takes Perrault to task for holding that ancient love poems, compared with modern, are rude and unpolished, because they lack gallantry: "It may be justly questioned, whether what Monsieur *Perrault* calls *Politeness*, be not very often rather an Aberration from, and Straining of Nature, than an Improvement of the Manners of the Age: If so, it may reasonably be supposed, that those that medled not with the Niceties of Ceremony and Breeding, before unpractised, rather contemned them as improper or unnatural, than omitted them because of the Roughness of the Manners of the Ages in which they lived. *Ovid* and *Tibullus* knew what Love was, in its tenderest Motions; they describe its Anxieties and Disappointments in a Manner that raises too many Passions, even in unconcerned Hearts." *Reflections*, pp. 51–52.

[27] See Marchamont Nedham's *Medela Medicinae*, 1665, and Richard F. Jones's *Ancients and Moderns*, p. 216.

Gildon appropriated *in toto,* and he applied it to love poetry. Repeating the concession he had made once before, he says:

> I shall never deny the Ancients their just Praise of the Invention of *Arts* and *Sciences*; but I cannot without contradicting my own Reason, allow them the Perfecters of 'em so far that they must be our uncontroverted Patterns and Standard: For our Physicians have found the Prescripts of *Hippocrates* very Defective: And as in Physic, so in Poetry, there must be a regard had to the Clime, Nature, and Customs of the People; for the Habits of the Mind as well as those of the Body, are influenc'd by them; and Love with the other Passions vary in their *Effects* as well as *Causes,* according to each Country and Age; nay, according to the very Constitution of each Person affected.

This fact, he concludes, renders fallacious any idea that the ancients should furnish immutable standards of literary excellence for the moderns.[28] In his insistence upon the principle of relativity, and in his emphasis upon the individual as opposed to the universal, Gildon takes a step toward romanticism.

The idea of a relative aesthetic appears again in Gildon's last essay,[29] which upholds the superiority of modern poetry in general over ancient. In answer to the champions of antiquity who would deny the moderns the title of poets because they did not strictly observe Aristotelian rules, he asserts that the dogmatic critics have mistaken the true purpose of poetry, which is pleasure. To achieve this end, he says, "regard must be had to the *Humour, Custom,* and *Inclination* of the Auditory; but an *English* audience will never be pleas'd with a dry, Jejune and formal Method that excludes Variety as the Religious observation of the Rules of *Aristotle* does."[30] In short, classical principles of art are not good for all time, and if pleasure, the true purpose of poetry, is to be achieved, a different art, determined by the age and nation which produce it, is required.

[28] *Miscellaneous Letters and Essays,* p. 210.

[29] "To my Honoured and Ingenious Friend Mr. Harrington, for the Modern Poets against the Ancients." Throughout most of the seventeenth century the controversy between the ancients and moderns in England was almost exclusively concerned with science. Even Wotton himself gave the palm to the ancients in the arts. But toward the end of this century and in the next, literature became the center of the quarrel. In a way, my article merely indicates the influence which the first stage of the controversy exerted upon the second.

[30] *Miscellaneous Letters and Essays,* p. 223.

Gildon does not loom large in the history of criticism, but in his defense of Shakespeare, attack on authority, hostility to imitation, idea of a relative aesthetic, insistence on the aesthetic purpose of poetry, and belief in the possibility of the advancement of literature, what influence he exerted made for the liberalizing of the neo-classical spirit.

Throughout the criticism of this age one finds frequent allusions to the scientific movement and arguments drawn from it. In fact, the frequency with which they occur when any liberal sentiment is expressed, indicates the strength and widespread nature of the influence. One writer, who advocated the spending of more time on the study of English and less on that of the classical languages, remarks that since "our *Navigators*, *Traders*, *Astronomers* and *Mathematicians*, *Physicians* and *Surgeons*, by Benefit of longer Time and Experience, have gone beyond the Ancients in their Arts and Knowledge; is there any good Reason why we should be behind them in Wit and Language?"[31] The habit of introducing the scientific parallel became so common as to appear in comedy. In the passage referred to, one character remarks that he would as soon receive medical treatment by the rules of Hippocrates and Galen as see a play written by the rules of Aristotle and Horace.[32] To this view Farquhar, a practical and successful dramatist, would certainly have subscribed, for in his essay on comedy he inveighs against Aristotle's authority and tries to undermine his reputation as a critic. "I will have a tug with *ipse dixit*, tho' I dye for 't," he declares. After stoutly denying "that we live in the decay of Time, and the Dotage of the World is fall'n to our Share," he exclaims,

No, no, Sir, *ipse dixit* is remov'd long ago, and all the Rubbish of old Philosophy, that in a manner bury'd the Judgment of Mankind for many Centuries, is now carry'd off; the vast Tomes of *Aristotle* and his Commentatore are all taken to pieces, and their Infallibility is lost with all Persons of a free and unprejudic'd Reason.

[31] *Many Advantages of a Good Language*, 1724, p. 25.

[32] The play is Thomas Killigrew's *Chit-Chat*, 1719, Act IV, Sc. 2. See *Critical Remarks on the Four Taking Plays of this Season . . . By Corinna, a Country Parson's Wife*, 1719, p. 52.

This being so, he asks, "by what Authority shou'd *Aristotle's* Rules of Poetry stand so fixt and immutable?"[33]

## III

In 1716 Sir Richard Blackmore, a physician and a poet of small ability, published an *Essay upon Epic Poetry*,[34] the primary purpose of which was to overthrow some of the most cherished neo-classical principles of the epic. A scientist himself and a fellow of the College of Physicians, he undoubtedly was familiar with that stream of scientific thought that had come down from the middle of the seventeenth century. At an earlier date he had expressed contempt for servile imitators of the ancients, and had voiced the hope that some good genius "would break the *Ice*, assert the *Liberty of Poetry*, and set up for an *Original* in *Writing* in a way accommodated to the *Religion, Manners*, and other *Circumstances* we are now under."[35] When after sixteen years no such hero arose, he engaged in this more elaborate attack on antiquity. He has not proceeded far in his essay before he launches upon a short history of the scientific revolt, which needs to be quoted in full if his position is to be clearly understood. After speaking of the blind obedience to Aristotle on the part of his earlier followers, he says:

The voluminous Lucubrations of these idle Students, who only copy'd and expounded their Leader's Sentiments, which they follow'd with a blind Obedience, were esteem'd the only valuable Productions of Philosophy. At length arose some famous Worthies, who animated by a generous Impulse to deliver *Europe* from the basest Servitude, that of the Understanding, attack'd *Aristotle* and his Adherents with great Vigour, declar'd against all arbitrary Impositions on the Mind, and asserted the Liberty of Reflection and a Power of examining Evidence, and judging for themselves. These excellent Persons, who deserv'd so well of Mankind, by vindicating the Dignity of Humane Nature, and standing up for its Rights and Prerogatives, against the Usurpation

[33] See "A Discourse upon Comedy, in Reference to the English Stage," 1702, in *Critical Essays of the Eighteenth Century, 1700–1725*, ed. W. H. Durham, pp. 263–64.
[34] This essay is found in *Essays upon Several Subjects*, 1716.
[35] See the Preface to *A Paraphrase upon the Book of Job*, 1700.

of a particular Sect, having by an impartial Search discover'd that the Peripatetick System had nothing in it for its support, but precarious and unevident Principles, effectually expos'd its Weakness, and soon brought the greatest Authority, that was ever establish'd in the Schools, into general Contempt.

The purpose of this lenthy preamble is clearly visible in the next passage, in which he expresses surprise that the revolution in science was not extended to cover literature as well. "But when," he continues,

these extraordinary Men, by encouraging the free Exercise of Reason, had infus'd an active Ferment into the Minds of an ignorant and slothful Generation, by the Operation of which they were excited to throw off the yoke of *Aristotle* in Matters of Philosophy, it is wonderful that the Effect was not more extensive. They had as great Reason to have proceeded to the Examination of his Rules in the Art of Poetry, and to have made Enquiry if those were settled on better Foundations.

Blackmore believes that the collapse of Aristotle's authority in science should have inspired scepticism regarding its validity in poetry. The realization that such had not been the case moved him to denounce the dogmatic critics of his day, and to associate them with the incorrigible and subservient Aristotelians of the preceding age. "But," he says,

I know not how it came to pass, his [i.e., Aristotle's] Notions and Precepts in this Art have still remain'd unquestion'd and untry'd. The modern Criticks, contemning the Examples of the Philosophers, have still proceeded in the old beaten Track, of believing and admiring whatever *Aristotle* advances on the Subjects, where the Muses are concern'd. They are all like their submissive Predecessors, mere Expositors, scarce excepting *Bossu* himself, of the writings of that great Man, and have made no Improvements, nor asserted the Liberty of Poetry, as the other freer Spirits have vindicated that of Philosophy. It's clear, that *Aristotle* form'd all his Axioms and Doctrines in Poetry, from the Patterns of *Homer* and other *Greek* Writers; and without assigning any Reason of his Positions, relies for the Truth of them on his own, or the Authority of those Authors. But it is not the Authority of the greatest Masters, but solid and convincing Evidence, that must engage our Belief, and make us subscribe to any Maxims in any Art or Science whatsoever.[36]

[36] *Essays upon Several Subjects,* pp. 10 ff.

In view of the intensity of the earlier scientific rebellion against antiquity, and of the number of important men who were engaged in it, Blackmore's surprise that the revolt was not extended is not strange. But what he does not seem to realize is that as the seventeenth century advanced, the spirit of literature, and, to a limited extent, the universities, remained humanistic, while science pursued a largely independent course. It became, in fact, the target for the ridicule of the greatest writers of the time, such as Swift and, later, Pope. Sir Richard, however, was only partially correct, as the examples of Dryden and Gildon show, and his own essay reveals one more critic inspired by the independence of science and rebelling against the domination of the classics. That his inspiration came from science is further revealed in his attitude toward Aristotle, which in one passage is expressed in words so reminiscent of the earlier upholders of the experimental philosophy as to seem almost like direct quotation:

I look upon *Aristotle* as a great Genius, and a Person of more than common Erudition; but will no more submit to him as a Law-giver of the Poets, than of the Philosophers. I shall always pay Respect and Deference to his Judgment and Opinions, tho not acquiesce in them as infallible and decisive Decrees.

It is not that he loves Aristotle less, but liberty more. He would not in general, he says, condemn Aristotle's rules, but "I shall use the same Liberty in adding any new Opinions on this Subject, which in my Judgment will improve the Art of Poetry."[37] He even looks with some tolerance upon one of the chief ideas of the supporters of the ancients, namely, that the works of antiquity have demonstrated their excellence in being approved by so many nations for so many ages. Yet he strenuously denies that this fact is proof of their infallibility. "Universality and Antiquity," he says, "are to be look'd on with Respect and Reverence; but since they have been often produc'd to support manifest Errors in Philosophy as well as in Religion, and have therefore been often rejected, why should they be regarded as infallible in Poetry?"[38] Blackmore recognized in this idea of universal and repeated consent one of the strongest

[37] *Ibid.*, pp. 14–15.  [38] *Ibid.*, p. 160.

supports of authority. He introduces it more frequently and answers it more elaborately than any other opinion. Fortunately, if science had demonstrated anything, it had shown that the life of error may indeed be long, that many ideas had down through the ages met with wide approval, only to be overthrown at last by some experimental scientist. Thus the new science offered him the soundest possible reasons for refuting the idea, and he makes full use of them. "*Aristotle's* Notions in Philosophy," he says,

> were, for many Ages, as universally receiv'd by the learned World as *Homer's* Poetry, and esteem'd as the Dictates of the most profound Judgment and Oracles of Reason; yet, after he had reign'd in the Schools many Centuries with uncontested Authority, upon Examination he was discover'd to have no just Claim to this great Dignity; he was found out to be an Usurper, strip'd of his Titles and Regalia, and not only degraded, but treated with the greatest Contempt. . . . It is vain to urge the Suffrages of Antiquity, against clear and solid Argument. In this Case Citations are neither pertinent nor useful, for the Authors of former Ages are disqualify'd from giving their Votes in a Matter of this Nature; no length of Time, no not three Thousand Years, is a sufficient Prescription to bar the Claim of Reason, which has an undoubted Prerogative to seize upon its Rights, when, and wherever they are discover'd.[39]

The chief consideration which intensifies Sir Richard's hostility to authority is the loss of liberty which the latter entails, and with this loss of liberty the impossibility of any development in poetry. Looking upon the great advance which had been made in science since the overthrow of ancient dictates, he ardently desires the same progress for poetry. "If Men," he says,

> from a generous Principle of Liberty, would renounce the unjust, tho prevailing Power of Authority, and claim their natural Right of entring into the Reason of Things, and judging for themselves, it is highly probable that the Art of Poetry might be carry'd on to greater Degrees of Perfection, and be improv'd, as Philosophy has been.

He discovers another happy result of this freedom in the discrediting of the pettifogging critics who would place literature

[39] *Essays upon Several Subjects*, pp. 166–67.

in the strait jacket of neo-classical rules and judge its excellence solely by classical examples. He promises that

When thus unfetter'd and disingag'd from a slavish Dependence upon celebrated Writers, Men would soon disregard the crude and unreasonable Assertions frequently laid down by injudicious Commentators and superficial Grammarians, whose Attainments consist in a Collection of Examples, and an Ability to explain the *Roman* and *Grecian* Authors: Nor will a modern Heroick Work be any longer acquitted or condemn'd merely as it bears a Conformity or Dissimilitude to the *Iliad* or the *Aeneid*."[40]

Instead, Blackmore thinks, critics will find it necessary to advance substantial grounds for their critical appraisals, and a more fruitful investigation of the nature of art will follow.

Sir Richard takes the occasion to answer what is almost the only possible objection to the evidence which he derives from the history of science. "Neither is it sufficient to alledge," he says,

that *Aristotle* has express'd greater Judgment and Accuracy in his Discourses on Poetry, than in his Philosophical Productions; and therefore, tho the last, upon a just Tryal, have been exploded, yet the first have been esteem'd in all Ages by the Learned World as masterly Instructions, and continue undisputed to this Day; for this is still to press us only with the Authority of *Aristotle* and his Commentators. If his Rules and Precepts of Poetry ought to be so highly regarded, it must be upon this Account, That stronger Reasons can be produc'd in Defence of these, than of his System of Natural Science: But how can this appear, if we take his Writings on the Art of Poetry upon Content, and do not by an impartial Examination make it clear, that the Evidence of Reason is on their Side; which was wanting to support his Philosophy? And this, as far as I know, has not been attempted.[41]

The argument opposed here by Blackmore was potentially the most powerful one advanced against the deadly scientific parallel, and had been employed in France by such defenders of the ancients as Dacier. Many years earlier Gildon had acknowledged that the poets of Greece still maintained their glory though

[40] *Ibid.*, pp. 12–13.
[41] *Ibid.*, pp. 13–14.

Greek science had been overthrown, but he had pursued the theme no further, for he was then writing against the ancients.[42]

In the long interval, however, that elapsed between his early and later criticism, he underwent a transformation in his critical views, and became one of the narrowest and most dogmatic of neo-classical critics, a complete critical apostate. In a work published five years after Blackmore's essay, he attacks the critical doctor severely for maintaining the same opinions which he himself in the preceding century had espoused with such enthusiasm. He seizes especially upon the argument which Blackmore had tried to answer, and which asserts that some distinction must be drawn between what might be called the naturalistic and the humanistic works of Aristotle. But Gildon muffs his opportunity, for he contents himself with the argument that Aristotle's philosophy had not received the approbation of all ages, that it was introduced by the Schoolmen to support Catholic theology, and that in this limited field only was it given an authoritative character. Since, he says, its authority did not arise

from the universal consent of all men, and in all ages and nations where his philosophy had appear'd, . . . the instance which *Sir Richard* gives is very defective, not to say unfair, when he puts that, which was forc'd upon mankind, on the same bottom with what was voluntarily receiv'd, from the evidence of the truth and reason that was found in those works

---

[42] "I will yield that *Greece* had Great Poets, notwithstanding all those Monstrous Faults and Absurdities they abound with; tho he [Rymer] will not allow the *English* any Honour, because they have been guilty of Errors. Nay, I'll say more, that the Poetry of *Greece* was her most valuable Learning, for that still maintains its Share of Glory and Esteem, whilst her Philosophy is now exploded by the Universal Reason of Mankind. *Homer, Pindar, Sophocles,* and *Euripides* will, as long as they are understood, preserve their Characters of Excellent Poets, tho the *Stagyrite* with all his Volumes, is now shrunk from the Ostentatious Title of the *Philosopher* to that of a good *Critic,* or *Grammarian.*" (*Miscellaneous Letters and Essays,* p. 221.) Other critics than Gildon found it necessary to recognize the overthrow of Aristotle's authority in science. Rymer says, "And however cryed down in the Schools, and vilified by some modern Philosophers; since Men have had a taste for *good sense,* and could discern the beauties of correct writing, he [Aristotle] is prefer'd in the *politest* Courts of *Europe,* and by the *Poets* held in great veneration." "Preface to Rapin," *Critical Essays of the Seventeenth Century,* ed. J. E. Spingarn, II, 164.

of *Aristotle*, that have met with that universal approbation which his
*poetics*, his *rhetorics*, his *politics*, and his *ethics* have found.[43]

Because Gildon noticed only the history of Aristotle's scientific
and humanistic works, and did not inquire into the difference between their natures, he failed to grasp a distinction that might
have furnished him much more cogent proofs than the pitiful
evidence he advances.

The development of the thought-movement which we have
been following did not proceed independently of France, where
the controversy between the ancients and moderns was still active, and was at this time especially concerned with Homer. In
fact, Blackmore's essay was partly inspired by this controversy,
and reveals distinct indebtedness to a treatise by one of the supporters of the moderns, the Abbé Terrasson, which, in the year
Sir Richard's essay appeared, was translated into English by
Francis Brerewood under the title *A Discourse of Ancient and
Modern Learning*. It is not my purpose to enter into the complexities of Anglo-French relations in this matter, except to
indicate one difference between the movements in the two countries. Terrasson attacks the authority of the ancients as a bar to
the progress of poetry and a dishonor to the mind of man, and
he introduces the popular parallel from science, but he does all
this merely to install Le Bossu in Aristotle's chair of authority—
a wretched substitution—and to move French neo-classical poets
into the place vacated by Homer and other ancient worthies.
The French critic shows how the development of Cartesian
science and French classicism went hand in hand, and he argues
the superiority of modern writers over ancient, because the
former observed more consistently the unities, decorum, and
other neo-classical principles, originally based upon the ancients.[44]
In short, the freedom from classical authority which the French
moderns demanded furnished merely the opportunity to place

[43] *The Laws of Poetry*, 1721, pp. 263–64. Wotton points out that though
science is unlimited and therefore capable of progressing, poetry is a limited art
and not necessarily capable of advancing. (*Reflections*, pp. 46–47.) He seems
to have recognized the fact that art does not necessarily obey the same law of
progress which science follows.
[44] See pp. x, xv, lviii–lxi, lxxiii, lxxxvii, lxxxix, xci, xcii–xciv.

stronger chains upon themselves.[45] The freedom desired in England was more of a true liberty, and since the moderns whose cause the critics were defending were in large part Elizabethans, especially Shakespeare, the upholders of modernity were essentially contending for a more liberal art. So the controversy in France, deeply influenced by Descartes, made for neo-classicism, while the same controversy in England, reflecting Bacon, moved toward romanticism.

Blackmore, however, did not move far in that direction. But he did insist upon the necessity of a sceptical attitude, upon the liberty of examining and scrutinizing received opinions, and upon the privilege of making additions to critical principles. He does not hesitate to disagree firmly with Le Bossu, to whom Terrasson would hand Aristotle's sceptre. Inspired by the precedent of science, he expresses vigorous dissent from various neo-classical rules, maintaining, for instance, that the epic hero need not be virtuous; that the action need not be prosperous; that the sufferings and calamities of a hero are as fitting material for an epic as his actions and exploits; and that the poem need not embody a moral.[46] Unfortunately, the liberty of departing from received opinions played him false, if his own epics be taken as proof, for they well deserve Pope's satire in the second book of the *Dunciad*, where they are represented as quite capable of putting the most hardened critic to sleep.

## IV

Nowhere is the difference between the French and English revolts from the ancients more clearly revealed and the note of

[45] Cf. Ker, I, xxiii. Wotton says, "In Poetry likewise he [Perrault] sets Monsieur *Boileau* against *Horace*, Monsieur *Corneille* and Monsieur *Moliere* against the Ancient *Dramatick* Poets. In short, though he owns that some amongst the Ancients had very exalted Genius's, so that it may, perhaps, be very hard to find any Thing that comes near the Force of some of the Ancient Pieces, in either Kind, amongst our Modern Writers, yet he affirms, that Poetry and Oratory are now at a greater heighth than ever they were, because there have been many Rules found out since Virgil's and Horace's Time; and the old Rules likewise have been more carefully scanned than ever they were before." *Reflections*, pp. 46–47.

[46] *Essays upon Several Subjects*, pp. 49, 52, 77, 78–79.

liberty more loudly struck than in the next and last critic to be
considered. In 1759, a year so far removed from seventeenth-
century science that one might well suppose its influence was
already spent, Edward Young published an essay entitled *Conjectures on Original Composition*, which upholds original as opposed to imitative writing, and which is one of several critical
works that definitely mark the turning of the literary tide from
neo-classicism to romanticism. Though its own originality can
easily be exaggerated, it contains complete, distinct, and confident statements of ideas and attitudes which before had, for the
most part, received only brief, sporadic, or subdued expression:
hostility to the authority of the ancients; insistence upon freedom from restraining rules; liberty to widen the domain of
poetry; depreciation of reason and learning; emphasis upon inspired genius and creative imagination; the organic as opposed
to the mechanical theory of art; and belief in the magical and
transporting power of verse. All these show how far the treatise
is removed from the critical dogmas of the preceding hundred
years. Admittedly inspired by Bacon, it is saturated with his
spirit and strewn with his ideas, as well as touched by his eloquence. Young speaks of Bacon as one "under the shadow of
whose great name I would shelter my present attempt in favour
of originals." And, indeed, the general position and attitude of
the two men are remarkably similar. Just as Bacon, perceiving
the stagnation of learning and the inadequacies of knowledge to
be due to servile submission to antiquity, in ringing tones called
upon his fellow men to arouse themselves, throw off their fetters,
and begin independent investigation of nature; so Young, with
the same reforming zeal, urges men to arise, strike off the chains
of classical authority, and allow their own genius full play, for
"The wide field of Nature . . . lies open before it, where it
may range unconfined, make what discoveries it can, and sport
with its infinite objects uncontrolled, as far as visible nature extends." I cannot refrain from comparing with this passage the
promise which the Baconian spirit in Thomas Sprat made to the
experimental scientists of his day: "The Beautiful Bosom of
*Nature* will be Expos'd to our view: we shall enter into its

*Garden,* and tast of its *Fruits,* and satisfy our selves with its *plenty.*"[47]

In analyzing the obstacles standing in the way of the development of poetry, a development which the independent activity of poetic genius could make possible, Young draws heavily upon the reasons Bacon gave for the stagnation of science. In fact, he quotes the Lord Chancellor as follows: "Men seek not to know their own stock and abilities; but fancy their possessions to be greater, and their abilities less, than they really are."[48] "Which," Young adds, "is, in effect, saying, That we ought to exert more than we do; and that, on exertion, our probability of success is greater than we conceive."[49] In another passage Young repeats the idea that men do not know their own abilities. Thus he applies to his own purposes what had been advanced for the reformation of science. Bacon's idea that the advancement of learning is checked by the diffidence and despair which men derive from the belief that it is impossible to go beyond the ancients, finds emphatic expression in the later critic.[50] "Illustri-

[47] *History of the Royal Society,* 1667, p. 327.

[48] The quotation is the opening sentence of the Preface to the *Great Instauration.* Bacon continues: "Hence it follows that either from an extravagant estimate of the value of the arts they possess, they seek no further, or else from too mean an estimate of their own powers, they spend their strength in small matters and never put it fairly to the trial in those which go to the main. These are as the pillars of fate set in the path of knowledge, for men have neither desire nor hope to encourage them to penetrate further." The idea that men do not put their abilities to the test is also clearly expressed by Young: "Its [the mind's] bounds are as unknown as those of creation; since the birth of which, perhaps, not one has so far exerted, as not to leave his possibilities beyond his attainments, his powers beyond his exploits. Forming our judgments altogether by what *has* been done, without knowing, or at all inquiring what possibly might have been done, we naturally fall into too mean an opinion of the human mind," and think that it is impossible to surpass Homer.

[49] Bacon says that more might be expected from the modern age than from antiquity, "if it but knew its own strength and chose to essay and exert it." *The Works of Francis Bacon,* ed. Spedding, Ellis, and Heath (new ed., 1889), IV, 82.

[50] According to Bacon, the principal impediment to knowledge "hath been in despair or diffidence, and the strong apprehension of the difficulty, obscurity, and the infiniteness which belongeth to the invention of knowledge, and that men have not known their own strength." This fact, he says, has caused some to depend on authorities. Elsewhere he asserts that accepted authorities instill in men the belief that they can do nothing either by art or industry, a belief which

ous examples," he says, "engross, prejudice, and intimidate." And he gives this command to modern poets: "Let not great examples, or authorities browbeat thy reason into too great a diffidence of thyself."[51] Like his great predecessor, Young was concerned with inspiring in men confidence in their powers and also a hope of success independent of the ancients. For this purpose Lord Verulam had found it necessary to combat the theory of nature's decay, and later scientists continued to attack it. Young attaches the same importance to a refutation of the idea. Again and again he insists that modern powers lie under no necessary inferiority, that time cannot be held responsible for the lack of modern achievements, and that the mind's teeming time is not past.[52] He utilizes to good effect Bacon's paradox, *Antiquitas sæculi juventus mundi*; that, as regards the world, the moderns are the ancients.[53] From this he draws the same conclusion as the philosopher, namely, that the moderns must be richer in judgment and knowledge.[54] By nature, our critic says,

"tend[s] wholly to the unfair circumscription of human power, and to a deliberate and factitious despair; which not only disturbs the auguries of hope, but also cuts the sinews and spur of industry, and throws away the chances of experience itself." Bacon, *op. cit.*, III, 249; IV, 86.

[51] Young makes use of the giant-and-dwarf figure, which appears repeatedly in the seventeenth-century controversy between the ancients and moderns: "Too formidable an idea of their [the ancients'] superiority, like a spectre, would fright us out of a proper use of our wits; and dwarf our understanding, by making a giant of theirs. Too great awe for them lays genius under restraint, and denies it that free scope, that full elbow-room, which is requisite for striking its most masterly strokes."

[52] Other references to the theory are found in Young's assertion that an impartial Providence scatters talents indifferently through all periods of time, and that different portions of understanding are not allotted to different periods. For this reason he holds that nature cannot be blamed for modern inferiority.

[53] "And to speak truly *Antiquitas sæculi juventus mundi*. These times are the ancient time, when the world is ancient and not those which we account ancient *ordine retrogrado*, by a computation backward from ourselves." (Bacon, *op. cit.*, III, 291.) Young says: "though we are the moderns, the world is an ancient; more ancient far, than when they whom we most admire filled it with their fame."

[54] "For the old age of the world is to be accounted the true antiquity; and this is the attribute of our own times, not of that earlier age of the world in which the ancients lived; and which, though in respect of us it was the elder, yet in respect of the world it was the younger. And truly as we look for greater knowledge of human things and a riper judgment in the old man than in the young, because of his experience and of the number and variety of the things

we are as strong as the ancients, by time we stand on higher ground.

Another essential idea of Bacon's and one emphasized by later scientists, seized upon Young's mind—the idea of the liberty to investigate and to reason upon the results. As we have seen, this attitude inspired all the critics we have discussed with a similar desire for liberty to depart from established rules and models, and to introduce innovations into art. Like them, Young argues for this freedom, which he considers essential to original writing. "Originals," he says, "soar in the regions of liberty; imitations move in fetters." Even more prominent in his essay is the idea of progress, which had inspired and encouraged seventeenth-century scientists, and which had hardened their faces against antiquity because its authority was an obstacle to advancement. Young contrasts the discoveries which originals may make with the sterility of imitations and their inability to go beyond the beaten paths of classical art.[55] Originals, he asserts, extend the republic of letters, and add a new province to its domain. They enable a poet not only to explore more fully the regions of nature, but also to survey the purely imaginary world. "In the fairyland of fancy," he says, "genius may wander wild;

---

which he has seen and heard and thought of; so in like manner from our age, if it but knew its own strength and chose to essay and exert it, much more might fairly be expected than from the ancient times. . . ." (Bacon, *op. cit.*, IV, 82.) The last part of this quotation contains the gist of Young's essay, which calls upon men to know their own powers and exert them fearlessly and independently.

[55] "*Imitators*," Young says, "only give us a sort of duplicates of what we had, possibly much better, before; increasing the mere drug of books, while all that makes them valuable, *knowledge* and *genius*, are at a stand." And elsewhere he enlarges upon the fewness of originals: "So few are our *Originals*, that, if all other books were to be burnt, the letter'd world would resemble some metropolis in flames, where a few incombustible buildings . . . lift their heads, in melancholy grandeur amid the mighty ruin." Cf. Bacon, *op. cit.*, IV, 13–14: "For let a man look carefully into all that variety of books with which the arts and sciences abound, he will find everywhere endless repetitions of the same thing, varying in the method of treatment, but not in substance, insomuch that the whole stock, numerous as it appears at first view, proves on examination to be but scanty. . . . Observe also, that if sciences of this kind had any life in them, that could never have come to pass which has been the case now for many ages—that they stand almost at a stay, without receiving any augmentations worthy of the human race; . . ."

there it has creative power, and may reign arbitrarily over its own empire of chimeras."[56] The relatively timid pleas for liberty to go beyond the ancients in imitation of nature has grown into the bold demand for liberty to go even beyond nature. In pleading for literary progress, Young introduces, as earlier critics had done, the encouraging example of progress in scientific knowledge. After painting a bright picture of the future development of art, he concludes: "What a rant, say you, is here? —I partly grant it. Yet, consider, my friend! knowledge physical, mathematical, moral, and divine increases; all arts and sciences are making considerable advance, and why may not poetry go forward with this advancement."[57] As examples of originals he mentions Milton and Shakespeare, but not these only, for he says, "in natural and mathematical knowledge, we have great originals already—Bacon, Boyle, Newton." Thus he draws closer together experimental science and creative poetry, and shows that the essential meaning he gives to the term "original" applies equally well to both.

The reference to Shakespeare merits comment. There is

[56] After quoting Bacon's opinion that the moderns underestimate their own abilities, Young says, "Nor have I *Bacon's* opinion only, but his assistance too, on my side. His mighty mind travelled round the intellectual world; and with a more than eagle's eye, saw, and has pointed out, blank spaces, or dark spots in it, on which the human mind never shone: Some of these have been enlightened since; some are benighted still." Bacon's assistance must have taken the form of inspiring Young to find the blank spots in the poetic world, and to show how a new province might be added to the literary domain, "the fairyland of fancy," for he says in the next sentence, "Moreover, so boundless are the bold excursions of the human mind, that in the vast void beyond real existence, it can call forth shadowy beings, and unknown worlds, as numerous, as bright, and perhaps as lasting, as the stars; such quite original beauties we may call paradisaical."

[57] Young finds definite evidence of the superiority of modern over ancient genius in the fact that the world has progressed in virtue, and since virtue assists genius, the latter must be greater than in former times. Thus, for his belief in the possibility of literary progress he draws support from the idea of progress in the religious and moral world, as well as from the advancement of science; but since his general indebtedness to Bacon and the scientific movement is so much more extensive and pronounced than to any other source, we are safe in inferring that the influence of the latter in this matter was correspondingly greater. Before Young's treatise appeared there had been considerable discussion concerning progress in religion and morality, upon which science exerted no negligible influence. See R. S. Crane, *Modern Philology*, XXXI (1933–34), 273–306, 349–82; especially pp. 373–74.

much praise of the poet in the essay, so much that the reader feels that he had a great deal to do with Young's idea of originality, but Shakespeare is not introduced for his dramatic excellence only; he is primarily considered as a means toward an end. Just as in the scientific movement great discoveries were employed, not for their intrinsic value, but because their excellence furnished proof for the validity of the principles of experimental science, which were themselves the matter of most concern, so Shakespeare is introduced to furnish proof of the principles of original composition. This is only an analogy, but it contributes something to an understanding of the similarity between the natures of the scientific and literary programs and between the means used to establish them.

There are other echoes of Bacon and of the scientific movement in Young, such as the belief that imitation of or reliance on antiquity prevents that progress in the liberal arts which the mechanical enjoy, because the latter try to go beyond their predecessors, while the former slavishly follow them.[58] And there are some figures of speech borrowed from Bacon, e.g., "a stream cannot rise higher than its source."[59] That Young was well

[58] In speaking of the evil effects of imitation, Young says, "*First*, it deprives the liberal and politer arts of an advantage, which the mechanic enjoy: In these men are ever endeavoring to go beyond their predecessors; in the former, to follow them. And since copies surpass not their *Originals*, as streams rise not higher than their spring, rarely so high; hence, while arts mechanic are in perpetual progress and increase, the liberal are in retrogradation and decay." Bacon was very fond of the contrast: "In arts mechanical the first device comes shortest and time addeth and perfecteth. But in sciences of conceit the first author goeth furthest and time leeseth and corrupteth" (*op. cit.*, III, 226); and in speaking of the way in which authority prevents progress, he says, "hence it hath comen in arts mechanical the first deviser comes shortest, and time addeth and perfecteth: but in sciences the first author goeth furthest, and time leeseth and corrupteth." (*Ibid.*, III, 289–90.) Elsewhere he dwells longer upon the comparison: "all the tradition and succession of schools is still a succession of masters and scholars, not of inventors and those who bring to further perfection the things invented. In the mechanical arts we do not find it so; they, on the contrary, as having in them some breath of life, are continually growing and becoming more perfect. . . . Philosophy and the intellectual sciences, on the contrary, stand like statues, worshipped and celebrated, but not moved or advanced. Nay, they sometimes flourish most in the hands of the first author, and afterwards degenerate." *Ibid.*, IV, 14; cf. IV, 74–75.

[59] Young uses the figure to show that imitations prevent the progress of poetry because they cannot surpass their models, and Bacon employs it to illustrate his conviction that reliance upon Aristotle prevents the progress of knowl-

aware of the scientific movement in the seventeenth century is revealed in a specific reference to "the dispute over ancient and modern learning," a dispute which extended with varying intensity from the founding of the Royal Society in 1662 down to Temple and Wotton. The elaboration of other details is hardly necessary; a thorough treatment of the subject would require an article in itself.[60] Furthermore, what is more important than any details of similarity is the spirit and purpose of Young's proposed reformation. He is really trying to do for poetry what Bacon did for science, free it from the domination of the ancients, and put it on the right road to improvement. He could very well have called his essay *The Advancement of Poetry*.

## V

The ways in which the scientific movement extended its liberalizing aid to literary criticism were various. It did much to develop a sceptical and critical attitude of mind, and, in the case of Dryden, may very well have fostered his inductive

edge, which is "like a water that will never arise again higher than the level from which it fell." *Op. cit.*, III, 227; cf. *ibid.*, III, 290; IV, 16.

[60] A few other similarities may be mentioned. Young enlarges upon the fame accorded originals: "Fame, fond of new glories, sounds her trumpet in triumph at its [an original's] birth"; Bacon says, "the introduction of famous discoveries appears to hold by far the first place among human actions; and this was the judgment of the former ages." (*Op. cit.*, IV, 113.) Young comments upon the assistance which the ancients can lend the modern in enabling them to surpass the productions of antiquity: "Have we not their [the ancients'] beauties as stars to guide; their defects as rocks to be shunned?" Among the reasons given for the hope that his age may surpass the ancients, Bacon lists "the noble monuments of ancient writers, which shine like so many lights before us." (*Op. cit.*, V, 110.) In explaining the obstacles to progress, both Young and Bacon use the figure of master and pupil, the former stating that advancement would be possible "if ancients and moderns were no longer considered as masters and pupils," and the latter asserting that the traditional philosophy possessed no life, for "all the tradition and succession of schools is still a succession of masters and scholars." (*Op. cit.*, IV, 14.) Bacon says (*op. cit.*, III, 291) that one error induced by the worship of antiquity "is a distrust that anything should now be found out, which the world should have missed and passed over so long"; and Young declares that the reason why originals are so few is not that "the writer's harvest is over, the great reapers of antiquity having left nothing to be gleaned after them." Young merely points Bacon's ideas and expressions in a new direction. Brandl has noted Young's indebtedness, in thought and style, to the *Novum Organum*, I, 129. See *Jahrbuch der deutschen Shakespeare-Gesellschaft*, XXXIX (1903), 10–11.

method of reasoning. But the most important assistance it offered was directed toward the overthrow of classical authority.
Since the end of the Middle Ages the attack on authority had
proceeded with little interruption. Authority in religion had
been rejected in the Reformation; authority in government had
been contested in the Commonwealth; authority in learning or
science had been overthrown in the Restoration, and now authority was being expelled from its last stronghold—literature.
Since the situation in criticism was exactly analogous to the
earlier situation in science, it is not strange that the revolt of the
latter should have inspired a similar revolt in the literary world.
In this rebellion science assisted in two ways. First, it set an example of, and furnished a precedent for, the abandonment of
submission to the dictates of antiquity. The mere fact that in one
field of intellectual activity an increasing number of illustrious
men had turned their backs upon the ancients could not but make
its influence felt in other fields. Second, it had demonstrated the
fallibility of those who had been considered infallible authorities. Again and again it had revealed the erroneous nature of
traditional theories and ideas in every branch of science, and had
thrown light on places which the ignorance of past ages left dark.
Science had refuted in no uncertain manner that basic argument
of conservatism, the consent of many men and many ages, by
proving that many beliefs which had received such consent were
totally false. Certainly the literary critic, looking at the shattered ruins of an erstwhile potent authority, could hardly fail to
harbor misgivings regarding its validity in poetry.

Another way in which scientific attitudes induced like views
in literature is revealed in the idea of progress or advancement.
The title itself of Bacon's *Advancement of Learning* discloses
the spirit which both inspired and motivated scientific activities
in the seventeenth century. This desire for advancement science
communicated to poetry. But it did more than that. By its discoveries it justified its own attitudes and partly realized its own
hopes, and in doing so presented a stimulating example to literature. Critics came to see in the worship of classical authority
the same obstacle to the progress of poetry which had barred the
advancement of learning, and in the progress which science had

achieved by overthrowing this authority, they discovered a hope
that by pursuing the same course poetry could go forward, its
domain could be widened, and its liberty enlarged.

And finally, in combating the enervating idea of nature's
decay, science was fighting not only its own battle but that of
every aspect of modernity. This obstinate theory was slow to
die. Arising in the sixteenth century and assuming the form of
moral degeneration, it convinced the Elizabethans that theirs
was an iron age, in which vice and wretchedness were the lot of
man; in the seventeenth century it wore the guise of intellectual
decay, and assured the moderns that their inferiority could never
hope to go beyond the ancients in the discovery of scientific truth;
and in the seventeenth and eighteenth centuries it whispered in
the ear of the trembling poet that his enfeebled genius left him
no other recourse than to follow meekly in the beaten paths of
classical art, first laid out in the prime and vigor of nature.[61]
Opposition to the theory was by no means confined to science, but
the latter opposed it more vigorously and consistently than any
other antagonist, and when condemnation of the idea is found in
conjunction with other characteristics of the scientific movement,
it may very well be ascribed to the influence of the latter.

Indeed, most of the ideas and attitudes which I have attributed to the influence of science may occasionally be found in
nonscientific quarters, but nowhere were they given the publicity
nor so widely and so earnestly advocated as by the scientists. The
experimental philosophy literally had to fight its way through
to final acceptance, and when it emerged victorious, its recognized
importance and prestige gave added force to each of its constitu-

[61] Cf. Pope's *Essay on Criticism*, I, 189, 196–98:

> Hail, Bards triumphant! born in happier days,

. . . . . . . . . .

> The last, the meanest of your sons inspire,
> (That on weak wings, from far, pursues your flights,
> Glows while he reads, but trembles as he writes)

. . . . . . . . . .

On the history of the theory of decline, see J. B. Bury, *The Idea of Prog-
ress*, 1928, pp. 44–49, 78–97; Richard F. Jones, "The Background of *The
Battle of the Books*" (*Washington University Studies*, VII, Humanistic Series
II [1920], pp. 104–16), and *Ancients and Moderns*, pp. 23–42.

ent elements. Furthermore, it may be noted that in regard to the critics discussed in this article no idea has been ascribed to the influence of the scientific movement except when attended by a clear and unmistakable reference to it.

In showing the influence of science on the literary criticism of the neo-classical period, I do not in any way wish to imply that it was the only liberalizing agent active at this time. Literary history is complex, and its phenomena are not to be explained by a formula nor reduced to the simplicity of a diagram. The character of neo-classicism in England was by no means homogeneous. There were inconsistencies and contradictions, uncertainties and doubts. For the most part, the age found itself in a critical dilemma, inasmuch as it had intellectually embraced a critical creed which did not justify its literary tastes. Dryden says: "Impartially speaking, the French are as much better critics than the English, as they are worse poets." And yet the French poets had conformed much more closely to the rules laid down by their critics than the English, especially the Elizabethans, whom Dryden has chiefly in mind. The age tried to escape from its dilemma through its beauties-and-faults criticism, in which beauties were referred to taste, and faults to the rules, but inevitably the beauties cast suspicion upon the faults. Throughout the period Shakespeare, Spenser, and other poets exerted an unremitting pull upon the closed circle of critical dogma, from which they had been excluded, but which under their influence was slowly widening to encompass them. When to this fact is added the strong nationalistic spirit which resented the spectacle of English poets being devastated by a criticism essentially foreign, or, as one critic puts it, English poets being tried by a foreign jury, we can easily see that there were other forces moving in the same direction as the one which we have been discussing. But disregarding the question of the relative strength of the influence which the scientific movement exerted on criticism, we may safely assert that when the experimental scientists of the seventeenth century went forth under the banner of liberty and progress to wage war on authority, they were battling for more causes than their own.

# SCIENCE AND ENGLISH PROSE STYLE
# IN THE THIRD QUARTER
# OF THE SEVENTEENTH CENTURY*

## Richard Foster Jones

ITERARY style, like human personality, is a compound
exceedingly difficult of analysis, for when its more obvious constituents are made clear, there still remains an
illusive element, consciousness of which leaves the analyst with
the unpleasant sensation of not having reached the bottom of the
matter. As the most complex phenomenon in literature, style is
the resultant of all the forces, known and unknown, underlying
literary development, and the method and extent of the contribution made by each of these forces are a matter of probable
inference rather than of positive demonstration. For that reason,
any attempt, however ambitious, to account for the style of a
literary epoch must be content with pointing out those more obvious influences that are combined and reflected in speech and
writing, and with ignoring other factors which may escape detection. Under the protection of this confession I shall attempt to
make manifest what seems to me the most important influence
instrumental in changing the luxuriant prose of the Commonwealth into that of a diametrically opposite nature in the Restoration.

To one who is familiar with the writers of the Puritan re-
gime, it would be rash to maintain that the style of this period is
homogeneous, but probably every one can agree that the dominating manner of writing was that revealed in the great figures of

* Reprinted, with minor corrections, from *Publications of the Modern
Language Association*, Vol. XLV (1930), by permission of the publishers.

Jeremy Taylor, Sir Thomas Browne, and John Milton, and lesser writers like Nathanael Culverwell. As is well known, this style is characterized by various rhetorical devices such as figures, tropes, metaphors, and similes, or similitudes, to use a term of the period. The sentences are long, often obscurely involved, and rhythmical, developing in writers like Browne a stately cadence, which, in the studied effect of inversions, is the prose counterpart of Milton's blank verse. The penchant for interlarding a work with Latin and Greek quotations is also apparent. The diction reveals a host of exotic words, many Latinisms, and frequently poetic phraseology of rare beauty. Against this style there arose a movement which later became an organized revolt, and which in the course of its condemnation of the old developed for itself a new standard of expression. The spirit animating the revolt had its origin in the scientific movement that determined the intellectual complexion of the seventeenth century. It is the purpose of this article to show that the attacks on the old, as well as the formulation of a new, style find consistent expression in those associated with the new science, that the first organized scientific body in England, the Royal Society, definitely adopted a linguistic platform which exerted a powerful influence on the style of its members even in writings other than scientific, and that the foremost exponents of the new style were members of this society and in most cases deeply interested in science.

Since Bacon stimulated and, to a certain extent, determined the scientific development of this period, one should search first in his writings for evidence of a stylistic standard. Without insisting upon a direct connection between his views and the movement that arose near the middle of the century, it would be foolish to underestimate the possible influence of one whose words were reverenced by later scientific reformers of style. At the very outset, however, we may say that his own style was quite different from that advocated by the scientists. "Ornamented with the riches of rhetoric," as it is, it everywhere reveals tropes, figures, and similitudes. For this reason his followers, though worshiping his ideas, never refer to his manner of expression as a model. Sprat, it is true, cites him as an example, but for poets and wits, not for writers of serious prose.[1] Rawley, Bacon's chaplain and biographer, represents his patron as opposed to fine writing, and tells us that in composing his works, the philosopher "would often ask if the meaning were expressed plainly enough, as being one that accounted words to be but subservient or ministerial to matter, and not the principal."[2] Yet even Rawley must have been aware that plainness is not a characteristic quality of Bacon's prose, for he immediately adds the rather meaningless statement, "And if his style were polite, it was because he would do no otherwise." Regardless of his own style, however, Bacon attacks all manner of rhetorical devices because they lead to the first distemper of learning, "when men study words and not matter," and he holds that similitudes and ornaments of speech render the detection and correction of errors very difficult.[3] Moreover, near the beginning of the *Magna Instauratio* he reveals a stylistic attitude which, though not apparent in his own practice, is essentially the same as that later maintained by his followers. "It being part of my design," he says, "to set everything forth, as far as may be, plainly and perspicuously (for nakedness of the mind is still, as nakedness of the body once was, the companion of innocence and simplicity), let me first explain the order and plan of the work."[4] While his antagonism to rhetoric and his advocacy of a naked style may not have inspired the stylistic revolt, they had their origin in the

[1] *History of the Royal Society*, pp. 416–17. Earlier in the volume he had found in Bacon's prose traits quite different from those demanded by the Royal Society. See p. 36. See also R. Boyle, *Works*, ed. T. Birch, V, 39.

[2] *The Works of Francis Bacon*, ed. Spedding, Ellis, and Heath, (new ed., 7 vols., 1879–90), I, 11.

[3] *Ibid.*, III, 282–84. The first reference contains his famous explanation of, and attack on, Ciceronianism. Though his own prose reveals elements that ally him to the Anti-Ciceronians, his emphasis upon a plain style is quite foreign to them; furthermore, as will be noted later, he was so far from approving their style that he considered it one of the distempers of learning.

[4] *Ibid.*, IV, 22. In a *Preparative towards a Natural and Experimental History* he lists rhetorical ornaments among the factors which increase the difficulty of, while adding nothing to, the work. "And for all that concerns ornaments of speech, similitudes, treasury of eloquence, and such like emptinesses, let it be utterly dismissed." IV, 254.

same scientific spirit that animated the later reformers of prose, who express views similar to his.

The immediate influence of Bacon's words must have been slight, for the exuberant prose of the Elizabethans continued on to the more highly developed and poetic style of the Commonwealth. In 1646, however, is heard again the plea for a plain style; this time in John Wilkins' *Ecclesiastes, or a Discourse Concerning the Gift of Preaching*. Wilkins, who later became the prime mover in the establishment of the Royal Society, had been for a number of years deeply interested in science, and was at this moment an enthusiastic member of a small group of men who met weekly in London to put into practice the Baconian experimental philosophy. It was the spirit of the latter that prompted him to say, as regards the "phrase" that should be used in preaching,

It must be plain and naturall, not being darkned with the affectation of Scholasticall harshnesse, or Rhetoricall flourishes. Obscurity in the discourse is an argument of ignorance in the minde. The greatest learning is to be seen in the greatest plainnesse . . . When the notion it self is good, the best way to set it off, is in the most obvious plain expression . . . And it will not become the Majesty of a Divine Embassage, to be garnished out with flaunting affected eloquence. How unsuitable it is to the expectation of a hungry soul, who comes unto this ordinance with a desire of spiritual comfort and instruction, and there to hear onely a starched speech full of puerile worded Rhetorick? 'Tis a sign of low thoughts and designs, when a mans chief study is about the polishing of his phrase and words. . . . Such a one speaks onely from his mouth, and not from his heart.

The same opinion is continued in another passage, concerning which we must remember that the epithet "solid" was so consistently applied to the new philosophy as opposed to the old that the expression "solid business" is equivalent to scientific matters. "It must be full, without empty and needlesse Tautologies, which are to be avoided in every solid business, much more in sacred. Our expressions should be so close, that they may not be obscure, and so plain that they may not seem vain and tedious."[5] A glance at Wilkins' own writings discovers a prac-

---

[5] *Ecclesiastes, or a Discourse concerning the Gift of Preaching as it falls under the Rules of Art*, 1646, p. 72.

tice consistent with his theory, and William Lloyd, in a funeral sermon on him, truly says,

He spoke solid truth, with as little shew of Art as was possible. He exprest all things in their true and Natural colours; with that aptness and plainness of Speech, that grave Natural way of Elocution, that shewed he had no design upon his hearers. His plainness was best for the instruction of the simple . . . He applied him self rather to their understanding than Affections . . . In his Writings he was Judicious and plain, like one that valued not the Circumstances so much as the substance.

Two years later the same contempt for the superficial fineries of verbal dress appears in William Petty, one of the outstanding members of the little group which, about the middle of the century, met weekly in Petty's lodgings at Oxford for the purpose of carrying on experiments, a group that later merged with a similar body in London to form the Royal Society. Petty was especially interested in the practical aspect of science, devoting much of his time to inventions of various sorts. In communicating some matters of scientific nature to Samuel Hartlib, he says,

I shall desire you to shew them unto no more than needs you must, since they can please only those few that are real Friends to the Design of Realities, not those who are tickled only with Rhetorical Prefaces, Transitions and Epilogues, and charmed with fine Allusions and Metaphors.[6]

The expression "Friends to the Design of Realities" is interesting in this case, for it means nothing more than subscribers to the new philosophy, and thus the quotation shows that Petty makes style a distinguishing mark between the experimental philosophers and those who held to the old tradition. This remarkable sensitiveness to matters of style on the part of the scientists, which is revealed in their thinking it necessary to confess, and vindicate, their lack of rhetorical ornament, appears again in a work by Francis Glisson, a famous physician of the time, and a prominent member of the London group of Baconians which

[6] *The Advice of W. P. to Mr. Samuel Hartlib, for the Advancement of some particular Parts of Learning*, London, 1648; *Harleian Miscellany*, 1810, VI, 2.

was formed in 1645. He concludes his Preface in the following manner:

> Finally expect no flashes of Rhetorick and Courtly-Language;
> Nobis licet esse tam dicertis,
> Musas qui colimus severiores.

And indeed the conditions of the matter forbids all such painting; in such a manner,

> Ornari res ipsa negat, contenti doceri.[7]

The next opposition to rhetorical ornament is discovered in Hobbes's *Leviathan*, 1651. Though now chiefly remembered for his psychological and political philosophy, Hobbes was, according to his own statement, most interested in natural science.[8] His philosophical interests were developed in France along with Descartes, Gassendi, and Mersenne, but in his earlier years he had been a companion of Bacon, and from the latter he may have caught his scientific enthusiasm. In his characteristically blunt fashion, Hobbes tells us that there is nothing he distrusts more than elocution, and that he has rejected the ornament of classical quotations because there is no longer any virtue in ancient authority.[9] He permits a counselor to use only significant, proper, and brief language, and forbids them *"obscure, confused,* and

---

[7] *A Treatise of the Rickets*, 1651. (This is a translation of the Latin edition which appeared the preceding year.) Mention might here be made of John Dury's *The Reformed School* (c. 1649), a passage from which (p. 49) reads: "Whatsoever in the teaching of Tongues doth not tend to make them a help unto Traditionall knowledge, by the manifestation of Reall Truths in Sciences, is superfluous, and not to be insisted upon, especially towards Children, whence followeth that the Curious study of Criticismes and observations of Styles in Authors and of straines of wit, which speak nothing of Reality in Sciences, are to be left to such as delight in vanityes more than in Truths." Dury belonged to that group of educational reformers which centered around Comenius, and to which Samuel Hartlib also belonged. Their philosophy, which is shot through with the spirit of scientific utilitarianism, was largely inspired by Bacon, and properly falls in the scientific movement. Dury's emphasis upon "reality" manifests the same attitude as is revealed in the quotation from Petty, and clearly indicates that the materialistic nature of the new science, with its insistence upon direct sense-observation of natural phenomena, was the chief source of this craving for a plain style. For an extended discussion of the influence of the Baconian philosophy upon educational theory, see Foster Watson, *The Beginning of the Teaching of Modern Subjects in England*, chap. vi.

[8] See end of the *Leviathan*.

[9] *Leviathan*, ed. A. R. Waller, pp. 526–27.

*ambiguous Expressions, also all metaphoricall Speeches, tending to the stirring up of Passion,"* which are useful only to deceive.[10] In speaking of that antithetical pair dear to the seventeenth-century critic—judgment and fancy—he lays down the law, as the Royal Society did later, that—

> In Demonstration, in Councell, and all rigourous search of Truth, Judgement does all; except sometimes the understanding have need to be opened by some apt similitude; and then there is so much use of Fancy. But for Metaphors, they are in this case utterly excluded. For seeing they openly professe deceit; to admit them into Councell, or Reasoning, were manifest folly.

And again, "in a Sermon, or in publique, or before persons un-known, or whom we ought to reverence, there is no Gingling of words that will not be accounted folly."[11] Among the four abuses of speech, he lists the metaphorical use of words, "that is, in other sense than that they are ordained for; and thereby de-ceive others."[12] He insists that "Metaphors and Tropes of speach" are no true grounds for reasoning, and one of the causes for absurd conclusions he ascribes "to the use of Metaphors, Tropes, and other Rhetoricall figures, in stead of words proper."[13] He concludes by saying:

> The Light of humane minds is Perspicuous Words, but by exact defini-tions first snuffed, and purged from ambiguity; *Reason* is the *Pace;* Encrease of *Science,* the *way;* and the benefit of man-kind, the *end.* And on the contrary, Metaphors, and sensless and ambiguous words, are like *ignes fatui;* and reasoning upon them, is wandering amongst in-numerable absurdities.[14]

The same scientifically induced materialism so characteristic of Hobbes appears in John Webster's *Academiarum Examen,* 1653. Webster was a chaplain in the Parliamentarian army, and an early and ardent follower of Bacon. In the work mentioned above he vehemently attacks the old philosophy, and fervently recommends a reformation of the universities in the way of the substitution of experimental science for the Aristotelianized di-vinity and natural philosophy dominant there. But he is not

[10] *Ibid.,* p. 185.    [11] *Ibid.,* pp. 43–44.
[12] *Ibid.,* pp. 14–15.    [13] *Ibid.,* pp. 21, 25.    [14] *Ibid.,* p. 26.

content with attacking these only; he would place distinctly below the new science such subjects as rhetoric, oratory, and the like, which, he says,

serve for adornation, and are as it were the outward dress and attire of more solid sciences; first they might tollerably pass, if there were not too much affectation towards them, and too much pretious time spent about them, while more excellent and necessary learning [i.e., experimental philosophy] lies neglected and passed by: For we do in these ornamental arts, as people usually do in the world, who take more care often time about the goods of fortune, than about the good of the body it self or the goods of the mind, regarding the shell more than the kernel, and the shadow more than the Substance.[15]

A similar dislike for an ornate style and a corresponding approval of plainness in expression may be found in Robert Boyle, a scientist so illustrious it would be impertinent to comment on his connection with the new movement. In his *Some Considerations Touching the Style of the Holy Scriptures,* written about 1653 though not published until 1661, he expresses the view that when verbal ornaments are spared, they are not missed, and that some writings expressed in the plainest language outshine other subjects decked with the gaudiest expressions. Nor does he ascribe any importance to an objection that the Bible is destitute of eloquence and unadorned with the flowers of rhetoric, an objection which, he says, "a philosopher [i.e., a scientist] would not look upon as the most considerable."[16]

We also find the Baconian spirit stirring in out-of-the-way places. In 1660 Joshua Childrey published his *Britannia Baconia,* which is in reality a natural history of England, Scotland, and Wales, and the title of which indicates its connection with the new science. The author worshiped Bacon, and regarded his words with almost superstitious awe, trying in all humility of spirit to put into practice the precepts of the great master. He, too, was imbued with a scorn of fine language, and with a feeling that science demanded a style more suited to its purposes. "I have endeavour'd," he says in the Preface, "to tell my tale as plainly as might be, both that I might be understood of all, and

---

[15] *Leviathan,* ed. A. R. Waller, p. 88.
[16] See Boyle's *Works,* ed. T. Birch, II, 92, 136; III, 2, 512; V, 54.

that I might not disfigure the face of Truth by daubing it over with the paint of Language." He then proceeds to emphasize the fact that clear and accurate expression is just as essential to the communication of truth as careful observation is to its discovery, and he implies his conviction that the prevailing style was inimical to its proper presentation. A like attitude continues to be manifested in this branch of science, if for the moment we may step beyond the chronological limits of this article. Robert Plot, in the *Natural History of Oxfordshire*, 1676, says,

> And these [natural and artificial phenomena] I intend to deliver as succinctly as may be, in a plain, easie unartificial Stile, studiously avoiding all ornaments of Language, it being my purpose to treat of Things, and therefore would have the Reader expect nothing less than Words.[17]

Ten years later, in the *Natural History of Staffordshire*, he is still making the same stylistic pronouncement, though the need for it had long ceased to exist. Certainly hostility to the style of the Commonwealth must have been deeply imbedded in scientists to cause this one to say in 1686, at a time when rhetoric was no longer in favor with any one of importance,

> I shall make all *Relations* (as formerly) in a plain familiar Stile, without the Ornaments of *Rhetorick*, least the matter be obscured by too much *illustration;* and with all the imaginable brevity that perspicuity will bear.[18]

The foregoing quotations are sufficiently numerous and emphatic to indicate that repugnance to the prevailing style and a feeling for the need of a simpler, more direct manner of expression were a characteristic feature of the new science from its very inception. To us it seems quite natural that science should be antipathetic to rhetoric, but in this period some unique factors tended to accentuate this antipathy. Above everything else, the experimental philosophy was characterized by a savage attack upon "Aristotelity," to use Hobbes's term, in the course of which the chief charge was brought against the wordiness of Peripateticism.[19] Again and again the new scientists stigmatized the tradi-

---

[17] P. 2.   [18] P. 1.

[19] Numerous references might be given to support this statement, but I shall quote only one writer, who figures in this study. "*Aristotelian Philosophy*

tional philosophy for being concerned only with words having no concrete significance and representing only figments of the imagination. Thus verbal superfluity became suspect. Allied to this attitude was the feeling for concrete reality, which naturally eschewed the verbal luxuriance of figurative language and the more subtle effects of imaginative expression. All this led to an insistence upon a direct, unadorned style which should be concrete in idea, and clear and economical in expression, in short, to use a phrase of the period, "the marriage of words and things."[20]

When the experimental philosophers were joined in a royally protected society, 1662, it was inevitable that what had been the more or less sporadic and scattered, but still representative, attacks on prose expression should be combined and strengthened into an organized revolt. So we are not surprised to find that in the statutes of the Royal Society, published in 1728, Chapter V, Article IV, reads:

> In all Reports of Experiments to be brought into the Society, the Matter of Fact shall be barely stated, without any Prefaces, Apologies, or Rhetorical Flourishes, and entered so into the Register-Book, by order of the Society.

But the full importance of this requirement is not revealed until

---

is a huddle of *words* and *terms insignificant*." And again, speaking of entities, modes, and formalities, "What a number of words here have nothing answering them? . . . To wrest names from their known meaning to Senses most alien, and to darken *speech by words without knowledge*; are none of the most inconsiderable faults of this *Philosophy* . . . Thus these *Verbosities* do emasculate the Understanding; and render it slight and frivolous, as its objects." Joseph Glanvill, *Vanity of Dogmatizing*, 1661, pp. 150 ff. He also speaks of the verbal emptiness of Aristotle's philosophy.

[20] One stylistic vice obviously came under the ban of the experimental philosophers. The latter's violent attack upon the ancients and upon authority in general did much to depreciate the value of Latin and Greek quotations. Glanvill, in the *Vanity of Dogmatizing*, attacks this habit on the ground that reliance on antiquity is no longer to be countenanced, so that appeals to it are impertinent and futile. "'Twas this vain Idolizing of Authors, which gave birth to that silly vanity of *impertinent citations*; and inducing Authority in things neither requiring, nor deserving it. That saying was much more observable, *That men have beards, and women none*; because quoted from *Beza*; and that other *Pax res bona est*; because brought in with a, *said St. Austin*." (Pp. 142 ff.) In 1678 he says that "the custom is worn out everywhere except in remote, dark corners." (*An Essay Concerning Preaching*, pp. 18 ff.) See also Hobbes's view of the same matter given earlier in this article.

we read Thomas Sprat's *History of the Royal Society,* 1667, in
an oft-quoted pasage of which the author makes clear the Society's intense opposition to rhetorical prose, and outlines the
ideal of a new style which had already crystallized and upon
which it was vehemently insisting. Sprat's words throw so much
light on the movement which we are tracing that I shall give
them in full, even at the risk of bringing before the reader's eye
that with which he is already familiar.

Thus they have directed, judg'd, conjectur'd upon, and improved
*Experiments.* But lastly, in these, and all other businesses, that have come
under their care; there is one thing more, about which the *Society* has
been most sollicitous; and that is, the manner of their *Discourse*: which,
unless they had been very watchful to keep in due temper, the whole
spirit and vigour of their *Design,* had been soon eaten out, by the luxury
and redundance of *speech.* The ill effects of this superfluity of talking,
have already overwhelm'd most other *Arts* and *Professions;* insomuch,
that when I consider the means of *happy living,* and the causes of their
corruption, I can hardly forbear recanting what I said before; and concluding, that *eloquence* ought to be banish'd out of *civil Societies,* as a
thing fatal to Peace and good Manners. To this opinion I should wholly
incline; if I did not find, that it is a Weapon, which may be as easily
procur'd by *bad* men, as *good:* and that, if these should onely cast it away,
and those retain it; the *naked Innocence* of vertue, would be upon all
occasions expos'd to the *armed Malice* of the wicked. This is the chief
reason, that should now keep up the Ornaments of speaking, in any request: since they are so much degenerated from their original usefulness.
They were at first, no doubt, an admirable Instrument in the hands of
*Wise Men:* when they were onely employ'd to describe *Goodness, Honesty, Obedience;* in larger, fairer, and more moving Images: to represent *Truth,* cloth'd with Bodies; and to bring *Knowledg* back again to
our very senses, from whence it was at first deriv'd to our understandings.
But now they are generally chang'd to worse uses: They make the *Fancy*
disgust the best things, if they come sound, and unadorn'd: they are in
open defiance against *Reason;* professing, not to hold much correspondence with that; but with its Slaves, *the Passions:* they give the mind a
motion too changeable, and bewitching, to consist with *right practice.*
Who can behold, without indignation, how many mists and uncertainties,
these specious *Tropes* and *Figures* have brought on our Knowledg? How
many rewards, which are due to more profitable, and difficult *Arts,* have
been still snatch'd away by the easie vanity of *fine speaking?* For now

I am warm'd with this just *Anger*, I cannot with-hold my self, from betraying the shallowness of all these seeming Mysteries; upon which, *we Writers*, and *Speakers*, look so bigg. And, in few words, I dare say; that of all the Studies of men, nothing may be sooner obtain'd, than this vicious abundance of *Phrase*, this trick of *Metaphors*, this volubility of *Tongue*, which makes so great a noise in the World. But I spend words in vain; for the evil is now so inveterate, that it is hard to know whom to *blame*, or where to begin to *reform*. We all value one another so much, upon this beautiful deceipt; and labour so long after it, in the years of our education: that we cannot but ever after think kinder of it, than it deserves. And indeed, in most other parts of Learning, I look on it to be a thing almost utterly desperate in its cure: and I think, it may be plac'd amongst those *general mischiefs*; such, as the *dissention* of Christian Princes, the *want of practice* in Religion, and the like; which have been so long spoken against, that men are become insensible about them; every one shifting off the fault from himself to others; and so they are only made bare common places of complaint. It will suffice my present purpose, to point out, what has been done by the *Royal Society*, towards the correcting of its excesses in *Natural* Philosophy; to which it is, of all others, a most profest enemy.[21]

This earnest indictment of the earlier mode of expression does not represent the sentiments of Sprat only. The *History* was written at the instigation and under the auspices of the Royal Society, was closely followed by the members during its composition, and when finished was heartily approved by the same body, so that we may look upon Sprat's attitude as typical of that of his colleagues.[22] Furthermore, in the next paragraph Sprat describes in terse and effective manner the style required by the Society of all papers presented to it.

They have therefore been most rigorous in putting in execution, the only Remedy, that can be found for this *extravagance:* and that has been, a constant Resolution, to reject all the amplifications, disgressions, and swellings of style: to return back to the primitive purity, and shortness, when men deliver'd so many *things*, almost in an equal number of *words*. They have exacted from all their members, a close, naked, natural way of speaking; positive expressions; clear senses; a native easiness: bring-

[21] Pp. 111–13.
[22] Cf. Thomas Birch, *History of the Royal Society*, II, 3, 47, 51, 138, 161, 163, 197 (hereafter cited as *Hist. Roy. Soc.*).

ing all things as near the Mathematical plainness, as they can: and preferring the language of Artizans, Countrymen, and Merchants, before
that, of Wits, or Scholars.[23]

The great importance of this discussion of style relative to
other matters canvassed in Sprat's *History* is made clear by comments upon the book itself, in which the manner of expression
is the characteristic most remarked.   In an ode which was prefixed
to the *History*, and which will later be treated more in full,
Cowley notices, and with great praise, only the style of the work.
In the next year Glanvill thinks it necessary to praise its stylistic
qualities in a passage which expresses the desired ideal as eluci-
dated by Sprat and renders a fairly accurate criticism of the latter's prose.  The book, he says,

is writ in a way of so *judicious* a *gravity* and so *prudent* and *modest* an
*expression*, with so much *clearness* of *sense*, and such a *natural fluency*
of *genuine eloquence:* So that I know it will both *profit* and entertain

[23] P. 113.  Sprat believed that English writers in general were freer from
stylistic vices than the French. "There might be," he says, with an eye on
France, "a whole Volume compos'd in comparing the Chastity, the newnesse,
the vigour of many of our *English* Fancies, with the corrupt, and the swelling
Metaphors, wherewith some of our Neighbors, who most admire themselves,
do still adorn their books." And again, "We have had many Philosophers, of
a strong, vigorous, and forcible judgment, of happy and laborious hands, of a
sincere, a modest, a solid, and unaffected expression, such who have not thought
it enough to set up for Philosophers, only to have got a large stock of fine words,
and to have insinuated into the acquaintance of some great Philosophers of the
age." (*Observations on Monsieur de Sorbier's Voyage into England*, 1665, pp.
265, 271. See also Sprat, *History of the Royal Society*, pp. 40–41.) Evelyn expresses the same sentiment, only he makes a luxuriant prose style a characteristic of the whole French nation. "The Reader will find," he remarks in the
Preface to his translation of a French treatise on painting, "in this discourse
(though somewhat verbose, according to the style of this overflowing nation)
divers useful remarks." (*Miscellaneous Writings of John Evelyn*, ed. W.
Upcott, 1825, p. 559.) Another sturdy Englishman expresses the same sentiment in more emphatic words: "And indeed however our smoother tongued
Neighbours may put in a claim for those bewitcheries of speech that flow from
Gloss and Chimingness; yet I verily believe that there is no tongue under
heaven, that goes beyond our English for speaking manly strong and full."
(Nathaniel Fairfax, *A Treatise of the Bulk and Selvedge of the World*, 1674,
"To the Reader.") In view of the common opinion that French influence
played a great part in the simplification of English prose, these quotations are
worthy of note. Furthermore, not a single stylistic reformer in England, as far
as my knowledge extends, ever refers, directly or indirectly, to any influence
from across the Channel.

you. And I say further, that you may remember to do your self this right, That the *Style* of that Book hath all the *properties* that can recommend any thing to an *ingenious relish:* For 'tis *manly,* and yet *plain; natural* and yet not *careless:* The *Epithets* are *genuine,* the *Words proper* and *familiar,* the *Periods smooth* and of *middle* proportion: It is not *broken* with *ends* of *Latin,* nor *impertinent Quotations;* nor made *harsh* by *hard* words, or *needless terms* of *Art;* Not rendred *intricate* by long *Parentheses,* nor *gaudy* by *flanting* [*sic*] *Metaphors;* not *tedious* by *wide fetches* and *circumferences* of *Speech,* nor *dark* by too much *curtness* of *Expression:* 'Tis not *loose* and *unjointed, rugged* and *uneven;* but as *polite* and as *fast* as *Marble;* and briefly avoids all the *notorious defects,* and wants none of the *proper* ornaments of Language.[24]

It is remarkable how sensitive the scientists were to the problem of expression. We may say without exaggeration that their program called for stylistic reform as loudly as for reformation in philosophy. Moreover, this attitude was in the public mind indissolubly associated with the Society.[25]

Such, then, was the stand firmly taken by the first scientific society in England as regards expression in prose composition. Naturally its stylistic ideal was reflected in the scientific writings of its members.[26] The question next arises, did it actually influence the style of nonscientific writings of the day? Fortunately we have two examples, one of which is remarkable, of men whose style was radically changed under the pressure exerted by the

[24] *Plus Ultra,* p. 84.

[25] The following quotation from Sprat's *History* clearly evinces the important place granted style in the obligations of the scientists. In fact, it shows that the experimental philosophers considered a reformation in current methods of expression essential to the advancement of science. "Their [members of the Royal Society] purpose is, in short, to make faithful *Records,* of all the Works of *Nature,* or *Art,* which can come within their reach: that so the present Age, and posterity, may be able to put a mark on the Errors, which have been strengthened by long prescription: to restore the Truths, that have lain neglected: to push on those, which are already known, to more various uses: and to make the way more passable, to what remains unreveal'd. This is the compass of their Design. And to accomplish this, they have indeavor'd, to separate the knowledge of *Nature,* from the colours of *Rhetorick,* the devices of *Fancy,* or the delightful deceit of *Fables.*" Pp. 61–62.

[26] See P. H. Hembt, "The Influence of Early Science on Formative English, 1645–1675," *Journal of Chemical Education,* III, 1051, and C. S. Duncan, *The New Science and English Literature,* pp. 147–54.

Society. In 1661 Joseph Glanvill, later the most ardent defender of the Royal Society, published his *Vanity of Dogmatizing*, the contents of which time prevents me from describing,
except to say that within its narrow compass it gathered all the
new threads of philosophical thought that traversed the mid-
seventeenth century. It is written in a highly rhetorical, exuberant, one might even say flamboyant, style, animated by an
enthusiasm great enough to justify the charge of its being rhap-
sodical. The modern note sounded by Glanvill, however, must
have brought him into sympathetic contact with some fellows
of the Royal Society, and thus have whetted his desire to become
a member of that body. At any rate, when, near the end of 1664,
he published a second edition entitled *Scepsis Scientifica*,[27] he
prefixed an "Address to the Royal Society," in which he eulo-
gized the new philosophy in general and that company in particular. This composition has all the earmarks of being a bid for
an invitation to join the philosophers, and such an inference is
borne out by the fact that on December 7, 1664, Lord Brereton
presented the book to the Royal Society, and, after the "Address" had been read, proposed the author as a candidate for
membership.[28] What especially interests us in the dedication is
the following passage found near the conclusion:

I found so faint an inclination [toward publishing the work again] that
I could have been well content to suffer it to have slipt into the state of
*eternal silence* and *oblivion*. For I must confess that *way of writing* to
be less agreeable to my *present relish* and *Genius;* which is more gratified
with *manly sense,* flowing in a *natural* and *unaffected Eloquence,* than
in the *musick* and curiosity of *fine Metaphors* and *dancing periods*. To
which measure of my present humour, I had indeavour'd to reduce the
style of these Papers; but that I was loth to give my self that trouble in
an Affair, to which I was grown too *cold* to be much concern'd in. And

[27] This version is accessible in a modern edition by John Owen, 1885. All
references are to this edition.
[28] See Birch, *Hist. Roy. Soc.*, I, 500. Glanvill's purpose is also suggested
by a change introduced in the body of the work. A passage in the *Vanity*, p. 240,
reads, "And the sole Instances of those illustrious Heroes, *Cartes, Gassendus,
Galileo, Tycho, Harvey, More, Digby*; will strike dead the opinion of the
worlds decay, and conclude it, in its *Prime*." In the *Scepsis*, p. 209, there is substituted for the names given above "that Constellation of Illustrious Worthies,
which compose the Royal Society."

this *inactivity* of temper perswaded me, I might reasonably expect a pardon from the *ingenious*, for faults committed in an immaturity of *Age* and *Judgment*, that would excuse them.[29]

Here we have a man desiring admission to the Royal Society, who with humility of spirit apologizes for his past sins, and with obvious alacrity swears allegiance to a stylistic creed that might otherwise have barred his entrance. I would not wish, however, to insinuate that his conversion was not sincere, for later events prove otherwise. But though he had evidently come under the influence of the scientists, and had experienced a true change of heart in stylistic matters, his open apology was evidently intended to serve a purpose. When we remember that less than four years separated the two editions, the reference to the immaturity of youth provokes a smile. It is significant that a man seeking admission into the Society considered it necessary to place himself in the proper position as to style.[30]

[29] In an earlier passage he gives another excuse for this style though at the same time suggesting the immaturity of youth as one. After speaking of some ingenious people laboring under the prejudices of education and customary belief, he says, "For Such it was then that the ensuing *Essay* was designed; which therefore wears a dress that possibly is not so suitable to the graver *Geniuses*, who have outgrown all *gayeties of style and youthful* relishes; But yet perhaps is not improper for the persons, for whom it was prepared. And there is nothing in *words* and *styles* but *suitableness*, that makes them *acceptable* and *effective*. If therefore this Discourse, such as it is, may tend to the removal of any *accidental* disadvantages from *capable Ingenuities*, and the preparing them for *inquiry*, I know you have so noble an *ardour* for the benefit of Mankind, as to pardon a *weak* and *defective* performance to a *laudable* and *well-directed* intention." (P. liv.) In still another passage he touches upon this all-important matter: "And 'Tis none of the least considerable expectations that may be reasonably had of your Society, that 'twill discredit that *toyishness* of *wanton fancy*; and pluck the misapplyed name of the *Wits*, from those conceited Humourists that have assum'd it; to bestow it upon the more *manly spirit* and *genius*, that playes not tricks with *words*, nor frolicks with the *Caprices* of *froathy imagination*." (P. lxv.) These words clearly indicate the popular association of stylistic reform with the Society, and the important place such a reformation occupied in the scientific movement.

[30] This case furnishes strong support to Herford's contention that Browne's style was the obstacle in the way of his joining the Royal Society. Browne had early become notorious for his style. In *The Philosophicall Touchstone, or Observations Upon Sir Kenelm Digbe's Discourses*, 1645, an attack on the *Religio Medici*, Alexander Ross says, "Your Rhetoricall descriptions (which are both uselesse in and destructive of *Philosophy*) make the soule sometimes equall with God, sometimes no better than a corruptible body; . . . If you lay the fault

A number of changes are introduced into the *Scepsis,* but, as the author states, very few as regards style, and they are concerned only with the substitution of simpler and more usual words for coined words or unusual Latinisms.[31] This change, however, reveals that he was moving in the direction of the new manner of expression demanded by the scientists. It is a stroke of good fortune for our purposes that in 1676 Glanvill published a third abbreviated version of the *Vanity of Dogmatizing,* as the first of seven essays combined to form a volume with the title, *Essays on Several Important Subjects in Philosophy and Religion.*[32] A comparison of this essay with the first version affords

of this upon your *Rhetoricall* expressions, I must answer you, that *Rhetorick* in such a subject may be well spared: use your *Rhetorick* when you will work upon the *affections,* but not when you will *informe* the *understanding.* Rhetorick . . . ought not to be used, but with great discretion, especially in abstruse questions . . . If you will dispute like a *Philosopher,* you must lay aside *Rhetorick,* and use *Philosophicall* termes; otherwise you will do as the fish *Sepia,* to wit, you'l so thicken the waters of your discourse, with the *liquor* that cometh out of your mouth, that you will make your self *invisible,* and delude the Reader, which is the fashion of those, who dare not confide in the strength of their arguments; whereas *naked* truth cares not for such *dressings,* nor seeks she after such *corners.*" (P. 92.) Ross has nothing but scorn for "Rhetoricall flourishes" and "Tullian pigments." See C. H. Herford's edition of Browne's works, Everyman's Library, p. xiv.

[31] Ferris Greenslet in *Joseph Glanvill,* 1900, pp. 200–201, has listed all such verbal changes, which amount to less than a score. Dr. Greenslet notices the difference between Glanvill's early and later work in the matter of diction, clearness, and simplicity, as well as in the quality of imagination. But since he failed to compare the *Vanity* with the version that appeared in the *Essays,* he did not perceive the extent or fully understand the nature of the author's stylistic evolution. Though he attributes the change in part to the influence of science, he failed to perceive the conscious and decisive nature of the influence which the Royal Society exerted on Glanvill. He is correct in detecting Bacon in the concrete imagery and balanced brevity of sentence structure, but he limits Browne's influence too narrowly to words. Though he accurately characterizes Glanvill's later style as simple, plain, reasonable, he is not sufficiently aware of the profound change that had taken place. See chapter vii.

[32] Concerning this essay, "Against Confidence in Philosophy," a passage in the preface to the volume reads: "[It] is quite changed in the way of Writing, and in the Order. Methought I was somewhat fetter'd and tied in doing it, and could not express my self with that ease, freedom, and fulness which possibly I might have commanded amid fresh thoughts: yet 'tis so alter'd as to be in a manner new." A comparison of the two versions reveals that chapters xvi, xvii, xviii, and xix, attacking Aristotle and the Peripatetic philosophy, as well as chapters i, ii, vi, xi, xx, xxi, and xxii, have been omitted almost *in toto;* that

nothing short of a revelation. Under the influence of the Royal Society the author's changed stylistic standards had established complete control over his writing, and had caused him to revise with a ruthless hand work written under the inspiration of the great prose writers of the Commonwealth. Furthermore, though in the second edition he had contented himself with an apology, leaving the style little changed, he would not permit the treatise to go forth again until it had become "quite changed in the way of writing." It is hardly necessary to do more than display parallel passages to show what science was doing to prose.

That all bodies both *Animal, Vegetable,* and *Inanimate,* are form'd out of such particles of matter, which by reason of their figures, will not cohære or lie together, but in such an order as is necessary to such a specifical formation, and that therein they naturally of themselves concurre, and reside, is a pretty conceit, and there are *experiments* that credit it. If after a decoction of *hearbs* in a Winter-night, we expose the liquor to the frigid air; we may observe in the morning under a crust of Ice, the perfect appearance both in *figure,* and *colour,* of the *Plants* that were taken from it. But if we break the *aqueous Crystal,* those pretty *images* dis-appear and are present[ly] dissolved.

Now these *airy Vegetables* are presumed to have been made, by

And there is an experiment . . . That after a decoction of Herbs in a frosty Night, the shape of the Plants will appear under the Ice in the Morning: which Images are supposed to be made by the congregated *Effluvia* of the Plants themselves, which loosly wandring up and down in the Water, at last settle in their natural place and order, and so make up an appearance of the Herbs from whence they were emitted. *Essays,* p. 11.

---

there is much beneficial rearrangement of material; and that much other material has been either left out or highly condensed. These changes, together with the compression in style, have caused the treatise to shrink to a fourth or a fifth of its first dimensions. A passage in the "Epistle Dedicatory" again calls attention to a change in his stylistic taste: "They [the essays] were some of them written several years ago, and had trial of the World in divers Editions: Now they come abroad together (with some things that are *new*) reduced to such an Order, as is most agreeable to my present judgment."

the reliques of these *plantal emis-sions* whose avolation was pre-vented by the *condensed inclosure.* And therefore playing up and down for a while within their liquid prison, they at last settle to-gether in their natural order, and the *Atomes* of each part finding out their proper place, at length rest in their methodical Situation, till by breaking the *Ice* they are disturbed, and those counterfeit *compositions* are scatter'd into their first *Indivisibles. Vanity,* p. 46.

Gone is the Brownesque "swelling" sentence at the begin-ning of the first passage, and the touch of beauty that adorned the account of the experiment has vanished; while the "vicious abundance of phrase" and "volubility of tongue" that charac-terize the remainder of the quotation have given way to the "plain and familiar words" and the "close, naked, natural way of speaking" of the latter version.

But this is so largely prosecuted by that wonder of men, the Great *Des-Cartes,* and is a Truth that shines so clear in the Eyes of all considering men; that to goe about industriously to prove it, were to light a candle to seek the Sun. *Vanity,* p. 28.

Upon which position all the Phi-losophy of *Des-Cartes* stands: And it is so clear, and so acknowl-edg'd a Truth, among all consid-ering Men, that I need not stay to prove it. *Essays,* p. 5.

For body cannot act on any thing but by motion; motion cannot be received but by quantative dimen-sion; the soul is a stranger to such gross substantiality, and hath noth-ing of quantity, but what it is cloathed with by our deceived phancies; and therefore how can we conceive under a passive sub-jection to material impressions. *Vanity,* p. 29.

For *Body* cannot act on anything, but by *Motion; Motion* cannot be receiv'd but by *Matter,* the *Soul* is altogether *immaterial;* and there-fore, how shall we apprehend it to be subject to *such Impressions. Es-says,* p. 6.

If we will take the literal evidence of our Eyes; the *Æthereal Coal* moves no more then this *Inferior clod doth. Vanity*, p. 78.

To *Sense* the *Sun stands still* also; *and no Eye* can perceive its *Actual* motion. *Essays*, p. 20.

And thus, while every age is but another shew of the former; 'tis no wonder, that Science hath not out-grown the dwarfishness of its *pristine stature*, and that the *Intellectual world* is such a *Microcosm. Vanity*, p. 138.

And thus while every Age is but an *other shew* of the *former*, 'tis no wonder that humane science is *no more* advanced above it's *ancient* Stature. *Essays*, p. 25.

In these passages there is an obvious change from "specious tropes" and "vicious abundance of phrase" to a "primitive purity and shortness," in which "positive expressions" and "native easiness" are manifest. The reduction of these "wide fetches and circumferences of speech" to a direct and "natural way of speaking" brings out in vivid relief not only the way in which the scientific spirit was destroying the sheer joy in language, but also how the definite linguistic stand taken by the Royal Society was producing results.[33]

Nor is the composition of our Bodies the only wonder; we are as

[33] Likewise, the enthusiastic, exclamatory, and picturesque elements of the following passage are strangely subdued to a quieter level. "What cement should untie [unite] heaven and earth, light and darkness, natures of so divers a make, of such disagreeing attributes, which have almost nothing, but *Being*, in common; This is a riddle, which must be left to the coming of *Elias*. How should a thought be united to a marble-statue, or a sun-beam to a lump of clay! The freezing of the words in the air in the northern climes, is as conceivable, as this strange union. That this active spark, this συμφυτον πνευμα [as the Stoicks call it] should be confined to a Prison it can so easily pervade, is of less facill apprehension, then that the light should be pent up in a box of Crystall, and kept from accompanying its source to the lower world: And to hang weights on the wings of the winde seems far more intelligible." (*Vanity*, p. 20.) "So that, what the *Cement* should be that unites *Heaven* and *Earth*, *Light* and *Darkness*, viz. Natures of so divers a make, and such disagreeing Attributes, is beyond the reach of any of our Faculties: We can as easily conceive how a thought should be united to a Statue, or a Sun-Beam to a piece of Clay: How words should be frozen in the Air, (as some say they are in the remote North) or how Light should be kept in a Box; as we can apprehend the *manner* of this *strange Union." Essays*, p. 4.

much non-plust by the most contemptible *Worm,* and *Plant,* we tread on. How is a drop of Dew organiz'd into an Insect, or a lump of Clay into animal Perfections? How are the Glories of the Field spun, and by what Pencil are they limn'd in their unaffected bravery? By whose direction is the nutriment so regularly distributed unto the respective parts, and how are they kept to their specifick uniformities? If we attempt Mechanical solutions, we shall never give an account, why the Woodcock doth not sometimes borrow colours of the Mag-pye, why the Lilly doth not exchange with the Daysie, or why it is not sometime painted with a blush of the Rose? Can *unguided matter* keep it self to such exact conformities, as not in the least spot to vary from the *species?* That divers Limners at a distance without either copy, or designe, should draw the same *Picture* to an undistinguishable exactness, both in form, colour, and features; this is more conceivable, then that *matter,* which is so diversified both in quantity, quality, motion, site, and infinite other circumstances, should frame it self so absolutely according to the Idea of it and its kind. And though the fury of that *Appelles,* who threw his Pencil in a desperate rage upon the Picture he had essayed to draw, once casually effected those lively representations, which his Art could not describe; yet 'tis not

*Blind Matter* may produce an elegant effect for once, by a great Chance; as the Painter accidentally gave the Grace to his Picture, by throwing his Pencil in rage, and disorder upon it; But then *constant* Uniformities, and Determinations to a *kind,* can be *no Results* of *unguided Motions."* *Essays,* p. 11.

likely, that one of a thousand such
præcipitancies should be crowned
with so an unexpected an issue.
For though *blind matter* might
reach some elegancies in individual
effects; yet specifick conformities
can be no *unadvised* productions,
but in greatest likelyhood, are reg-
ulated by the immediate efficiency
of some *knowing* agent. *Vanity*,
pp. 44 ff.

Here, indeed, is merciless pruning. The "amplification of style"
found in the extended illustrations, touched with beauty, of the
composition of bodies, has been unhesitatingly cut away, for
Glanvill's changed standard reveals in it only a "trick of flaunting metaphor," "specious tropes and figures," and he now feels
that the discussion has been rendered "tedious by wide fetches
and circumferences of speech." Certainly condensation could go
no further than is manifested in the later version. How completely has vanished the feeling for beauty in language, as well
as a spirit of enthusiasm and imaginative activity!

The process that had been inaugurated in the *Scepsis Scientifica* of reducing exotic and unusual words, or "hard words," to
more natural terms, as well as a constant striving for a simpler,
more direct expression, is carried still further in this last version,
as is made clear by the foregoing quotations and may be emphasized by further passages. "Which to us is utterly occult, and
without the ken of our Intellects" becomes "to which we are altogether stranger"; "those abstrusities, that lie more deep, and are
of a more mysterious alloy" = "the Difficulties that lie more
deep"; "those principiate foundations of knowledge" = "the
Instruments of knowledge"; "Plato credits this position with his
suffrage; affirming" = "Plato affirms"; "is a difficulty which
confidence may triumph over sooner, then conquer" = "is hardly
to be conceived"; "is but as the Birth of the labouring Mountains, Wind and Emptiness" = "stands yet unresolved"; "pre-
ponderate much greater magnitudes" = "outweigh much
heavier bodies."[34] And there are many verbal changes, always

[34] *Vanity*, pp. 26, 27, 29, 53, 137; *Essays*, pp. 5, 6, 13, 25.

making for greater simplicity or brevity, which may be represented by the following: "our employed mindes" = "we"; "material ειδωλα = "material Images"; "bodily distempers" = "diseases"; "doth much confer to" = "makes"; "education-prepossessions" = "first opinions"; "præterlapsed ages" = "past ages"; "world's Grand-ævity" = "greatest antiquity"; "midnight compositions" = "dreams."

Although it is true that Glanvill is reducing a book to the dimensions of an essay, and thus omits many ideas *in toto*, the comparisons placed before us reveal not a change in or omission of ideas, but an alteration in treatment and expression only.[35] In sentence structure the Brownesque inversions, as well as Browne's habit of overloading the first part of a sentence at the expense of the latter, are ironed out and straightened into a natural order in which verb follows subject, and object verb. Exclamatory sentences and rhetorical questions are subdued to direct assertions, the length of sentences is perceptibly decreased, and oratorical cadence has almost disappeared. The verbal reform, begun in the *Scepsis*, is continued in the substitution of simpler, more current words for the unusual Latinisms and exotic terms characteristic of Browne, while emotional and extravagant expressions are greatly tempered. There is general condensation in expression, an economy of words which deflates the verbosities and superfluous terms of the earlier style. Figurative language and poetic imagery, whether extended or brief, are abolished, curtailed, or restrained. Illustrations, in the description of which Glanvill had shown a feeling for beauty, are purged of all qualities except the essential one of expository clearness. All the glories of enthusiastic expression and all joy in beauty have faded into the common light of day. We find in a comparison of the two versions not only a change in style but also a vivid picture of the spirit of one age yielding to that of another.[36]

[35] It would be easy to quote many more parallel passages illustrating this change, but the reader should compare the two versions himself in order to realize fully the transformation that has taken place. It is hardly necessary to point out that all Glanvill's later works reveal the same stylistic evolution.

[36] Later Glanvill joined in the attack on pulpit eloquence, which arose about 1668, and his words show that science was by no means without its influence upon this attack. Furthermore, the terms used by the reformers of the pulpit are startlingly similar to those with which the scientists have made us

We have in the essays of Abraham Cowley what I take to be another example of the direct influence which the sentiments and regulations of the Royal Society were exerting upon writers. That there was a decided change in style between his early and later prose has been recognized by more than one scholar. Mr. A. A. Tilley in the *Cambridge History of English Literature* asserts that Cowley furnished a complete transition from the old to the new style in prose, his early work revealing stiff, cumbrous, and involved sentences, nearer to Jeremy Taylor than to Dryden, and unlike the conversational ease of the later essays composed during the last four or five years of his life. Mr. Tilley calls especial attention to the fine example of rhetorical prose in the latter part of *A Vision Concerning Oliver Cromwell*, published in 1661 though composed in 1659, contrasting with that the style of the *Essays*, which is neither stiff nor slovenly, and in which the use of metaphors is restrained, and the sentences are well turned.[37] Dr. A. B. Gough, in his edition of Cowley's prose works, also thinks that the style of the *Essays* reveals a decided advance in clarity and ease over the earlier prose.[38] Cowley's first biographer, in the year after the former's death, pointed out "that in the Prose of them [the *Essays*], there is little Curiosity of Ornament, but they are written in a lower and humbler style than the rest, and as an unfeigned Image of his Soul should be drawn without Flattery." Several passages in the essays themselves bear witness to the author's acquired depreciation of eloquence, in one of which he speaks slightingly of "Figures and Tropes of Speech" as only adorning discourse,[39] and in another he refers scornfully to the "tinckling" of oratory.[40] But the best expression of his changed attitudes appears

---

familiar. (See Glanvill, *Philosophia Pia*, pp. 73, 90–91; the last essay in *Essays on Several Important Subjects*, 1676, and *An Essay Concerning Right Preaching*, 1678, pp. 11–51.) For an account of Glanvill's vigorous defense of the Royal Society, consult the present writer's "The Background of *The Battle of the Books*," *Washington University Studies*, VII, Humanistic Series II (1920), 125–29.

[37] VIII, 431–33.
[38] P. 310.
[39] Abraham Cowley, *The Essays and Other Prose Writings*, ed. A. B. Gough, 1915, p. 143.
[40] *Ibid.*, p. 199.

in "The Garden," composed in 1666 and addressed to John Evelyn, where, after an opening paragraph, which misses much of being as rhetorical as the *Vision*, the author says, "You may wonder, Sir (for this seems a little too extravagant and Pindarical for *Prose*) what I mean by all this Preface."[41]

This change has generally been attributed to French influences, especially Montaigne, but we must remember that when the *Vision* and earlier prose works were written, Cowley had for some years been exposed to French influence without results. What possible factor comes into play between 1659, when the *Vision* was composed, and the composition of the *Essays*? In February 1660, Cowley was proposed for membership in, and in the following March was elected to, the "invisible college" that was soon to become the Royal Society.[42] In 1661 he published a *Proposition For the Advancement of Experimental Philosophy*, which was an elaborate plan for a "Philosophical College," and to which the structure of the Royal Society owed much. Upon his retirement into the country he severed formal relations with the Society, since he could no longer attend the meetings, and was not reckoned a member after the passing of the second charter of April 22, 1663. But his contact with the members was by no means broken nor his interest in science lost. In fact, Sprat says, "This labour about Natural Science was the perpetual and uninterrupted task of that obscure part of his Life." On December 7, 1664, at the same meeting at which Glanvill's *Scepsis* was presented to the Society, a committee was appointed to improve the English tongue, composed of more than a score of men, among them Dryden, Evelyn, Sprat, and Waller.[43] Naturally, Cowley, not being a member, does not appear in the list, but we learn from excellent authority that he

[41] *Ibid.*, p. 169.

[42] Birch, *Hist. Roy. Soc.*, I, 17.

[43] *Ibid.*, I, 499. The late Professor Emerson in "John Dryden and A British Academy" (*Proceedings of the British Academy*, X, 1924) calls attention to the fact that Cowley was not a member of this committee, and thinks that Evelyn's memory had played him false in mentioning Cowley. But we must remember that Evelyn does not say that Cowley and the others were members of the committee, and that there is no reason why both the poet and Clifford, who also was not a member, should not have met with the committee.

met with them.  On August 12, 1689, Evelyn wrote to Pepys,

> And in deede such [improving the English tongue] was once de-
> sign'd since the Restauration of Charles the Second (1665), and in
> order to it three or fowre Meetings were begun at Grey's Inn, by Mr.
> Cowley, Dr. Sprat, Mr. Waller, the D. of Buckingham, Matt. Clifford,
> Mr. Dryden, & some other promoters of it.  But by the death of the
> incomparable Mr. Cowley, distance & inconvenience of the place, the
> Contagion & other circumstances intervening, it crumbled away and
> came to nothing.

The important place here granted Cowley in the scheme is borne
out by what Sprat says in his *Life* of the poet: "we [Clifford and
Sprat] had persuaded him . . . to publish a Discourse concerning Style."  At the very time Sprat was writing the *History of
the Royal Society* with its pronounced opinions on style, he was
conferring with Cowley about improving the language and per-
suading him to write a discourse on style.  Certainly Cowley must
have been brought into direct and stimulating contact with the
stylistic convictions of the new philosophers.  This is made all
the clearer by his "Ode to the Royal Society," prefixed to Sprat's
history, in which he ardently praises Bacon, the new philosophy,
and the Society.  One stanza, however, is devoted to praise of
Sprat's work,

> "And ne're did Fortune better yet
>    Th' Historian to the Story fit:
>    As you [Royal Society] from all old Errors free
> And purge the Body of Philosophy;
>    So from all Modern Folies He
> Has vindicated Eloquence and Wit.
> His candid Stile like a clear Stream does slide
>    And his bright Fancy all the way
>    Does like the Sun-shine in it play;
> It does like *Thames,* the best of Rivers, glide
> Where the God does not rudely overturn,
>    But gently pour the Crystal Urn,
> And with judicious hand does the whole Current guide.
> T'has all the Beauties Nature can impart,
> And all the comely Dress without the paint of Art.

From this stanza we see that the only aspect of Sprat's volume which the poet notices is its style, that he attributed to his future biographer credit for purifying prose as the scientists had purified natural philosophy, and that he evidently approved Sprat's indictment of the traditional prose style and subscribed to the new standard that the scientists had formulated. Thus Cowley must have been keenly and sympathetically aware of the efforts made by the experimental philosophers to discredit the old methods of expression, and he must have come under the same influence that metamorphosed Glanvill. To seek for the cause of his stylistic evolution in any other quarter seems to me far-fetched, if not futile.

With the example of Glanvill and Cowley before us, may we not infer that the same pressure toward stylistic reform must have been brought to bear upon all members of the Society,[44]

[44] Another possible example of the influence of the Royal Society in sobering the style of its members is found in Samuel Parker, later bishop of Oxford, who in 1666 published *A Free and Impartial Censure of the Platonick Philosophie*, dedicated to Bathurst, then president of Trinity College, Oxford, and formerly a member of the Oxford group of Baconians, to which reference has already been made. Both in the dedication and in the body of the work (pp. 2, 64) Parker expresses his gratitude to Bathurst for turning him from the unprofitable study of the old scholastic philosophy to the new experimental science. Though disclosing the influence of both Hobbes and Descartes, the *Censure* reveals chiefly the influence of Bacon and his followers. Parker brings to bear upon Platonism the same arguments which the experimental philosophers had used, and were using, against Aristotelianism, namely, that, as regards natural phenomena anyway, its empty notions could not be tested by sense observations or experiments, the criteria of truth. From this attack on a philosophy which presumably is mainly words, he passes naturally to an onslaught upon a wordy and figurative style, which is fully in keeping with the attitude of the scientists, and in the composition of which he undoubtedly had an eye on the Cambridge Platonists. These latter, he says, "put us off with nothing but rampant Metaphors and Pompous Allegories, and other splendid but empty Schemes of speech . . . true Philosphie is too sober to descend to these wildernesses of Imagination, and too Rational to be cheated by them. She scorns, when she is in chase of Truth, to quarry upon trifling gaudy Phantasms: Her Game is in things not words . . . I remember I had not long conversed with Platonick Authors, when I took occasion to set it down as a note to my self, that though a huge lushious stile may relish sweet to childish and liquorish Fancies, yet it rather loaths and nauceats a discreet understanding then informs and nourishes it . . . Now to discourse of the Natures of things in Metaphors and Allegories is nothing else but to sport and trifle with empty words, because these Schemes do not express the Natures of Things, but only their Similitudes and Re-

and through them even upon the world outside? Furthermore, when we consider the notable array of men of affairs, noblemen, clergymen, and writers who were members of the Society, we must believe that the influence of the latter was indeed far-reaching. The many-sided Isaac Barrow, divine, mathematician, and classical scholar, by virtue of being professor of geometry at Gresham College, Lucasian professor of mathematics at Cambridge, 1663, and a very early member of the Royal Society, could hardly have escaped being influenced by the stylistic attitude of the Society. John Tillotson, another great exponent of the new style, "whose sermons at Lincoln's inn and St. Lawrence Jewry attracted large congregations," and became a stylistic pattern for the whole nation, was not elected a member of the Society until 1672.[45] Yet in another way he had come under its influence. As a son-in-law of John Wilkins, he was associated with the latter in the composition of *An Essay Towards a Real Character and a Philosophical Language*, 1668.[46] This remark-

semblances." (Pp. 73 ff.) And he continues his attack on metaphors at great length. But in spite of this expressed antipathy to rhetorical prose, the style of the *Censure* is far from being bare and unadorned. (Note, for instance, the following: "But when they pretend to be Natures Secretaries, to understand all her Intrigues, or to be Heavens Privadoes, talking of the Transactions there, like men lately drop'd thence encircled with *Glories*, and cloathed with the Garments of *Moses* & *Elias*," etc., p. 73.) He had been for only a short time a member of the Royal Society, and perhaps its influence had not had time to bear fruit. In his next important works, however, *A Discourse of Ecclesiastical Politie*, 1670, and *A Defence and Continuation of the Ecclesiastical Politie*, 1671, we note a decided toning down of his enthusiastic language, though he himself claims that he is pursuing a middle way between a bare and an ornate style. (*A Defence*, pp. 97–98.) Parker is treated more at length in my article on pulpit eloquence.

[45] *Cam. Hist. of Eng. Lit.*, VIII, 346, 423.

[46] "His [Tillotson's] joining with Dr. Wilkins in perfecting the scheme of a *real character and philosophical language*, the *essay* towards which was publish'd in 1668, led him to consider exactly the truth of language and style, in which no man was happier, or knew better the art of uniting dignity with simplicity, and tempering these so equally together, that neither his thoughts sunk, nor style swell'd; keeping always a due mean between flatness and false rhetoric. Together with the pomp of words he cut off likewise all superfluities and needless enlargements. He said what was just necessary to give clear ideas of things, and no more. He laid aside long and affected periods. His sentences were short and clear; and the whole thread was of a piece, plain and distinct. No affections of learning, no torturing of texts, no superficial strains,

able project had long been in Wilkins' mind, and in 1662 he was
prodded to develop it by the Royal Society, the members of
which were deeply interested in the matter.[47] The study of language naturally involves consideration of style, and we are not
surprised to find the stylistic attitude of science reflected in
various parts of the *Essay*.[48] In this way Tillotson must have
had impressed upon him the stylistic values of the new philosophy.[49]

Finally, Dryden, who asserted that whatever talent he had

no false thoughts, nor bold flights. All was solid and yet lively, and grave as
well as elegant . . . he retrench'd both the luxuriances of style, and the length
of sermons." Thomas Birch, *The Life of the Most Reverend Dr. John
Tillotson*, 2d ed., London, 1753, pp. 21–22.

[47] Birch, *Hist. Roy. Soc.*, I, 119; II, 265, 281, 283.

[48] In the Dedication a passage reads, "To which it will be proper for me to
add, That this design will likewise contribute much to the clearing of some of
our Modern differences in Religion, by unmasking many wild errors, that
shelter themselves under the disguise of affected phrases; which being Philosophically unfolded, and rendered according to the genuine and natural importance of Words, will appear to be inconsistencies and contradictions. And
several of those pretended, mysterious, profound notions, expressed in great
swelling words, whereby some men set up for reputation, being this way examined, will appear to be, either nonsense, or very flat and jejune." Later he
speaks of "the Common mischief that is done, and the many impostures and
cheats that are put upon men, under the disguise of affected insignificant
Phrases." On pp. 17–18, he says, "As for the ambiguity of words by reason
of *Metaphor* and *Phraseology*, this is in all instituted Languages so obvious
and so various, that it is needless to give any instances of it; . . . And though
the varieties of Phrases in Language may seem to contribute to the elegance and
ornament of Speech; yet, like other affected ornaments, they prejudice the native
simplicity of it, and contribute to the disguising of it with false appearances.
Besides that like other things of fashion, they are very changeable, every generation producing new ones; witness the present Age, especially the late times,
wherein this grand imposture of Phrases hath almost eaten out solid knowledge
in all professions; such men generally being of most esteem who are skilled in
these Canting forms of speech, though in nothing else." The same values that
appear in the previous discussions of style also appear in the use of such terms
as brevity, perspicuity, significancy, and facility of expression, and the like.
See pp. 319, 443, 447.

[49] That the Royal Society looked upon Wilkins as specially qualified for the
study of language or style is revealed in the fact that, though he was not appointed on the committee to improve the language, perhaps because he was too
busy with the *Essay*, he was ordered to attend the first meeting of the committee
and outline to them the proper method of procedure. Birch, *Hist. Roy. Soc.*,
II, 7.

for English prose was due to his having often read the works of
Tillotson,[50] was in a position to be even more directly influenced
by the persistent efforts of the scientists to purify prose expression. He joined the Royal Society the same year in which it
received the patronage of Charles II, and the poem addressed
to Dr. Charleton bears eloquent testimony to his admiration of
and interest in the new science. He, too, was a member of the
committee appointed to improve the tongue, at the meetings
of which, we may infer, he discussed stylistic matters with Cowley, Clifford, and Sprat. That he was no indifferent listener to
the scientific discussions of the Society is revealed in his answer
to the charge of being magisterial, preferred against him by Sir
Robert Howard: "I must crave leave to say, that my whole discourse was sceptical, according to the way of reasoning which was
used by Socrates, Plato, and all the Academics of old . . . and
which is imitated by the modest inquisitions of the Royal Society."[51] If he was so influenced in the method of presenting his
ideas, would he not likewise be influenced in the manner of his
expression, a matter considered no less important by the scientists?

Before concluding this article it may be advisable to distinguish between the revolution in style which we have outlined
and another stylistic movement of the century.[52] The Anti-

[50] Congreve's dedication of *Dryden's Dramatic Works*, quoted by Ker,
*Essays of John Dryden*, I, xxvii, n.

[51] "Defense of an Essay of Dramatic Poesy," *Essays of John Dryden*, ed.
Kerr, I, 124. Dryden in the Preface to *Religio Laici* called himself a sceptic in
philosophy, and Kerr, I, xv, speaks of him as "sceptical, tentative, disengaged."
How much of this quality was due to the scepticism of science that stretched
from Bacon to the Royal Society? See Bredvold's "Dryden, Hobbes, and the
Royal Society," *Mod. Phil.*, XXV (1928), 417–38.

[52] In discussing this paper, a fraction of which was read before one of the
groups of the Modern Language Association at Toronto in 1928, one scholar
maintained that there was some relation between the two movements and referred to Professor Morris Croll's very able articles on Anti-Ciceronianism.
During my own investigations I had discovered no such relationship, and a close
study of the problem has confirmed me in the belief that the two movements
were separate and distinct in that the scientific demand for stylistic reform
neither had its origin in, nor drew support from, the Anti-Ciceronian revolt.
For Professor Croll's theories consult the following: "Juste Lipse et le Mouve-
ment Anti-Cicéronien," (*Revue du Seizième Siècle*, Vol. II [1914]); " 'Attic'
Prose in the Seventeenth Century," (*Stud. in Philol.*, Vol. XVIII [1921]);

Ciceronian movement was the rhetorical counterpart of the revolt against that body of orthodox ideas, gathered largely from antiquity, in which the Renaissance was complacently resting. The rationalistic spirit of inquiry, especially in moral and political matters, which demanded a turning away from what appeared to be only the forms of knowledge to direct observation and the realities of life, also found it necessary to revolt against the Ciceronian style that was closely associated with orthodox philosophies. In the same way, the scientific movement, in the main engineered by Bacon, represented the abandonment of empty theories of nature for observation and experiment. It also announced a stylistic program, but one distinctly different from the Anti-Ciceronian. In short, the desire to discover knowledge which would more fully satisfy the demand for reality was responsible for both revolutions, but the stylistic movements that accompanied them pursued different and divergent courses. The Anti-Ciceronian style found its theories in Aristotle and its models in such Latin writers as Lucan, Juvenal, Persius, Tacitus, Pliny, and especially Seneca; science renounced Aristotle and all his works, and sought for no models in the ancients. Instead of a conscious literary style, such as the other movement was developing, the new philosophy found in the very nature of its material a manner of expression characterized by the lack of literary qualities. The former style, which was far from denying itself the assistance of rhetoric, made use of aphorism, antithesis, paradox, and especially metaphors; the latter, which eschewed all rhetorical flourishes, laid not the slightest claim to these qualities, and against metaphors, as this article has revealed, carried on constant and uncompromising warfare. Again, neologizing was a distinct characteristic of the Anti-Ciceronians, and freakish Latinisms and strange words were admitted into their works; the scientists, on the other hand, abhorred all such importations, preferring "the language of Artizans, Countrymen, and Merchants" to the "hard" words of scholars. Bacon, Hall, Johnson, and Wotton have been considered the Anti-Ciceronian leaders in England, but there is nothing that relates the last three to the

"Attic Prose: Lipsius, Montaigne, Bacon," (*Schelling Anniversary Papers*, 1923); "Muret and the History of 'Attic Prose,'" (*PMLA*, Vol. XXXIX [1924]).

stylistic propaganda of science. Bacon, it is true, attacked the study of style for its own sake, which, he claimed, was fostered by study of the classics, and his own style reveals Anti-Ciceronian characteristics, but in at least one passage in his works[53] he condemns this style—in fact, he considers it one of the distempers of learning—and elsewhere, as revealed near the beginning of this article, he states with approval the characteristics which were later embodied in the stylistic ideal of the scientists, and which do not belong to the other movement. Other examples of Anti-Ciceronianism in England are Donne, Burton, and Browne, with the first of whom the scientists were in no way concerned, while against the style of the latter two they were in open revolt. In fact, the inclusion of these men among the Anti-Ciceronians coerces the belief that one object of the scientific attack was not Ciceronianism but Anti-Ciceronianism. Finally, the absence of any reference on the part of the scientific reformers either to the movement in general, or to single representatives of the movement, strongly argues their indifference to, if not ignorance of, the movement as such.

There are, to be sure, certain resemblances between the two stylistic attitudes. In both "reality" is emphasized, but with the scientists the term generally means a material reality, while the Anti-Ciceronians used it to refer much more widely to rationalistic explanations of human experience. Though in both "things" are preferred to "words," the experimental philosophers had concrete objects in mind, while the others were thinking of intellectual or moral conceptions. Indeed, as has been said, both attitudes had their origin in that element in the Renaissance which turned from reliance on the authority of the ancients and their unsatisfying philosophy to a rationalistic examination of actual experience, but they developed in quite different directions. Neither is it significant that both object to musical phrases and pronounced rhythm in prose, though the Baconians were consistent in their practice, as cannot be said of the Anti-Ciceronians. Likewise, the former constantly emphasize clearness, which together with plainness was the cardinal tenet in their creed, but the latter, though sometimes including the word in their termi-

[53] See *Schelling Anniversary Papers*, pp. 138–39.

nology, frequently did not exemplify it in their practice. To the scientist brevity meant the excision of all rhetorical devices; to the others it meant studied brevity such as aphorisms, point, and the like. Again, appropriateness, propriety, is a term so general and common that its use by both parties is hardly indicative of any relationships, and, in fact, it signified one thing in science and another in moral matters, which constituted the most important element in the revolt against Cicero. One must be cautious in arguing a relationship from the mere occurrence of similar terms, for terms have a way of detaching themselves from their use and of becoming common property, a fact which may be illustrated by examples given earlier in this article. Alexander Ross objects strenuously to the "Tullian pigments" in Browne's style, an expression that seems immediately to identify him with the Anti-Ciceronians, but Ross was the most orthodox of the orthodox, vociferously opposed to everything new in science and philosophy, and so by no stretch of the imagination can he be included in that group. Browne, on the other hand, was not a Ciceronian, as the charge would imply, but an Anti-Ciceronian. Another example is revealed in the passage quoted from Samuel Parker, in which the expression "scheme of words" is used, and which thus would seem to place him among the enemies of Cicero, since the latter especially objected to the *schemata verborum* in Ciceronian style. But Parker employs the term with reference to metaphors, which are one of the *figurae sententiae*, and these latter are characteristic of the Anti-Ciceronians.

By far the clearest and most consistent explanation of the attacks of science upon rhetorical prose is discovered in the nature of the scientific movement. Above everything else the new science insisted upon the necessity of abandoning the empty notions of traditional philosophy, which seemed far removed from material objects, and of observing carefully and recording accurately all physical phenomena. In the concrete nature of the experimental philosophy is to be found the secret of the craving for a clear, accurate, plain style and the belief that such a style was essential to the attainment of scientific goals.[54] This obsession

[54] Probably the most remarkable example of this passion for concrete, material reality in language as well as in philosophy, is discovered in the startling

with the actual nature and appearance of things caused them to resent the interposing of any possible obstruction between observation and description, and gave rise to a stylistic taste which decreed that a rhetorical style, with its figurative language and musical cadence, was the product of folly, vanity, and immaturity, and was not appropriate to serious discourse. Furthermore, the interest in science, together with the wider growth of ration-

---

proposal advanced by Nathaniel Fairfax in the preface to *A Treatise of the Bulk and Selvedge of the World*, 1674. Fairfax displays a violent antipathy to all imported words in the English language, and in his own work he tries as far as possible to substitute English coinages for words of foreign origin, with grotesque results in some cases. Since he was a great admirer of the Royal Society and the experimental philosophy, which impressed him with its practical and utilitarian character, it is not strange to find him proclaiming an interest in things, not words. Thus he advocates the purification and enlargement of the English vocabulary, made necessary by the activities of the new scientists, through the introduction of plain, homely words, gathered from the fields and shops. He wishes to realize literally Sprat's "so many things in the same number of words," not difficult Latinisms but the common words of daily use, "words that answer works, by which all Learners are taught to do, and not make a Clatter." More of his sentiments are worth quoting: "Now the *Philosophy* of our day and Land being so much workful as the world knows it to be, methinks this of all times should be *the* time, wherein, if ever, we should gather up those scatter'd words of ours that speak works, rather than to suck in those of learned air from beyond Sea, which are as far off sometimes from the things they speak, as they are from us to whom they are spoken. Besides, it may well be doubted, whether Latine can now be made so fit to set forth things the writings of a *Working Philosophy* by, as our own Speech.—For we must know that almost all the old pieces of good Latine that we draw by, have been taken up by that sort of learning that is wont to be worded in the Schools, and spent in the setting to sale of such things as could best be glazed with the froth of ink, by the men of Closets. Whence he that is best skill'd in it, is so hard put to it, in the Kitchin, the Shop, and the Ship; and ever will be, though *Plautus* should be as well understood as *Tully*. For the words that are every day running to and fro in the Chat of Workers, have not been gotten into Books and put aboard for other Lands until this way of Knowing by Doing was started amongst us.—But as Learnings being lockt up in the Tongues of the Schools, or Love's being lickt up in more the womanly simprings of the lips, and the smiling kissing speeches of some others abroad, have been enough to enkindle in us a panting after, and fondness for some of those Outlandish dynns: So if the works of our own men shall be shipt over by words of our own tongue, it may happily make others who have love enough for the things, to seek as much after our words, as we upon other scores have done after theirs; the first draught being *English*, name and thing, doing and speaking." Cf. what Sprat says about the Royal Society's "preferring the language of Artizans, Countrymen, and Merchants, before that, of Wits, or Scholars."

alism, tended to create a distrust of the imagination, a distrust which in some cases was deepened by the growing feeling that fancy was associated with the passions, and, therefore, was a dangerous faculty of the mind. This latter attitude appears infrequently in the scientific revolt, but plays a great part in the attack on pulpit eloquence. Finally, scientific materialism exerted a distinct influence on ideas regarding the nature of language. A suggestion of this appears in Bacon, but it finds clear and definite expression in Hobbes, who claims that words are only the marks of things.[55] Thus the connotative value of words and their power to invest the creations of the imagination with life and being are summarily cast into the discard. Hobbes's idea is implied in the words of many of the scientists, and in Samuel Parker is again clearly stated.[56] Its most remarkable manifestation, however, is in John Wilkins' *Essay Towards a Real Character and a Philosophical Language*, 1668, in which words are literally reduced to marks, and which frankly confesses to making no provision at all for such creatures of the imagination as fairies, fauns, and the like on the ground that they have no existence in nature. With this conception of language in the background, is it strange that science came to grips with imaginative prose?

There were, of course, other factors co-operating with science in the simplification of English prose. Rationalism and the steady growth of the classical spirit made against all extravagancies. In explaining the attacks on intricacies of style, Mr. Spingarn mentions the substitution of general for technical terms, the preference for sceptical as opposed to dogmatic modes of thought and speech, the horror of pedantry, the trend toward precision of word and idea, and the attempt to make literature approximate conversation. In most of these matters the presence of the two factors just mentioned may be noted, but it should be remarked that science also was very much concerned with all but the last. Two characteristics of the scientific revolt, however, distinguish it from other stylistic influences, and justify the opinion that science exerted by far the most powerful force upon prose. First, the thoroughgoing nature of the stylistic reform

[55] *Leviathan*, ed. A. R. Waller, p. 14.
[56] *A Free and Impartial Censure*, p. 61.

advocated by the experimental philosophers, which, rejecting any compromise whatsoever with rhetoric, insisted upon an undefiled plainness and caused the issue at stake to be outlined sharply and distinctly. Perhaps of greater importance is the fact that reformation of style was a very significant part of a definite program adopted by a closely organized society of prominent men who were aggressively active in promulgating their views. The extent to which Glanvill's style changed under their discipline is a fair gauge of the influence that must have been exerted upon all members of the society, and, through them, upon the outside world.

# THE ATTACK ON PULPIT ELOQUENCE IN THE RESTORATION: AN EPISODE IN THE DEVELOPMENT OF THE NEO-CLASSICAL STANDARD FOR PROSE*

## RICHARD FOSTER JONES

ONE of the interesting phenomena in literary history is the sudden and decided change that came over English prose in the third quarter of the seventeenth century.[1] This stylistic revolution finds a ready, if not always a clearly realized, explanation in the rationalistic temper of the age, which demanded of prose a fitter medium for the expression of thought, and discountenanced appeals to the imagination and emotions. Hence the inference might easily be drawn that the change represented an unconscious substitution of one style for another, in that prose was naturally reacting to the altered intellectual outlook of men. Yet seldom indeed are literary revolutions achieved in such a manner, for they are as much the products of conscious effort as of unconscious change. Men are not so oblivious of their own standards nor so unobservant of their changing intellectual environment as to pass through a transition period without noting its character or deliberately

* Reprinted, with minor corrections, from *The Journal of English and Germanic Philology*, Vol. XXX (1931), by permission of the publishers.

[1] "The Restoration may be taken as the era of the formation of our present style. Imagination was tempered, transports diminished, judgment corrected itself, artifice began." A. H. Welsh, *Development of English Literature and Language*, 1882, II, 23.

assisting the cause to which they are bound. Such certainly was not the case with seventeenth-century prose. The substitution of a plain, direct, unadorned style for the elaborate and musical style of the Commonwealth was a change of which the age was quite conscious, and for which many stoutly battled.

In a previous article I have traced the important and direct influence which science exerted in the simplification of English prose.[2] There I showed how consistently and emphatically the representatives of the new science from its very beginning had manifested a stylistic attitude which reached its most elaborate expression in Sprat's *History of the Royal Society*, and which profoundly influenced some of the writers of the day. The standard thus established was inspired by the materialistic nature of the experimental philosophy, and was dictated by the need which that philosophy felt for an accurate, plain, and clear medium of expression. Since our necessities frequently assume the guise of virtues, the scientists evolved a stylistic taste which, rebelling against all rhetorical devices, placed a premium upon plainness. These new stylistic values soon spread from the scene of their origin, and, owing to the popularity of the new science and to the representative nature of the membership of the Royal Society, were widely disseminated. It is the purpose of the present article to follow the new standard of prose as it invades an alien field, and to discuss the many and earnest efforts made to impose upon sermons the same style that had been found most serviceable to science.

Prior to the restoration of Charles II, especially in the third and fourth decades of the century, the predominating style of preaching was characterized by affectations, fanciful conceits, metaphors, similes, plays upon words, antitheses, paradoxes, and the pedantic display of Greek and Latin quotations.[3] After 1660

[2] "Science and English Prose Style in the Third Quarter of the Seventeenth Century," *PMLA*, XLV (1930), 977–1009.

[3] See E. C. Dargan, *A History of Preaching*, 1912, II, 146, 153. For a discussion of the style of sermons on the Continent as well as in England during this period, consult J. E. Spingarn, *Critical Essays of the Seventeenth Century*, I, xxxvi–xlii. Professor G. P. Krapp discusses sermons up to and including Donne in *The Rise of English Literary Prose*, chap. iv. See also Fritz Pützer, *Prediger des Englischen Barock*, Bonn, 1929; and *The Works of Symon Patrick*, ed. Alex. Taylor, 1858, I, xcvii–ci.

the scientific ideal of style—plainness, directness, clearness—
steadily gained ascendency over the older manner of expression.[4]
This change was materially assisted by the determined efforts
of numerous stylistic reformers, the first of which appeared, as
we would expect, in scientific quarters. As early as 1646, John
Wilkins, in *Ecclesiastes*, which ran through nine editions in the
seventeenth century, had advocated a plain, natural, and clear
way of preaching. Some eight years later Robert Boyle found
in the Bible a style pleasing to a scientist, and concluded that the
plainest language was the most fitting garb for religious truth.[5]
But not only in definite statements do we find evidences of a new
standard for sermons. Early in the Restoration a few preachers
were exemplifying in their sermons the stylistic virtues for which
the scientists clamored. Tillotson, whose contact with the new
science was close, drew crowded congregations by virtue of his
simple, clear manner of speaking; indeed, he became so popular
that his sermons began to serve as models, and to him more than
to any one else has been ascribed the credit for the new kind of
preaching.[6] Thus reformation in the style of religious composi-

---

[4] "Pedantry, crabbed conceit, elaboration of metaphor or illustration, gave
way to advanced directness, and the English language was made to show of what
it was capable when it was not strained: style, casting off imitation, became direct
and plain. During the forty years which followed the return of Charles II,
English divines, in their treatment of serious themes, laid the foundation on
which Addison based his mastery over the language of his day." W. H. Hutton
in *Cam. Hist. of Eng. Lit.*, VIII, 335.

[5] In 1663 Meric Casaubon expressed doubt concerning the use of eloquence
in the pulpit, and indicated a growing opposition to it. "I do not deny," he
says, "but ardent and vehement speech is generally most plausible and powerful:
yet I find that some accounted learned and judicious have avoided it, as having
too much affinity, with madness and distraction." *The Question, To whom it
belonged Anciently to Preach*, p. 29.

[6] For a more extended treatment of Wilkins, Boyle, and Tillotson, see
*PMLA*, XLV (1930), 979, 983, 1002. Though Wilkins was never a popular
preacher, his sermons illustrated the new style as clearly as Tillotson's. Compare
William Lloyd's funeral sermon on Wilkins with Thomas Birch's description
of Tillotson's style, *The Life of Tillotson*, 1753, pp. 22–23. Another great
preacher and scientist, Isaac Barrow, illustrated the new style in his sermons, and
also expressed opinions in its behalf. In a discourse entitled "Against Foolish
Talking and Jesting" (found in *Illustrations of the Liturgy*, ed. James Brogden,
3 vols., 1842) he makes "foolish talking" consist of opposite tales, plays on
words, odd similitudes, startling metaphors, "in short, a manner of speaking out

tions was already under way, when the attack proper on pulpit eloquence began.

Robert South, who had for some years been public orator at Oxford, fired the opening gun in a sermon preached at Christ Church, April 30, 1668, and for the next decade hardly a year passed without witnessing one or more onslaughts upon rhetorical preaching.[7] Taking as his text Luke XXI, 15, "For I will give you a mouth and wisdom, which all your adversaries shall not be able to gainsay or resist," South interprets the expression "a mouth and wisdom" as meaning ability of speech, which, to suit his purpose, he analyzes into great clearness and perspicuity, an unaffected plainness and simplicity, and a suitable zeal and fervor. By the light of these standards he inveighs against "difficult nothings, rabbinical whimsies, and remote allusions, which no man of sense and solid reason can hear without weariness and contempt," and he maintains that only the ignorant are impressed with "highflown metaphors and allegories, attended and set off with scraps of Greek and Latin." South obviously discovered in the Bible the manner of expression that he wished to find,[8] for he draws his main argument from the Apostles, who, he claims,

---

of the simple and plain way (such as reason teacheth and proveth things by), which . . . doth affect and amuse the fancy, stirring in it some wonder, and breeding some delight thereto." (II, 372–73.) However, he permits the use of "exhorbitancies of speach" when men cannot be reached by reason.

[7] As will be noted on another page, Sprat had evidently, in the preceding year, meant to include sermons in his tirade against eloquence in general. *History of the Royal Society*, pp. 111–13.

[8] Before the middle of the century not only had no suspicion been attached to the use of rhetoric in sermons, but rhetorical devices had actually been advocated for religious discourses. In a work entitled *Sacred Eloquence: Or the Art of Rhetorick as it is layd down in the Scripture*, published in 1659, nine years after the author's death, John Prideaux, bishop of Worcester, drew up a rhetoric which defines all rhetorical terms such as tropes, metaphors, parables, similitudes and the like to be used in sermons, and which, in chapter v, recommends direct appeals to the affections of an audience. Furthermore, he takes all his numerous examples from the Bible, in which, he says, the metaphors, especially, "are eminent and numberless." Sacred eloquence he defines as "a Logicall kind of Rhetorick, to be used in Prayer, Preaching, or Conferences; to the Glory of God, and the convincing, instructing and strengthening our brethren." Instead of the Bible's justifying a plain style, to him it justified all manner of figures of speech.

used a plain, easy, obvious, and familiar style, in which nothing
was strained or far-fetched,

> no affected scheme, or airy fancies, above the reach or relish of an ordi-
> nary apprehension; no, nothing of all this; but their grand subject was
> truth, and consequently above all these petty arts and poor additions;
> as not being capable of any greater lustre or advantage than to appear
> just as it is. For there is a certain majesty in plainness; as the proclama-
> tion of a prince never frisks it in tropes or fine conceits, in numerous
> and well turned periods, but commands in sober, natural expressions.
> A substantial beauty, as it comes out of the hands of nature, needs neither
> paint nor patch; things never made to adorn, but to cover something
> that would be hid.[9]

This clearness of expression, he adds, made the Apostles' preaching irresistible, since the will can be effectively reached only
through reason and judgment. There is no evidence that South
was associated in any way with the scientific movement. In fact,
he actually attacked the Royal Society as being subversive to the
universities.[10] But the plain style advocated by him differs in
no respect from that which the scientists had pressed and were
pressing upon the world. One also senses in South an attitude
which was soon to become prevalent, namely, a natural distaste
for all verbal embellishments. South himself hardly lived up to
his ideal.[11]

Early in the following year appeared a work[12] which turned

[9] That South had the recently deceased Jeremy Taylor in mind is apparent
in what he says relative to St. Paul's manner of preaching: "Nothing here of *the
fringes of the northstar*; nothing of *the down of angels' wings, or the beautiful
locks of cherubims*: no starched similitude introduced with a 'Thus have I seen a
cloud rolling in its airy mansion,' and the like. No, these were sublimities above
the rise of the apostolic spirit." Some of South's ideas and expressions argue his
acquaintance with Wilkins' *Ecclesiastes*, and perhaps with Boyle's *Some Considerations Touching the Style of the Holy Scriptures*, and with Sprat's *History*.

[10] See John Evelyn's *Diary*, July 9, 1669. South, however, was neither
ignorant of nor unfriendly toward the new science. See his *Sermons*, 1843, IV,
114–17, 206.

[11] Cf. *The Classic Preachers of the English Church*, by J. E. Kempe, 1877,
chap. iii. A few years later South resumed his attack on rhetorical embellishments in two sermons entitled *A Discourse Against Long Extemporary Prayers*,
directed in the main against the dissenters.

[12] *A Friendly Debate Between a Conformist and a Non-Conformist. The
Third Edition*, 1669. The Preface is dated October 20, and the imprimatur

the attack on pulpit eloquence in a direction which it pursued until the end. The association of pedantic and rhetorical preaching with only the Puritans of Cromwell's day and the nonconformists of the Restoration was obviously too narrow.[18] In earlier days certainly royalist ministers—witness Jeremy Taylor—had been as guilty of eloquent preaching as the more fanatical "men of God," and sermons generally in the first half of the century had committed most of the stylistic sins attributed to the nonconformists. From this association, however, the stylistic revolt acquired all the virulence characteristic of the powerful reaction against the Puritans. "Fine preaching" soon became the rhetorical counterpart of fanatical religion; enthusiasm was detected as quickly in the first as in the second. On the other hand, a rational religion and a plain style were claimed by the con-

---

November 7, 1668. The popularity of the work is indicated by its reaching a fifth edition within a year of its first appearance. Baxter says that the book "was greedily read," and that it "did exceedingly fit the humours not only of the haters of the Non-conformists, but also of all the prophane despisers and deriders of serious Godliness." (*Reliquiae Baxterianae*, ed. M. Sylvester, 1696, Part III, pp. 39–43.) *A Continuation or Second Part* of Patrick's work appeared in the spring of 1669, and *A Further Continuation, or the Third Part*, dated October 13, 1669, was published in answer to *A Sober Answer to the Friendly Debate*, by Philagathus (Samuel Rolls, a Presbyterian divine), the Preface to which is dated June 1, 1669. Patrick was also attacked in *An Humble Apology for Non-Conformists, with modest and serious reflections upon the Friendly Debate . . . by a lover of truth and peace*, which he answered in "An Appendix to the Third Part of the Friendly Debate," dated January 13, 1670. In his *Autobiography* Patrick says that he was provoked to write his book by the great insolence of the dissenters, and that it "proved very acceptable, and had many editions." See *Works*, ed. A. Taylor, IX, 450.

[18] The Conformist says to his opponent, "As soon as you had cast out of doors all that was Old among us; if any Fellow did but light upon some new and pretty Fancy in Religion, or some odd unusual Expression, or perhaps some swelling words of Vanity, presently he set up for a Preacher, and cry'd himself for a man that had made some new discovery." (*A Friendly Debate*, pp. 34–35.) Patrick was by no means responsible for first suggesting this aspect of Puritanism. It must have been widely noted, for five years earlier Butler had attributed to his hero a style characterized by "hard" words, Latin and Greek quotations, and figures of speech:

> For Rhetoric, he could not ope
> His mouth, but out there flew a trope.

See *Hudibras*, Part I, Canto I, ll. 51–119.

forming clergy as their special possessions.[14] The author of *A Friendly Debate*, Simon Patrick, destined, first as bishop of Chichester and later of Ely, to play a worthy part in the established Church, had himself undergone a considerable stylistic change before he began to combat the style of the dissenters.[15] That rationalism played a part in this change is evidenced by Patrick's basing his argument squarely on the way in which the emotions should be aroused.[16] Since the nonconformists appealed to them through the imagination and senses, they "seek to please the itching Ears and gratifie the longings of their Fancies with new-found words, affected Expressions, and odd Phrases," and their audiences are affected only by pretty fancies, fine phrases,

[14] "[The nonconformists] have found out in lieu of Moral Vertue, a *Spiritual Divinity*, that is made up of nothing else but certain Trains and Schemes of Effeminate Follies and illiterate Enthusiasms; and instead of sober Devotion, a more spiritual and intimate way of Communion with God, that in truth, consists in little else but meeting together in private to prate Phrases, make Faces, and rail at Carnal Reason (i.e. in their sense all sober and sincere use of our Understanding in Spiritual Matters) whereby they have effectually turn'd all Religion into unaccountable Fancies and Enthusiasms, drest up with pompous and empty schemes of speech, and so embrace a few gawdy Metaphors and Allegories, instead of the substance of true and real Righteousness. And herein lies the most material difference between the sober Christians of the Church of *England* and our modern Sectaries, That we express the Precepts and Duties of the Gospel in plain and intelligible Terms, whilst they trifle them away by childish Metaphors and Allegories . . . and (what is more) the different Subdivisions among the Sects themselves are not so much distinguish'd by any real diversity of Opinions, as by variety of Phrases and Forms of Speech, that are the peculiar *Shibboleths* of each Tribe." Samuel Parker, *A Discourse of Ecclesiastical Politie*, 1670, pp. 74 ff.

[15] Compare, for instance, the style of *Mensa Mystica*, 1660, with that of the book under discussion. The former treatise contains numerous figures of speech—comparisons, metaphors, exclamatory sentences—and in general is much warmer, more enthusiastic, more sensitive to beauty, and more imaginative than his later work. Here is a typical example: "Our hearts must flame with love, our minds must reek with holy thoughts, our mouths must breeth forth praises like clouds of incense, and our hands must not be lifted up with nothing in them." (P. 47.) This is as bad as anything he reprehends in the nonconformists.

[16] "I have been taught, that there are two wayes to come at the Affections: One by the Senses and Imagination; and so we see people mightily affected with a Puppet-play, with a Beggar's tone, with a lamentable Look, or anything of like nature. The other is by the Reason and Judgment; when the evidence of any Truth convincing the Mind, engages the affections to its side, and makes them move according to its direction." *Friendly Debate*, p. 15.

verbal cadences, rhetorical figures, empty words, pretty similitudes, and shreds of authors. Thus they teach many things about
spiritual truths that are nothing but the creations of a heated
imagination. The conformists, however, appealing to the emotions only through the reason, employ a plain, proper, and familiar style. Here appear again the stylistic values of science,
changed in no jot or tittle from their earlier use, though now
applied to another type of prose composition. Here also appears
the rationalistic spirit which, permeating the whole period, insists upon the primacy of reason, manifests a distrust of the
imagination, and sees in language only an instrument for the
expression of intellectual concepts.[17]

The serious light in which the use of figurative language in
religious discourse, especially that of the Puritans, was viewed
becomes apparent in Samuel Parker's *A Discourse of Ecclesiastical Politie*, 1670. That great champion of intolerance, later
bishop of Oxford, advocates nothing less than an act of Parliament "to abridge Preachers the use of fulsome and lushious
Metaphors" in the belief that such measures would prevent
factions and

be an effectual Cure of all our present Distempers . . . For were Men
obliged to speak Sense as well as Truth, all the swelling *Mysteries of*

[17] See *A Friendly Debate*, pp. 15, 34–35, 37, 54, 85–86, 121–22, 142,
190–91, 197. Although rationalism undoubtedly played some part in Patrick's
stylistic attitude, the fact that his early work, composed at a time when he must
have been familiar with the rationalistic movement, by no means conformed to
the standards here expressed, whereas later volumes, composed after the scientific
attack on rhetoric had made great headway, are written in a much simpler style,
strongly suggests that his own views on style as well as his practice must also
have been indebted to the stand taken by the Royal Society. Though Patrick
did not become a member of the Society, he was wholeheartedly in favor of
the new science, as is clearly shown in his *A Brief Account of the new Sect
of Latitude-Men. Together with some reflections upon the New Philosophy*,
1662, in which he attacks Aristotelianism and the authority of the ancients,
pitting against them the discoveries of the moderns, particularly those indebted
to the telescope and microscope. He fully recognizes the importance of these
two inventions, and he also shows due appreciation of Boyle's experiments
with the air pump, Gilbert's work in terrestrial magnetism, Harvey's discovery
of the circulation of the blood, as well as of the work of Bacon, Galileo, and
others. In emphasis upon observation and experiment, opposition to Peripateticism, support of the moderns against the ancients, regard for the most distinguished scientists of the century, he is one with the experimental philosophers.

*Fanaticism* would immediately sink into flat and empty Nonsense; and they would be ashamed of such jejune and ridiculous Stuff as their admired and most profound Notions would appear to be, when they want the Varnish of fine Metaphors and glittering Allusions.[18]

The *Discourse* was not Parker's first attack upon rhetorical compositions. Four years earlier, after he had been converted to the experimental philosophy and had joined the Royal Society, he had taken up cudgels in behalf of the stylistic cause of science, and had attacked the Cambridge Platonists in the same way in which the scientists were belaboring Aristotelians and rhetorical writers.[19] He is now merely bringing to bear upon the style of the nonconformists the same values and standards that he had employed in behalf of science, and so it is not strange to find him clamoring for plain, perspicuous, and intelligible terms. The parallel between the scientific and clerical revolts in general is exact: the nonconformists correspond to the rhetorical writers of the commonwealth, and the conformists to the experimental philosophers, while the stylistic ideal remains the same.[20]

[18] P. 76. This proposal calls to mind the famous passage from Sprat's *History of the Royal Society*, published three years earlier, in which the author, considering the prevailing type of eloquence as injurious as international dissensions and hypocrisy in religion, and looking upon its cure as almost impossible, advocates the banishing of eloquence out of all civil societies. Although Sprat includes in his indictment "almost all arts and professions," he must have had sermons chiefly in mind. Needless to say, his attitude toward pulpit eloquence derives entirely from his scientific outlook and furnishes another link between the stylistic program of science and that of the pulpit reformers.

[19] *A Free and Impartial Censure of the Platonick Philosophie,* 1666, pp. 75 ff. Also see *PMLA,* XLV (1930), 1001. Parker was at first very much impressed by the work of the Platonists, but "when I came to survey it more closely I soon found it was nothing else but words." It was the new science that had opened his eyes.

[20] Cf. *A Discourse of Ecclesiastical Politie,* pp. 74 ff., and *A Free and Impartial Censure,* pp. 75 ff. In the following year Parker takes to task another stylistic vice which science had damned, namely, "Learned Shreds of Latin and Scholarlike Sayings of ancient Poets and Philosophers." And in a letter to the author, printed at the end of the same work, Patrick, who seems to have joined forces with Parker in a common cause, apologizes for some Greek quotations on the ground that "our Antagonist makes such a noise with them." (*A Defence and Continuation of a Discourse of Ecclesiastical Politie,* 1671, pp. 93–94, 735.) The antagonist was John Owen, who will be considered later. In his *Reproof to the Rehearsal Transprosed,* 1673, an attack on Marvel, Parker continued his stylistic campaign with such statements as "downright English is

The attack on the use of rhetoric in the pulpit received great impetus from the publication of a book which, because of its wit, humor, and sensational nature, achieved remarkable popularity and ran through many editions.[21] The author, John Eachard, became master of Catherine Hall, Cambridge, in 1675, and four years later vice-chancellor of the university. No single work in the whole movement did so much toward bringing the problem of style before the public or provoked so many replies. Parts of the book are expressed in such a manner as to impugn their seriousness, but the sections dealing with style seem serious enough. Among the causes producing contempt for the clergy, such as poor education, slight remuneration, and unfit men, the author emphasizes a meretricious style, which, he claims, sprang from the neglect of the study of English. No one before him had ever argued so earnestly for the study of the mother tongue, or attributed such dire results to its neglect. To ignorance of the possibilities of the English language and to reliance upon the classics he imputes all stylistic abuses, and the latter are described in picturesque language. Though Eachard does not specifically designate the nonconformists as the object of his scorn, they evidently are; but he had ministers of the older generation in mind as well.[22] He introduces no new element into the charge that had been, and was being, preferred against the former, except the emphasis upon the study of English, but he continues the attack upon the pedantic use of classical quotations, vaunting eloquence, hard words, fantastical phrases, and rhetorical devices

---

in some Cases as good a Flower as the fairest Trope in Aristotle's Rhetorick" (p. 30). The treatise is more remarkable for its sarcastic notice of Milton's *Areopagitica*, concerning the style of which Parker says, "Such fustian bumbast as this past for stately wit and sence in that Age of politeness and reformation." (P. 191.) Browne, Taylor, and Milton received scant courtesy during this period.

[21] *The Grounds and Occasions of the Contempt of the Clergy and Religion Enquir'd into; in a Letter written to R. L.* The treatise is dated at the end, August 8, 1670. (All references are to *Dr. Eachard's Works*, 11th ed., 1705.) Arber has reprinted it in his *English Garner*. Mr. Spingarn calls Eachard "the Jeremy Collier of the corrupt rhetoric of the pulpit." *Critical Essays of the Seventeenth Century*, I, xliv.

[22] See James Arderne, *Directions Concerning the Matter and Stile of Sermons*, 1671, p. 1.

in general. He is especially severe with "frightful metaphors" and similitudes, to find which, he says, the nonconformists

rake Heaven and Earth, down to the bottom of the Sea, then Rumble over all Arts and Sciences, ransack all Shops and Ware-houses, spare neither Camp nor City, but that they will have them. So fond are such deceived ones of these same gay words, that they count all Discourses empty, dull, and cloudy, unless bespangled with these Glitterings. Nay, so injudicious and impudent together will they sometimes be, that the *Almighty* himself is often in danger of being dishonored by these indiscreet and horrid Metaphor-Mongers: And when they thus Blaspheme the God of Heaven, by such unallowed Expressions, to make amends, they'll put you in an, *as it were,* forsooth, *As I may say.*[23]

The spirit of scientific rationalism is apparent in Eachard's attitude.[24] His opposition to rhetoric finds support in the fact that the latter obscures the truth, makes no appeal to the reason, and weakens the judgment. He echoes the strictures of the scientists in protesting against webs of empty speculations and useless, unprofitable, frothy expressions, and he draws upon the terms familiar to the new science in demanding that which is practical, solid, and useful expressed in plain, direct, intelligible, and common language. He is also imbued with the scientific spirit, when he contends that a luxuriant style prevents "more profitable searching into the Nature and Causes of things themselves."[25] But in nothing is the influence of the Royal Society more evident than in what he says about the proper words to be used in sermons. In this matter he only elaborates upon what Sprat had said about the virtuosi's "preferring the language of Artizans, Countrymen, and Merchants, before that of Wits and Scholars." Eachard complains that "if the Minister's words

[23] P. 38. See also pp. 24, 27, 32, 38–39, 41; and *Some Observations upon an Answer to an Enquiry,* 1671. *Dr. Eachard's Works,* pp. 56, 76.

[24] Eachard, though he gives us delightful caricatures of the Cartesian novice and the amateur Baconian of his day, had great respect for the Royal Society, and was especially interested in the part which clergymen played in its affairs. See *Some Observations upon an Answer to an Enquiry, Dr. Eachard's Works,* pp. 199 ff.

[25] See also p. 37. Cf. what Robert Boyle says about the empty phraseology of Peripateticism in contrast to the new science: "But these uninstructive terms [substantial forms, real qualities, etc.] do neither oblige nor conduct a man to deeper searches into the structure of things, nor the manner of being produced, and of operating one upon another." *Works,* ed. T. Birch, 1744, V, 43.

be such as the Constable uses, his Matter Plain and Practical, such as come to the common Market, he may pass possibly for an Honest, Well-meaning Man, but by no means for any Scholar." Some preachers, he continues, act "As if plain Words, useful and intelligible Instructions were not as good for an Esquire . . . as for him that holds the Plough, or mends Hedges."[26] Such hostility to "hard" words finds its ultimate inspiration in those who were striving for a plain and clear medium of expression in the scientific world.

The clearest evidence, however, for the participation of science in the formulation of a standard for sermons is contained in several treatises by Joseph Glanvill. In the year following Eachard's *Enquiry*, when the attack on the use of rhetorical devices in religious compositions was at its height, Glanvill published his *Philosophia Pia*,[27] one of several attempts written dur-

---

[26] Pp. 33, 35. The stylistic attitude which science did much to make popular appears also in *A Discourse Concerning the Knowledge of Jesus Christ*, 1674, by William Sherlock, rector of St. George's, Botolph Lane, London, and later dean of St. Paul's, of whom South said that he wrote both for and against every subject he touched upon. Sherlock manifests great grief at seeing so many "abused with Words and Phrases, which . . . signifie nothing," and declaims against men who "argue from Fancies and Allegories, which . . . have nothing solid and substantial in them." Since figurative language is only the "cheat and imposture of an Enthusiastic fancy," he concludes that "at this rate it were easie to make any thing of any thing, to find out some pretty words and phrases, and illusions, types of Metaphors, to countenance all the feats of Enthusiasm, and the more godly Romances of Popish Legends." In his eyes rhetoric is associated with the imagination, a deceptive faculty of the mind, which perverts the plainest sense, and makes men "dote upon words and phrases." See pp. 1, 55, 69–70, 81–82, 194, 254. Also consult *A Free and Impartial Inquiry into the Causes of that very great Esteem and Honour that the Nonconforming Preachers are generally in with their Followers. . . . By a Lover of the Church of England, and Unfeigned Piety*, 1673.

[27] This was reprinted, at the command, Glanvill says, of a person of great fame and learning, and with only slight verbal changes, as the fourth essay, entitled "The Usefulness of Real Philosophy to Theology," in *Essays on Several Important Subjects in Philosophy and Religion*, 1676. In an earlier article I have discussed Glanvill at length as affording the clearest example of the great revolution which the new science was working in style. (See *PMLA*, XLV [1930], 989–98.) He had, in his earlier days, been an enthusiastic Cartesian, as *The Vanity of Dogmatizing* makes clear; but a few years later, attaching himself to the Royal Society, he became an ardent disciple of Bacon and the most unreserved supporter of the experimental philosophy. It is to be noted that his style, when under the influence of Descartes, remained highly

ing this period to reconcile science and religion. In this work he is very explicit about the influence of experimental science on sermons. It teaches men, he says, to state things clearly; to pay less regard to the niceties in religion, and more to practical and certain knowledge. "The Real Philosophy," he continues, ends many "*disputes*, by taking men off *unnecessary Terms* of *Art*, which very often are the occasions of the Great Contests: If things were stated in *clear* and *plain* words, many Controversies would be at an end; and the Philosophy I am recommending inclines Men to *define* with *those* that are *simplest* and *plainest*; and thereby also very much promotes the Interests both of *truth* and *peace*."[28]

One cannot emphasize too much the relationship of the discussion of rhetoric to the peculiar conditions of the period which produced it. Sick of the religious controversies that had brought so much woe in their wake, men were beginning to discover in language the cause of the evil. Glanvill's sentiments had been

rhetorical, but when he came under the discipline of the scientists, it underwent a remarkable change toward simplicity and directness. Some scholars have discovered Descartes' influence on the English stylistic movement in the expression "mathematicall plainness," which Sprat employs in describing the style demanded by the Royal Society. (See Miss Marjorie Nicolson's interesting article, "The Early Stage of Cartesianism in England," *Stud. in Phil.*, XXVI [1929], 374.) But perhaps it is not necessary to cross the channel to find a source for these words. There was no mean mathematical tradition in England, embracing as it did Napier, Oughtred, and Wallis, the last of whom was closely associated with the Royal Society. Even though Bacon himself was no mathematician, mathematics was soon included in the general program of the Baconian philosophers. The following extract from a letter written by Dr. John Twysden to Oughtred, at some date between 1648 and 1652, shows that the stylistic quality under discussion could very well have been derived from England's own mathematicians. Speaking of Oughtred's *Clavis Mathematica*, Twysden says, "Neither truly did I find my expectation deceived; having with admiration often considered how it was possible (even in the hardest things of geometry) to deliver so much matter in so few words, yet with such demonstrative clearness and perspicuity: and hath often put me in mind of learned Mersennus his judgment (since dead) of it, that there was more matter comprehended in that little book than in Diophantes, and all the ancients." *Correspondence of Scientific Men of the Seventeenth Century*, ed. S. P. Rigaud, 1841, p. 66. For an important reference to Oughtred in this respect, see *Vindiciae Academiarum*, 1654, pp. 20–21.

[28] See *Philosophia Pia*, pp. 73, 90–91, 93–94; and *Essays on Several Important Subjects*, pp. 22, 25, 28.

foreshadowed by Sprat and anticipated by Parker in his proposal of a parliamentary act to abolish metaphors in order to end the distempers of the age.[29] The interpretation of rhetoric as "a cheat and imposture of an enthusiastic fancy" and the concomitant belief that the clouds raised by obscuring figures of speech were chiefly responsible for the religious factions that had rent England removed the discussion of style from a purely aesthetic and intellectual realm, and proposed it almost literally as a matter of life and death.[30] As strong as was the scientific hostility to luxuriant prose, when the spirit animating science had entered the religious world, the opposition grew much more intense. Yet after all, this spirit was only demanding for religious discourse what it had insisted upon for natural philosophy, a medium of expression that would represent real things just as they are, and thus remove controversies caused by mere fancies and the imaginative, empty, and obscuring verbosities with which they were expressed. It is not strange, then, to find Glanvill introducing the same values and employing the same phrases in formulating an ideal for sermons as had been introduced into the discussion of the proper scientific style.

Seven years later Glanvill is still harping upon the method of expressions proper to sermons. In a work written in defense of the "plain way" of preaching, he makes style a distinguishing mark between conformists and nonconformists in a manner reminiscent of Patrick's earlier distinction. The metaphors, obscure expressions, and odd schemes of speech of the dissenters, in his eyes, serve only to obscure their doctrines, "Whereas our Ministers represent the doctrine and instructions in clearness of thought and simplicity of speech."[31] He differentiates at some

---

[29] Also consult his *Reproof to the Rehearsal Transprosed*, 1673, pp. 56 ff. Just as Bacon and the experimental philosophers had discovered rhetoric to be one factor in the corruption of science, so the conformists attributed the corruption of religion to rhetorical devices.

[30] In the dedication to his *Essay Towards a Real Character and a Philosophical Language*, 1668, a design fostered by the Royal Society, Wilkins had pointed out, as a virtue of the language he was trying to establish, that it would "contribute much to the clearing of some of our Modern differences in Religion, by unmasking many wild errors, that shelter themselves under the disguise of affected phrases." See *PMLA*, XLV (1930), 1002, note 48.

[31] *A Seasonable Defence of Preaching: And the Plain Way of it*, 1678, p. 41.

length between men whose learning is concerned with languages and antiquities, or with school divinity and the spinosities of controversy, and

another sort of learned men, whose design hath been to study things, to furnish their minds with clear and right conceptions on human nature, the manners and actions of men, to turn their thoughts, after due preparation towards practical Theology, to make parochial charges, and to exercise themselves in frequent Preaching: and these are by their learning and knowledge inabled to speak with the most judgment, propriety, and plainness. For (as I intimated before) it requires parts and understanding to be plain. He must think distinctly and clearly that would teach so: and the true useful learning is the proper instrument to inable a man for that.[32]

Glanvill's words furnish an interesting, if not significant, parallel between the conforming clergy and the Baconian philosophers. One is opposed to futile controversy over theology, the other to disputatious Peripateticism; both emphasize the study of things rather than words; one observes human nature and conduct, the other, physical nature; one stresses practical theology, the other, the usefulness of the experimental philosophy; and finally, the first approves "exercise in frequent preaching," the second, the "doing" nature of the new science.

We need not go far afield to discover a possible channel through which the scientific spirit could have reached the pulpit. One of the most remarkable features of early science in England was the number of clergymen who were interested in it. Eachard comments on the number who were members of the Royal Society, and whom he considered as capable scientists as any of the others.[33] Glanvill also, in order to show that the Society was not inimical to religion, points to the impressive array of ecclesiastics

[32] See pp. 45–46. In another passage he returns to the same theme: "A man doth not shew his wit or learning by rolling in metaphors, and scattering his sentences of Greek and Latin, by abounding in high expressions, and talking in Clouds, but he is then learned, when his learning has clear'd his Understanding, and furnish'd it with full and distinct apprehension of things; when it enables him to make *hard* things *plain*; and conceptions that were *confused*, *distinct* and *orderly*; and he shews his learning by speaking good, strong, and plain Sense." P. 109.

[33] *Some Observations upon an Answer to an Enquiry*, pp. 119–22. (*Dr. Eachard's Works*, 1705.) See also Sprat's *History of the Royal Society*, p. 132.

who were fellows, among them the archbishops of Canterbury and York, and the bishops of Ely, London, Rochester, Salisbury, and Winchester.[34] These men could very well have transmitted the stylistic views of the Society to their own realm, and their influence would necessarily have been wide. In fact, Glanvill, who figures so largely in this and my previous article, expressly argues that the clerical members of the Society were responsible for the attack on Puritan rhetoric and for the formulation of a new standard for sermons. Furthermore, he attributes this activity of theirs directly to their training and interest in the experimental philosophy. In an essay entitled "Antifanatick *Theologie* and Free *Philosophy*,"[35] he borrows Bacon's fiction of the New Atlantis, and has the Father of Solomon's House, which he identifies with the Royal Society, describe the state of religion in Bensalem. The Father gives a most uncomplimentary picture of a religious sect, the Ataxites, who obviously represent the Puritans, and points out how the clerical members of Solomon's House remedied the situation. The latter underwent a rather strange training for their profession.

They were sensible, That knowledge was still *imperfect*, and capable of further growth, and therefore they looked forward into the *Moderns* also, who about their time, had imployed themselves in discovering the

[34] Preface to *Plus Ultra*, 1668. See also Caroline F. Richardson's *English Preachers and Preaching, 1640–1670*, chap. iv.

[35] The seventh essay in *Essays on Several Important Subjects In Philosophy and Religion*, 1676. The general purpose of this essay is to show that the application of the scientific spirit to religion was responsible for the reaction against Puritanism, and for the establishment of a rational religion. Glanvill himself was aware that his ideas might not meet with universal approval, although he advances them with utmost sincerity. "The *Seventh*," he says, "is entirely new. 'Tis a description of such a Genius in *Theology* and *Philosophy*, as I confess I my self like; and I believe some others may. But I blame no Mans different sentiment, who allows the liberty of judging that himself takes. I have borrowed the countenance, and colour of my Lord *Bacons* story; of which I have given the brief contents. The Essay is a mixture of an Idea, and a disguised History." Two other essays touch upon the same matter: the fourth, already discussed, and the fifth, "The Agreement of Reason and Religion." Though Glanvill ignores the influence of a wider rationalism than that embodied in the scientific movement, and though he is obviously engaged in enthusiastic propaganda for the new science, there may be some suggestion of truth in his theory that the scientific divines reformed religion in the same way as the experimental philosophers reformed science.

Defects of the Ancients, in reviving some of their neglected Doctrines; and advancing them by new Thoughts and Conceptions: They read, and consider'd all sorts of *late* Improvements in *Anatomy*, *Mathematicks*, *Natural History*, and *Mechanicks*, and acquainted themselves with the *Experimental Philosophy of Solomon's House*, and the other Promoters of it. So that there was not any valuable Discovery made, or *Notion* started in any part of *Real Learning*. And by this *Universal* way of proceeding, They furnish'd their Minds with great *variety* of *Conceptions*, and rendred themselves more capable of judging of the *Truth*, or *likelyhood* of any propos'd Hypothesis . . . They had the felicity of *clear* and *distinct thinking*.

By virtue of such a training they evolved a standard for sermons which was an exact replica of that demanded for scientific exposition. This standard Glanvill describes both negatively and positively. "They affected," he says, "no gayness of metaphors, or *prettiness* of *similitudes*: no tricks to be plaid with the *words* of their Texts"; but "whereas the *Ataxites* had made Religion a *fantastick*, and *unintelligible* thing . . . Those Divines labour'd much to reduce it to it's native *plainness*, and *simplicity* . . . Laying down the genuine notions of Theology, and all things relating to *Faith*, or *Practice*, with all possible perspicuity and plainness." And toward the end of the essay he elaborates at greater length upon the subject.

They did not involve their discourses in *needless words* of *Art*, or *subtle distinctions*; but spoke in the plainest, and most intelligible Terms: and distinguish'd things in the most easie and familiar manner that the matter of discourse would bear. They took this as an *establish'd Rule*, That *unwonted* words were *never* to be us'd, either in Pulpits, or elsewhere, when *common* ones would as fitly represent their meaning: and they always chose *such*, as the custom of speaking had rendred familiar in the Subjects on which they spoke, when *those* were *proper*, and *expressive*. . . . They effected not to ostentate *Learning*, by high-flown expressions, or ends of *Greek*, and *Latin*: They did not stuff their Sermons with numerous, needless *Quotations* . . . No, their Learning . . . abundantly appear'd to the intelligent, by the *judgment* and *strength*, the *reason* and *clearness* with which they spoke.[36]

[36] See pp. 9, 22, 26, 28, 31, 42, 44. If Glanvill's words were absolutely trustworthy, it would hardly be necessary to adduce any other evidence for the influence of science on pulpit eloquence; but unfortunately he is so intent on

Powerful though the influence of science was upon the new standard for religious discourse, it should by no means be emphasized to the exclusion of other factors. Rationalism, which was strong in the scientific movement, and which owed a great deal to Descartes, was rapidly dominating the minds of men, and appears frequently in the passages which have been discussed. More and more emphasis is laid upon the necessity of appealing to the mind through reason and clear statement. Together with the doctrine of the primacy of reason went a corresponding distrust of the imagination, which justified itself in two ways. The scientists came to view that faculty of the mind as an agent of deception, distorting, obscuring, and falsifying truth conceived of in a rationalistic manner. Hobbes, whenever he touches upon the matter, evinces such a view, and it appears frequently in those associated with the new science.[37] When morality and religion, however, were considered, the imagination underwent a moral interpretation, as well as retaining its deceptive quality. The influence of Stoicism, so pronounced during this period, is revealed in a tendency to condemn the imagination because it is associated with passions, which are natural enemies to the ethical

---

putting as much as possible to the credit of the Royal Society that he is capable of exaggerating whatever evidence appears for his thesis, and of being blind to the existence of other forces making for the same result. Yet there must be some truth in what he says, for he was not such a man as to make himself foolish with fallacious and absurd arguments.

Mention might here be made of Seth Ward, bishop of Salisbury, who had held the Savilian professorship of astronomy for the years 1649–61, and who had been an important member of the group of experimental scientists which for a number of years held weekly meetings at Oxford. In his *Apology for the Mysteries*, 1673, he says, "Concerning which things I shall not endeavour at a Rhetorical Harangue, but crave leave that I may be admitted to speak in a plain and humble Analytical and Didactical way of discourse." These words reveal not only the same sentiments, but almost the same words, that had previously been expressed by scientists relative to their scientific treatises. See *PMLA*, XLV (1930), 980–81.

[37] A somewhat extended discussion of the imagination is contained in Glanvill's *Vanity of Dogmatizing*, chap. xi, the purpose of which is to show how the imagination deceives. The chapter begins: "Fourthly, we *erre* and come short of *Science*, because we are so frequently mislead by the evil conduct of our *Imaginations*; whose irregular strength and importunity doth almost perpetually abuse us. Now to make a full and clear discovery of our *Phancies* deceptions; 'twill be requisite to look into the nature of that *mysterious faculty*." Cf. Hobbes's *Leviathan*, chap. ii.

and rational soul of man. Sprat denounces rhetorical ornaments because they hold correspondence with the passions, the slaves of reason.[38] Casaubon refers to those who opposed eloquence because they considered the emotions closely allied to madness and distraction.[39] It is in Simon Patrick's *Friendly Debate*, however, that this attitude is most fully developed. Finally, as a result of the various factors involved, science, rationalism, Stoicism, there developed a definite stylistic taste that was repelled by the vanity and folly of rhetoric in all kinds of compositions, and in sermons was especially shocked at what appeared to be almost blasphemous gaudiness. The many and strong terms of condemnation, which frequently border upon vituperation, represent not only a rational judgment but also a natural revulsion. Rhetoric was no longer fashionable in polite quarters.

Another aspect of the stylistic problem, but whether as a cause or an effect of the attack on rhetoric is not easily determined, appears in a growing consciousness of the distinction between poetry and prose.[40] Prose, as a distinct type of literature, was emerging in much more definite outline; its own peculiar properties were beginning to receive attention. In the seventeenth century these properties were noted chiefly in connection with style, though content is sometimes considered. In general, poetry was related more closely to the imagination and emotions, prose to the rational mind. South thinks the style of plays and romances entirely unsuitable to a preacher;[41] and Parker is willing to consider the Cambridge Platonists poets but not philosophers.[42] James Arderne advises clergymen not "to suffer your fancy to be tempted towards following of Poetick, or Romantick writings, the latter being good for nothing, and the other best in its own measures."[43] Especially does this conception of the different provinces proper to prose and poetry appear in the defense

---

[38] *History of the Royal Society*, p. 112.

[39] *The Question, To whom it belonged Anciently to Preach*, p. 29.

[40] See Miss Marjorie Nicolson's "The Early Stage of Cartesianism in England," *Stud. in Phil.*, XXVI (1929), 373.

[41] Sermon preached April 30, 1668.

[42] *A Free and Impartial Censure*, p. 75.

[43] *Directions Concerning the Matter and Stile of Sermons*, pp. 73–74.

of the figurative language used in the Bible, a defense imposed
upon those who were inclined to cite the Scriptures as a model
of a clear, plain style. Patrick defends David's use of rhetorical
figures on the ground that "his Psalms are pieces of Divine
Poetry, in which Passions are wont to be expressed much otherwise than they ought to do [be?] in plain and familiar speech";[44]
and William Sherlock explains "that there is a vast difference
between Poetical Descriptions, such as the Book of Canticles is,
and Practical Discourse for the Government of our Lives: the
first requires more Garnish and Ornament, and justifies the
most mysterious flights of Fancy; the second requires a plain
and simple dress, which may convey the Notions with ease and
perspicuity to the mind."[45]

On the other hand, prose itself was undergoing analysis and
division according to its content and purpose, and the style proper
to each species was beginning to be considered. So vigorously
and successfully had the scientists insisted upon an unadulterated
plainness that the reformers of pulpit eloquence were moved to
impose this stylistic ideal on compositions of an alien nature.
Although rationalism tended to bring both science and religion
to the same level, a difference in purpose, subject matter, and the
audience addressed was sure to be recognized in some quarters.
The purpose of scientific discourse is to demonstrate; of sermons,
to persuade and move; the material of one is concrete objects
and the laws governing them; of the other, spiritual truth; and
finally science addressed itself to those on a higher rational plane
than is apparent in the average congregation. It should also be
noted that science was primarily concerned with written discourse, and sermons with oral composition, in which rhetoric
has a more natural place.[46] In view of these differences it was
almost inevitable that the need of a style for sermons different

[44] *A Friendly Debate*, pp. 85–86.

[45] *A Defense and Continuation*, p. 168. In the sections devoted to style
in the third book of the *Rhetoric*, Aristotle insists upon the distinction between
the style of poetry and that of oratory.

[46] The fact, however, that thousands of sermons were published during
this period renders the simplification of their manner of expression a very important element in the evolution of prose style in general.

from that proper to scientific experiments and observations should make itself felt.

I can very well allow that in Philosophy [the term is generally used at this time as equivalent to science], where the Quality and Nature of things do not transcend and over-match words, the less Rhetorical ornaments, especially the fewer Metaphors, providing still that the phrase be pure and easie, the better. But in Divinity, where no expressions come fully up to the Mysteries of Faith, and where the things themselves are not capable of being declared in *Logical* and *Metaphysical* Terms; Metaphors may not only be allowed, but are most accommodated to the assisting us in our conceptions of Gospel-mysteries.[47]

In somewhat the same strain Arderne says, in advocating the necessity of metaphors to make clear the obscure, "I know this is wholly rejected by some, who consider not, that the poverty of conceptions, or scarcity of words constrains, that in every sentence almost the adjectives and epithets are in strictness metaphorical."[48] In spite of the great impetus given to the idea of a plain style by the enthusiastic Baconians, there were those who, in a critical spirit, were weighing and testing its suitability to non-scientific forms of prose.

The defense of figurative language, as was to be expected, devolved largely upon the shoulders of the nonconformists, who were compelled to find some shelter in the shower of abuse cast upon them.[49] But they were sensitive enough to the spirit of the

[47] Robert Ferguson, *The Interest of Reason*, pp. 279–80. See also pp. 342–43.
[48] *Directions Concerning the Matter and Stile of Sermons*, pp. 76–77.
[49] In speaking of the attacks made upon nonconformists because of their "Luscious and rampant Metaphors," Robert Ferguson says, "The due stating therefore the Nature and import of Metaphors, is become not only a seasonable, but a necessary piece of Service." (*Interest of Reason*, 1675, p. 279.) There is no doubt that there was some basis for the charges preferred against the style of the dissenters, as is evident from passages cited by their opponents from three of their number especially: Thomas Watson, William Bridge, and John Durant. The following quotation is more or less typical: "They say the *Marygold* opens and shuts with the Sun, when the Sun shines, it opens, when the Sun withdraws, it shuts, it opens and shuts according to the withdrawing and shining of the Sun: and so if your comforts be true, the more the righteousness of Christ opens before you, the more the Sun of righteousness shines upon you, the more you will be comforted," etc. (William Bridge, *The Freeness of the Grace and Love of God*, 1671, p. 49.) Still, one cannot help feeling that the object of attack was really wider than the nonconformists, that it was rhetoric in general.

age to be very guarded in advocating the use of rhetorical devices and to emphasize the importance of caution as much as they urged the usefulness and propriety of figures.[50] Metaphors and similitudes are to be employed only when there is need of such, when they are derived from a just analogy and founded in nature or the Scriptures, and when they are pertinent, not overnumerous, and used with prudence and reverence. When these conditions are met, rhetoric is justified by the practice of Christ and his apostles, by the recognized purpose of preaching, and by the grace, elegance, and efficacious communication of truth peculiar to it.[51] It is interesting to note that the inheritors of the Puritan tradition were the chief advocates of the imaginative elements in style. Certainly the most earnest defense of the beauty and pleasure found in rhetorical compositions occurs in what is probably the most ambitious attempt on the part of the nonconformists to rehabilitate rhetoric.[52] In fact, Robert Ferguson justifies a figurative style by the critical theories of poetry current in his day, which in turn had been contaminated by rhetorical theory.[53] "I take it for granted," he says, "that as Reason gives a Discourse its strength and Nerves, so Rhetoric

[50] Much that they say in this respect can be traced back as far as Aristotle. See the *Rhetoric*, Book III, chaps. ii–iv. Echoes of Aristotle are rather frequent during this period, but he furnished no argument for the plainness demanded by the scientists.

[51] See John Owen's Preface to Henry Lukin's *An Introduction to the Holy Scripture*, 1669; and D. T.'s *Hieragonisticon: or Corah's Doom, Being an Answer to Two Letters of Enquiry into the Grounds and Occasions of the Contempt of the Clergy and Religion*, 1672, p. 148. Owen, the most prominent of the dissenters, is evidently answering Patrick's *Friendly Debate*. D. T. handles Eachard very severely, calling him names and laughing at his advocacy of the study of English. In another work, *Truth and Innocence Vindicated*, 1669 (1670), written in answer to the *Ecclesiastical Politie*, Owen turns the tables on Parker by accusing him of using swelling words, ambiguous terms, and rhetorical flourishes, and by insisting upon the importance of clearness and perspicuity in style. Owen, however, defends the nonconformists' use of rhetoric on the ground that their figures of speech are necessary to express "Gospel Mysteries" and are found in the Scriptures. See pp. 19–20, 84.

[52] *The Interest of Reason in Religion. With the Import and Use of Scripture-Metaphors; . . . With Reflections on several Late Writings, especially Mr. Sherlocks Discourse concerning the Knowledg of Jesus Christ*, 1675.

[53] For a study of the earlier contamination of poetical theory by rhetoric, see D. L. Clark's *Rhetoric and Poetry in the Renaissance*, 1922.

gives it its Colour," an idea borrowed intact from Hobbes's psychological analysis of poetry.[54] The *dulce et utile* underlines much that he says regarding the virtues of figurative language, and the decorum of expression is emphasized.[55]

The first argument against rhetorical preaching which Ferguson felt compelled to answer was that based upon the style of the Bible, which had been proposed as a model of plainness. In his reply he does not entirely escape obscurity and inconsistency, as was inevitable in any attempt to characterize as a whole style of such different kinds of composition as are found in the Scriptures.[56] He emphatically states that there is hardly a single

[54] "Judgment begets the strength and structure, and Fancy begets the ornaments of a Poem." (J. E. Spingarn, *Critical Essays of the Seventeenth Century*, II, 59.) In substituting "rhetoric" for "fancy," and "colours" for "ornaments," Ferguson throws into high relief the essentially rhetorical nature of Hobbes's poetic theory. Likewise, when he applies the other theories, which also belong to the rhetorical tradition, to sermons, he is only restoring to its proper realm that which had been foisted upon poetry.

[55] "The strongest Arguments when delivered dryly, as they do not so delight and please, so neither do they so enlighten and instruct, as when clothed in a bright and flourishing Character. The same things nakedly and bluntly represented, do not make so great an impression, as when embellished with handsome Language. Nor is there anything more persuasive as well as delightful, than to find good words accompanying excellent Sense. And the better any subject is, the more worthy it ought to be accounted of a rich and polished, though not of a gaudy Dress. And indeed elegant expressions are impertinently bestowed, where the matter and sense are not considerable. Nor is there a greater evidence of Folly in a Speaker or Writer, than to affect a loftiness of expression on a mean and petty Subject. Words being manifestative of conceptions and things, ought to be proportionate to the Themes whereof we treat, and the ideas we have of them. Where there is not something substantial and weighty underneath, a dazling stile serves only to amuse the Reader, and to palliate the weakness of the Discourse." Ferguson, *op. cit.*, pp. 357 ff.

[56] This fact probably accounts for two contradictory criticisms of the Bible mentioned by Ferguson: "As upon the one hand the Scripture is blam'd as Dull, flat and unaffecting by men of a wanton and prophane wit, because of its not being adorned with Flowers of Rhetorick; so upon the other hand, there are some who find fault with it as dark and obscure, because of the many Rhetorical Tropes and Figures which it is replenished with." (*Op. cit.*, p. 354.) Though the King James version of the Bible has profoundly influenced English literature, there is little or no evidence that it played a part in the stylistic revolt under discussion. Robert Boyle even holds that the Bible has suffered in being translated. (See *Works*, ed. Birch, II, 120.) Discussions of the style of the Bible during this period are really numerous enough to justify a separate article.

figure of speech that is not to be found in the Bible,[57] but he also discovers in it brevity, perspicuity, simplicity, and even plainness. This apparent contradiction he would explain by distinguishing between the true eloquence of the Bible and that false kind which consists of a flourish of painted words or a smooth structure of periods, and which, influencing the affections only, does not leave as lasting an impression as that produced by reason. This latter eloquence he attributes to the ancient sophists and demagogues, and he inveighs just as sternly as the conformists against empty schemes of speech, grandiloquency, bewitching smoothness, flourishes of wit, and flowers of language. In short, he objects to that type of oratory that emphasizes beauty of style irrespective of thought.[58] The majestic eloquence of the Scriptures, on the other hand, is always appropriate to the thought expressed.

There are no empty frigid phraseologies in the Bible, but where the expressions are most splendid, and lofty, there are Notions and things enough to fill them out. God did not design to endite the Scripture in a pompous tumid stile, to amuse our fancies, or meerly strike to our Imaginations with the greater force, but to instruct us in a calm and sedate way; and therefore under the most stately dress of words, there always lyes a richer quarry of things and Truths.[59]

In chapter ii, entitled "Of the Import and Use of Scripture-Metaphors," he embarks upon a long and much needed discussion of metaphors, both as found in the Bible and as proper to sermons.[60] The purpose of the former, he points out, is not "to

[57] Cf. John Prïdeaux, *Sacred Eloquence*, 1659, mentioned earlier in this article.

[58] "The Stile of the most reputed Oratours is for the most part too pompous and flatulent for the subjects they treat of; neither the Images which they form in their minds, nor the Arrayment of them in Words, are adapted and proportioned to things . . . and their discourses are like a load of flesh in the body of man, that serves only to embarass it with an unprofitable weight. But to imagine so of God, or to ascribe . . . *great swelling words of vanity* to him . . . or to think that in the enditing the Bible, he did . . . only feed us with gaudy phantasms, poetical Schemes, and luxuriant phrases, is to impeach more than one of his perfections." Ferguson, *op. cit.*, p. 163.

[59] *The Interest of Reason*, p. 160.

[60] Ferguson admits that some of the nonconformists of the preceding age may have been guilty of the charges brought against them, but he would ex-

impregnate our minds with gawdy Phantasms, but to adjust the Mysteries of Religion to the weakness of our Capacities."[61] They are drawn from the whole field of nature, as well as from the manners and possessions of man, so that to understand them clearly one must be acquainted with natural philosophy and the customs of Oriental nations. Without such knowledge, a "luxurious Fancy will be apt to frame very wild and absurd Notions out of Metaphors."[62] As regards the figures that may lawfully be used in sermons, he lays down the following rules: they must be modest, clean, easy, and common; they must "carry a due Proportion, Analogy, and Similitude to the things they are brought to illustrate"; and they must never be employed except when the preacher is thoroughly familiar with the value and use of the terms in their original sense. Of all the rules for the employment of metaphors laid down by the rhetoricians, he considers of most importance those which forbid too numerous figures and which insist upon the intelligibility of metaphors to the audience addressed. Figures from classical mythology he would ban entirely.[63] The nonconformists would not, like the scientists, sweep away all metaphors, but they imposed strict laws upon the use of them.

As has been noted on a previous page, Ferguson acknowledges that a plain style, while not suitable to sermons, is proper to scientific exposition, and in other passages he draws at great length a distinction between preaching and compositions devoted to reasoning, argument, and demonstration. In the latter, he claims, rhetoric has no place, since it is always accompanied by neglect of logic, and since argument weighs more heavily than fine language. Not only do verbal ornaments fail to convince; they even cast suspicion on the cause for which they are employed. "Metaphorick flourishes," he says, "may . . . be useful to illustrate and brighten Truth when it is once established,

cuse them on the ground of the poor taste of their day. He thinks that in his own age trifling with words and phrases and puerile affectation of cadences were no longer relished. See pp. 295–96.

[61] P. 343.
[62] See pp. 345–57.
[63] See pp. 301, 345–47, 367 ff.

but the naked and plain mode of disputing conduceth only to the conviction and demonstration of it."[64] Sermons, on the other hand, may avail themselves of all the rhetorical devices which are legitimately employed in other compositions.[65]

But the nonconformists were not alone in advocating a cautious use of rhetoric in the pulpit. Several years before Ferguson's volume appeared, James Arderne had published a treatise, inspired by Eachard's *Enquiry* of the previous year, which proposed to establish the proper style for sermons.[66] Advocating a diction not far removed from the ideal of science, he condemns archaisms, compounds,[67] and neologisms. "In short," he says, "chuse words as well as you can, wholly *English*, and such as are the images of your meaning, and which serve to humour the aim of the sentence whereof they are a part: and of words thus qualified, take those which most readily offer themselves." But he fully recognizes the beauty and grace which figurative language may lend to a discourse, as well as the need of figures to express abstract conceptions. Yet, though he considers that a bare, plain style is likely to become flat and mean, he warns against permitting a grave and majestic one to become inflated and bombastic. Furthermore, he lays down some of the rules regarding the use of figures which Ferguson was later to draw up; namely, that they should be proper, intelligible, and not too numerous.[68] Those who upheld figurative language against the stylistic ideal of science ransacked all the principles of rhetoric for precautions in the use of metaphors and similitudes, a fact which bears testi-

[64] P. 360.

[65] "But as to the usage of Metaphors in Popular Sermons, and practical Discourses, the Case is otherwise. Whatsoever is pleadable in their behalf upon any occasion, serves to justify the usurpation of them in Discourses *ad Populum* and *Didactical* Writings. The Inducements and Motives of their allowance in Rhetorical Tracts, Orations, or whatever else doth best admit these Ornaments of Eloquence, do all of them evince their agreeableness to the Oratory of the Pulpit." P. 360.

[66] *Directions Concerning the Matter and Stile of Sermons, Written to W. S. a young Deacon, by J. A.,* 1671. Arderne was at this time curate of St. Botolph's, Aldersgate, but some years later became dean of Chester.

[67] The mention of this verbal type is probably due to Aristotle's having accorded it some notice. See the *Rhetoric*, III, iii, 1.

[68] See pp. 22 ff., 43–44, 49–50, 68–70, 73–76.

mony not only to other influences of the day, but also to the deep impression which the experimental philosophy had made upon stylistic views.[69]

Finally, we discover a defense of rhetoric in quarters where we would least expect it, in Joseph Glanvill's *An Essay Concerning Preaching*, 1678. The first part of the treatise reveals the same scientific values that have hitherto characterized his ideas regarding style: hostility to "hard" words; distrust of the imagination; condemnation of rhetoric, especially metaphors; and insistence upon what is plain, solid, and useful. Toward the end of the essay, however, he begins to weaken in his stand. At first, he apologizes for departing from his ideal of plainness, which is still dear to his heart, on the ground that the mob cannot appreciate it. Only the wisest, he informs us, are moved by the appeal which plainness makes to the mind; the common people have not capacity for much knowledge, for "their affections are raised by figures and earnestness and passionate representations . . . so that however little you may think these, they must be heeded, and suited to the capacity, and genius of your hearers." He makes another quarter-turn, when he says that, though "fullness of sense and compactness of writing are real excellencies," the spoken word is hard to follow, and thus amplifications, a certain "laxness of style," and the representation of "the same thing in different colors and lights" are necessary to sermons. At last, facing fully about, he engages in an unabashed defense of rhetorical preaching, which is a flat contradiction to the stylistic views held by him ever since he became a member of the Royal Society.

I do not by this reprehend all Wit whatever in Preaching, nor any thing that is truly such: For true Wit is a perfection in our faculties, chiefly

---

[69] Sherlock, who, however, in his own day enjoyed no reputation for consistency, after he had been taken to task by Ferguson for his advocacy of a plain style, thought it necessary to modify his position in the following manner: "I was not so silly as to oppose a sober use of Metaphors, no not in matters of Religion, as Mr. Ferguson would fain insinuate; . . . my quarrel with them is, that they confound and darken the most plain and material notions in Religion by metaphorical Descriptions." (*A Defence and Continuation of a Discourse*, 1675, pp. 162–63.) In this last statement, Sherlock assumes the exact attitude maintained by the scientists.

in the understanding and imagination; Wit in the understanding is a sagacity to find out the nature, relations, and consequences of things: Wit in the imagination, is a quickness in the phancy to give things proper Images; now the more of these in Sermons, the more judgment and spirit, and life: and without Wit of these kinds, Preaching is dull and unedifying. The Preacher should indeavour to speak sharp and quick thoughts, and to set them out in lively colours; This is proper, grave, and manly wit, but the other, that which consists in inversions of sentences, and playing with words, and the like, is vile and contemptible fooling.[70]

He issues a caution, however, against going out of the way in order to introduce rhetorical ornaments. These sentiments represent a distinctly alien element in Glanvill's conception of style, and indicate the introduction of some specific influence at this point in his career. The source of this influence is, I think, to be sought in France.[71]

The reformation of pulpit eloquence began earlier in France than in England and continued until late in the century.[72] The earliest attack on rhetorical preaching seems to have been Sirmond's *Le Prédicateur*, 1638, which I have not had the opportunity of examining. In 1652, Balzac, whose style, however, was by no means considered a model, published his *Socrate Crestien* in which he frowned upon the use of rhetoric in religious observances and condemned rhetorical paraphrases of the Scriptures.[73] Furthermore, Port-Royal had developed a style proper to Christian humility, which Jacquinet describes as "mortifiée et

---

[70] *An Essay Concerning Preaching*, p. 71. See also pp. 55, 63.

[71] It is evident that the upholders of the proper use of rhetoric in sermons were greatly influenced, both in what they condemned and in what they commended, by the Anti-Ciceronian movement. We might almost go so far as to say that in the dispute between the conformists and the nonconformists we have a clash between Anti-Ciceronianism and the stylistic program of science. See Professor Croll's articles on Anti-Ciceronianism in *Stud. in Phil.*, Vol. XVIII (1921); *Schelling Anniversary Papers*, 1928; and *PMLA*, Vol. XXXIX (1924).

[72] For a treatment of the French movement see Sainte-Beuve's *Port Royal*, and P. Jacquinet's *Des Prédicateurs du XVIIᵉ Siècle avant Bossuet*, 2d ed., 1885.

[73] Discourse 6, 7. Another attack on pulpit eloquence, which I have not seen, is Gueret's *Entretiens sur l'Eloquence de la Chaire et du Barreau*, 1666. A number of years later, in 1687, Bouhours attacked the conceits used in sermons. *La Manière de Bien Penser dans les Ouvrages D'Esprit*, 1687, pp. 55 ff.

pénitente," and which was free from ornamentation.[74] But the most important channel through which French influence in this matter reached England was Rapin's *Réflexions sur l'Usage de l'Eloquence de ce Temps*, 1672, which was translated the same year into English.[75] In it we find almost all the ideas that appear in the nonconformists and in that part of Glanvill's essay which has just been discussed. Though some of these ideas were too general to be ascribed to Rapin alone, the accumulated similarities between French and English treatises are significant. Rapin distinguishes between the true eloquence of the Bible and the false rhetoric of the sophists, with its far-fetched figures and out-of-the-way ornaments. He cautions preachers against too numerous figures and demands that metaphors be proportioned to ideas. Pointing out the large number of figures found in the Bible, he upholds rhetorical language for the ornament, grace, and force which it imparts to a discourse. For this reason, and because rhetoric is needed to move the common man, he opposes a bare and unadorned style. It is a "natural" eloquence that he approves, an eloquence in which thought is emphasized and those ornaments only are admitted which are appropriate to thought. While it is impossible to state definitely that Ferguson and Glanvill were influenced by Rapin, the evidence points that way.[76]

[74] *Des Prédicateurs*, p. 340.

[75] Rapin's popularity in England in the 1670's was considerable, owing in some degree to Rymer's translation of his treatise on poetry, 1674.

[76] *The Whole Critical Works of Mon^r Rapin*, translated by Basil Kennet, 3d ed., 1731, II, 1–106, *passim*. Mr. Spingarn refers to Voltaire's assertion, that Bourdaloue was responsible for the transformation of English preaching, with the remark that Burnet (*Supplement to Burnet's History of my own Time*, ed. H. C. Foxcroft, pp. 96, 467) bears Voltaire out. But to me Burnet's words seem to point in the opposite direction. In 1664 Burnet went to France to study the manner of preaching followed there, and though he was displeased with that of the Jesuits, he liked the manner of the secular clergy. "I took a good tincture of their way—indeed more than Scotland could well bear and much more than England could endure; but I have worn off some gestures that looked too like acting, and yet the way of preaching in which I still hold is . . . very like the way of the secular clergy of the Port Royal." If these words mean anything, they indicate that Burnet's French method of preaching was distinctly at odds with the ideal of simplicity which was being established in England. Furthermore, Tillotson's sermons had already illustrated the new style of preaching by the time Burnet went to France. See *Critical Essays of the Seventeenth Century*, ed. Spingarn, I, xli.

In general, the French, with whom the scientific movement was not so strong as with the English, left much more room for rhetoric in the simplification of prose. For the most part, their problem was to replace false eloquence with true, sophistic with rhetoric. The English, on the other hand, were imbued with a scientific spirit which impelled them to cast into the discard all rhetorical devices and ornaments and to adopt plainness for their ideal. The scientists were so intent on the actual nature of things that they resented any form of expression that did not match exactly the thing described. To them the truths of nature possessed a vivid reality which was in constant danger of being dimmed when expressed in language. Language was almost considered a necessary evil of communication. Words sank to the low estate of "marks," mere tags to be attached to things. The world has never witnessed such a thoroughgoing materialism, such a passion for the substantial (in its literal sense) and the matter-of-fact as characterized the mid-seventeenth century. The reformers of the pulpit brought the same spirit to religion, and strove to introduce the same exactitude in the use of words expressing moral and religious truths. Finally, the English were by nature more practical, more materialistic, more utilitarian in their philosophy, and less given to the refinements of civilization than the French. The difference between the two people is reflected in the difference between Bacon and Descartes, experimental science and mechanistic philosophy, the Royal Society and the French Academy.[77]

[77] That the English were well aware of this difference is revealed in numerous passages, but nowhere more clearly than in Sprat's *History of the Royal Society*. Though ostensibly apologizing for his lack of eloquence in comparison with the elegant style of Pelisson's history of the French Academy, Sprat hardly conceals a sturdy pride in his manner of expression. "I have onely this to allege in my excuse; that as they undertook the advancement of the Elegance of Speech, so it became their *History*, to have some resemblance to their enterprize: Whereas the intention of ours, being not the Artifice of Words, but a bare knowledge of things; my fault may be esteem'd the less, that I have written of *Philosophers*, without any ornament of *Eloquence* . . . I hope now, it will not be thought a vain digression, if I step aside, to recommend the forming of such an *Assembly* [as the French Academy] to the Gentlemen of our Nation. I know indeed, that the *English Genius* is not so airy, and discursive as that of some of our neighbors, but that we generally love to have Reason set out in plain, undeceiving expressions; as much, as they to have it deliver'd with

Needless to say, the scientific ideal of expression, with its bareness and lack of color, was hardly appropriate to artistic uses. In Defoe's works it did achieve great results, but in the prose of Temple, Addison, and Steele other stylistic elements are quite apparent. Yet science, in its aggressive attacks on the old luxuriant prose, had cleared the ground, and had, indeed, laid a foundation of clearness and directness upon which could be erected a more artistic structure. At the end of the century John Hughes proposed, as the four fundamental elements of an ideal style, propriety, perspicuity, elegance, and cadence,[78] to the first two of which the scientific movement had made a definite contribution. But though in belles-lettres the plain style of the scientists underwent much improvement, in the pulpit it seems to have held its own for a considerable time, and may have been in part responsible for the desiccation of religion which disgraced the neo-classical period. In 1672 Dryden speaks as if the old method of preaching were still existent,[79] but some ten years later, according to Evelyn, it was no longer fashionable since the pulpit "is grown into a far more profitable way, of plaine and practical discourses, of which sort this Nation, or any other, never had greater plenty, or more profitable."[80] Eleven years later, Wotton, who was upholding the superiority of the moderns

colour and beauty. And besides this, I understand well enough, that they have one great assistance to the growth of Oratory, which to us is wanting; that is, that their Nobility live commonly close together in their Cities, and ours for the most part scattered in their Country Houses . . . They prefer the Pleasures of the Town; we, those of the Field: whereas it is from the frequent conversations in Cities, that the Humour, and Wit, and Variety, and Elegance of Language, are chiefly to be fetch'd." Pp. 40–41.

[78] *Critical Essays of the Eighteenth Century*, ed. W. H. Durham, p. 80.

[79] *Essays of John Dryden*, ed. W. P. Ker, I, 173–74.

[80] *Diary*, July 15, 1683. Evelyn is speaking about a sermon in the old style, which, he significantly says, was preached by "a stranger, an *old* man" [my italics]. The same year, Patrick, perhaps taking to himself some of the glory thereof, asserts that "never did men more endeavour orderly discourse, and aim at plain, unaffected speech, than they do now in the Church of England: where good sense, in the most easy and familiar words, is now looked upon as the principal commendation of sermons." (*Works*, ed. A. Taylor, VI, 410.) In the following year another remarks to the same effect that the "florid strain of preaching is almost quite worn out, and is become now as ridiculous as it was once admired." G. Burnet's Preface to his translation of More's *Utopia*. See also his *Discourse of the Pastoral Care*, 1692, pp. 108–9, 111–13.

over the ancients, felt constrained to yield the point in eloquence because even in the pulpit "very few meet with Applause, who do not confine themselves to speak with the severity of a Philosopher."[81] And finally, Swift in *A Letter to a Young Clergyman* advances a standard for sermons which is exactly the same that we have been tracing. This treatise, with its many echoes of Eachard, would hardly have been out of place had it appeared in 1670 instead of 1721.[82]

[81] *Reflections upon Ancient and Modern Learning,* 3d ed., 1705, p. 35. Wotton explains the inferiority of modern eloquence on the ground of "the Humour of the Age," which makes men suspect a trick in everything said in courts or in Parliament to move the passions, "And therefore when Men have spoken to the Point, in as few Words as the Matter will bear, it is expected they should hold their Tongues." Cf. what Locke says about rhetoric being the art of deceiving. *Essay of Human Understanding,* Book III, chap. x.

[82] A contrary idea of the style suitable for religious compositions is found in Hughes's essay. Though he thinks that science "requires a grave *didactick* Style, agreeable to the Plainness and Simplicity of Truth and Reason" and that history should wear a plain dress, he claims that "*Morality* and *Divinity* are capable of all the Ornaments of Wit and Fancy." See p. 85. The nonconformists had, of course, made the same distinction years before.

# SCIENCE AND LANGUAGE IN ENGLAND OF THE MID-SEVENTEENTH CENTURY*

RICHARD FOSTER JONES

IN two previous articles I have attempted to prove the influence which science exerted upon the style of English prose, both secular and religious, during the Restoration.[1] Both treatises were more interested in showing the nature and extent of this influence than in making plain its origin. I did mention the probable source of the stylistic views associated with early science, but with little elaboration or documentation.[2] It is the purpose of the present article to furnish a more substantial basis for the theory that in the attitude of science toward language is to be discovered the most important origin of the stylistic reformation with which the scientists were enthusiastically concerned.

In investigating any matter of a scientific import in England of the seventeenth century, one must always take Bacon into consideration, for from him radiated waves of life-giving power which penetrated the farthest nooks and crannies of the period. While there is implied in his constant opposing of nature to books a certain antipathy to language, we discover more definite information concerning this antipathy in the *Novum Organum*.[3] Of the "Idols" that possess the human mind, he considers the Idols of the Market-place (i.e., language) the most trouble-

---

* Reprinted, with minor corrections, from *The Journal of English and Germanic Philology*, Vol. XXXI (1932), by permission of the publishers.

[1] *PMLA*, XLV (1930), 977–1009; and *Jour. Eng. Ger. Philol.*, XXX (1931), 188–217.

[2] *PMLA*, XLV (1930), 1008; *Jour. Eng. Ger. Philol.*, XXX (1931), 215.

[3] See Book I, Aphorisms XLIII, LIX, LX.

some, maintaining that these alone had "rendered philosophy and the sciences sophistical and inactive." He justifies such a belief on the ground that since words were invented to satisfy inferior intellects, they either stand for things that do not exist at all, or inaccurately represent the truths of nature. This fact, he holds, was responsible for the violent disputes characteristic of the Middle Ages and Renaissance, which were really concerned with words rather than with realities.[4] In this connection Bacon stresses, as Hobbes did later, and, like Hobbes, inspired by mathematics, the importance of definitions, but he thinks that in dealing with material things definitions themselves may be of little avail, since they are composed of words, and "those words beget others." The materialistic origin of this depreciation of language is further revealed in his listing, in ascending degrees of faultiness, first, names of substances; second, names of actions; and third, names of qualities. In short, Bacon condemned language because it foisted upon the world ideas that had no basis in reality, or confused and distorted the real truths of nature, so that knowledge of them became impossible.

A somewhat hidden but none the less real reason for the distrust of language felt by the early Baconians lay in the difference between the ways of acquiring knowledge adopted by the old and new sciences. Books were the storehouse of the former, experiment and observation of nature the means of acquiring the latter. To master the traditional science which prevailed during the Renaissance, a study of Latin and Greek was necessary, so that a philological training was, as Huxley pointed out several centuries later, the essential qualification of a scientist of that day; but with the advent of Bacon willingness to experiment and observe was proposed as the prime characteristic of a scientist. Thus the opposition between language and observed phenomena became established, and language, inseparably associated with the erroneous science of the past, attracted the suspicion adhering to the latter. George Thompson, one of many who were trying to introduce the new method into the practice of medicine, some-

---

[4] The emptiness and wordiness of disputatious Peripateticism, which departed from all material reality, became, of course, the main charge which ardent scientists of the seventeenth century brought against the old science.

times with ludicrous results, indignantly assails Henry Stubbe, a fanatical enemy of the Royal Society, for attacking "all true-hearted virtuous, intelligent Disciples of our Lord *Bacon*," and he assures Stubbe that

'Tis *Works*, not *Words*; *Things* not *Thinking*; *Pyrotechnie* [chemistry], not *Philologie*; *Operation*, not merely *Speculation*, must justifie us Physicians. Forbear then hereafter to be so wrongfully Satyrical against our Noble Experimentators, who questionless are entred into the right way of detecting the Truth of things.[5]

Another upholder of the new medicine declares that the only benefit one may derive from studying Galen is "to manage a discourse about fruitless Notions with Elegancy. With this weapon, the Tongue, tis likely *Galen* himself prevailed over all other Physicians in the Court of the Emperor Antoninus; . . . And yet for all his height of Eloquence we see his Principles to be but streight and shallow."[6]

Another scientist, much greater than those mentioned, but one whose linguistic and stylistic views were sometimes inconsistent, reveals on more than one occasion his low opinion of philological study. Boyle considers rhetoric and deductive logic as matters of small importance, and styles himself "a much greater studier than prizer of languages," though, as may be noted in the quotation given below, he bestowed little enough study upon words. In an autobiographical note found among his papers, he makes clear the reason for his pronounced antipathy to philology:

. . . those excellent sciences, the mathematics, having been the first I addicated myself to, and was fond of, and experimental philosophy with its key, chemistry, succeeding them in my esteem and applications; my propensity and value for real learning gave me so much aversion and contempt for the empty study of words, that not only I have visited divers countries, whose languages I could never vouchafe to study, but

---

[5] Μισοχυμίας, 1671, pp. 31, 40.

[6] Marchamont Nedham, *Medela Medicinæ*, 1665, p. 256. In *An Answer to a Letter of Inquiry*, 1671, p. 37, one who signs himself W. S., and who was enthusiastic over the new science, declares "[When they go from School to the University] they leave behind them skill in tongues as a more jejune and barren kind of Employment. The more we grow towards men, the more we understand that *Words* are invented only to signifie *Things*; and while we are studying the Nature of Things we grudge the time that is spent, in hunting the Etymology of a word to its first Theam."

I could never be induced to learn the native tongue of the kingdom, I was born and for some years bred in [Ireland].[7]

So strong indeed was the antagonism to language engendered by the new science that even those who had devoted their lives to linguistic studies were inclined to depreciate their own profession. In a letter to John Collins, a mathematician and fellow of the Royal Society, Edward Bernard, an orientalist of some note who two years later was to join the society, admits that with the exception of mathematics his

study is literal [i.e., linguistic], and so beside the fame and regard of this age and inferior, in the nature of the thing, if I may speak as fits the schools, to real learning. I must profess that there is [a] great deal of difference, as I esteem, between what is notional only and what is also useful, between the derivation of a word and the solution of a problem.[8]

The whole tenor of his letter reveals the hope and belief that science will grow and thrive at the universities. His own field of study is totally ignored.

Another example of this depreciation of language under the influence of the scientific movement appears in the vigorous attacks on the teaching of the classics in the schools.[9] Under the lead of Comenius, Dury, and others inspired by the Baconian philosophy, the study of the ancient languages was severely reprehended during the period in which Puritanism was triumphant. The spirit of utility, which derived its strength from the new science, and which recommended the latter to the Puritans, demanded that language be considered only a means to an end, and thus insisted upon the easiest possible method of learning it,

[7] *Works*, ed. T. Birch, I, 11, 29–30; V, 229. Another manifestation of this effort to dethrone language in favor of material things is found in John Webster (*Academiarum Examen*, 1653, p. 20), who considered language as only subservient to true learning, whereas natural philosophy of itself conferred knowledge.

[8] Letter dated April 3, 1671, *Correspondence of Scientific Men of the Seventeenth Century*, ed. S. P. Rigaud, 1841, I, 158–59.

[9] For a treatment of Bacon's influence on educational theory in England at this time, see Foster Watson's *The Beginnings of the Teaching of Modern Subjects in England*, chap. vi. Watson shows how the study of things was constantly and strongly emphasized in opposition to the study of words.

and upon its subordination to the useful study of nature. John Dury, insisting that the true end of science is "to make use of the Creatures for that whereunto God hath made them," maintains that "Tongues are no further finally useful then to enlarge Traditionall Learning; and without their subordination unto Arts and Sciences, they are worth nothing towards the advancement of our Happiness."[10] This critical attitude toward linguistic study was by no means confined to this age or to the proponents of the new science. It appears in the essayists and other writers on education and kindred matters.[11] The most vigorous condemnation, however, of the study of languages is found in the *Academiarum Examen*, 1653, of John Webster, a Puritan and an enthusiastic Baconian, who expressly advocated the substitution of the new science for the classical studies in the universities.

The knowledge of Tongues beareth a great noise in the world, and much of our precious time is spent in attaining some smattering and small skill in them . . . before we arrive at any competent perfection in them, and yet that doth scarcely compensate our great pains; nor when obtained do they answer our longing, and vast expectations. For there is not much profit or emolument by them, besides those two great and necessary uses to inable to read, understand, and interpret or translate the works and writings of other men . . . that thereby we may gather some of their hidden treasure; and also to inable men to converse with people of other nations, and so fit men for foreign negotiations, trade and the like.

Since man's knowledge is in no way increased by the mere knowing of languages, he believed that little time should be spent upon them.

Now for a Carpenter to spend seven years time about the sharpning and preparing of his instruments, and then had no further skill how to imploy them, were ridiculous and wearisome; so for Schollars to spend divers years for some small scantling and smattering in the tongues, having for the most part got no further knowledge, but like Parrats to babble and

---

[10] *The Reformed School* (1650?), pp. 42, 47. See also *PMLA*, XLV (1930), 981, note 7.

[11] See T. C., *Moral Discourses*, 1655, pp. 50 ff., and Francis Osborne, *A Miscellany*, 1659, p. 78. The avenue, however, through which the scientists reached their conclusions was different from the approach adopted by the others, especially as regards the emphasis placed upon the materialistic nature of truth.

prattle, that whereby the intellect is in no way inriched, is but toylsome, and almost lost labour.[12]

An indirect way of attacking the study of the classical languages is revealed in the effort to show that Latin, generally considered the most perfect of tongues, was exceedingly defective. Wilkins, in arguing the virtues of his universal character, takes great pains to point out the inconsistencies, illogicalities, anomalies, irregularities, and complexities of Latin, and he emphasizes the difficulty of learning it because of the unusually large number of rules, which he, daring to differ from Bacon, "that incomparable Man," considered a serious defect. The tendency throughout the comparison of his own invented symbols with Latin is to depreciate and discourage the study of the latter.[13]

It is difficult for us to realize the extremes to which this distrust of language was carried. Its frequent appearance during the formative period of modern science bears conclusive testimony to the fact that all verbal media of communication were considered one of the greatest obstacles to the advancement of learning. Yet even the scientists realized that language was at least a necessary evil, if they wished to share their discoveries with others. This realization inspired in them a desire to reduce language to its simplest terms, to make it as accurate, concrete, and clear an image of the material world as was possible. In no one is this attempt more clearly displayed than in William Petty, a versatile and practical scientist and one of the founders of the Royal Society. Influenced by, though not so materialistic as, Hobbes, Petty manifests a desire for clear definitions, and toward this end seeks to place language on a purely materialistic basis, to curtail all verbal superfluity and insignificancy, in short, to sweep away all the fogginess of words.[14] Believing that, "whereas all

---

[12] P. 21. The third chapter of Webster's book discusses the study of language, in which the author emphasizes the utilitarian purpose of education, denies the usefulness of all speculative subjects, depreciates linguistic studies, and opposes the teaching of grammar. He would substitute the "symbolic, hieroglyphical, and emblematical ways of writing" (p. 24), with special emphasis upon a universal character.

[13] *Essay Towards a Real Character and a Philosophical Language*, 1668, pp. 443 ff.

[14] See *The Petty Papers*, ed. Marquis of Lansdowne, 2 vols., 1927; and the *Petty-Southwell Correspondence, 1676–1687*, ed. Marquis of Lansdowne, 1928.

writings ought to be description of things, they are now onely of words, opinions, theories,"[15] he attempted to draw up "A Dictionary of Sensible Words" which would show "what sensible Matter, Thing, Motion or Action, every word therein doth meane and signify."[16] Speaking elsewhere of this dictionary, he expresses as clear a linguistic counterpart of the mechanical philosophy as one could wish for:

That Dictionary I have often mentioned was intended to translate all words used in Argument and Important matters into words that are *Signa Rerum* and *Motuum*. But the Treasury of *Sensata* are the many Miscelany papers of my Scripture, which I add and subtract, Compose and distribute as Printers do their Letters.[17]

Not content with reducing all physical phenomena to matter and motion, scientists desired to impose the limitations of the same terms upon language, since they believed that only by making language correspond more closely to the truths of nature was it possible to advance knowledge.[18]

This latter idea, indeed, lay at the bottom of all their linguistic and stylistic views. In discussing the vague conception of "nature" current in his own day, Boyle says, "On this occasion, I must not forbear to take notice, that the unskilful use of terms of far less extent and importance, and also less ambiguous, than the word nature is, has been, and still is, no small impediment to the progress of sound philosophy."[19] He amplifies his statement by

[15] *Petty-Southwell Correspondence*, p. 324.

[16] *The Petty Papers*, I, 150–51. He further elaborates upon his purpose as intending to show what words have the same meaning, many meanings, or no meaning at all; what words are the names of other words, are merely auxiliary, or are ornamental.

[17] *Petty-Southwell Correspondence*, p. 324.

[18] Petty pays tribute to Boyle as one who "understand[s] the true use and signification of words, whereby to register and compute your own conceptions." See also *Advice of W. P. to Mr. Samuel Hartlib*, 1648, *Harleian Miscellany*, VI, 11–12. This materialistic conception of language finds frequent expression throughout the period, as, for instance, in *The Displaying of Supposed Witchcraft*, 1677, p. 21. John Webster, the author, evidently influenced by Bacon, holds that "words are but the making forth of those notions that we have of things, and ought to be subjected to things, and not things to words: if our notions do not agree with the things themselves, then we have received false *Idola* or images of them."

[19] *A Free Inquiry into the Vulgarly Received Notion of Nature*, written in 1666 though published twenty years later. See *Works*, ed. Birch, 1744, IV, 419.

pointing out that most physicians, chemists, and naturalists were content to explain phenomena by means of such expressions as "real qualities," "natural powers," "faculties," and the like, which do not clearly represent anything in the physical world. Such a quiescence in ignorance sufficiently explains why the Baconians considered a reformation of language as important as a change in philosophy. In this respect Boyle may be again quoted, although confirmative passages could easily be brought from other sources.

And I confess I could heartily wish, that philosophers, and other learned men (whom the rest in time would follow) would by common (though perhaps tacit) consent, introduce some more significant and less ambiguous terms and expressions in the room of the too licenciously abused word nature, and the forms of speech, that depend upon it; or would, at least, decline the use of it as much as conveniently they can; and where they think they must employ it, would add a word or two, to declare in what clear and determinate sense they use it.[20]

The position of the scientists was that the truth of ideas regarding nature was dependent upon accuracy of language, and that the advancement of science must necessarily wait upon the introduction of greater precision and clarity into the use of words. This linguistic reformation was to be achieved by a constant narrowing of terms through strict definition, and by the employment of words that would be exactly equivalent, not to hazy conceptions bred in the minds of men by the loose usage of the past, but to the objective truths of nature. They were seeking an objective rather than subjective, materialistic rather than psychological basis for language.

In his *History of the Royal Society*, Sprat speaks of the attempt of the new scientists to reduce their style to "a Mathematicall plainness,"[21] an expression that is more significant than may be realized. For certainly the remarkable development of mathematics in the seventeenth century, to which Descartes contributed much, and especially the improved mathematical symbols that were coming into use,[22] exerted no small influence

---

[20] *Works*, ed. Birch, IV, 365.    [21] P. 113.
[22] See Florian Cajori, *A History of Mathematics*, 2d ed., 1919, pp. 139, 157.

upon conceptions of what language should be. Hobbes, in his emphasis upon definition and in his general deductive method, to say nothing of his unfailing interest in mathematics, reveals how much the latter had influenced him, and, indeed, the movement toward clear definitions characteristic of this period drew much of its inspiration from mathematics. The Malmesbury philosopher considered words only the marks of things, just as mathematical symbols possess no virtue in themselves, but merely stand for quantities and relationships. Seth Ward, professor of astronomy at Oxford and an early upholder of the new science, declares that the change from the traditional verbose mathematical writing to "the Symbolicall way, invented by *Vieta,* advanced by Harriot, perfected by Mr. *Oughtred* and *Des Cartes*" made him hope

that the same course might be taken in other things (the affections of quantity, the object of universall *Mathematicks,* seeming to be an Argument too slender to engrosse this benefit). My first proposall was to find whether other things might not as well be designed by Symbols, and herein I was presently resolved that Symboles might be found for every *thing* and *notion.*[23]

The period witnessed frequent efforts to employ the analogy between mathematical symbols and verbal terms. Samuel Parker, an ardent convert to the experimental philosophy who at times reveals the influence of Hobbes, in attacking the cloudy terms used by the Cambridge Platonists, insists that "the use of Words is not to explaine the Natures of Things, but only to stand as marks and signes in their stead, as Arithmetical figures are only notes of Numbers; and therefore Names are as unable to explaine abstracted Natures, as figures are to solve *Arithmetical Problems.*"[24] Influenced by the new developments in mathematics, scientists wished to degrade language to the same colorless symbolism which had proved so successful in mathematics, so that words would have no more character than the $x$, $y$, $z$ of algebra.

The mathematical spirit is also apparent in the remarkable

[23] *Vindiciae Academiarum,* 1654, pp. 20–21.
[24] *A Free and Impartial Censure of the Platonick Philosophie,* 1666, p. 61.

development of various schemes for a universal language which appeared at this time.[25] Seth Ward was of the opinion that "an Universall Character might easily be made wherein all Nations might communicate together, just as they do in numbers and in species. And to effect this is indeed the design of such as hitherto have done any thing concerning an Universall Character."[26] At first the seeming necessity of a multitude of characters in the schemes that had been proposed made him dubious of their feasibility,

But it did presently occur to me that by the helpe of Logick and Mathematicks this might soone receive a mightly advantage, for all Discourses being resolved in sentences, those into Words, words signifying either simple notions or being resolvible into simple notions, it is manifest, that if all the sorts of simple notions be found out, and have Symboles assigned to them, those will be extreamly few in respect of the other, (which are indeed Characters of words, such as *Tullius Tiro's*) the reason of their composition easily known, and the most compounded ones at once will be comprehended, and yet will represent to the very eye all the elements of their composition, and so deliver the natures of things: and exact discources may be made demonstratively without any other paines then is used in these operations of specious Analytics.[27]

Ward also expresses a firm conviction that such a design would

[25] For a discussion of these schemes consult Otto Funke's *Zum Weltsprachenproblem in England im 17. Jahrhundert*, Heidelberg, 1929 (*Anglistische Forschungen*, Heft 69). Funke, however, fails to mention Henry Edmunson's *Lingua Linguarum*, 1658, and Samuel Hartlib's *Common Writing*, 1647, the latter antedating by several years the earliest work he discusses. Bacon (*Advancement of Learning*, Book VI, chap. i) did much to stimulate interest in the matter. See Funke, *op. cit.*, pp. 1 ff; Wilkins, *Essay Towards a Real Character*, 1668, p. 13; Edmunson, *Lingua Linguarum*, 1658, Dedication; John Webster, *Academiarum Examen*, 1653, pp. 24–25; Cave Beck, *Universal Character*, 1657, "To the Reader," and prefatory poem signed by Jos. Waite.

[26] *Vindiciae Academiarum*, pp. 20–21. Boyle had expressed the same idea in a letter to Hartlib dated March 19, 1647: "If the design of the *Real Character* take effect, it will in good part make amends to mankind for what their pride lost them at the tower of *Babel*. And truly, since our arithmetical characters are understood by all the nations of *Europe*, the same way, though every several people express that comprehension with its own particular language, I conceive no impossibility, that opposes the doing that in words, that we see already done in numbers." *Works*, ed. Birch, I, 22.

[27] *Loc. cit.* It is worthy of note that one of the early attempts to construct a universal language advocated the substitution of numbers for letters and syllables. See Cave Beck's *Universal Character*, 1657.

prove of great assistance to the advancement of learning, that is reall Learning, by which I understand that *Mathematicks* and *Naturall Philosophy*, and the grounds of *Physick*. . . . Such a Language as this (where every word were a definition and contain'd the nature of the thing) might not unjustly be termed a naturall Language, and would afford that which the *Cabalists* and *Rosycrucians* have vainely sought for in the Hebrew, And in the names of things assigned by Adam."[28]

The effort to create a universal language was in part inspired by the desire to rectify the multiplicity of tongues, the "curse of Babel." With the rise of the new science, men were especially impressed with the need of some common medium whereby the discoveries of one country might be transmitted to another. Owing to the attack on the authority of the ancients, Latin, which had hitherto met the need, was in process of being depreciated and discarded. Furthermore, it was difficult to learn, and scientists resented spending too much time on the study of words.[29] Two other considerations, however, exerted a powerful influence on the movement. One was the desire to discover a language which would avoid the defects, real and supposed, of all established tongues, defects of which the age was acutely conscious. The other was the conviction that words should so match things that a word might not only stand as a symbol of a thing, but should also indicate its nature. The first of these two considerations manifests science's wide dissatisfaction with language in general. One linguistic inventor, who drew his inspiration from Bacon and the Baconians, expressed the belief that a universal character, "if happily contrived so as to avoid all Equivocal

---

[28] *Loc. cit.* John Wallis, a co-worker of Ward's in mathematics and the new science, was somewhat dubious of the practicability of such a language. See *Defence of the Royal Society*, 1678, pp. 16–17. It is beside our purpose to enter into a discussion of the speculations regarding the language Adam spoke in the Garden of Eden, and the names he gave things, which was considered the "natural language," except to say that Ward was not the only one to associate a universal character with this language. See John Webster, *Academiarum Examen*, pp. 18–32.

[29] As early as 1638 John Wilkins held that a universal language would "mightily conduce to the spreading and promoting of all Arts and Sciences: Because that great part of our Time which is now required to the Learning of Words, might then be employed in the Study of Things." *Mercury*, 3d ed., 1707, pp. 55–56.

words, Anomalous variations, and superfluous Synonomas with
which all Languages are encumbred, and rendred difficult to the
learner, would much advantage mankind in their civil commerce
and be a singular means of propagating all sorts of Learning and
true Religion."[30] Dalgarno, who, assisted by Boyle, Wilkins,
Ward, Bathurst, Petty, and Wallis,[31] men who composed the
Oxford group of experimenters, produced in 1661 his universal
language under the title *Ars Signorum*, claimed that the purpose
of his work was to show

a way to remedy the difficulties and absurdities which all languages are
clogged with . . . by cutting off all redundancy, rectifying all anomaly,
taking away all ambiguity and aequivocation. . . . In a word, designing
not only to remedie the confusion of languages, by giving a much more
easie medium of communication than any yet known, but also to cure
even Philosophy itself of the disease of Sophisms and Logomachies; as
also to provide her with more wieldy and manageable instruments of
operation, for defining, dividing, demonstrating etc.[32]

The defects of language were in large part considered responsible for the confused and false ideas of nature which the old
philosophy maintained. It was an authentic sense of the dangers
inherent in all known tongues, ancient and modern, that determined the linguistic and stylistic views of the early scientists.

The climax of this movement toward a universal language
was reached in John Wilkins' ambitious *Essay Towards a Real
Character and a Philosophical Language*, 1668, a work sponsored by the Royal Society. From our point of view, the *Essay*
is, indeed, a quixotic book, but to his own age it was a noble, if
somewhat impractical, achievement. The first part of the treatise
is devoted to showing the imperfections which, inherent in all
tongues, should be remedied by a language constructed according to the rules of art. A single passage clearly reveals the
author's attitude:

As for the ambiguity of words by reason of *Metaphor* and *Phraseology*,
this is in all instituted Languages so obvious and so various, that it is

[30] Cave Beck, *The Universal Character*, 1657, "To the Reader."
[31] Dalgarno paid particular tribute to Ward and Wilkins for assistance rendered. See Funke, *op. cit.*, p. 46. It is interesting to note that Ward, Wallis,
and Wilkins were all mathematicians.
[32] Quoted in Funke, *op. cit.*, p. 16.

needless to give any instances of it; every Language having some peculiar phrases belonging to it, which, if they were to be translated *verbatim* into another Tongue, would seem wild and insignificant. In which our English doth too much abound, witness those words of *Break, Bring, Cast, Cleare, Come, Cut, Draw, Fall, Hand, Keep, Day, make, Pass, Put, Run, Set, Stand, Take,* none of which have less than thirty or forty, and some of them about a hundred several senses, according to their use in Phrases, as may be seen in the Dictionary. And though the varieties of Phrases in Language may seem to contribute to the elegance and ornament of Speech; yet, like other affected ornaments, they prejudice the native simplicity of it, and contribute to the disguising of it with false appearances. Besides that, like other things of fashion, they are very changeable, every generation producing new ones; witness the present Age, especially in late times, wherein this grand imposture of Phrases hath almost eaten out solid knowledge in all professions; such men generally being of most esteem who are skilled in these Canting forms of speech, though in nothing else.[33]

More than to any other linguistic defect, scientists objected to a word's possessing many meanings or the same meaning as another word, and especially to the use of metaphors. The desire to make the word match the thing, to be in a strict sense a description of a thing or action, explains their exaggerated antipathy to metaphors and such figures of speech.

The chief means whereby the linquistic reformers would obviate the deficiencies of existing tongues was to be found in symbols so constructed as to indicate the exact nature of things. Dalgarno was the first to undertake the task, but it was Wilkins who carried the idea to its farthest application. He attempted to classify everything in the universe, and then by a combination of straight lines, curves, hooks, loops, and dots, to devise for each thing a symbol which would denote its genus and species.[34]

[33] Pp. 17–18. Wilkins believed that such a design as he was promoting "would exceedingly abbreviate the number of words, prevent much circumlocution, contribute to perspicuity and distinctness, and very much promote the elegance and significancy of speech." (P. 319.) As noted on an earlier page, he discusses at length the imperfections of language, especially Latin, and claims that his invented symbols remove all such defects. (Pp. 443 ff.)

[34] In the use of lines and dots Wilkins had been anticipated many years by Samuel Hartlib's *Common Writing*, 1647. Hartlib, however, was intent only on devising a character for international use; he was not concerned with making the symbol display the nature of the thing.

For those creations of the imagination, such as fairies, which lie beyond the realm of nature, he frankly made no provision, claiming that since they did not exist, they should not be represented in language. At last Hobbes's conception of words as only the marks of things had been literally realized. Wilkins' undertaking represents the lowest state to which language was degraded. Barred from representing the creations of the imagination and stripped of all connotations from past usage, language was to become nothing more than the dead symbols of mathematical equations.[35]

By way of summary, we may say that the linguistic views of seventeenth-century scientists were characterized by a suspicion of language arising out of its association with the old science, which seemed to depend more upon words than upon nature, and out of a feeling that all instituted languages tended to obscure rather than to describe realities. Linguistic defects were discovered in the imperfect meanings given to words, in the many meanings ascribed to a single word, in the figurative use of words, in the multiplication of words through synonyms, and in the number, irregularities, and inconsistencies of grammatical rules. The vividness with which material reality was conceived filled the scientists with alarm lest that reality should be lost through

[35] The scientists, it is true, influenced largely by the French Academy, were concerned with the improvement of the English language. But it must be noted that they considered such an undertaking much inferior to the true goal of the Royal Society. Sprat devotes several pages to the matter, advocating a society to "set a mark on ill Words; correct those, which are to be retained; admit and establish the good; and make some emendations in the Accent, and Grammar." But he considered such a design of less moment than experimental philosophy. The Royal Society did appoint a committee to reform the mother tongue, but after a few meetings the project came to nought. Even while advocating, largely under the influence of the French, this linguistic undertaking, they were careful to emphasize its inferiority to the more important scientific movement. In the dedication to his *Essay* Wilkins says, "Now if those famous Assemblies [Academia de la Crusca and French Academy] consisting of the great Wits of their Age and Nations, did judge this Work of Dictionary-making, for the polishing of their Language, worthy of their united labour and studies; Certainly then, the Design here proposed [universal character], ought not to be thought unworthy of such assistance; it being as much to be preferred before that, as *things* are better then *words*, as *real knowledge* is beyond *elegancy of speech*, as the *general good of* mankind, is beyond that of any *particular Countrey* or *Nation*."

a faulty medium of communication and lest the manner of expression should usurp an importance belonging to the thing described. The result was a linguistic ideal which reduced language to its simplest terms, a single word being exactly equivalent to a single thing, and which, influenced by the unusual developments in mathematics, sought to degrade words to symbols of the same colorless nature as characterized those of mathematics. The effort to realize this ideal resulted in various schemes for a universal language and real character, in which words finally became marks, but marks which indicated the exact nature of the thing. It is hard to overemphasize the fact that science in its youth considered the linguistic problem as important as the problem of the true scientific method.

What stylistic standards would naturally develop out of this conception of language? Certainly none other than those which almost invariably appear whenever the scientists touch upon style. There should be little figurative language, especially metaphors, which falsely describe actions and things. There should be no verbal superfluity, but rather an economy of words sufficient to match exactly the phenomenon. Words should be the plainest possible, with intelligible, clear, and unequivocal meanings, preferably common words which are closer to material realities. There should be no emphasis upon or interest in the mode of expression for its own sake. Rhetorical ornaments and sheer delight in language represent a pernicious misplacing of emphasis, and in the end destroy the solid and fruitful elements in knowledge. What need is there to bring in Seneca and Aristotle to explain what is so easily explicable without them? As far as I can discover, not a single Baconian in any discussion of style mentions either one. I do not say that the two ancient worthies were without influence on style in the seventeenth century, but I am of the opinion that they had nothing to do with the stylistic views of science, which, as I have shown elsewhere, were quite different from Anti-Ciceronianism as described by Professor Croll.[36]

[36] See *PMLA*, XLV (1930), 1004–6. I do not wish in any way to depreciate Professor Croll's very valuable articles, which have thrown much light on English prose of the first half of the seventeenth century. I think, however,

In a recent review of one of my articles[37] Mr. Croll holds that the style advocated and adopted by the scientists was actually the Anti-Ciceronian style modified by some changes. These changes, however, even as described by him, were so important and far-reaching as to justify us in considering the result a new style. If my impression is correct, he implies that language is a minor, and structure or form a major, element in expression, and that the latter remained constant throughout the century. He sees in seventeenth-century prose a homogeneity which would certainly confound most literary historians, who have considered the Restoration an important turning point in the development of prose style. Any theory which places Sir Thomas Browne and John Dryden, Jeremy Taylor and John Tillotson in the same stylistic category is puzzling.[38]

In the same review Professor Crane opposes two objections to my article. The first asserts that the scientists insisted upon plainness of expression only in scientific works, and that they believed other subjects demanded other styles. One has only to turn to a single familiar passage in Sprat's *History of the Royal Society* (pp. 111–13), a *locus classicus* in seventeenth-century opinions on style, to see how Sprat applies his antagonism to rhetoric and his advocacy of a plain style to "most other Arts and Professions." Furthermore, in a previous article I have attempted to show how the stylistic ideal of science was carried over into an alien field.[39] The distinction which the scientific advocates of plainness were chiefly interested in drawing was that

---

that he has tried to comprehend too many phenomena within the limits of his theory, with the result that many contradictions have arisen, which are hard to explain away.

[37] See *Philological Quarterly*, X (1931), 184–85.

[38] It seems hardly conceivable to me that the same spirit or movement which inspired the style of Browne, who is considered a thoroughgoing Anti-Ciceronian, should have incited the scientists to attack that style. Can we believe that when Glanvill, coming under the influence of the Royal Society, apologized for his earlier imitation of Browne's manner of expression, he was moved by the same spirit that had prompted him to adopt it? That his later prose should reveal some of Browne's characteristics is not surprising. It is hardly to be expected that any revision could have eradicated every vestige of his earlier model.

[39] "The Attack on Pulpit Eloquence in the Restoration," *Jour. Eng. Ger. Philol.*, XXX (1931), 188–217.

between poetry and prose.[40] That the passage in Sprat's *History* from which Mr. Crane quotes has poets, dramatists, and satirists in mind for the most part seems clear to me. Certainly Sprat is not speaking of argumentative or expository prose. With the exception of Boyle[41] there is little disposition on the part of scientists to establish categories of prose style.[42]

The second objection denies the truth of my statement that "science renounced Aristotle and all his works" which Mr. Crane interprets literally. My position is that science had foresworn allegiance to the authority of Aristotle, and had renounced all the evil consequences of such an allegiance. Against this position Mr. Crane's citations resolve themselves into inferences. The first is that since Hobbes translated Aristotle's *Rhetoric*, he subscribed to the latter's views. Is it not, however, just as permissible to infer that since this translation, made in the course of his tutoring William Cavendish (1633?) and before he had revealed any interest in science, was never published, the translator did not consider it worthy of publication? One has only to compare Aristotle's and Hobbes's opinions of metaphors to see how little the latter is indebted to the former. The second inference is that since Cowley, in outlining the studies of youths entering into an "Apprenticeship in Natural Philosophy," mentions Cicero, Quintilian, and Aristotle, he considered these men authorities on prose style. Though the passage is by no means clear, it seems to refer to Cicero and Quintilian as aids to poets, while the reference to Aristotle reads, "For the Morals and Rhetorick *Aristotle* may suffice; or *Hermogenes* and *Longinus*

[40] *Ibid.*, XXX, 205–6.

[41] Boyle expressed almost every stylistic view known to his age. Unfortunately the particular edition of Bacon's works to which Crane refers is not accessible to me; so I am not sure what passages he has in mind. Though Bacon lies outside of the field I am treating, and though in places he expresses stylistic views quite different from those of his followers, in other passages he anticipates their attitude. The chapter in which he formally discusses rhetoric (*Advancement of Learning*, VI, 3) reveals no stylistic classifications, but it does reveal an appreciation of rhetoric which the experimentalists of the mid-century could hardly have approved. In fact, Sprat, in his attack on rhetorical devices (*History of the Royal Society*, 111–13) seems to be answering this very chapter.

[42] Toward the end of his life Glanvill weakened in his stand for a plain style in the pulpit, and Barrow would permit rhetoric in sermons as a last resort.

be added for the latter." The mention of Hermogenes, whom Mr. Crane fails to notice, as an "authority" destroys whatever significance there otherwise might have been in the naming of Aristotle, for their rhetorical theories diverged widely. It seems clear that Cowley is only listing in perfunctory fashion well-known writers on rhetoric. One could hardly ask for clearer evidence of the fact that Anti-Ciceronianism meant nothing to the scientists than is revealed in the assigning of these two men to the study of youths, Aristotle, the mainstay of the Anti-Ciceronians, and Hermogenes, the rhetorician of the Ciceronians.[43] The complete absence, as far as I can discover, of references to or quotations from Aristotle, in the various passages in which the Baconians express their stylistic views, renders me very doubtful of his having influenced them at all. Professor Crane's failure to cite such references strengthens that doubt.

[43] In describing the growth of Ciceronianism Bacon says, "Then grew the flowing and watery vein of Osorius, the Portugal bishop, to be in price. Then did Sturmius spend such infinite and curious pains upon Cicero the orator and Hermogenes the rhetorician." *Works*, ed. Spedding, Ellis, and Heath (London, 1887), III, 283.

# A BIBLIOGRAPHY
## OF THE PUBLISHED WRITINGS OF
## RICHARD FOSTER JONES

BOOKS AND ARTICLES

1919. *Lewis Theobald: His Contribution to English Scholarship, With Some Unpublished Letters.* New York: Columbia University Press. xi + 363 pp.

1920. "Another of Pope's Schemes," *Modern Language Notes*, XXXV, 346–51.
"The Background of *The Battle of the Books*," *Washington University Studies*, VII, Humanistic Series II, 99–162.

1922. "Some Reflections on the English Romantic Revival," *ibid.*, IX, 293–314.

1923. "Nationalism and Imagism in Modern American Poetry," *ibid.*, Sixth Series, XI, 97–130.

1925. "A Conjecture on the Wife of Bath's Prologue," *Journal of English and Germanic Philology*, XXIV, 512–47.
"Eclogue Types in English Poetry of the Eighteenth Century," *ibid.*, pp. 33–60.

1926. "Richard Mulcaster's View of the English Language," *Washington University Studies*, XIII, 267–303.

1928. "Romanticism on Trial," *English Journal*, XVII, 67–68.

1929. (Ed.) *Seventeenth-Century Literature.* (*Nelson's English Readings*, Vol. III.) New York: Thomas Nelson & Sons. 423 pp.
(Ed.) *Eighteenth-Century Literature.* (*Ibid.*, Vol. IV.) New York: Thomas Nelson & Sons. 416 pp.

1930. "Science and English Prose Style in the Third Quarter of the Seventeenth Century," *Publications of the Modern Language Association*, XLV, 977–1009.

1931. "The Attack on Pulpit Eloquence in the Restoration: An Episode in the Development of the Neo-Classical Standard for Prose," *Journal of English and Germanic Philology*, XXX, 188–217.

"The Originality of 'Absalom and Achitophel,' " *Modern Language Notes*, XLVI, 211–18.

"Reply to A. H. Nethercot, Concerning Cowley's Prose Style," *Publications of the Modern Language Association*, XLVI, 965–67.

1932. "Science and Language in England of the Mid-Seventeenth Century," *Journal of English and Germanic Philology*, XXXI, 315–31.

1933. "Romanticism Reconsidered," *Sewanee Review*, XLI, 3–25.

1936. *Ancients and Moderns: A Study of the Background of the "Battle of the Books."* ("Washington University Studies, New Series, Language and Literature," No. 6.) xi + 358 pp.

1937. (Ed.) *Francis Bacon: Essays, Advancement of Learning, New Atlantis, and Other Pieces.* Garden City, N.Y.: Doubleday, Doran. xxxiv + 491 pp.

1939. "Puritanism, Science, and Christ Church," *Isis*, XXXI, 65–67

1940. "Science and Criticism in the Neo-Classical Age of English Literature," *Journal of the History of Ideas*, I, 381–412.

1942. "The Moral Sense of Simplicity," in *Studies in Honor of Frederick W. Shipley.* ("Washington University Studies, New Series, Language and Literature," No. 14.) pp. 265–87.

1949. "The Background of the Attack on Science in the Age of Pope," in *Pope and His Contemporaries: Essays Presented to George Sherburn.* New York: Oxford University Press, pp. 96–113.

SELECTED REVIEWS

1930. *The Grub-Street Journal*, James T. Hillhouse (Durham, N.C.: Duke University Press, 1928), in *Journal of English and Germanic Philology*, XXIX, 311–12.

1931. *Prediger der Englischen Barock. Stilistich Untersucht*, Fritz Pützer (Bonn, 1929), in *Journal of English and Germanic Philology*, XXX, 416–17.

1932. *Atala, or the Love and Constancy of Two Savages in the Desert*, translated from the French of F. A. Chateaubriand by Caleb Bingham, edited by William Leonard Schwartz (Stanford, Calif.: Stanford University Press, 1930); and *The Letters of Sarah Byng Osborn, 1721–1773*, ed. John McCelland (Stanford, Calif.: Stanford University Press, 1930), in *Modern Language Notes*, XLVII, 130–31.

1933. *English Devotional Literature (Prose) 1600–1640*, Helen C. White ("University of Wisconsin Studies in Language and Literature," No. 29 [Madison, 1931]), in *Journal of English and Germanic Philology*, XXXII, 104–7.

1937. *William Whitehead—Poeta Laureatus, eine Studie zu den Literarischen Stromungen um die Mitte des 18. Jahrhunderts*, August Bitter ("Studien zur Englischen Philologie," Vol. LXXVIII [Halle-Soale, 1933]), and *The Works of Thomas Purney*, ed. H. O. White ("The Percy Reprints," No. XII [New York: Oxford University Press, 1933]), in *Modern Language Notes*, LII, 533–34.

1938. *John Donne and the New Philosophy*, Charles Monroe Coffin ("Columbia University Studies in English and Comparative Literature," No. 126 [New York: Columbia University Press, 1937]), in *Sewanee Review*, XLVI, 261–63.

1939. *Thomas Fuller's "The Holy State and the Profane State,"* ed. Maximilian Groff Walten ("Columbia University Studies in English and Comparative Literature," No. 136; 2 vols. [New York: Columbia University Press, 1938]), and *The Formation of Thomas Fuller's Holy and Profane State*, Walter E. Houghton, Jr. ("Harvard Studies in English," Vol. XIX [Cambridge, Mass.: Harvard University Press, 1938]), in *Journal of English and Germanic Philology*, XXXVIII, 641–43.

*Mythology and the Romantic Tradition in English Poetry*, Douglas Bush (Cambridge, Mass.; Harvard University Press, 1937), in *The Classical Journal*, XXXV, 113–14.

1940. "Science, Technology, and Society in Seventeenth Century England," Robert K. Merton, *Osiris*, Vol. II, Part 2 (Bruges, 1938), in *Isis*, XXI, 438–41.

*The White Doe of Rylston, by William Wordsworth: A Critical Edition*, Alice Pattee Comparetti ("Cornell Studies in English," Vol. XXIX [Ithaca, N.Y.: Cornell University Press, 1940]), in *Journal of English and Germanic Philology*, XL, 303–4.

1941. *Sir William Temple: The Man and His Work*, Homer E. Woodbridge ("The Modern Language Association of America, Monograph Series," Vol. XII, 1940), in *Journal of English and Germanic Philology*, XL, 416–18.

*The Road to Tryermaine: A Study of the History, Background, and Purposes of Coleridge's "Cristabel,"* Arthur H. Nethercot (Chicago: University of Chicago Press, 1939), in *Journal of English and Germanic Philology*, XL, 154–55.

1945. *Francis Bacon on Communication and Rhetoric or: The Art of Applying Reason to Imagination for the Better Moving of the Will*, Karl R. Wallace (Chapel Hill, N.C.: University of North Carolina Press, 1943), in *Modern Language Quarterly*, VI, 235–36.

1947. *Four Essays on "Gulliver's Travels,"* Arthur E. Case (Princeton, N.J.: Princeton University Press, 1945), in *Modern Language Notes*, LXII, 206–8.

# THE INVENTION OF THE
# ETHICAL CALCULUS

## Louis I. Bredvold

---

T HE prediction is not infrequently heard in our day that the moral and political sciences, once they have achieved the absolute precision of the physical sciences, will solve all the problems of human society that have plagued man through the ages. This prediction is usually presented as a new discovery, a new hope, a revelation made possible to this latter age by the astonishing recent progress in the physical sciences. It may be of some interest, therefore, to observe that it is not at all new, that it has, in fact, had a history of more than three hundred years. A glance back over some of its earlier manifestations will indicate its importance in the thought of the seventeenth and eighteenth centuries, and illustrate, as well, its postulates and its characteristic mode of demonstration.

In its genesis and early development in the seventeenth century, this hope of a millennium through exact science was quite independent of the experimental and inductive method championed by Bacon, and as a mode of Utopian thought even a direct contrast to *The New Atlantis*. Its inception was in the minds of mathematical scientists, and its formulation was controlled by the methods and ideals of mathematical reasoning. It promised to develop infallible conclusions from unquestionable first principles. Its proponents had necessarily to proceed by deduction, not by induction, in their attempts to excogitate and realize it.

Already in the seventeenth century, which was so amazingly rich in mathematical discoveries, the imagination of mankind was profoundly impressed by two aspects of mathematics: first, its infallibility as a form of reasoning, in striking contrast to the inconclusiveness, not to say futility, of most other forms of philosophizing, in which the continuous argument seems only so much evidence of the insolubility of the problem; second, the successful application of mathematics to the phenomena of motion, especially to astronomy. What could be more natural than to extend the application of this admirable instrument of the mind to the study of all the realms of human experience? The idea had a number of distinguished exponents in the seventeenth century, most of them probably inspired by Descartes.

Without inquiring into the obscurer historical origins of this idea, we may begin with the first important moment in its career, its revelation to Descartes in an extraordinary dream on the night of November 10, 1619, to which he himself traced his philosophical mission. It seems probable that this dream was brought on by his intense preoccupation at this time with physics and mathematics and that it was in fact the intuitive grasp of the great philosophical system which he labored henceforth to elaborate. He recorded in his diary that he was filled with enthusiasm, and that he had discovered the "foundations of the Admirable Science"—*mirabilis Scientiae fundamenta reperirem.*[1] In the light of his later work, this could only mean that Descartes at this time first glimpsed the possibility of applying the infallible method of mathematics to all the phenomena of the universe and every department of thought. His metaphysics and mathematics are but fragments of the comprehensive a priori system he aspired to construct. He conceived of his new Method as a "universal mathematical science," beginning like geometry with incontestable axioms and deducing through a series of theorems absolutely certain conclusions. This complete and homogeneous system would include not only physics, but medicine and ethics. For, as he explained in the Preface to his *Principles of Philosophy,*

all Philosophy is like a tree, of which Metaphysics is the root, Physics the trunk, and all the other sciences the branches that grow out of this

[1] Jacques Maritain, *The Dream of Descartes* (New York, 1944), pp. 13–29.

trunk, which are reduced to three principal, namely, Medicine, Mechanics, and Ethics. By the science of Morals, I understand the highest and most perfect which, presupposing an entire knowledge of the other sciences, is the last degree of wisdom.[2]

One of the pathetic frustrations of Descartes was his inability to make progress on an a priori Medicine, "based in infallible demonstration," as he described it to Mersenne in 1630, a Medicine which was to be so absolutely certain that it would give mankind conquest over sickness, the infirmities of age, and perhaps even over death itself. Unfortunately, the system had not yet been developed to the point of efficacy when death called on Descartes.[3]

As to the Ethics which he planned as part of his universal science, he seems to have devoted less time and effort to this subject than to Medicine. Nevertheless he assured his friend Chanut in a letter (June 15, 1646) that his studies in Physics had been of great service to him in reaching sure foundations in Ethics, and that he had found certainty easier to demonstrate in Ethics than in some aspects of Medicine:

> Je vour dirai, en confidence, que la notion telle quelle de la Physique, que j'ai tâché d'acquérir, m'a grandement servi pour établir des fondements certains en la Morale; et que je me suis plus aisément satisfait en ce point qu'en plusieurs autres touchant la Médicine, auxquels j'ai néanmoins employé beaucoup plus de temps.[4]

Such was the plan of the "universal science" of Descartes, and he lived and died convinced of the possibility of a complete mathematical philosophy of the universe, including human life and personality, if he could only be given the necessary funds for research, for which he repeatedly appealed in his publications. His actual achievements are but fragments of this great plan. But he bequeathed to his successors his method of constructing ethics as a deductive and infallible science, perhaps itself essentially mathematical, but at least proceeding by a kind of reason-

[2] Descartes, *The Method, Meditations, and Selections from the Principles*, translated by John Veitch, 6th ed. (Edinburgh, 1879), p. 184.

[3] Henri Gouhier, *La Pensée Religieuse de Descartes* (Paris, 1924), pp. 66–72, 142–48; also *The Discourse on Method*, Parts 5 and 6.

[4] Gouhier, *op. cit.*, p. 150.

ing analogous to that of mathematics. When Pascal wrote his little essay on the virtues and limitations of the *"esprit de géométrie"* he had in mind the pretensions of Cartesianism.

Quite independently of Descartes, his English contemporary Thomas Hobbes developed an ethical and political philosophy under the same mathematical inspiration, but with a different set of axioms and consequently different conclusions. Geometry, said Hobbes, "is the only science that it hath pleased God hitherto to bestow on mankind."[5] He proposed to reduce, by strict geometrical reasoning, psychology, ethics, and politics to equally exact sciences. Mankind has hitherto relied only on Experience as the source of ethical and political knowledge; by this means, however, we can acquire only Prudence, useful as that may be. But by means of Science, he said, we may acquire Sapience, which is infallible.[6] Reasoning is, indeed, but a kind of arithmetic: "when a man *Reasoneth*, he does nothing else but conceive a sum total, from *Addition* of parcels; or conceive a Remainder, from *Substraction* of one sum from another."[7] But reasoning is also analogous to geometrical demonstration. The process consists, first, "in apt imposing of Names"; second, in "getting a good and orderly Method in proceeding from the Elements, which are Names, to Assertions made by Connexion of one of them to another; and so to Syllogismes, which are the Connexions of one Assertion to another, till we come to a knowledge of all the Consequences of names appertaining to the subject in hand; and that is it, men call Science."[8] A science of human nature worked out in this way could be predictive, and therefore an infallible guide in morals and politics. Hobbes struck a very modern note in the Epistle Dedicatory to *De Cive*:

And truly the geometricians have very admirably performed their part. . . . If the moral philosophers had as happily discharged their duty, I know not what could have been added by human industry to the completion of that happiness, which is consistent with human life. For were the nature of human actions as distinctly known, as the nature of quantity in geometrical figures, the strength of avarice and ambition,

[5] *Leviathan*, ed. A. R. Waller (Cambridge, 1904), p. 17.
[6] *Ibid.*, p. 27.
[7] *Ibid.*, p. 21.
[8] *Ibid.*, p. 25.

which is sustained by the erroneous opinions of the vulgar, as touching the nature of right and wrong, would presently faint and languish; and mankind should enjoy such an immortal peace, that (unless it were for habitation, on supposition that the earth should grow too narrow for her inhabitants) there would hardly be left any pretence for war.[9]

Such a Utopian political philosophy Hobbes sought to evolve by borrowing the methods of science and mathematics.

We are told that geometry may be either Euclidean or non-Euclidean, depending on the initial choice of axioms. When ethics and politics are developed by a similar deductive method the whole system necessarily depends on the selection of first principles. Hobbes founded his system on the new "philosophy of motion," the great discovery made in his time that motion can be measured and calculated mathematically. As man is part of the material cosmos and his psychology and conduct nothing but a variety of "motions," Hobbes put human nature entirely within the realm of physical (and presumably mathematical) laws. Man is a bundle of appetites and desires, and the only way his bellicose selfishness can be restrained for the purposes of an orderly society is for all men to convey to government an absolute power, under which the first duty of the subject is absolute obedience, if not, indeed, as a French commentator has suggested, habitual hypocrisy. Government can exist, Hobbes said, only by such complete submission. Sovereign power, once we have established it, may put a subject to death at will, as David did Uriah, without offending against any juridical principle. "For though the action be against the law of Nature, as being contrary to Equity," said Hobbes (who sometimes used the terminology of idealistic ethics, only to empty it of any ideal meaning), "yet it was not an injury to *Uriah*; but to *God*. Not to *Uriah*, because the right to do what he pleased, was given [David] by Uriah himself: and yet to *God*, because *David* was God's subject; and prohibited all Iniquity by the law of Nature."[10] Such was the promise of happiness to man in this, the first complete Utopia evolved under the influence of the mathematico-physical method. But a theory of human society

[9] *De Cive*, ed. Sterling P. Lamprecht (New York, 1949), p. 3.
[10] *Leviathan*, ed. A. R. Waller, p. 150.

according to which the sovereign power may be as cruel and arbitrary as it pleases, without the victim having the right even to think that his sufferings are injuries, could hardly appeal to the common sense of mankind.

With a different set of axioms, however, the geometrical method of deduction could be used equally effectively against Hobbism, as in Cumberland's *De Legibus Naturae Disquisitio Philosophica*, published in 1672. In the latter part of the seventeenth century this new *ars demonstrandi* had attained great prestige as a method of investigation as well as of presentation. Spinoza, who died in 1677, left in manuscript his great ethical treatise with the title *Ethica More Geometrico Demonstrata*. Against this Cartesian pretension to universal mathematics Bishop Huet directed his *Censura Philosophiae Cartesianae* (1689). But the idea of reducing ethics and law to an exact demonstrative science was a legacy from the seventeenth to the eighteenth century. One has only to look at the title page of Christian Wolff's treatise on legal theory, published at Halle in 1749: *Jus Gentium methodo scientifica pertractum: In quibus ex ipsa hominis natura continuo nexu omnes obligationes et jura omnia deducuntur.* However, Wolff adopted an unusually rigoristic method of presentation, and by his time the exposition of ethics and politics *more geometrico* usually assumed a more informal appearance.

Another line of development, more strictly mathematical, leads from Descartes to Leibnitz. Here one discovers the now forgotten professor at the University of Jena, Erhard Weigel (1625–1699), who was in his day a public figure, enjoying a high reputation even beyond the boundaries of the learned world. Among his many publications was an *Ethica Euclidea*, mentioned by Leibnitz in a letter in 1663. If we may judge his speculations from his *Idea Matheseos Universae* (1669), he held that the basic principles of all knowledge are to be discovered in a science called *Pantometria*, to which moral philosophy and jurisprudence as well as metaphysics must be subordinated. This *Pantometria* is of course his version of the "Admirable Science" which was revealed to Descartes in his dream in 1619. Leibnitz was a student at Jena in 1663, and he recalled many years later that

Weigel had been ingenious in inventing diagrams to represent moral aspects and relations, but Leibnitz judged these as unsatisfactory as "serving the memory in the retention and arrangement of its ideas rather than the judgment in the acquisition of demonstrative knowledge."[11] For Leibnitz was also haunted by the dream of a General or Universal Science, but he was great enough to see the inadequacies of Descartes and the futility of some of the efforts of Weigel.

The earliest attempts of Leibnitz were directed toward the solution of political questions by the geometrical method. In 1669, when he was twenty-five years old, he tried to settle by this method the selection of a new king for Poland. He published at Danzig a little book, *Specimen demonstrationum politicarum pro eligendo rege Polonarum*, presenting his argument in the geometrical style of sixty propositions, accompanied by corollaries, and thus demonstrating that three candidates should be excluded and the fourth elected. Two years later, when he was in Paris on a diplomatic mission, he tried a second *Specimen demonstrationis politicae* on Louis XIV, in which the geometrical method indicated that the French monarch should dispatch his armies from the Low Countries to Egypt to break the power of the Turk. But neither specimen of political demonstration had any influence on the course of events.

These were, however, youthful efforts, and Leibnitz soon undertook a more ambitious project, closer allied to the calculus than to geometry, and in method contributing to the development of modern symbolic logic. He was far too subtle to be satisfied with such crude statements as that of Hobbes, that reasoning is merely a kind of arithmetic, using the processes of addition and subtraction. What he sought to achieve was the Cartesian idea of a universal mathematical science, but he also understood from the beginning that the logic and mathematics available to Descartes were inadequate for this purpose. Before 1680 he began work on an encyclopedic treatise, of which only plans and fragments remain. The resemblance of his plan to that of Descartes is obvious. He believed that he could discover a

---

[11] Leibnitz, *New Essays concerning Human Understanding*, Alfred G. Langley, trans. (New York, 1896), p. 436.

"general science" (*Scientia generalis*) which would include not only geometry (in a transcendent form) and mechanics (based on Geometry), but also a "*Logique civile*" or "*Logique de la vie*," which would provide a calculation of probabilities applicable to all practical questions and in particular to legal problems.[12] For this purpose he devised a sort of symbolic mathematical logic which he called "*la charactéristique universelle*," by which he hoped to reduce all reasoning to a combination of signs, to a calculation. In a letter written about 1690 to the Duke of Hanover he said: "Et comme j'ay eu le bonheur de perfectionner considerablement l'art d'inventer ou Analyse des Mathematiciens, j'ay commencé à avoir certaines vues toutes nouvelles, pour reduire tous les raisonnemens humains à une espece de calcul . . ."[13] This new Characteristic (a new way of thinking as well as of writing) he called "*le juge des controverses*," and he regarded it as an infallible method of settling disputes. "If controversies were to arise," he said, "there would be no more need of disputation between two philosophers than between two accountants. For it would suffice for them to take their pencils in their hands, to sit down to their slates, and to say to each other (with a friend to witness, if they liked), 'Let us calculate.' "[14] This new mathematical method was therefore to decide with certainty all questions in practical affairs, all moral, political, and social questions, and, as Couturat has put it, "nous permettra, soit de prévoir l'avenir comme si nous avions assisté aux conseils de Dieu et surpris le secret de la création, soit de diriger sûrement notre conduite dans toutes les conjonctures."[15]

As this *furor mathematicus* continued unabated into the eighteenth century it is not surprising to find it mentioned in *The Dunciad*. Pope was no master of mathematics, but we may reasonably assume that he knew that its sober champion, Dr. Arbuthnot, specifically rejected the notion of an infallible deductive science of politics.[16] It seems likely that Pope had

[12] Louis Couturat, *La Logique de Leibnitz* (Paris, 1901), p. 141.

[13] *Ibid.*, p. 84, note 3.

[14] *Ibid.*, p. 98, note 3. Translation quoted from J. G. Hibben, *The Philosophy of the Enlightenment* (New York, 1910), p. 165.

[15] Couturat, *op. cit.*, p. 240.

[16] Lester M. Beattie, *John Arbuthnot* (Cambridge, Mass., 1935), p. 338.

something more than circle-squarers in mind when Dulness triumphs over Science, Wit, and Logic, but "Mad *Mathesis* alone was unconfined." When religious Mystery is described as expiring in Mathematics, the allusion may be to that ardent theologian *more geometrico*, Samuel Clarke, as well as to the Deists. The only mathematician to be honored by name in either the text or notes of Book IV was the Scottish John Craig, who in 1699 published a curious book with the title *Theologiae Christianae Principia Mathematica*. Craig worked out a calculus of moral evidence and its decay with time; his figures showed that in 1699 the evidence in favor of the truth of the Gospel was equivalent to the testimony of twenty-eight contemporary disciples, but that it would diminish to zero in the year 3144.[17]

Had Pope been less chary of names in Book IV he might have included Francis Hutcheson, who announced on the title page of his *Inquiry into the Original of our Ideas of Beauty and Virtue* (1725) a section devoted to "an attempt to introduce a Mathematical Calculation in subjects of Morality." Only an extended quotation can do justice to this attempt.

To find a *universal Canon* to compute the *Morality* of any Actions, with all their Circumstances, when we *judge* of the Actions done by our selves, or by others, we must observe the following *Propositions*, or *Axioms*.

1. The *moral Importance* of any *Agent*, or the *Quantity of publick Good* produc'd by him, is in a *compound Ratio* of his *Benevolence* and *Abilitys*: or (by substituting the initial Letters for the Words, as M = Moment of Good, and $\mu$ = Moment of Evil) M = B $\times$ A.

2. In like manner, the *Moment* of *private Good*, or *Interest* produc'd by any Person to himself, is in a *compound Ratio* of his *Self-Love*, and *Abilitys*: or (substituting the initial Letters) I = S $\times$ A.

3. When in comparing the *Virtue* of two Actions, the *Abilitys* of the *Agents* are equal; the *Moment* of *publick Good* produc'd by them in like Circumstances, is as the *Benevolence*: or M = B $\times$ 1.

4. When *Benevolence* in two *Agents* is equal, and other Circumstances alike; the *Moment* of *publick Good* is as the Abilitys: or M = A $\times$ 1.

5. The *Virtue* then of *Agents*, or their *Benevolence*, is always di-

[17] *Dunciad*, Book IV, ll. 31, 647, and 462, and article on Craig in *D.N.B.*

*rectly* as the *Moment* of *Good* produc'd in like Circumstances, and *inversly* as their *Abilitys*: or $B = \dfrac{M}{A}$.

6. But as the natural Consequences of our Actions are various, some *good* to our selves, and *evil* to the Publick; and others *evil* to our selves, and *good* to the Publick; or either *useful* both to our selves and others, or *pernicious* to both; the entire Motive to good Actions is not always *Benevolence alone*; or Motive to Evil, *Malice alone*; (nay, this last is seldom any Motive at all) but in most Actions we must look upon *Self-Love* as another Force, sometimes conspiring with Benevolence, and assisting it, when we are excited by Views of *private Interest,* as well as *publick Good*; and sometimes opposing *Benevolence,* when the good action is any *difficult* or *painful* in the Performance, or *detrimental* in *its* Consequences to the *Agent.* In the former Case, $M = B + S \times A = BA + SA$; and therefore $BA = M - SA = M - I$, and $B = \dfrac{M - I}{A}$. In the latter Case, $M = B - S \times A = BA - SA$; therefore

$$BA = M + SA = M + I, \text{ and } B = \dfrac{M + I}{A}.\text{[18]}$$

On this effort Sterne commented pertinently that Hutcheson "plus's and minus's you to heaven or hell, by algebraic equations —so that none but an expert mathematician can ever be able to settle his accounts with S. Peter—and perhaps S. Matthew, who had been an officer in the customs, must be called in to audit them."[19] But there is also the basic difficulty, both theoretical and practical, of resolving these equations of capital letters into the numerical equivalents proper in any given case, without which there can be no real computation. Hutcheson showed no interest in this problem, nor any awareness of it. "Strict logicians," said Hazlitt in his essay on Jeremy Bentham, "are licensed visionaries."

These flights of algebraic fancy appear trivial and futile from a distance of two hundred years, though there are even now social psychologists who believe they can reduce the behavior of man to mathematical formulas. But these trivialities are symptomatic of the mathematical ground-tone of the age. The eighteenth

[18] *Inquiry,* 2d ed. (1726), pp. 182–84.
[19] William R. Scott, *Francis Hutcheson* (Cambridge, 1900), p. 32, note.

century felt that it was ever on the very verge of a complete and final understanding of the nature of man, that the intellectual conquest of man over his own weaknesses was the next immediate step after the intellectual conquest so recently achieved over nature. The Utopianism of the age might be defined as the aspiration of every radical thinker to be the Newton of Ethics or the Newton of Politics. In this age, though the enthusiasm over the algebraic method gradually lapsed, the spirit of geometry really came into its own and achieved a general ascendency over the minds of men, even intruding, as Joseph Warton protested, into "polite literature."[20] It may therefore be correct to say with Gustave Lanson that the spirit of Cartesianism really reached its ascendency after 1700, when the reputation of Descartes as scientist was already on the decline.[21] Fontenelle, the Perpetual Secretary of the Academy of Sciences, has described the diffusion of this modern spirit at the opening of the century:

L'esprit géométrique n'est pas si attaché à la géométrie, qu'il n'en puisse être tiré, et transporté à d'autres connaissances. Un ouvrage de morale, de politique, de critique, peut-être même d'éloquence, en sera plus beau, toutes choses d'ailleurs égales, s'il est fait de main de géomètre. L'ordre, la netteté, la précision, l'exactitude qui règnent dans les bons livres depuis un certain temps, pourraient bien avoir leur première source dans cet esprit géométrique, qui se répand plus que jamais, et qui en quelque façon se communique de proche en proche à ceux même qui ne connaissent pas la géométrie. Quelquefois un grand homme donne le ton à tout son siècle; celui à qui on pourrait le plus légitimement accorder la gloire d'avoir établi un nouvel art de raisonner était un excellent géomètre.[22]

Geometrical reasoning is deductive, and there was of course nothing new about deductive reasoning as such. Nor was there anything new in the observation that geometry could begin with a few exact definitions and deduce from them a whole volume of exact demonstration. The novelty of the "modern" geometrical spirit was the application of the same method to writing whole

[20] Joseph Warton, *Essay on Pope* (1782), I, 209.

[21] Gustave Lanson, *Études d'Histoire Littéraire* (Paris, 1930), p. 81.

[22] Fontenelle, *Preface sur l'Utilité des Mathématiques et de la Physique,* *Oeuvres* (Paris, 1825), I, 54.

volumes of exact demonstration of the science of human nature. The French *philosophes* and their English counterparts, the Utilitarians, were geometricians in the sense that they constructed their systems of psychology, ethics, and politics by the a priori method and believed that by its use they were writing exact and irrefutable demonstrations. As is well known, it was this basic method that Burke attacked so vigorously and insistently: "Aristotle, the great master of reasoning, cautions us, and with great weight and propriety, against this species of delusive geometrical accuracy in moral arguments, as the most fallacious of all sophistry."[23] The archetype of this method may be examined in Locke, whose name its promulgators so often coupled with that of Newton.

In the *Essay Concerning Human Understanding* Locke repeatedly affirmed his conviction that morality is as capable of demonstration as mathematics, and with the same certainty.[24]

For certainty being but the perception of the agreement or disagreement of our ideas, and demonstration nothing but the perception of such agreement, by the intervention of other ideas or mediums; our moral ideas, as well as mathematical, being archetypes themselves, and so adequate and complete ideas; all the agreement or disagreement which we shall find in them will produce real knowledge, as well as in mathematical figures.[25]

Locke explained that he believed mathematical demonstration to be applicable to other modes than quantity. But it is a significant fact that Locke himself has in various places in the *Essay* exposed to the sharpest criticism every step necessary in any such extension of mathematical reasoning. The first step is, of course, to provide the axioms of ethical science by choosing correctly (not wisely, for there is no wisdom in mathematics), and defining precisely, a set of basic concepts. Now it is notorious how difficult it is to get any general assent, even among philosophers, either to the choice or the definition. Locke would not begin, as Hobbes did, with the concept of motion: the "true ground of morality,"

[23] Quoted by Elie Halévy, *The Growth of Philosophic Radicalism*, English translation (London, 1949), p. 158.
[24] *Essay*, I, ii, 1; III, xi, 16; IV, iii, 18–19; IV, iv, 7–9; IV, xii, 8.
[25] *Essay*, IV, iv, 7.

he thought, "can only be the will and law of God."[26] We can only suppose that, had Locke undertaken to write a system of ethics, as Molyneux asked him to, he would have developed the concept of the Law of Nature, in the manner of Cumberland. He would have chosen his own terms to define, despite objections from Hobbists or other heretics. Such first principles are obviously too controversial to serve the purpose of geometrical axioms. Moreover, when he encountered definitions which he disagreed with he appealed, empiricist as he naturally was, to the experience of mankind, which is not a generally recognized source of mathematical certainty. He heaped scorn on Descartes' proof that the soul is a thinking substance: "It is but defining the soul to be 'a substance that thinks,' and the business is done. . . . No definitions that I know, no suppositions of any sect, are of force enough to destroy constant experience."[27] From Locke's own pages it would appear that the authors of the geometrical science of morality are able to contest one another's axioms and that they are unable to find initial definitions that are not themselves prepositions requiring proof.

As for the next step, that of elaborating the theorems and corollaries of our hypothetical science, we could not do better than heed the warnings of Locke in his famous chapter on "trifling propositions" (IV, viii). For one great danger of a deductive social science is circularity of reasoning, in which the predicate of a proposition is already implicit in our idea of the subject. Such propositions "have a certainty in them," Locke said, "but it is only a verbal certainty, but not instructive." The useful propositions are such as "affirm something of another, which is a necessary consequence of its precise complex idea, but not contained in it."[28] But such propositions, as Locke explicitly stated, are possible only in dealing with the relations between abstract ideas, and ethics can therefore become as certain as mathematics only on the conditions that it become as abstract as mathematics. The demonstrative science of morality thus turns out to be a coherent, but self-contained, system spun out of definitions. As

[26] *Essay*, I, ii, 6; IV, iii, 18.
[27] *Essay*, II, i, 10–19.
[28] *Essay*, IV, viii, 8.

the youthful Berkeley commented: "To demonstrate morality it seemed one need only make a dictionary of words, and see which included which. . . . Locke's instances of demonstration in morality are, according to his own rule, trifling propositions."[29]

The pertinence of such strictures becomes evident when we examine Locke's first illustration of the kind of moral science he hopes for:

> The *relation* of other *modes* may certainly be perceived, as well as those of number and extension: and I cannot see why they should not also be capable of demonstration, if due methods were thought on to examine or pursue their agreement or disagreement. "Where there is no property there is no injustice," is a proposition as certain as any demonstration in Euclid: for the idea of property being a right to anything, and the idea to which the name "injustice" is given being the invasion or violation of that right, it is evident that these ideas, being thus established, and these names annexed to them, I can as certainly know this proposition to be true, as that a triangle has three angles equal to two right ones.[30]

It is perhaps instructive to observe how Locke here lapses, not only into a trifling proposition, but into a monstrous definition which defies common sense and "constant experience." Under Locke's science of morality the concept of justice would have no application outside the law of property, and the case of Uriah would be as desperate as under the political absolutism of Hobbes —unless both Bathsheba and Uriah's life were defined as property.

Such abuses of deductive reasoning vitiate the whole mass of ethical and political speculation left us by the geometrical spirit of the eighteenth century. They are the enthusiasms of a mathematical faith that would leap over all difficulties, that felt itself strong enough to move mountains. William Godwin needs for his system the proposition that truth will inevitably triumph over error if it is adequately communicated. How is this proposition to be established as true? "In strict consideration," says Godwin, "it will not admit of debate. Man is a rational being. If there be any man who is incapable of making inferences for

[29] John Wild, *George Berkeley* (Cambridge, Mass., 1936), p. 29.
[30] *Essay*, IV, iii, 18.

himself, or of understanding, when stated in the most explicit terms, the inferences of another, him we consider as an abortive production, and not in strictness belonging to the human species. It is absurd therefore to say that sound reasoning and truth cannot be communicated by one man to another."[31]  And thus, as Locke said of Descartes' definition of the soul, the business is done. We do not read Godwin because of this kind of demonstration; on the contrary, we neglect him and most of the other ambitious speculatists of his century just because of the unreality which pervades their work. Their reliance on the geometrical method to produce an infallible social science proved to be their grand mistake, and is the chief explanation of that neglect and indifference which they have suffered since their own time. Such is the verdict pronounced upon them by posterity, and never more authoritatively than by Gustave Lanson:

On a surtout reproché à la philosophie de xviiie siècle son abus de l'à priori. Tous les faiseurs de systèmes posent des principes, donnent des définitions, et ils tirent des conséquences sans avoir songé à établir leurs principes ni à justifier leurs définitions. . . . Ils ne songent pas à se demander si la réalité autirise leurs principes ou leurs définitions: ils trouvent la réalité au terme de leur analyse; et s'ils ne la trouvent pas, ils la condamnent. Leur méthode n'est ni critique, ni historique, ni expérimentale: elle est purement analytique. La réalité est citée par eux pour être jugée par leurs systèmes. Ils sont portés à prendre toutes les idées claires et distinctes pour des idées vraies; il leur parait impossible qu'un enchaînement nécessaire d'idées claires et distinctes ne représente pas en définitive la nature réelle, et, dans les domaines oú s'exerce la liberté humaine, n'exprime pas la seule realité légitime: en sorte que toute réalité qui n'y est pas conforme doit disparaître et faire place à une réalité conforme. Tout ce qu'il y a de hardi, de décisif, d'a priori et de révolutionnaire dans l'esprit philosophique est de pure essence cartésienne.[32]

Such a brief survey has of necessity unduly simplified the history of this "new way of ideas," and many names and many illustrative publications have been passed over without mention. By way of further qualification, it is not the intention here to

---

[31] *Political Justice*, F. E. L. Priestley, ed. (Toronto, 1946), I, 88.

[32] Lanson, *op. cit.*, p. 92.

deny that the social thinkers of the seventeenth and eighteenth centuries enriched their treatises with a multitude of empirical data and that the dissemination of their ideas had great practical consequences. The important development of the use of statistics, the application of mathematics to games of chance and to economic and sociological phenomena, any calculation of so-called laws of probability, fall outside the scope of this survey; for probability is obviously not certainty, and their difference constitutes that basic theoretical and practical disparity between social science and physical science which the Utopian theorists so resolutely ignored. The "unit idea" with which we have been concerned is the idea of a universal science with a universal method, applicable to human nature as well as to physical nature; since the seventeenth century it has been obvious that the method of any such science must be mathematical. It is the premises of the mathematical method in ethics and politics that are here in question, and this brief survey of their history and application may suggest some tentative reservations as to their theoretical and practical soundness.

# THE CONVERSATION OF THE
# AUGUSTANS

## Herbert Davis

IT is curious that Swift should have prefaced his *Hints Towards an Essay on Conversation* with the remark that few obvious subjects have been so seldom, or, at least, so slightly handled; for it was a subject which had received frequent attention during the seventeenth century from those writers who had concerned themselves with the manners and behaviour of the young prince or the courtier or the gentleman as well as from the moralists who addressed themselves to a wider audience on the proper government of the tongue. And during Swift's lifetime there continued to come from the press in England a series of translations and adaptations of books providing models of polite conversation and handbooks devoted to this useful art. The subject had been touched upon in various ways in almost all the Renaissance books of manners, like Giovanni della Casa's *Galateo*, of which an English abridgment was printed in 1663 under the title, *The Refin'd Courtier*. This went into three editions before the end of the seventeenth century, and a new version was published by Lintott in 1703, entitled *Galateo of Manners: or, Instructions to a Young Gentleman How to Behave Himself in Conversation &c.* While Swift was still continuing to gather materials for his great work, new translations also appeared of Castiglione's *Courtier* and Guazzo's *Art of Conversation*. But the subject was handled more specifically in the popular handbooks translated from the French such as *The Art of Pleasing in Conversation*, by Pierre d'Ortigue, Sieur de Vaumorière, attributed by the publishers to Cardinal Richelieu. This also seems to have served as a French conversation book, as the French and English texts were often printed side by side, and in this form it was finally revised, corrected, improved, and enlarged by Mr. Ozell in 1736, for which notable work he is mentioned in the Introduction to Swift's *Polite Conversation*. Five editions of the *Reflexions upon Ridicule* of the Abbé Morvan de Bellegarde appeared between 1706 and 1739 and a translation of his *Models of Conversation for Persons of Polite Education* appeared as late as 1765.

But perhaps we should not be surprised that Swift does not bother to take notice of these books, much less read them; for their nature and their style may be indicated by the following examples:

This Complaisance which I pretend to teach, is an Art to regulate our Words and behaviour in such a manner as may engage the love and respect of those with whom we converse, by distributing our praises where the quality or merit of the person require it.

Men are formed for society. Business, decorum, and the necessity of commerce obliges them often to see and converse with one another. . . . The great art of pleasing in conversation is to proportion it to the level of the company you are in.

The complaisance one is obliged to practise towards the Sex, impresses a certain tincture of politeness not easily to be acquired elsewhere . . . The bent brow assumes a more gay and sprightly air, every action grows less constrained and more free, and their physiognomy barters Meditation's pensive garb for a more lively livery.

He is even less likely to have taken any notice of the contributions of his own countrymen and contemporaries like Abel Roper or Daniel Defoe. He does not appear even to have been stirred by any of these productions to parody the books of manners or the models of conversation. He is concerned with the subject directly as his own experience provides him with growing opportunities to observe himself the manners and behaviour of polite society. He is prompted to write, as he himself tells us,

by mere indignation, to reflect that so useful and innocent a pleasure, so fitted for every period and condition of life, and so much in all men's power, should be so much neglected and abused.

He is not concerned with conversation as one of the arts of the courtier or as an accomplishment for ladies and gentlemen who wish to enter polite society, but as a human privilege common to all civilized societies. He would have approved of the point of view expressed by St. Évremond:

> Conversation is an Advantage peculiar to Man, as well as Reason. 'Tis the Bond of Society, and by it the Commerce of a Civil Life is kept up. The Mind communicates its Thoughts, and the Heart expresses its Inclinations; in short, Friendship is contracted and kept up by this Means . . .
>
> To live then as Man, 'tis necessary to converse with Men; 'tis fit Conversation should be the most agreeable Pleasure of Life.

Later on, he was to describe his ideal of conversation as it might be among rational creatures, when he was privileged to listen to the discourse of the Houyhnhnms—

> where nothing passed but what was useful, expressed in the fewest and most significant words: . . . where no Person spoke without being pleased himself, and pleasing his companions: where there was no interruption, tediousness, heat or difference of sentiments.

In rather similar terms he describes the conversation which in his own experience he had always found wholly agreeable, the conversation of Stella, which he set himself to record immediately after her death.

> People of all sorts were never more easy than in her company. . . . All of us who had the happiness of her friendship agreed unanimously that in an afternoon or evening's conversation she never failed before we parted of delivering the best thing that was said in the company.

Two days later, as he takes up his task again on the night of her funeral, he returns to the subject of her conversation:

> She never had the least absence of mind in conversation, nor given to interruption, or appeared eager to put in her word, by waiting impatiently until another had done. She spoke in a most agreeable voice, in the plainest words, never hesitating, except out of modesty before new faces, where she was somewhat reserved: nor, among her nearest friends ever spoke much at a time. She was but little versed in the common topics of female chat; scandal, censure and detraction, never came out of her mouth . . .

And again, in the later paragraphs added from time to time, he points out that for this reason she rather chose men for her companions—

yet no man was on the rack to entertain her, for she easily descended to anything that was innocent and diverting. . . . She was never positive in arguing; and she usually treated those who were so, in a manner which well enough gratified that unhappy disposition; yet in such a sort as made it very contemptible, and at the same time did some hurt to the owners.

Swift added a very small collection of the bon mots of Stella, which it must be confessed do not give us a very brilliant sample of their conversation, though indicating the kind of witty sallies which pleased them.

I have sometimes wondered whether we might not possibly detect some better indication of the quality of the conversation of the Augustans at their best among the "Thoughts on Various Subjects," which are to be found in the first two volumes of the *Miscellanies*, published jointly by Swift and Pope in 1727. For the editors promise to include things in which they have casually had any share, particularly those written in conjunction with their friends Dr. Arbuthnot and Mr. Gay. These *Miscellanies* were in fact to be regarded as the casual amusements of the Scriblerus Club—"not our Studies, but our Follies; not our Works, but our Idlenesses." It may therefore be permissible to consider some of the "Thoughts" as a collection of the bon mots of the Scriblerians, even if in their printed form they have been carefully cut and polished. For, unless I am mistaken, they have not always the same impersonal and aphoristic quality as those *Various Thoughts, Moral and Diverting*, dated October 1, 1706, which Swift had himself written and included in his *Miscellanies in Prose and Verse*, published in 1711. It is to be noted that in the later joint volumes one or two are printed with initials indicating that the original remark was due to Arbuthnot or Henley or T. K. And in Swift's own copy of the *Miscellanies*, now in the possession of Lord Rothschild, which is corrected and annotated in his own hand, there are pencilled points in the margin against all those *Thoughts*, which Mr. John Hayward has included in his recent edition of the *Selected Prose Works of Jonathan Swift*, published by the Cresset Press in 1949. As these include the initialed remarks I have just referred to, I am doubtful whether he is right in thinking that Swift was marking only those which he recognized as his own, although he may have been noting those for which he was responsible because he had put them down. If not all coined by him, they may well have been treasured by him as the choicest fruits of the conversation of the Scriblerians. For instance, this sentence, attributed to Arbuthnot, sounds to my ears like a stroke of wit occurring in the agreeable game of conversation—"We may see the small value God has for Riches, by the People he gives them to." Such a remark has a dangerous quality which would make it unfit for every sort of company; yet it displays the kind of wit which needs for full enjoyment the company of a small select group who will understand and respond and carry on the game fearlessly.

There are indeed many remarks in this little collection which indicate that the company was under no restraint. There was nothing in the atmosphere in which they conversed to subdue their spirits. They could play away merrily without any need of muting their instruments. Great ministers may be mentioned, even kings, in terms that would not do at court—

A King may be a Tool, a thing of Straw; but if he serves to frighten our Enemies, and secure our Property, it's well enough: A Scarecrow is a thing of Straw, but it protects the Corn.—

for the recognized Wit may claim something of the freedom of the Fool, as Swift well knew, boasting that he would make full use of it:

The greatest advantage I know of being thought a Wit by the World, is that it gives one the greater freedom of playing the Fool.

In this company, where all are wits, in this Augustan conversation, one may give oneself away completely; one need not be afraid of truth or wisdom, however much they may reveal the absurdities of the world or expose the weaknesses of man's nature.

The World is a thing we must of necessity either laugh at, or be angry at; if we laugh at it, they say we are proud; if we are angry at it, they say we are ill-natur'd.

We have just Religion enough to make us *Hate*, but not enough to make us *Love* one another.

But in this company, too, one might even hope for real understanding and a harmony unknown among the strife of political parties and the clamour of rival sects. In the possibility of experiencing among a few choice spirits the highest pleasure of rational beings, in the perfection of the art of conversation, the bond of society, and the means of fostering friendship, they believed that there might be a chance to create a little world of harmony and peace.

There is nothing wanting to make all rational and disinterested People in the World, of one Religion, but that they should talk together every Day.

If Swift was not himself the first to utter this remarkable statement, he at least set his mark against it, as a thought that he had treasured and approved. Even if it should only be regarded as the momentary product of an agreeable conversation in the friendly company of men of wit and understanding, it is hardly the sort of doctrine we should expect from him. For this is indeed a new way of salvation, not by praying together or working together or fighting together, but "that they should talk together every day."

And yet it is this very belief in the importance of conversation between rational and disinterested people and this preoccupation with the agreeable art of conversation that is a key to the understanding of many things in Swift's life and work, and perhaps also to some of the qualities of Augustan literature. It is, for instance, this almost extravagant notion of conversation that sharpens and intensifies his satire against all the things in society which at various levels threaten to ruin it.

It is this which drove him to develop the role of Bickerstaff, "whose pleasant writings," as Steele said, "had created an Inclination in the Town towards any Thing that could appear in the same Disguise." Though it is difficult to be quite sure how far Swift had a hand in the *Tatler* at first, Steele clearly acknowledges that "a certain uncommon Way of Thinking, and a Turn in Conversation peculiar to that agreeable Gentleman rendered his Company very advantageous to one whose Imagination was to be continually employed upon obvious and common Subjects." In fact, the *Tatler* began as another of the fruits of the actual conversation of the Augustans, and although later Steele seemed to Swift to have forfeited all right to be considered as a friend or as a rational and disinterested person because of the violence of party hatred which developed in him, Swift could claim with justice that in the days of his power he had tried to help Steele and had wished to remain on friendly terms with those whom he admired in spite of their politics. He continued to express his great admiration for Addison, and in the Preface to their *Miscellanies* joined with Pope in apologizing for anything in their writings that had reflected upon the two distinguished members of the Kit-Kat Club whom they wished to associate with themselves in the full fellowship of the Augustans.

In regard to two Persons only, we wish our Raillery though ever so tender or Resentment, though ever so just, had not been indulged. We speak of Sir *John Vanbrugh*, who was a Man of Wit, and of Honour; and of Mr. *Addison*, whose Name deserves all Respect from every Lover of Learning.

It may be said, of course, that Sir John Vanbrugh had won Swift's respect as a notorious victim and enemy of the Duchess of Marlborough, whose treatment of the architect of Blenheim must have justified to Swift's mind the worst he had ever said of her. But Pope and Swift would have recognized in his very successful plays some of the qualities of conversation, which he, like Congreve, had transferred to the theatre for the purposes of satire and comedy; and they did not wish to be separated from any of those rational and disinterested spirits who were engaged in different ways in the same task of refining the conversation of the age.

That task had been clearly described in Swift's letter to Isaac Bickerstaff, which was printed in the *Tatler* of September 28, 1710: it was to prevent the corruption of the English language and be "the instrument of introducing into our style that simplicity, which is the best and truest ornament of most Things in human life, which the politer Ages always aimed at in their Building and Dress, (*Simplex munditiis*) as well as their productions of wit." If the art of conversation was to be maintained as a means of easy and agreeable communication between civilized men and women the language of conversation must be kept free from all pedantries, all technical jargon, and all fashionable affectations. The witty and the clever and the learned must alike be reminded that the greatest virtues are modesty and common sense:

> Fine sense and exalted sense are not half so useful as common sense: There are forty men of wit for one man of sense: And he that will carry about him nothing but gold, will be every day at a loss for want of readier change.

And again:

> Modesty, if it were to be recommended for nothing else, this were enough, that the pretending to little leaves a man at ease, whereas boasting requires a perpetual labour to appear what he is not: If we have sense, modesty best proves it to others; if we have none, it best hides our want of it.

The lack of any kind of pretension in language—that is the secret of power; that simplicity and ease which comes of modesty and good sense at the same time avoids all obscurity and allows the full effect of all that is there to be perceived and felt. We may have to admit that in his impatience at all kinds of pedantry Swift pushes his argument against "hard words" and technical terms to the point of absurdity; and Dr. Johnson had no difficulty in replying with good effect. Any lexicographer's feelings would be outraged by some of the things Swift says in his *Letter to the Lord Treasurer*, containing a "Proposal for Correcting, Improving and Ascertaining the English Tongue," or even in his *Letter to a Young Clergy-Man*. But in exalting the art of conversation, and in making the standards of that art his criterion for all forms of communication through language, he was obliged to emphasize those virtues which insure that everyone in the company will be easy, because there is nothing that they will not understand. Nevertheless, if the English learned tradition is a little less liable to certain forms of professionalism and pedantry than other traditions, this may be in part due to the strength of this Augustan tradition and to a fear of becoming a victim of that

Bickerstaffian laughter which is still liable to break over the heads of the unwary.

The danger of this tradition is that in trying to avoid the learned jargon of academies and schools it may easily degenerate to the level of the mere club, and sink into emptiness and ease to the exclusion of the more vigorous intellectual activities. Most of the Augustans were clubmen of some kind or other, even if the club was very small and did not long survive as a unit, like the Scriblerus Club for which Swift was himself largely responsible. The Brothers Club had seemed to him too large as well as too extravagant to serve the purposes of conversation, and new members had constantly been introduced in spite of Swift's opposition. He was doubtless happiest and easiest in a select group of men united in the bonds of friendship. But in one very important respect Swift was not a clubman at all, for at the end of his "Essay on Conversation" he makes a vigorous protest against the custom which had for some time past arisen in English society of excluding women, except in parties at play, or dancing, or in the pursuit of an amour. That he regards as the chief cause of the degeneracy of manners after the Restoration; it had been very different before in that great age to which he always looked back with the highest admiration.

I take the highest period of politeness in England (and it is of the same date in France) to have been the peaceable part of King Charles the First's reign; and from what we read of those times, as well as from the accounts I have formerly met with from some who lived in that court, the methods then used for raising and cultivating conversation, were altogether different from ours. Several ladies, whom we find celebrated by the poets of that age, had assemblies at their houses, where persons of the best understanding, and of both sexes, met to pass the evenings in discoursing upon whatever agreeable subjects were occasionally started.

It was because of this belief in the value of conversation in a mixed society, which is of course strongly emphasized in the French tradition,[1] that Swift satirizes so violently the manners of the modern Lady, whose habits and tastes have put an end to

---

[1] Cf., for example, the chapter in which the Abbé de Bellegarde discusses the advantage of "converse with the Fair Sex" as a part of the education of a young man for polite society, and particularly as a way of civilizing the scholar and pedant.

the possibility of all agreeable conversation. For instance, in *The Journal of a Modern Lady*, in his hard rough lines he gives a Hogarthian picture of a fashionable tea-party:

> But let me now a while survey
> Our Madam o'er her Ev'ning Tea;
> Surrounded with her Noisy Clans
> Of Prudes, Coquets and Harridans;
>
> . . . . . . . . . . .
>
> Or how should I, alas! relate
> The sum of all their senseless Prate,
> Their Inuendoes, Hints and Slanders
> Their Meanings lewd, and double Entendres?
>
> . . . . . . . . . . .
>
> Now Voices over Voices rise;
> While each to be the loudest vies,
> They contradict, affirm, dispute,
> No single Tongue one Moment mute;
> All mad to speak, and none to hearken,
> They set the very Lap-Dog barking;
> Their Chattering makes a louder Din
> Than Fishwives o'er a Cup of Gin:
> Not Schoolboys at a Barring out
> Raised ever such incessant Rout:
> The jumbling Particles of Matter
> In Chaos made not such a clatter:
> Far less the Rabble roar and rail,
> When drunk with sour Election Ale.

And it was likewise because of his firm belief in the importance of women's influence in refining the manners of society, and providing the right atmosphere for agreeable conversation, that he continued far more seriously than either Addison or Steele, at all times in public and in private, in verse and in prose, to concern himself with the education of women. In his *Letter to a Young Lady on Her Marriage* he is entirely concerned to prepare her to take her proper place in her husband's circle of friends, and it may be noted that he is even more insistent in recommending to women the importance of mixed society:

I advise that your Company at home should consist of Men rather than Women. To say the Truth, I never yet knew a tolerable Woman to be fond of her own Sex: I confess, when both are mixt and well chosen, and put their best Qualities forward, there may be an Intercourse of Civility and Good-will; which, with the Addition of some Degree of Sense, can make Conversation or any Amusement agreeable. But a Knot of Ladies, got together by themselves, is a very School of Impertinence and Detraction; and it is well if those be the worst.

He then recommends a course of study and a suitable circle of acquaintance by which to correct her taste and judgment, and promises that thus she may, in time, hope to become a reasonable and agreeable companion.

Among his friends in Dublin and in the country during the latter part of his life in Ireland he maintained a rigorous discipline, always striving by a mixture of raillery and compliment to provide himself with a society for easy conversation. How important this was to him may be realized from the almost tender solicitude with which he addresses Delany, when an incident had occurred in which the crudity of one of Sheridan's jests had threatened to disturb the pleasant relations among them:

> Bestow your friend some good Advice;
> One Hint from you will set him right,
> And teach him how to be polite.
>
> . . . . . . . . . . . .
>
> What use in life to make men fret,
> Part in worse humour than they met?
> Thus all society is lost,
> Men laugh at one another's cost:
> And half the company is teazed
> That came together to be pleased:
> For all buffoons have most in view
> To please themselves by vexing you.

He looks for such pleasure from the proper mingling of humour and raillery and wit that his anger is aroused by the "pert Dunces of Mankind" who cannot distinguish between raillery and gross abuse, but

> To show their Parts, will scold and rail,
> Like Porters o'er a Pot of Ale.

He does not exaggerate when he says that for the whole of

the latter half of his life he had been careful to observe the habits of conversation of society on all occasions, and that he had taken more than thirty years in the preparation of his treatise on Polite Conversation. In this "perfection of folly," as he himself called it, he promises to deal with the subject finally. He will establish the whole art of conversation in England by providing wit and humour suitable for all occasions and companies, which can never be outdated because every single sample has been already fixed by traditional usage for at least a hundred years. When he was too ill and deaf himself to enjoy company any longer it must have afforded him a grim amusement to go on collecting material for this strange comedy of dullness; but when he had finished the dialogue he could give full play in the introductory essay to his feelings of indignation at the abuse of this innocent pleasure. This feeling is mingled with his disgust at the flat stupidity of the tasteless moneyed society of the Whig Hanoverian era, already so violently expressed in his *Rhapsody on Poetry* and in his *Directions for a Birthday Song*. In the same mood of irony he now writes with pride and eloquence of the glories of his own dear country, which has outdone all the nations of Europe in advancing the art of polite conversation to the greatest height it is capable of reaching. Here he will provide all that anyone could want with perfect models, far better than any of these Frenchmen or Italians, a collection so full and complete that all the genius and politeness of England is summed up in it. It had cost him such pains to be sure that nothing was irrecoverably lost forever that he might well expect at a proper juncture the public thanks of both Houses of Parliament—

I may venture to affirm, without the least violation of modesty, that there is no man, now alive, who hath, by many degrees so just pretensions as myself, to the highest encouragement from the crown, the parliament, and the ministry, towards bringing this work to its due perfection. I have been assured, that several great heroes of antiquity were worshipped as gods, upon the merit of having civilized a fierce and barbarous people. It is manifest, I could have no other intentions.

If only his treatise had been published some years ago, it would have prevented the corruption of hundreds of thousands, by turning the nobility and gentry from politics to politeness; for politeness is the firmest foundation upon which loyalty can be supported.

For thus happily sings the divine Mr. Tibbalds, or Theobalds, in one of his birthday poems:

> I am no schollard; but I am polite:
> Therefore be sure I am no Jacobite.

Hear likewise our most illustrious laureat Mr. Colley Cibber:

> Who in his talk can't speak a polite thing,
> Will never loyal be to George our King.

And even on the title page, which imitates the form of the books which provided models of conversation, he points his satire directly against the influence of the court of George II; his models of conversation are "according to the polite mode and method now used at court, and in the best companies of England."

Swift must now have felt that he had at last dealt thoroughly with this subject which thirty years earlier had seemed to him to have been too seldom or too slightly handled. He may have noticed an essay which was written by Lord Chesterfield, *Common Sense*, No. 54, dated February 11, 1738, concerned with a fresh menace to conversation, which he had overlooked. This was the new kind of table-talk introduced as a result of the fashionable interest in French cooking and the absorption of all the company in discussing the merits of each dish.

The frugal meal was antiently the time of unbending the mind by chearful and improving conversation, and the table-talk of ingenious men has been thought worth transmitting to posterity. The meal is now at once the most frivolous and the most serious part of life. The mind is bent to the utmost, and all the attention exerted, for what? The critical examination of compound dishes: and if any two or three people happen to start some useful or agreeable subject of conversation, they are soon interrupted, and overpowered by the extatic interjections of, excellent! exquisite! delicious! Pray taste this, you never eat a better thing in your life. Is that good? Is it tender? Is it seasoned enough? Would it have been better so? Of such wretched stuff as this does the present table-talk wholly consist, in open defiance of all conversation and common sense.

Within Swift's lifetime there also appeared another "Essay on Conversation," which is of interest as being the work of Fielding, and included by him in the first volume of his *Miscellanies*, 1743. In the traditional manner he discusses first the whole aspect of social intercourse—the art of pleasing or doing good to one another—and the proper behaviour on specific occasions to be expected from persons of good breeding and good manners; and then separately he considers the art of conversation with respect to the use of words in discourse, which is the chief means to bring delight and pleasure to mankind. But he is evidently a little weary of the Olympian airs of the Augustans, if we may judge from the tone of this passage:

the highest Pleasure which we are capable of enjoying in Conversation, is to be met with only in the Society of Persons whose Understanding is pretty near on an Equality with our own: nor is this Equality only necessary to enable Men of exalted Genius and extensive Knowledge to taste the sublimer Pleasures of communicating their refined Ideas to each other; but it is likewise necessary to the inferior Happiness of every subordinate Degree of Society, down to the very lowest.

On this he bases all his subsequent advice. Since we cannot expect always to find this equality in general society, certain things must be avoided, like pedantry or unlimited raillery, if conversation is to be agreeable to all. He does not challenge the Augustan ideal; like them he regards it as the chief art of human life, but he is more aware that it is also necessary to the happiness of the subordinate levels of society.

It is not my intention to trace the discussion of these ideas any further, but rather to consider briefly the powerful influence they exercized over all forms of Augustan literature.

Professor James Sutherland has already pointed out in his *Preface to Eighteenth Century Poetry* that it is necessary for a proper understanding of the century not to forget the value then placed upon good conversation. He notes that the very qualities of that conversation are also the qualities of its most characteristic prose and poetry. "The poetry of that century, however remote its diction may sometimes be from the idiom of contemporary speech, has at least this in common with conversation that it is consciously addressed to someone else." The poet "is not murmuring to himself alone." I would go so far as to say that the poetry of the Augustans is at its best when it is most conversational in tone; when it is topical, easy, and gay; when it is intimate, whether it is serving the purpose of compliment or raillery. Such poetry must obviously not embarrass us by a display of passion or by a striving for originality or by a show of unconventional learning. It is not intended for meditation or hard study; it is written to be passed round after dinner and enjoyed in company. Swift gives us a glimpse of such a scene in the *Journal to Stella*, October 15, 1710:

> After dinner came in Lord Peterborow: we renewed our acquaintance and he grew mightily fond of me. They began to talk of a paper of verses called *Sid Hamet*. Mr. Harley repeated part, and then pulled them out, and gave them to a gentleman at the table to read, though they had all read them often: Lord Peterborow would let nobody read them but himself: so he did; and Mr. Harley bobbed me at every line to take notice of the Beauties. Prior rallied Lord Peterborow for author of them: and Lord Peterborow said, he knew them to be his; and Prior then turned it upon me, and I on him. I am not guessed at all in town to be the author; yet so it is: but that is a secret only to you. Ten to one whether you see them in Ireland; yet here they run prodigiously.

It is the ideal of the Augustan poet to be

> Blest with each talent, and each art to please
> And born to write, converse and live with ease.

There are still, of course, formal occasions of public mourning or of national rejoicing when he may need to use a more elaborate ceremonial; there are still poet laureates and their odes— but all the most significant poetry of the Augustans is modulated inevitably to a conversational rhythm. This is certainly true of Swift; it is perhaps almost equally true of Pope and Prior and Parnell and Gay.

But it was not only in familiar verse, in satire and in comedy and in pieces of wit, humour, and raillery that we find these qualities of good conversation. They appear also in the more serious prose of the time and account for the peculiar ease and urbanity which mark the writings of the moralists and philosophers. They affect the tone of that most popular preacher of the day, the Spectator in his Saturday sermons, even when he is venturing to speak of Eternity and describe his vision of the Golden

Scales, an image used almost a century earlier by another famous preacher, the Dean of St. Paul's in his Second Prebend Sermon. The contrast between these two passages provides a startling illustration of the change in the way in which such topics could be dealt with. Donne's voice is the voice of one preaching to himself out of the depths of his own religious experience, "like an Angel out of a cloud," as Walton had said, as with his magnificent rhetoric he lifts us up through all the afflictions and sufferings of mortal life to the final pinnacle of despair, where the human soul recognizes its utter worthlessness before God:

mine enemy is not an imaginary enemy, fortune, nor a transitory enemy, malice in great persons, but a reall and an irresistible, and an inexorable and an everlasting enemy, the Lord of Hosts himselfe, the Almighty God himselfe, the Almighty God himselfe only knows the waight of this affliction and except he put in that *pondus gloriae*, that exceeding waight of an eternal glory, with his own hand into the other scale, we are waighed downe, we are swallowed up irreparably, irrevocably, irrecoverably, irremediably.

How different is this from the urbane conversation of Addison, who had been "entertaining himself" with comparing the use of this image of the scales in Homer and Virgil, in the Bible and in Milton:

These several amusing thoughts having taken possession of my mind some time before I went to sleep, and mingling with my ordinary ideas, raised in my imagination a very odd kind of vision. . . . I saw, methought, a pair of golden scales . . . and great heaps of weights thrown down on each side of them.

With these he makes several experiments, not being able to tell the real weight of them until he has put them in the scales.

This I found by several instances, for upon my laying a weight in one of the scales, which was inscribed by the word Eternity; though I threw in that of time, prosperity, affliction, wealth, poverty, interest, success, with any other weights, which in my hand seemed very ponderous, they were not able to stir the opposite balance, nor could they have prevailed, though assisted with the weight of the sun, the stars, and the earth.

Here for a moment there is a danger that the easy, urbane style might be disturbed by a note of solemnity—the very word "prevailed" might bring to some the echo of a sterner music—but at once we are brought back again to the table, and the game proceeds pleasantly, until at last we are gaily trying in the golden scales the balance between the sexes, or weighing Whigs against Tories.

The same conversational quality, the same awareness of the presence of a polite audience may be found in the writings of the philosophers. We find it, for instance, in the *Three Dialogues* of Berkeley, even when his design is no less than "plainly to demonstrate the reality and perfection of humane knowledge, the incorporeal nature of the soul, and the immediate providence of a Deity." Note the insinuating address of the Preface of the 1713 edition, as he places himself on the side of the ordinary readers against the prejudices of the professional philosophers:

> . . . it has been my Aim to introduce the Notions I advance, into the Mind, in the most easy and familiar manner; especially, because they carry with them a great Opposition to the Prejudices of Philosophers, which have so far prevailed against the common Sense and natural Notions of Mankind.
>
> . . .
>
> . . . methinks, this Return to the simple Dictates of Nature, after having wandered thorow the wild Mazes of Philosophy, is not unpleasant. It is like coming home from a long Voyage: A Man reflects with Pleasure on the many Difficulties and Perplexities he has passed thorow, sets his Heart at ease, and enjoys himself with more Satisfaction for the future.

That expresses very pleasantly the complacence and confident satisfaction of the Augustans, who felt that the spirit of man after long and strange wanderings had come back at last to a comfortable home, where it could with ease and pleasure concern itself with its own particular human affairs. There they were anxious to inculcate good manners and an urbanity in discourse which would put the company at ease with one another. It might impose restraints and set certain limits; it would be on its guard against eccentricities and extravagance and enthusiasm; but it would be able to tolerate a great variety of gifts, for it valued wit and raillery and humour; and, finally, it would assume that the company would always be ready to explore in their conversation and in their writings all the many delightful vagaries of the comedy of human life.

# SOME ASPECTS OF MEDICINE REFLECTED IN SEVENTEENTH-CENTURY LITERATURE WITH SPECIAL REFERENCE TO THE PLAGUE OF 1665

## John F. Fulton

L ATE into dark December nights of the year 1664 London citizens sat up to watch a new blazing star, with "mighty talk" thereupon. King Charles II. and his Queen gazed out of the windows at Whitehall. About east it rose, reaching no great altitude, and sank below the south-west horizon between two and three o'clock. In a week or two it was gone, then letters came from Vienna notifying the like sight of a brilliant comet, and "in the ayre the appearance of a Coffin, which causes great anxiety of thought amongst the people." . . . In March there came into the heavens a yet brighter comet, visible two hours after midnight, and so continuing till daylight. With such ominous portents the Great Plague in London was ushered in.[1]

To endeavor to write the history of medicine using contemporary literature as one's chief source of information would, of course, be folly, but to write it without examining the prose, poetry, and drama of a given era is to ignore a rich source of information concerning the social forces resulting from or impinging upon events in medicine. Such an event was the great plague in London in 1665.

Richard F. Jones has long aimed to bridge the gap between science and letters and in so doing has been a source of inspiration to many in the sciences who believe that humanistic values must be maintained in our general educational programs and especially

[1] W. G. Bell, *The Great Plague in London in 1665* (London: John Lane, The Bodley Head, 1924), p. 1.

in the teaching of the sciences themselves. Previously I have attempted to trace the impact of scientific discovery on the literature of the seventeenth and eighteenth centuries;[2] I must now pay tribute to Professor Jones by examining some aspects of medicine in the literature of the seventeenth century, particularly the progress of the great plague as reflected in the diarists of the period, Evelyn and Pepys, whose journals have long been a source of information about their life and times. What they recorded about the plague is of especial interest, and it has been used extensively by Walter George Bell in his history of the plague years, a detailed study published in 1924 which can be enthusiastically recommended as background material to any who wish to pursue the subject closely. Bell devotes considerable attention to the best-known literary piece about the plague, long the principal source of information about it—Daniel Defoe's *Journal of the Plague Year*.[3] Although based primarily on fact, this volume must be looked upon as a novel and not a documented historical treatise; furthermore, it did not appear until 1722, fifty-seven years later, when rumors of a plague in Marseilles set Defoe's imaginative mind to work on reconstructing events in London which had occurred when he was five years old. The story was dramatic in itself, but Defoe took a few liberties nonetheless. The result was an immediate and continuing success, and nearly two centuries were to pass before another student of the plague called into question some aspects of Defoe's fascinating account.

In approaching a study of the plague it must be remembered that the population of London at that time was something less than five hundred thousand, that probably half of the populace fled from the city as the plague spread, and that the most conservative figures indicate that at least a hundred thousand, or approximately half the remaining population of London, suc-

[2] J. F. Fulton, *Humanism in an Age of Science. Being a Ludwig Mond Lecture Delivered at the Manchester School of Medicine 6 October 1949* (New York: Henry Schuman, 1950).

[3] Daniel Defoe, *A Journal of the Plague Year: Being Observations or Memorials, of the Most Remarkable Occurrences, as Well Public as Private, Which Happened in London During the Last Great Visitation in 1665. Written by a Citizen Who Continued All the While in London. Never Made Publick Before* (London: 1722).

cumbed. The *Bills of Mortality*[4] which were published weekly
show the rise and fall of plague incidence during the summer
and autumn of 1665 (and even into the winter and spring of
1666), and while the final summation for the year indicates a
total of 68,596 having died of the plague, all authorities believe
this an underestimate because many deaths were unrecorded and
also because there were many deaths from undiagnosed "fever"
and especially "spotted fever" which in all likelihood could
largely be attributed to the epidemic scourge.

The plague was a disease of the poor. It had been twenty
years since it had appeared in London in epidemic proportions,
but the crowded, dirty tenements where sanitary science was unknown, the open sewers and careless disposal of refuse offered
fertile breeding ground for the disease when it appeared in viru-
lent form in 1665. The King and his court and large numbers of
the educated and the wealthy fled the city, leaving but a few of
the more courageous of their number to carry on the business of
the city. Among these were John Evelyn and Samuel Pepys.
Evelyn had just been appointed one of the commissioners to care
for the sick and wounded and prisoners of war from the recently
declared war with Holland; Pepys was Surveyor-General of the
Victualling Office, and as such he functioned as an undersecretary
of the Royal Navy. On July 3 Pepys entered in his journal:
". . . Resolving from this night forwards to close all my letters,
if possible, and end all my business at the office by daylight, and I
shall go near to do it and put all my affairs in the world in good
order, the season growing so sickly, that it is much to be feared
how a man can escape having a share with others in it, for which
the good Lord God bless me, or to be fitted to receive it."[5] Six
days later he mentioned the "solemn fast day"—the fast which

[4] *London's Dreadful Visitation: or, a Collection of All the Bills of Mortality for This Present Year; Beginning the 27th of December 1664, and
Ending the 19th of December Following: as Also, the General or Whole Year's
Bill: According to the Report Made to the King's Most Excellent Majesty, by
the Company of Parish-Clerks of London, &c.* (London: E. Cotes, 1665).

[5] H. B. Wheatley (ed.), *The Diary of Samuel Pepys, M.A. F.R.S.*
(London: G. Bell and Sons, Ltd., 1920), V, 2. All the quotations which
follow are from the Wheatley edition.

was to be observed within the cities of London and Westminster and adjacent places on the first Wednesday of every month for the duration of the plague.

Both Pepys and Evelyn followed the weekly *Bills of Mortality* and carefully recorded the growing number of deaths and their concern over the seriousness of the situation. On the 28th of August Evelyn wrote: "The contagion still increasing and growing now all about us, I sent my Wife and whole family (two or three necessary servants excepted) to my Brother's at Wotton, being resolved to stay at my house myselfe, and to looke after my charge, trusting in the providence and goodnesse of God."[6] Evelyn, to take his mind off the melancholy subject, regularly joined his friends of the Royal Society who were carrying on their experiments without interruption. "On my returne I call'd at Durdans, where I found Dr. Wilkins, Sʳ Wᵐ Petty, and Mr. Hooke, contriving chariots, new rigging for ships, a wheele for one to run races in, and other mechanical inventions; perhaps three such persons together were not to be found elsewhere in Europe for parts and ingenuity" (1665, August 4).

During the week of September 5 to 12 the deaths reached a new high, 6,988 being recorded. There were also 364 deaths from fever and 157 from spotted fever during that week. Evelyn recorded on the 7th: "Came home [from Chatham], there perishing neere 10,000 poor creatures weekly; however, I went all along the citty and suburbs from Kent Streete to St. James's, a dismal passage, and dangerous to see so many coffines expos'd in the streetes, now thin of people; the shops shut up, and all in mourneful silence, not knowing whose turn might be next. I went to yᵉ Duke of Albemarle for a pest-ship, to wait on our infected men, who were not a few."

Pepys also gives us a vivid picture of the plague-stricken city (August 12): "The people die so, that now it seems they are fain to carry the dead to be buried by day-light, the nights not sufficing to do it in. And my Lord Mayor commands people to be within at nine at night all, as they say, that the sick may have

[6] H. B. Wheatley (ed.), *Diary of John Evelyn Esq.*, F.R.S. (London: Bickers and Son, 1906), II, 186.

liberty to go abroad for ayre." He also makes other comments on the measures that had to be resorted to in burying the plague victims:

> I went away and walked to Greenwich, in my way seeing a coffin with a dead body therein, dead of the plague, lying in an open close belonging to Coome farme, which was carried out last night, and the parish have not appointed any body to bury it; but only set a watch there day and night, that nobody should go thither or come thence, which is a most cruel thing: this disease making us more cruel to one another than if we are doggs. (August 22)

And again:

> Church being done, my Lord Bruncker, Sir J. Minnes, and I up to the Vestry at the desire of the Justices of the Peace, Sir Theo. Biddulph and Sir W. Boreman and Alderman Hooker, in order to the doing something for the keeping of the plague from growing; but Lord! to consider the madness of the people of the town, who will (because they are forbid) come in crowds along with the dead corps to see them buried; but we agreed on some orders for the prevention thereof. Among other stories, one was very passionate, methought, of a complaint brought against a man in the towne for taking a child from London from an infested house. Alderman Hooker told us it was the child of a very able citizen in Gracious Street, a saddler, who had buried all the rest of his children of the plague, and himself and wife now being shut up and in despair of escaping, did desire only to save the life of this little child; and so prevailed to have it received stark-naked into the arms of a friend, who brought it (having put it into new fresh clothes) to Greenwich; where upon hearing the story, we did agree it should be permitted to be received and kept in the towne. (September 3)

These measures—the closing of the shops, night burials, isolation of patients, and quarantine of houses—described by Evelyn and Pepys were the result of *Orders Conceived and Published by the Lord Mayor and Aldermen of the City of London, Concerning the Infection of the Plague*, "printed by James Flesher, Printer to the Honourable City of London." This extremely rare brochure of eight leaves is undated but it is believed to have been published in May or June of 1665.[7] The *Orders*

---

[7] W. G. Bell, *op. cit.*, pp. 73 ff. The Historical Library at Yale is fortunate in possessing one of the few copies of these *Orders* still extant.

revealed some appreciation of the public health problems involved, but its framers reckoned without the panic which prevailed throughout the city as the plague increased in violence, leaving far too few to cope with the desperate situation. The enlightened clause which permitted a man owning two houses to isolate those sick with the plague in one with proper care, and thus to give those still healthy a chance to escape infection, was not in practice allowed because of the mistaken fear that contagion would thus be more widely spread.

If there could be anything amusing about the picture which London presented when the plague was at its height in September, it is to be found in a diary entry made by Pepys on the 3d: "Up; and put on my coloured silk suit very fine, and my new periwigg, bought a good while since, but durst not wear, because the plague was in Westminster when I bought it; and it is a wonder what will be the fashion after the plague is done, as to periwiggs, for nobody will dare to buy any haire, for fear of the infection, that it had been cut off of the heads of people dead of the plague."

In the light of later knowledge the attempts of seventeenth-century London to cope with the disaster which had befallen it are full of pathos. Even the parochial division of the city government, with its sharp distinction between the City and the adjoining parishes and its jealously individualistic separate officers, conspired against any efficient handling of the emergency. And, as Bell points out, "neither law nor civil administration, nor medicine itself, had any real enlightenment." Had physicians had the wit to learn the lesson of former plagues, or even the wisdom to enforce the *Orders*, many who died might have been saved.

Evelyn, whose duty it was to find homes or nursing establishments for the sick and wounded returning from the war, had a glimmering of the importance of segregation. He suggested at this time the construction of an infirmary—in the immediate future it would obviate the necessity of farming the men out in homes where they were open to infection and in the long run it would save public monies because of the obvious economy of one official establishment over numerous private accommodations.

Evelyn retained an interest in medicine throughout his life, and there are many informative references in his diary to physicians and current developments in medicine. I should like to quote, although an earlier entry, his excellent description of a "cure" which had gained great popularity:

His Majestie began first to *touch for y^e evil*, according to custome, thus: his Ma^tie sitting under his state in the Banquetting house, the chirurgeons cause the sick to be brought or led up to the throne, where they kneeling, y^e King strokes their faces or cheekes with both his hands at once, at which instant a chaplaine in his formalities says, "He put his hands upon them and he healed them." This is sayd to every one in particular. When they have ben all touch'd they come up again in the same order, and the other chaplaine kneeling, and having angel gold strung on white ribbon on his arme, delivers them one by one to his Ma^tie, who puts them about the necks of the touched as they passe, whilst the first chaplaine repeats, "this is y^e true light who come into y^e world." Then followes an Epistle (as at first a Gospell) with the Liturgy, prayers for the sick, with some alteration, lastly y^e blessing; and then the Lo. Chamberlaine and the Comptroller of the Household bring a basin, ewer and towell, for his Ma^tie to wash. (1660, July 6)

John Aubrey also described the prevailing belief in the miraculous powers of the King. "Arise Evans had a fungous Nose, and said, it was reveal'd to him, that the King's Hand would Cure him: And at the first coming of King Charles II into St. Jame's Park he kiss'd the King's Hand, and rubb'd his Nose with it; which disturb'd the King, but Cured him."[8]

But the refreshing breeze of skepticism was beginning to blow ever so gently. "Dr. Ralph Bathurst, Dean of Wells and one of the Chaplains to King Charles, who is no Superstitious Man," Aubrey recorded, "protested to me that the curing of the King's Evill by the Touch of the King does puzzle his Philosophie: for whether they were of the House of Yorke, or Lancaster, it did. 'Tis true (indeed) there are Prayers read at the Touching, but neither the King minds them nor the Chaplains."

[8] O. L. Dick, "The Life and Times of John Aubrey," in *Aubrey's Brief Lives. Edited from the Original Manuscripts and with an Introduction by Oliver Lawson Dick* (London: Secker and Warburg, 1949), p. lxix.

And Aubrey further wrote: "In Somersetshire 'tis confidently reported that some were Cured of the King's evil, by the Touch of the Duke of Monmouth: The Lord Chancellor Bacon saith, That Imagination is next Kin to Miracle-working Faith."[9]

As Richard Jones has frequently pointed out, the seventeenth century was an era of vast intellectual readjustment in which men were beginning to break with classical authority, especially in the sphere of medicine and science. Men were commencing to turn to Nature for answers to their questions where previously they had been content to follow the ancients or whatever practice superstition dictated. "Till about the yeare 1649," Aubrey explained, "when Experimental Philosophy was first cultivated by a Club at Oxford, 'twas held a strange presumption for a Man to attempt an Innovation in Learnings; and not to be good Manners, to be more knowing than his Neighbours and Forefathers; even to attempt an improvement in Husbandry (though it succeeded with profit) was look'd upon with an ill Eie. Their Neighbours did scorne to follow it, though not to doe it was to their own Detriment. 'Twas held a Sin to make a Scrutinie into the Waies of Nature; Whereas it is certainly a profound part of Religion to glorify God in his Workes; and to take no notice at all of what is dayly offered before our Eyes is grosse Stupidity."[10] Altogether, Aubrey concluded, that "in those times, to have had an inventive and enquiring Witt, was accounted Affectation, which censure the famous Dr. William Harvey could not escape for his admirable Discovery of the Circulation of the Blood."[11] A hint of this is given in the reference to Ent made by Dryden in his laudatory verse addressed to Dr. Walter Charleton and published in Charleton's book, *Chorea Gigantum, or, the Most Famous Antiquity of Great-Britan Vulgarly Called Stone-heng, Standing on Salisbury Plain, Restored to the Danes.* Ent, a distinguished member of the Royal College of Physicians, was a staunch supporter of Harvey in the furor which attended his announcement of the discovery of the circulation.

[9] *Ibid.*
[10] *Ibid.*, p. xlii.
[11] *Ibid.*

> . . . The World to *Bacon* does not onely owe
> Its present Knowledge, but its future too.
> Gilbert shall live, till *Load-stones* cease to draw
> Or *British* Fleets the boundless Ocean awe.
> And noble *Boyle*, not less in *Nature* seen,
> Than his great Brother read in *States* and *Men.*
> The *Circling* streams, once thought but pools,
>                                of blood
> (Whether Life's fewel, or the Bodie's food)
> From dark Oblivion *Harvey's* name shall save·
> While *Ent* keeps all the honour that he gave.

Among the most vehement and vocal in forcing upon the common man recognition of the new experimental philosophy so actively espoused by the early members of the Royal Society were a large number of physicians. Of the group of 132 charter members of the Royal Society, enumerated in their first election list of 1663, there were twenty-five physicians. These, to be sure, were the more conventional and socially prominent within the profession. But there were also some "irregulars," such as Noah Biggs and George Starkey. About Biggs there appears to be no information; Starkey was a Bermudian who, during his attendance at Harvard College (he was graduated in the Class of 1646), was encouraged in his interest in chemistry by the younger John Winthrop. He gave up a medical practice in Boston and moved to London about 1650 and there became a friend of Robert Boyle, to whom he dedicated his *Nature's Explication and Helmont's Vindication*, published in 1657. Starkey died in 1665 of the plague, contemporary sources naming him among some members of the College of Physicians who had the courage to dissect the corpse of a plague victim and who were thus infected. Bell, however, believes there was probably no dissection other than that recorded by Dr. George Thomson in his *Loimotomia; or the Pest Anatomized* (1666)[12] and that Starkey was a victim to his devotion to his patients. But this point need not concern us here. Biggs and Starkey are important to this discussion because of their vigorous attacks on medical practices of the times, on slavish devotion to classical authority,

[12] W. G. Bell, *op. cit.*, pp. 203–6.

and for an equally vigorous espousal of the experimental method. In a remarkable book, *Matæotechnia Medicinæ Praxeos*,[13] which was discussed by Richard Jones in his *Ancients and Moderns*,[14] Biggs carries his attack to the universities, believing their stagnation to be due to their unquestioning reliance on the teachings of the ancients. The "humble motion for the reformation of the universities" promised in his subtitle gives no hint of the impassioned plea for reform which he urged upon them. He advocated a "thorough and early plowing up the fallow ground of the universities, that she [*sic*] may be laboriously rummig'd in her stupendous bulk of blinde learning, and her rubbish cast out, and no longer be a *Quagmire* of pittiful learned idleness" (p. 230).

Starkey, in his aforementioned volume,[15] writes in the same vehement style, and as with Biggs his enthusiasm sometimes outran his judgment. But Richard Jones points out[16] that "no treatise discloses ardent loyalty to the ideal of the experimental and observational method more clearly than the following pas-

---

[13] Noah Biggs, *Matæotechnia Medicinæ Praxeos. The Vanity of the Craft of Physick. Or, a New Dispensatory. Wherein Is Dissected the Errors, Ignorance, Impostures and Supinities of the Schools, in Their Main Pillars of Purges, Blood-Letting, Fontanels or Issues, and Diet, &c. and the Particular Medicines of the Shops. With an Humble Motion for the Reformation of the Universities, and the Whole Landscap of Physick, and Discovering the Terra Incognita of Chymistrie. To the Parliament of England. By Noah Biggs, Chymiatrophilos* (London: Printed for Edward Blackmore, 1651).

[14] R. F. Jones, *Ancients and Moderns; A Study of the Background of the "Battle of the Books"* ("Washington University Studies, New Series, Language and Literature," No. 6 [St. Louis, 1936]), pp. 104–5, 138–39.

[15] George Starkey, *Natures Explication and Helmont's Vindication, or a Short and Sure Way to a Long and Sound Life: Being a Necessary and Full Apology for Chymical Medicaments, and a Vindication of Their Excellency Against Those Unworthy Reproaches Cast on the Art and Its Professors (such as were Paracelsus and Helmont) by Galenists, Usually Called Methodists. Whose Method So Adored, Is Examined, and Their Art Weighed in the Ballance of Sound Reason and True Philosophy, and Are Found Too Light in Reference to Their Promises, and Their Patients Expectation. The Remedy of Which Defects Is Taught, and Effectual Medicaments Discovered for the Effectual Cure of All Both Acute and Chronical Diseases. By George Starkey, a Philosopher Made by the Fire, and a Professor of That Medicine Which Is Real and Not Histrionical* (London: Thomas Alsop, 1657).

[16] R. F. Jones, *op. cit.*, p. 142.

sage, which glorifies even Starkey's confused conception of true science":

> Yet I know that although I consume and spend whatever moneys I can borrow from my bare necessity, or at utmost my most absolute conveniency, in Furnaces, Coals, and Glasses, with the Bee making Honey, but not for my self, yet the experience, which through Gods blessing this industry hath brought, doth and will bring me, will make my name live, when the names of hundreds, that bark and snarl at me, and load me with unworthy reproaches, shall lie buried in perpetual oblivion. . . . Whatever I do get I lay out in future discoveries, and all to do good to an ungrateful generation: oft times running in debt for conveniencies, and necessaries, and sparing out of my belly to find out new experiments in Medicine.[17]

Since that time there have been many George Starkeys who laid out everything "in future discoveries . . . oft times running in debt for conveniencies and necessaries," but the scientific progress thus dearly purchased has been no less thrilling than were its beginnings. Although science in the course of time has given us, among its many advantages, infinitely better means of communication than were available in the seventeenth century, it has at the same time pushed us farther apart, and the humanist and the scientist have lost the common ground where they were wont to meet for mutual stimulation. It seems to me that our salvation, as educators or individuals, lies in a return to the *spirit* of that age when those engaged in creating or fostering the art and literature of the period and those in medicine and the embryo sciences were interested in one another's fields and had some understanding of what transpired across the boundaries. In the words of the philosopher Josiah Royce, "Science is, or ought to be, poetry, and poetry is knowledge, and the humanity of the future will not divide life but will unite it."

[17] George Starkey, *op. cit.*, pp. 224–25.

# JOHN FOXE AND
# THE PURITAN REVOLUTION

### William Haller

In *An Harborowe for Faithfull and Trewe Subjects*, a spirited refutation, published in 1559, of *The Monstruous Regiment of Women*, John Aylmer, later Bishop of London, declared that his fellow countrymen ought to thank God seven times a day that they were born Englishmen and not Italians, Frenchmen, or Germans. For England was a land of plenty, abounding in beef and mutton, butter, cheese, and eggs, beer and ale, besides wool, lead, cloth, tin, and leather, and God and his angels fought on her side against her foreign foes. "God is English," declared a gloss in the margin. "For you fight," continued the text, "not only in the quarel of your country: but also and chieflye in defence of hys true religion, and of his deare sonne Christe." England says to her children:

God hathe brought forthe in me, the greatest and excellentest treasure that he hath, for your comfort and al the worldes. He would that out of my wombe should come that servaunt of his your brother John Wyclefe, who begate Husse, who begat Luther, who begat truth. What greter honour could you or I have, then that it pleased Christ as it were in a second birth to be borne again of me among you?

And a gloss in the margin reiterates, "Christes second birth in England."

Aylmer was hardly the first and certainly not the last Englishman to embrace the idea which he stated with such engaging assurance.[1] But for the generations that came after the accession

---

[1] "O blessed peace, oh happy Prince, O fortunate people: The lyuing God is onely the English God." John Lyly, *Euphues and his England*, 1580. (*Works*, II, 210, R. W. Bond, ed.)

of Elizabeth, at least down to the Puritan Revolution, the full authoritative explication of that idea was the work of Aylmer's companion in exile under Mary, John Foxe. The so-called "Book of Martyrs" was much more than the title by which it came to be popularly known implies. *Actes and Monuments of Matters Most Speciall and Memorable, Happenyng in the Church, with an Universall History of the Same,* as the work was actually entitled, was designed by the author to set before his countrymen in overwhelming detail a conception of universal history and of England's place in history, a conception which continued to prevail in the English mind long after the book had gone out of fashion though not out of use and memory. The pivotal fact of history, as Foxe presented it, involving every nation, institution, and individual, was the struggle of Christ and Antichrist for the soul of man. The climax of that struggle began with the Reformation, the Reformation began in England, and in England it was destined to reach its culmination in the final overthrow of Antichrist and the triumph of Christ and his church. Elizabethan chroniclers presented a view of English history which centered attention on the crown and the achievement of national unity under the crown. The view presented by Foxe centered on the English church in relation to the church at large and hence on England's place in the world, her historic calling and destiny. Though the one view appealed especially to Protestant sentiment, the two were not commonly regarded as anything but complementary until they were brought into conflict by the Puritan preachers at the outbreak of revolution in 1640.

Foxe was not, of course, by modern standards, an objective critical historian. Every page of his book is colored by religious and national prejudice, and the probity as well as the soundness of his scholarship has been challenged.[2] But such criticism is here beside the point. The point is that he supplied his countrymen with what seemed an authoritative account of the past, focused

[2] See especially S. R. Maitland, *Essays on . . . the Reformation in England,* 1849, and other writings. The most temperate and judicious account of Foxe so far published is J. F. Mozley, *John Foxe and His Book,* London, 1940. The fullest account of the bibliographical history of *Actes and Monuments* and of certain aspects of its reputation and influence is to be found in L. M. Oliver, "The Acts and Monuments of John Foxe," 1945, an unpublished Harvard dissertation.

upon England, her recent experience and present position in the world. The nature and scope of his accomplishment become clear when we follow the development of his book from its small beginning in 1554 to the final full-blown folios of 1583. The first draft of the work, *Commentarii rerum in ecclesia gestarum per totam Europam, persecutionum, à Vuicleui temporibus ad hanc aetatem descriptio. Liber primus,* was an octavo of 212 leaves, published at Strasbourg in 1554. In 1559 this had become a folio of 750 pages, *Rerum in Ecclesia gestarum,* published at Basel. In that year the author returned to England, and in 1563 published the first English version of his work, a folio of 1,741 pages, called *Actes and Monuments of These Latter and Perilous Dayes.* A second edition in two volumes and some twenty-three hundred pages followed in 1570, a third in 1576, and a fourth with the title in its final form in 1583. Foxe died in 1587, but his book was again reprinted in 1596, in 1620, in 1632, and in the crucial year of 1641. In 1571 convocation ordered that a copy be set up along with the Bible in cathedral churches and that every archbishop, bishop, archdeacon, dean, and resident canon should keep a copy in hall or dining room for servants and visitors. It was also installed in many parish churches, where we are told it can still sometimes be found.[3]

The point in history at which Foxe began his account of the church remained always for him a point of central significance. The *Commentarii* began with an account of Wycliffe and the Lollards, followed by some brief notice of Huss, Jerome of Prague, and Savonarola. The first book of *Rerum in Ecclesia gestarum* began at the same point, gave some additional account of Luther, went on in a second book to Henry VIII and Edward VI, and filled four remaining books with reports of current troubles of the author's countrymen under Mary. So far the work could be described as a history of the English church from the fourteenth century, focused on the contemporary situation with incidental reference to Continental reformers. It grew to its final proportions by the accretion of more tales of martyrs of all ages and countries but also by the extension of the general historical narrative before and after Wycliffe, who con-

[3] Mozley, *op. cit.,* 147.

tinued to hold a key position in the whole story. Before Wycliffe, Foxe carried his account farther and farther back into the history of England and of the church at large. After Wycliffe he gave more space to foreign reformers, but still more to fifteenth- and sixteenth-century English events, and most of all to the late unhappy time under Mary. He dedicated the work in its English form to Elizabeth, with the statement that, though the book might not serve for her reading or for that of the learned, being written in the vulgar tongue, she should consider the need of the ignorant flock committed to her government. "Who, as they have bene long . . . wrapt in blindnesse for lacke specially of Gods word, and partly also for wanting the light of history, pity I thought but that such should be helped, their ignoraunce relieved, and simplicity instructed."

The history of the church, as Foxe presented it, was the story of a decline and fall brought on by the willful corruption of men, followed by the attempted repression of God's word and the persecution of his faithful, but concluding through grace in the recovery of the gospel, the restoration of the church, and the certain hope of redemption. The process of recovery began with Wycliffe, who first brought back the light of the word to the people, and although Huss and Luther had carried reformation forward on the Continent, responsibility for its fulfillment still rested upon Wycliffe's countrymen, who had, therefore, been ever since the special objects of Antichrist's attack. This theme Foxe elaborated in ever greater detail in successive editions of his book after his return to England in 1559. In the first English version of *Actes and Monuments* he led up to Wycliffe and the Lollards with an account in a hundred eighteen pages of the previous history of the church from the beginning. By 1583 this introduction had grown to over four hundred pages, and his account of history after Wycliffe had grown on a corresponding scale. In 1563 he took only some four hundred pages in all to reach Henry VIII. Twenty years later he took over twice that number. Though many of the added pages were occupied with the last agonies of martyrs, these legends and the pictures which accompanied them were introduced not simply for the sensational effect which they undoubtedly had but still more for driving home to Englishmen the lesson of history in which they were framed.

The history of the church, Foxe explains, falls into five periods as foreshadowed by the mystic numerology of Revelation 11 and 12.[4] The first, of three hundred years, to which he devotes Book I of the final version of *Actes and Monuments*, was the time of the purity of the church and of its persecution by heathen emperors. Then came the second period of three hundred years, during which the church flourished in peace, thanks to Constantine, whose British connections were duly noted. In this period the Britons were Christianized by Joseph of Arimathea and missionaries sent by the Apostle Philip. But the Britons were conquered by Saxons, the Saxons were presently converted by Augustine, coming from Rome, and in the next three-hundred-year period, from Egbert to the Conqueror, the church began to decline, and though Alfred endeavored to promote piety and learning, the corrupting influence of the Roman clergy and of the monastic orders began to creep in.

This brings Foxe to the three hundred years from William the Conqueror to Wycliffe, "wherein is described the proud and misordered raigne of Antichrist, beginning to stirre in the Church of Christ." The two preceding books had given an account of British and Saxon times against the background of the general history of the church and of the growing power of the Bishop of Rome. Now Foxe tells the story of English kings down to Edward III, focused upon the struggle of English rulers to maintain the independence of the English crown and the English church against the aggressions of the papacy and its instruments. The stories of Henry and Becket, John and Langton are paralleled by stories of the strife of popes and emperors on the Continent. A woodcut depicts the emperor Henry IV with his wife and child barefoot in the snow at Canossa while monks and bishops jeer from behind castle walls and the pope sits beside the fire with a concubine in his lap. Another depicts Pope Alexander treading on the neck of the emperor Frederick. The meaning of all this seemed unmistakable. For a thousand years, Foxe

[4] Unless otherwise indicated, references to *Actes and Monuments* from this point on are to the edition of 1583.

says at the conclusion of his fourth book, Satan had been chained up and the church free from oppression. But "about this time," that is, toward the end of the thirteenth century, the evil one began "to be lo[o]sed and to come abroad, according to the forewarning of S. Johns Revalation." And if anyone thought this was not so, "let him consider and ponder well the tragicall rages, the miserable and most sorrowfull persecutions, murders, and vexations of these latter 300. yeares now following, and . . . he will be put out of all doubt to know, that not only Antechrist is already come, but also to know where he sitteth, & how he is now falling apace . . . to his decay and confusion."

So with the "fift Booke Conteyning the last 300. yeares from the loosing out of Satan" Foxe arrives at the crucial point in the story and in the case against Rome. Antichrist's way was to promote ignorance and superstition among the people, reduce their rulers to his tyrannous authority, and pursue true believers with fire and sword. But such also had been the way and purpose of the Bishop of Rome ever since the rise of Hildebrand. Hence, it was obvious, the pope was Antichrist. When, however, Antichrist in the person of the pope had raged unchecked for about a hundred years, the Lord began to move learned and faithful men here and there to withstand him, and in England, finally, he raised up Wycliffe. "Thys is out of all doubt, that at what time all the worlde was in most desperate and vile estate, & that the lamentable ignorance and darknes of God his truth had overshadowed the whole earth: this man stepped forth like a valiant champion." Like the morning star, like the moon at full, like the sun, "so doeth he shine and glister in the temple and Church of God." Christians had forgotten everything but the mere name of Christ, knowing nothing of scripture and true doctrine, nothing of "the greatnes & strength of sinne, of true works, of grace and free justification [,] of liberty of a Christian man." Instead of Peter and Paul, men studied Aquinas and Scotus and the "sentences" of the fathers collected by Peter Lombard. "The people were taught to worship no other thing but that which they did see, and did see almost nothing whiche they did not worship." With this introduction, the author goes on in the ensuing two-hundred-odd pages to relate the struggles and sufferings of

Wycliffe and his followers, the Lollards in England, Huss and Jerome of Prague on the Continent. But important as Wycliffe was, he merely represented the historic primacy of England in the promotion of the faith. In the preface to his sixth book Foxe declared that it was not true that the faith which now prevailed among his countrymen had sprung up only within the last twenty or thirty years. "This profession," he had shown and would further show, "hath bene spread abroade in Englande of olde and aunciient time, not onely . . . from the time of Wyckleffe, but hathe continually from time to time sparkled abroade, although the flames thereof have never so perfectly burst out, as they have done within these hundred yeares and more."

The sixth book of the *Actes and Monuments* told of the war of Antichrist upon the saints in England and abroad in the fifteenth century, and the remaining half of the entire work, comprising in the second and subsequent editions a second volume, was devoted entirely to Henry VIII, Edward, and Mary. The first volume concluded with a summing up entitled "The proude primacie of Popes paynted out in Tables, in order of their rising up by little and little, from faythfull Bishops and Martyrs, to become Lords and governors over King and kingdomes, exalting themselves in the Temple of God, above all that is called God, &c. 2. Thessalonions. 2." This summation was accompanied by a series of twelve woodcuts, each filling nearly half a folio page. The first in the series depicted Christian martyrs enduring torments at the behest of a heathen emperor, but the series as a whole was devoted not to the torments and triumphs of the saints but to the step-by-step usurpation of power in church and state by successive popes and the degradation at their hands of kings and emperors. Constantine is shown embracing the Christian bishops, but after that we see the emperor kissing the pope's toe, the pope crowning the emperor with his foot, King John surrendering his crown to the legate, and finally the pope carried shoulder high in triumph with kings and emperors trudging before him. As a tailpiece to the volume we see justice with her scales, and the Bible outweighing the decretals of the pope, plus bells, beads, and crosses. Christ and His apostles stand on one side looking on, and on the other the devil vainly tugs at the scale and the pope, attended by monks and bishops, pours in money. The first page of the second volume shows Henry VIII on his throne, crown on head and sword in hand, with the pope under his feet, lamented over by Fisher, Pole, and a rout of monks, while Cranmer with Cromwell behind him hands the sacred book to the king. In the second volume, Foxe tells the story of the progress of reformation on the Continent after Jerome and Huss. He acknowledges Luther as the chief agent appointed by the Lord to subvert the papacy, but he does not let his readers forget that Luther was the disciple of Huss, who was the disciple of Wycliffe. After Luther, he goes through the roll of German, Swiss, French, Italian, and Spanish Protestants, giving little attention, however, to Calvin. He then returns to his own country and his main theme, praising the Lord, "Who by his mightie power and brightnes of his word, hath revealed this great enemie of his so manifestly to the eyes of all men, who before was hid in the Church so coulourably, that almost few Christians could espye him."

The nature of Foxe's accomplishment as an historian is clear. Elizabeth's accession seemed to him an act of providence, her survival and success essential to the maintenance of the true religion. Thus the interest of the Protestant cause became one with that of the crown and the nation. Any threat to the safety and independence of either church or crown was seen as a threat to the safety and independence of both, and piety and patriotism together moved the historian to show that such had always been the case. Yet, writing in order to excite faith and loyalty in the people, he realized that the stories with which he filled his pages, of kings defending their authority and saints suffering for their beliefs, must be made to sound convincing in spite of the great weight of tradition opposed to the idea they represented. For this purpose he made use of two devices, aside from that of narrative art itself. One, of the greatest importance, has already been indicated. It was to show that the history of the church squared at every step with the prophetic vision of St. John. Each was used as the key to unlock the meaning of the other, leading readers to conclude that the mutual canceling out of two incomprehensibles left no mystery in either but only inescapable certainty in both. The other way to convince readers of the validity of such an account of the past was to make them feel that what they were told, unlike the accounts of monkish chroniclers and other agents of Rome, was an unprejudiced statement of facts derived from original records or reported directly to the author by the parties concerned or other witnesses. How genuinely impartial and disingenuous Foxe was in his choice and use of primary sources is immaterial. He created the impression in men ready to believe that he was telling the truth as he found it, uncolored by partisanship and undistorted by invention or tradition. The very hugeness of his book proved, very likely, to be a help, certainly no deterrent, in gaining and holding the attention of readers. They did not have to read the whole book to get at the story or the idea, and yet the stories and the pictures, which also told the story, led them on and on or brought them back to read more and more. Besides, there were convenient helps for finding one's way about in the book, a calendar of saints, martyrs, and other personages, tables and summaries, an index with directions for its use, subtitles, running heads, glosses, and pictures.

But Foxe's gift for narrative was his best reliance. History, as he wrote it, always came back to the story of an individual, to story after story, told with unflagging energy and conviction. Yet every individual case was charged with the whole meaning of history as he conceived it. The blood of English martyrs of yesterday was shown to be one with the blood of all the martyrs back to Nero. All history was one. God revealed himself alike in his works and his word. The Old Testament told of Christ and the church, prefigured in the patriarchs, prophets, judges, and kings of the chosen people. The New Testament told of Christ's coming and the institution of his church on earth. Revelation foreshadowed the whole course of the church up to the Reformation and on to the end of time. And the record of scripture was confirmed and extended in history as recorded by men. The story of every saint was the story in brief of the church itself, the story always of the age-long war of Christ and Antichrist in which every soul was involved and in which England in particular was called by God to play a very particular part. Thus, to the stock question of their opponents, "Where

was your church before Luther?" Protestants in general were
taught to reply, "With the apostles, with the martyrs under the
heathen emperors, at Rome with Peter and Paul and their successors until Antichrist usurped the chair of Peter and the dragon
drove the true church into the wilderness." And the English
Protestants were taught by Foxe to answer that the true church
since apostolic times had always in some guise or other been
present in England, that in England, though continually beset,
it had never been overwhelmed, that in England the Reformation had begun and had spread thence to all the world, and that
in England it was now or soon or eventually, if Englishmen did
their part, to be finally consummated and the power of Antichrist brought to an end. Foxe concludes his dedicatory epistle
to the church universal by declaring:

And for asmuch as it is the good will of our God, that Sathan thus
should be let lose amongst us for a short time: yet let us strive in the
meane while what wee can to amende the malice of the tyme with
mutuall humanitie. They that be in errour, let them not disdayne to
learne. They which have greater talentes of knowledge committed, instruct in simplicitie them that be simple. No man liveth in that common
wealth where nothing is amisse. But yet because God hath so placed us
Englishmen here in one common wealth, also in one Church as in one
shippe together: let us not mangle or devide the shippe, which being
devided perisheth: but every man serve in his order with dilligence,
wherein he is called . . . that wee professing one Christ, may in one
unitie of doctrine gather ourselves into one Arke of the true Church together, where we continuing stedfast in fayth may at the last luckely
be conducted to the joyfull porte of our desired landing place by hys
heavenly grace.

In the year after the Armada, the whole matter was neatly
summed up in "A speciall note of England," prefixed by
Timothy Bright to his abridgement of Foxe's book.[5] England,
he said, was the first kingdom that "universallie embraced the
Gospel." Constantine, an Englishman, was the first Christian
emperor. Wycliffe first openly challenged the pope, Henry VIII
was the first king to renounce him, Edward VI the first to abolish

---

[5] *An Abridgement of the Booke of Acts and Monumentes of the Church
. . . by Timothe Bright, Doctor of Physicke, for Such as Either Through Want
of Leysure, or Abilitie, Have Not the Use of So Necessary an History,* 1589.

popish superstition, and Elizabeth, "the verie Maul of the pope," was "a Mother of Christian princes." In brief, England was "the first [nation] that embraced the Gospel: the onely establisher of it throughout the world: and the first reformed." In the edition of Foxe's book which appeared in 1632, a significant "continuation" by a later hand told how Protestants were massacred in France while England was miraculously delivered from Spanish invasion and gunpowder treason. In the face of these two obvious interventions by Providence in their behalf, who could deny that Englishmen held a special place in the favor of the Lord and a special responsibility for the fulfillment of his purposes on earth?

"But so it is," Foxe wrote in 1576, "I cannot tel how, the elder the world waxeth, the longer it continueth, the nerer it hasteneth to his end, the more Satan rageth: geving still new matter of writing bookes and volumes." By the time the Long Parliament met in November 1640, the conception of history and of England's historic relation to the church, set forth in seven editions of the *Actes and Monuments*, was still very much alive in men's minds, and the new crisis gave it new force and meaning. One of the first actions of the House of Commons was to summon Cornelius Burges and Stephen Marshall to address its members on a special fast day on November 17, 1640.[6] As spokesmen for the brotherhood of preachers whom Laud had attempted to silence, both declared that the Lord required that his word should be preached and that Parliament should see that his will was obeyed instantly at whatever cost. But Parliament would probably not have defied the king on the strength of such assurances alone. Men who took such pains to make sure of legal historical justification for revolution in the civil state expected no less of those who sought revolution in the ecclesiastical state. The preachers had to make clear that their demands were in accord not only with scripture but also with divine intention as revealed in the history of the church and of the realm of England. This they found not difficult. They brought into the pulpit, adapted to their own purposes, the ideas which the Eng-

[6] Cornelius Burges, *A Sermon Preached to the Honourable House of Commons . . . Novem. 17. 1640*, 1641; Stephen Marshall, *A Sermon Preached Before the Honourable House of Commons . . . November 17. 1640*, 1641.

lish people had been imbibing from Foxe for the past eighty years. Everybody knew, or at any rate few were prepared to deny, that Antichrist, in one guise or another, had for a long time been endeavoring to stifle the preaching of the word in England. For he knew that, if the word were preached in England, his power everywhere would presently come to an end. But the great bulwark of free preaching in England had been the independence of the English crown. Therefore papists, foreign and homebred, had labored to subject English monarchs to the will of the pope. Now, however, the repressors of free preaching were the English bishops, who had misled the king and were attempting to thwart the will of Parliament.

In their sermons on November 17, both Burges and Marshall began by setting forth the familiar doctrine of calling and covenant, each taking as his text a case from the history of the chosen people in the Old Testament. In that used by Burges (Jeremiah 50:5) the Lord has kept his promise to deliver the people from Babylon and has set their faces again toward Zion. In Marshall's text (II Chronicles 15:2) the Lord has granted victory to Asa the king. In each case a prophet is at hand to give warning that, as God is in covenant with his chosen ones, they are in covenant with him to do his work, rebuild Zion, and overthrow false gods and their priests. This being interpreted, meant, of course, that Parliament was in covenant with the Lord to erect everywhere a preaching ministry and that the Lord could be depended upon to bring to success the work he had appointed to be done. But Parliament was bound not simply by the force of analogy to Old Testament instances. It was committed also by England's historic destiny. The step it was called upon to take was simply the next step in the long course of divinely directed events which made up human history, especially English history. God's purpose would be fulfilled, whatever Parliament might do, but Parliament had nevertheless been chosen to be the instrument of its next advance. "The hand of the Diall *makes* not the Clock to go," Marshall said, "but shewes how it doth go."

Both he and Burges made much of the fact that the day of this, the first fast day of the new Parliament, fell on the anniversary of Queen Elizabeth's accession, and though the coincidence had not happened by intention, neither would it have happened, they were certain, except through God's providence. It gave them, at any rate, their cue for calling up, in the light of the doctrine they had been expounding, the legend which their countrymen had come to believe as historic fact. Their audience heard again that the pope was Antichrist, and that England as the champion of the true faith had always been his chosen enemy. Henry VIII had driven him out, Edward had begun to reform the church, Mary had brought popery back, and Elizabeth had struggled with the "hydra" of stout "popelings" at home, aided by potent and dangerous abetters abroad. Nevertheless, in spite of Antichrist, the Lord has never ceased to favor England. He delivered her out of Babylon and preserved her from the Spanish invasion, from gunpowder treason, and from many other dangers. Preachers and audience both knew, moreover, that Laud, try as he might, had never succeeded in completely silencing the pulpit. "All the Nations in *Christendome*," Marshall could say, "have been in grievous perplexities many yeers round about us: we have bin hitherto kept as another Land of *Goshen*, where light hath still shined, when all others have been in darknes." And yet God's favor always brought with it a responsibility never to be forgotten. "All your counsels and advising will bee nothing, if God say, *I will stay no longer in* England," and this he will surely do if Parliament now fails to complete the reformation of the church by removing the last vestige of the ancient enemy's power to restrain the preaching of God's word. For, "the preaching of the Word is the *Scepter* of Christs Kingdome, the *glory* of a Nation, the *Chariot* upon which life & salvation comes riding."

The English bishops, whether they were fighting Antichrist's battle or not, clearly lost the first engagement in the war of ideas with the Puritan pulpit. Clarendon said that Burges and Marshall had a greater hold upon Parliament in 1640 than the Archbishop of Canterbury had ever had upon the court and that the preachers did more than Parliament itself to spread the wildfire of rebellion in 1642.[7] Charles acknowledged that, unless he

[7] Clarendon, *History*, I, 401; II, 319–21.

could count on the loyalty of the pulpit, he could expect to derive small comfort out of commanding the militia.[8] Burges and Marshall in their sermons at that first Parliamentary fast-day service gave the cue to their fellows for preaching a holy war in which England's historic responsibility for true religion was poised fatefully against the duty of obedience to the crown. But a greater voice than that of any preacher also took up the theme, and set it, as was his habit, in a larger context.

Milton professed that history should be written with brevity, clarity, freedom from partisanship, and critical evaluation of sources.[9] His first venture upon the writing of history was, however, the tract, *Of Reformation in England*, an account of the English Reformation conceived in the tradition and spirit of Foxe and issued in support of Marshall and his associates. It opens with the statement that the writer knows nothing "more worthy to take up the whole passion of pitty, on the one side, and joy on the other: then to consider first, the foule and sudden corruption, and then after many a tedious age, the long deferr'd, but much more wonderfull and happy reformation of the *Church* in these latter dayes." Again we hear, summarized in Milton's pregnant rhetoric, the story of the steady promotion of ignorance and superstition by a venal priesthood for its own aggrandisement, of the glorious recovery of the Bible and the revival of learning, of the testimony of the martyrs "shaking the *Powers* of *Darknesse*, and scorning the *fiery rage* of the old *red Dragon*." Again, too, we hear that England, through divine favor, had been the first to blow the evangelic trumpet to the nations and hold up a new lamp to Christendom, and again we are told that other reformers but lit their tapers at Wycliffe's preaching. Again, too, the question is asked, why, after so favoring England, did God permit popes and prelates, through five or six kings' reigns, to stifle truth. And the answer, running through the tracts against the bishops, the divorce tracts, and *Areopagitica*, is still the same. England has been greatly tried because she has been greatly trusted, because she has been given a great part to play.

[8] Godfrey Davies, *The Early Stuarts*, p. 141.
[9] *Familiar Letters, Works* (Columbia) XII, 90–95, 101–3.

Now once again by all concurrence of signs, and by the generall instinct of holy and devout men, as they daily and solemnly expresse their thoughts, God is decreeing to begin some new and great period in his Church, ev'n to the reforming of Reformation itself: what does he then but reveal Himself to his servants, and as his manner is, first to his English-men.[10]

This, of course, was not history written according to Milton's preferred classical models, with brevity, clarity, and detachment. It was history written, as history often is, passionately in support of a cause, history written in the apocalyptical mood of the *Actes and Monuments*, suited to the Puritan interest in the crisis of the early 1640's. That is to say, Milton is the prophet and propagandist of a particular reform, conceived and urged as the fulfillment of England's destiny and responsibility revealed in her history and the history of the church at large. And this continued to be his theme when his zeal led him beyond the limits set for revolution by the Puritan preachers. He would have Parliament reform marriage because England had so often in the past been granted the honor of giving out reformation to the world.[11] Who but the English Constantine had baptized the Roman empire? Who "but *Alcuin* and *Wicklef* our Country men open'd the eyes of *Europe*, the one in arts, the other in Religion."[12] And the great argument for unlicensed printing was framed in an historical account of censorship as one of the devices of the Roman Antichrist, contrary to ancient, to Christian, and to English belief and practice. Milton by that time had concluded that, as there had been nothing to choose between the popish clergy and the English prelates, so now there was nothing to choose between new presbyter and old priest. His *History of Britain*, whatever his professed theory concerning the duty of an historian, became, as he went on and as 1649 approached, a bitter attack upon the clerical mind and character in any guise at any time. In that nation, "so pliant and so prone to seek after knowledge," of which he would have had Lords and Commons remember that they were a part as well as the governors, the ministry of the word was no longer to be the privilege of a clerical caste

[10] *Areopagitica, Works* (Columbia) IV, 340.
[11] *Doctrine and Discipline of Divorce, Works* (Columbia) III, 376–77.
[12] *Op. cit.*, p. 377.

but the responsibility of anyone gifted with the ability to learn and teach. He did not, however, cease to be the great spokesman for the ideas which Foxe had set forth at the beginning of England's heroic age. History he still conceived as falling into the pattern of corruption, fall, and betrayal, of present struggle and always imminent recovery, and England he conceived as always singled out to play a very special role in history and to bear a very special responsibility.

Ideas, like the books in which they are conveyed, are indeed not absolutely dead things, though by the generations that live by them they may be discovered to have strange roots. As the eighteenth century drew near, men made ready to put much that had been said in the age before into different language if not out of mind. Nevertheless, it is not to be overlooked that Foxe's *Actes and Monuments* was republished in 1684 for the ninth but by no means for the last time.

# POPE ON WIT:
## THE *ESSAY ON CRITICISM*

### Edward Niles Hooker

SINCE the publication of Tillotson's admirable study we have become increasingly aware of the extraordinary art of Pope's verse. That awareness, however, has not led us insistently enough to suspect that the *Essay on Criticism* has something to say, something neither trivial nor commonplace, and worthy of the artistry with which the ideas are set forth. Supposing that Pope never could make up his mind about certain crucial terms such as *wit* and *nature*, we are tempted to regard the poem as a mélange of confused and sometimes contradictory assertions or as a potpourri of Augustan clichés. Poor addled Pope (one recent editor intimates) employed the word *wit* throughout the *Essay on Criticism* in seven different senses; and we can conclude, if we like, that he knew no better.

To the acute and subtle mind of Empson we stand indebted for the explicit recognition that the *Essay* has a solid core of intelligible meaning, or perhaps a complex of meanings, coherent and applicable, and revolving around what he regards as the key word, *wit*.[1] A close reading of the poem leaves no room for doubting that Pope intended to convey what seemed to him the significant facts about the place of wit in literature, and that for some reason it struck him as particularly desirable to do so. To understand the *Essay*, therefore, we should address ourselves to three questions. Why, in an essay devoted to the principles of criticism, does Pope lavish space and attention on wit rather than

[1] "Wit in the *Essay on Criticism*," *Hudson Review*, Vol. II, No. 4 (Winter 1950), pp. 559–77.

on taste? Second, what controversies being agitated at the time he was composing the poem would have led Pope to take a stand, and how is that stand established in the *Essay*? And third, what body of contemporary thought, more or less parallel to his own, was available to him as he wrote, and how can it illumine the direction and implications of his thinking?

In the first place, Pope at the start, after describing the highest form of artistic talent in the poet as true genius, and the highest gift of the critic as true taste, proceeds to the principle that the best critics are those who excel as authors (lines 15–16).[2] True taste, therefore, is best revealed in the operations of genius. That genius and taste "have so intimate a Connection" is not an idea peculiar to Pope; as one of his contemporaries remarked, "there are Cases where they cannot be . . . separated, without almost taking away their Functions."[3] A discussion of the art of criticism would be idle unless it expounded taste by revealing the ways and standards of genius.

Or, since genius is distressingly rare, one may, like Pope, examine the ways of wit, that more inclusive thing, conceived of as literary talent or as the distinguishing element in literature, the breath of life informing the dull clay. As Dryden had proclaimed, "The composition of all poems is, or ought to be, of wit . . ."[4] He meant, not ingenuity, but a spark. The special gift of those who create literature is to "invigorate their conceptions, and strike Life into a whole Piece"; what would otherwise remain leaden or sluggish is magically transformed by Flame and Strength of Sense.[5] Nothing could be more natural than that Homer and Virgil, authors who possessed such qualities in the highest degree, should be called "these Two supreme Wits."[6] Fire, invention, and imagination became inextricably associated with wit; they were the life-giving forces—so David

---

[2] References to and quotations from the *Essay on Criticism* are based on George Sherburn's edition, *Selections from Pope* (New York: Nelson and Sons, n.d.).

[3] Anon., *The Polite Arts* (1749), p. 15.

[4] Preface to *Annus Mirabilis*, in *Essays of Dryden*, ed. W. P. Ker, I, 14.

[5] Antony Blackwall, *An Introduction to the Classics* (6th ed., 1746), p. 12.

[6] *Ibid.*, p. 18.

Abercromby meant when he said that "we never write wittily, but when our Imagination is exalted to a certain degree of heat, destructive to our cold dulness."[7] In the words of John Oldmixon, a minor contemporary of both Dryden and Pope: "Every Thing that pleases in Writing is with us . . . resolved into Wit, whether it be in the Thought or the Expression."[8] When John Sheffield, Duke of Buckingham, said in his *Essay upon Poetry*, " 'Tis Wit and Sence that is the Subject here,"[9] he had in mind much the same idea that Blackwall owned when he remarked of Horace, "His Sprightliness of Imagination is temper'd with Judgment; and he is both a pleasant Wit, and a Man of Prudence."[10] Sense and judgment are the solid, useful stuff with which the writer works, but wit is the magic that lifts the stuff to the plane of belles-lettres. A critic must understand wit if he is to talk of literature. And in an essay on literary criticism we should expect Pope to deal in generous measure with the problem of wit.

But in 1711 there were additional reasons why he had to confront the subject, reasons general and reasons personal. As for the general reasons, no one at the time could have forgotten that outburst of hostilities in 1698–1700, in which the righteous had beset the wits—and had driven them to cover. It is true, of course, that the attack had been directed overtly against specific forms of wit, the facetious varieties which played with sex and trifled with religion and morality. But underneath lay an impulse more sinister, more dangerous, which denied the worth of literature itself (or what we think of as creative writing).

The psychological basis for the hostility can be found in Dryden's friend Walter Charleton, who observed that in works of wit "Phansie ought to have the upper hand, because all Poems, of what sort soever, please chiefly by Novelty."[11] How this remark becomes significant will appear when it is set beside Charleton's definition of Fancy as the faculty by which we conceive simi-

[7] *Discourse of Wit* (1685), p. 180.
[8] *Essay on Criticism* (1728), p. 44.
[9] In *Critical Essays of the 17th Century*, ed. Spingarn, II, 288.
[10] *Introduction to the Classics*, p. 21.
[11] *Brief Discourse concerning the Different Wits of Men* (1669), p. 25.

larities "in objects really unlike, and pleasantly confound them in discourse: Which by its unexpected Fineness and allusion, surprizing the Hearer, renders him less curious of the truth of what is said."[12] In an age when the utilitarian and scientific movement had grown to giant size, an art which pleased by confounding truth and deceiving men was bound to be viewed with hostility. All wit came under attack.

The philosophic and moral basis for the hostility was well stated by Malebranche, who wrote:[13]

But that which is most opposite to the efficacy of the Grace of Christ, is that which in the Language of the World is call'd Wit; for the better the Imagination is furnish'd, the more dangerous it is; subtilty, delicacy, vivacity and spaciousness of Imagination, great qualities in the Eyes of Men, are the most prolifick and the most general causes of the blindness of the Mind and the corruption of the Heart.

Without intending to betray her own cause Margaret, Duchess of Newcastle, made this humble request:[14]

> Give me a Wit, whose Fancy's not confin'd;
> That buildeth on it self, with no Brain join'd. . . .

Exactly what many had suspected! The current prejudice against wit was vigorously put by Ferrand Spence, who viewed it as nothing but the froth and ferment of the soul, beclouding reason and sinking rational pursuits into the miasma of fantasy.[15]

In the few years preceding the publication of Pope's *Essay* the agitation concerning wit was intensified, partly because of the appearance of the *Letter concerning Enthusiasm* (1707) and *Sensus Communis* (1709), both of which, by pleading for the complete freedom of wit and raillery, even in the most serious matters, sent shivers of horror down the spines of some English and Continental readers. Both were speedily translated into French, and both reviewed in 1709 by the indefatigable Jean Le Clerc, who warned concerning the former: "*Le livre mérite d'être lû avec attention, pour ne pas lui donner un sens et un but,*

---

[12] *Brief Discourse*, pp. 20–21.
[13] *A Treatise of Morality*, trans. James Shipton (1699), p. 114.
[14] *Poems, or, Several Fancies in Verse* (3d ed., 1668), p. 224.
[15] Preface to trans. of St. Évremond, *Miscellanea* (1686), sig. A9*v*–A10*r*.

*qu'il n'a point.*[16]   But whether they read attentively or not, many readers detected the sense and aim which was not really present (to Le Clerc). There soon issued a long and bitter retort called *Bart'lemy Fair: or, an Enquiry After Wit; In Which Due Respect Is Had to a Letter Concerning Enthusiasm* (1709). This work takes Shaftesbury's *Letter* to be primarily an assault on religion, and sees wit as a mode of enquiry that would unsettle everything, morals and government alike. Of the terrible menace lurking in wit the anonymous author bitterly remarks: "To be Witty, if a Man knows how, is the only way to please. Wit is the Salt that gives a goût to any Carrion: Nothing so Profane, or Lewd, but shall be relish'd if it pass for Wit."[17]

Such objections are obviously directed against, not true wit, but the abuse of it. Yet wit easily lent itself to abuse, and the contemporary mind distrusted it as a likely enemy to all goodness. With almost uncanny prescience the learned Dr. Samuel Clarke answered part of Shaftesbury's contentions a few years before they were printed. In a series of sermons preached at St. Paul's in 1705, he denounced the sort of men who pretend to seek for truth and to explode falsehood by means of wit:[18]

. . . whatsoever things are profane, impure, filthy, dishonourable and absurd; these things they make it their business to represent as harmless and indifferent, and to laugh Men out of their natural shame and abhorrence of them; nay, even to recommend them with their utmost Wit. Such Men as these, are not to be argued with, till they can be persuaded to use Arguments instead of Drollery. For Banter is not capable of being answered by Reason: not because it has any strength in it; but because it runs out of all the bounds of Reason and good Sense, by extravagantly joining together such Images, as have not in themselves any manner of Similitude or Connexion; by which means all things are alike easy to be rendered ridiculous. . . .

Wit appeared to many good men as a threat to decency because it walked regularly with irreligion and vice. Thus James Buerdsell, fellow of Brasenose College, complained in 1700 that "the prevailing Humour of Scepticism" had become "so extremly Mod-

[16] *Bibliotheque Choisie*, XIX (Amsterdam, 1709), 431.

[17] P. 18.

[18] *Works of Samuel Clarke* (4 vols., 1738), II, 603-4.

ish, that no Person can be that self-admir'd thing, a Wit, without it."[19] In the same year young Samuel Parker, of Trinity College, Oxford, deplored the sad fact that "Dissoluteness and Irreligion are made the Livery of Wit, and no body must be conscious of good parts, but he loses the credit of them unless he take care to finish 'em with Immoralities."[20]

Because wit, having become fashionable, began to appear as the natural ally of the scoffer, undermining religion and morals, it seemed to constitute a menace to society—a menace that must be understood if one is to feel the force of Swift's digressions on wit in the *Tale of a Tub* (1704). The threat, obvious to large numbers of intelligent men, was aggravated by the appearance of Shaftesbury's essays, at the very time when Pope meditated on the problems of wit and criticism.

One must not forget that the publication of the *Tatler* and the *Spectator*, both by their nature and their purpose, affected the debate: by their nature, for they were seen to follow in the footsteps of Montaigne, one of the greatest of modern wits; and by their purpose, for they proposed to temper wit with morality and to enliven morality with wit. Wit *could* be made an ally of goodness, they demonstrated forcefully—and so successfully that it was possible two decades later for the author of the Preface to the *Plain Dealer* to assume general agreement when he remarked that periodical essays are composed in the finest taste

when they cloath good Sense with Humour, and embellish good Morals with Wit; when they instruct Familiarly, and reprove Pleasantly; when they don't swell above Comprehension, nor sink below Delicacy: In short, when they adapt the Wisdom of the Antients to the Gust of the Moderns, and constrain Montaigne's Pleasantry within Bickerstaffe's Compass.

Much of the *Tatler* and *Spectator* papers was devoted to exposing false wit in social life, discrediting the antics of the unseemly biters and banterers, the scatterbrained and volatile, the uncouth leapers and slappers, the hollow laughers, the pert coxcombs. False wit in literature was attended to by Addison in the *Spectator*. Underlying these endeavors is the assumption that wit needed to be defended, and that it could be restored to its rightful

[19] *Discourses and Essays on Several Subjects* (Oxford, 1700), p. 205.
[20] *Six Philosophical Essays* (1700), p. 18.

place by stripping it of the gaudy and unclean adornments which thoughtless admirers had forced upon it. And at least since the time of Cowley's ode "Of Wit," the separation of true from false wit had been a regular mode of defending literature itself.

But besides these general reasons Pope had a personal stake in the argument over wit. The subject had interested him for years before the *Essay on Criticism* was published, as the correspondence with Walsh shows. It was in his correspondence with Wycherley, however, that the subject became crucial—and almost necessarily so. For in the late years of Dryden and the early years of Pope, Wycherley had become the very symbol of the poet of wit.

The trouble began with Wycherley's belated urge for recognition as a nondramatic poet, signalized by the publication in 1704 of his *Miscellany Poems*. Preceding the poems is a Preface that remains one of the unreadable wonders of our language. It is wit gone mad, an avalanche of simile and metaphor, a breathless flow of whim and fancy, out of which, now and then, there half emerges, here and there, a globule of meaning; after which a cloud of darkness settles, and the reader gropes his way blindly toward the poems that follow (where he is not to fare much better).

Little enthusiasm greeted the *Miscellany Poems*. But Wycherley, undaunted, commenced almost immediately to plan a new collection which should contain some unpublished verses and some revised and corrected versions of poems already printed. This time, however, he showed no unseemly haste in afflicting printer and public. Instead, he passed copies around to his friends for advice and correction. Among others so honored was Alexander Pope.

Pope, as we know, took this responsibility seriously. In Wycherley's letter dated February 5, 1705/6[21] we discover that our bold youth was already pruning excrescences from the elder bard's disorganized fancies. On April 10, Pope was explaining with admirable candor that some of the poems were so wretched that "to render them very good, would require a great addition, and almost the entire new writing of them." Wych-

[21] Pope, *Works*, ed. Elwin-Courthope, VI, 26.

erley's chaos sprang from a false conception of wit. For great wits such as John Donne, said Pope, like great merchants take least pains to set out their valuable goods, whereas the "haberdashers of small wit" spare no decorations to present their little wares as seductively as possible.[22] As the business of lopping and grafting proceeded, Wycherley's assumed meekness wore thin, until a minor explosion occurred in 1707. Pope had set about to produce a semblance of logical order in the poem on Dullness, subjecting it to radical alterations; such amiable helpfulness provoked Wycherley to this response on November 22:[23]

And now for the pains you have taken to recommend my Dulness, by making it more methodical, I give you a thousand thanks, since true and natural dulness is shown more by its pretence to form and method, as the sprightliness of wit by its despising both.

Here was a home-thrust, impelled by some resentment and hostility. Pope's letter, dated one week later, shows that he was aware of the resentment; nevertheless he replied patiently: "To methodize in your case, is full as necessary as to strike out; otherwise you had better destroy the whole frame, and reduce them into single thoughts in prose, like Rochefoucauld, as I have more than once hinted to you."[24] As for the alleged incompatibility of wit and method, Pope urged that this is true only for the trivial forms of wit embodied in fancy or conceit; but as for true wit, which is propriety, why, that requires method not only to give perspicuity and harmony of parts, but also to insure that each detail will receive its increment of meaning and beauty from the surrounding elements.

This strange contest of wills lasted from 1706 until 1710 at least. In the latter year, on April 11, Wycherley wrote to Pope in protest against the extent to which the younger man was improving his verses. By your tuning of my Welsh harp, he said, my rough sense is to become less offensive to the fastidious ears of those finicky critics who deal rather in sound than in meaning.[25] Wit shines with a native luster that defies the need of polish.

As Wycherley saw it, there was a generous, libertine spirit

[22] Elwin-Courthope, VI, 28.    [23] *Ibid.*, VI, 33.
[24] *Ibid.*, VI, 34–35.    [25] *Ibid.*, VI, 44.

in wit, too free to be confined, and too noble to be sacrificed for smoothness or regularity. Taking form as a novel simile, a brilliant metaphor, a dazzling paradox, or a smart aphorism, wit is its own justification wherever it happens to appear. Some of Wycherley's contemporaries were wont to say of great wits that their "careless, irregular and boldest Strokes are most admirable."[26] For wit in writing is the sign of a fertility of mind, of multitudinous thoughts crowding in upon one or flying out toward the most sublime and exalted objects, of a capacity for wide-ranging speculation that soars above man's necessities and desires, of a flame and agitation of soul that little minds and men of action cannot comprehend.[27] To sacrifice such flashes of wit to an ordered design, to a carefully conceived framework, is to sacrifice poetry itself. Even the feebler manifestations of wit are sacred; we recall that Wycherley had composed a Panegyrick upon Puns.

Pope's artistic conscience told him that such scintillation, when it failed to fit into its proper place and contribute to the effect of the whole, was false wit because it was bad art. And he must have understood that such irresponsible, uncontrolled flashes, lacking any relationship with artistic purpose and solid sense, had contributed to the disrepute into which wit had fallen. As he was driven to correct and revise Wycherley's manuscripts, he was impelled to defend himself, and true wit as well, by reaching a coherent view of literature that would justify his own practice. It was a bold step for a virtually unknown young author to set himself against the most famous wit surviving from the glamorous court of Charles II. But he might draw comfort and support from the fact that a few of the distinguished men of the time had expressed concepts of wit similar to his own. Little by little his ideas take form; we can see them developing in his correspondence, especially that with Wycherley. He told Spence later that he had formulated the substance of the *Essay on Criticism* in prose before he undertook the poem.

One passage in the poem that would seem to have Wycherley

[26] Cf. John Dennis, *Critical Works*, II (Baltimore, 1943), 381.

[27] *Ibid.*, II, 383. Thus Dennis wrote to Wycherley, knowing he was addressing a sympathetic spirit.

in mind is that contained in lines 289–304, where he speaks of
the writers addicted to conceits and glittering thoughts, specious
prodigalities which are valued by their creators not because they
are essential parts of the meaning or because they fit into the
places where they are thrown, but because they startle and surprise or raise admiration for their makers' liveliness. These are
diseases. Works so constructed are "One glaring Chaos and wild
heap of wit"—an extraordinarily apt description of Wycherley's
*Miscellany Poems* of 1704.

But there is a clearer and more specific connection between
the correspondence and the poem visible in the passage comprising lines 494–507. Here Pope describes the unhappiness that
wit brings to those who possess it by stirring up malice and envy
in the dull and ignorant. This, as we learn from a letter dated
November 20, 1707,[28] was a subject which he had treated in his
reorganization of Wycherley's poem on Dullness. If his distinguished correspondent failed to appreciate the addition, nothing prevented the use of it in a new poem.

By an interesting association of ideas Pope proceeds from
here, through a short transitional passage (lines 508–25) dealing with the shame and disgrace that wit suffers at the hands of
its friends, to the conclusion of Part II. This concluding section
(lines 526–55) completes the subject of Dullness and likewise
fulfills the thought developed in lines 408–51, where Pope describes two types of false wit, one caused by servile dullness and
the other by modes and current folly. In the closing lines of
Part II two more kinds of false wit are exposed: that which
grows out of the union of dullness with bawdry, and that which
springs from dullness and irreligion. The interesting feature of
Pope's strategy in this passage is that these two abuses of wit are
made to appear as temporary phases in a historical process, the
first brought about by the dissoluteness, luxury, and idleness in
the reign of Charles II, and the second, by the license and im-
piety allowed in the reign of William III. These particular
manifestations of false wit (both of them "modes in wit" and
"current folly") are sharply dissociated from true wit by art-
fully fixing them in past reigns, which Pope had no need to de-

[28] Elwin-Courthope, VI, 32.

fend, especially as, out of the Wit's Titans who flourished in these two reigns, the last surviving member and champion was none other than William Wycherley.

It would take a monograph to show in detail how the analysis of false wit (with which Part II of the *Essay* is largely concerned) responds to particular literary developments in Pope's age, and this is not the point where such an investigation could be most profitable. We must still ask ourselves, what did Pope mean by true wit, and what Augustan writers whose thoughts were taking a similar direction can help us to comprehend the import of his view?

In the course of exposing false wit, Pope suggests two criteria by which true wit may be determined. First, it belongs not to the part but to the whole. It is the master idea which informs every portion of the body and gives life and energy; it is the joint force of all components, and not the beauty, regularity, or brilliance of any one feature. It unites the parts, and prevents undue attention from falling on any one; and no part has goodness or badness in itself except in its relation to the whole. And if the whole is properly informed with wit, it gives a generous pleasure, warming the mind with rapture so that we are delighted though we know not why, so delighted that we cannot be disturbed by trivial faults in the execution.

The second test is, that it must take its course from nature, that is, from truth. But not necessarily from the worn or commonplace; enough that we recognize, when we encounter it in art, its essential agreement with the frame of our minds, with universal human experience. So far from being commonplace, the whole piece gives the effect of boldness, not because of style or artifice but because new life, energy, and insight have been added. It comes with the graces of expression, which tend to heighten the outlines of truth rather than to disguise or conceal them. The expression, in fact, should be as modestly plain as the subject and form permit; and sprightly wit is so far from adhering to it that the expression may rather be said to set off the wit. Nature alone is not true wit until it becomes animated and is drawn into a unity by the shaping spirit.

It is in Part I of the *Essay*, however, where we must look for a fuller account of the relationship of wit and art in the production of poetry.

Pope begins by specifying genius as the quality necessary in the poet, and taste in the critic, but notes that the two functions ideally should coincide. Genius is a synonym for wit, and after the first sixteen lines the former word is discarded in favor of the latter. Wit, then, is a quality that must be present at birth, and it is apportioned to men in varying measure and strength. If it is the genuine poetic gift, it may be fitted for only one type of poetry. Each man must discover his own special strength and cultivate only that for which he is specially fitted.

Along with genius (or taste) we can expect to find at least a rudimentary sense, or judgment, which is just as much the gift of heaven as wit. This sense needs developing; otherwise it is easily perverted, either by the formulas of academic learning or by the distortions of fashion. But nature, to protect us, herself provides the standard of good judgment: an impulse that leads us to prefer the lasting and universal over the ephemeral and local.

This thought is first suggested in lines 19–27, and is taken up again for further development in lines 68–87. Again we are assured that nature furnishes us with a just and universal standard of judgment. But nature also provides the life, force, and beauty that a work of genius requires; it is the source and end as well as the test of art. From this fund art draws its supplies, and proceeds quietly, unobtrusively, to endow all parts of the body with spirit and vigor.

At this point it is easy for the reader to become confused, for the principle of control, which at the start of the passage was called *judgment*, has now become *art*; a few lines later it appears as *wit*, and by the end of the passage it has been transformed back to *judgment* again. Perhaps the most perplexing lines are the oft-quoted:

> Some, to whom Heaven in wit has been profuse,
> Want as much more to turn it to its use. . . .

The lines lend themselves to ridicule, and Pope knew all too well that they left him open to banter. Yet, with his marvelous gift of lucidity to aid him, he left the couplet as we see it. Why? Presumably because it seemed to be the best way of putting something that was very difficult to express.

He found it difficult because it involved a question on which the credit of literature depended. For Pope's contemporaries, encouraged by Locke, were erecting a wall between wit and judgment and attempting to deposit the most valued achievements of mankind on the side of the wall occupied by judgment. This way of thinking is well described by Sir William Temple in his essay "Of Poetry." In the usual acceptation, he says, man's goal is taken to be profit or pleasure. The faculty of the mind conversant with profit is wisdom; that conversant with pleasure is wit (or the vein that produces poetry). To wisdom is attributed "the Inventions or Productions of things generally esteemed the most necessary, useful, or profitable to Human Life"; and to wit, "those Writings or Discourses which are the most Pleasing or Entertaining."[29] Wit may borrow from wisdom, of course, but its own proper role is to dazzle the eyes and tickle the ears and cut capers; it has no insight of its own, no peculiar way of thinking, nothing to offer but toys.

Into this pitfall Pope had no desire to plunge. Nor was he tempted by the compromise that seduced many of his contemporaries: to say that the essence of poetry is fable, design, or structure (product of the faculty to which we assign reason, judgment, and wisdom).[30] If the core of literature is provided by the plain rational faculty, then it is conceivable that whatever is valuable in it could be conveyed more profitably in another way (say, in plain didactic prose), without the fuss and feathers of literary art. But apart from that, the compromise effectively disinherits most of the kinds of poetry, for only epic, tragedy, and comedy necessarily have fables.

To Pope, wit and judgment, as they operate in literature, are married. In this union, so long as they are in a healthy state,

[29] In Spingarn, III, 73–74.

[30] For a rather typical expression of the idea, see Mary Astell (?), *Bart'lemy Fair* (1709), p. 80: "Colouring is the least of the Matter, both in Wit and Painting; a few bold Strokes never made an Artist; the Attitudes, Proportions, and above all the Design, shew the Masterly Genius." Cf. also Dennis, *Critical Works*, II, 46.

they work together as a single faculty. As for the meaning of *wit* in the perplexed couplet, we must go back to the early lines in the poem, where we are told that genius and taste must ideally coincide; or, as the thought is expanded, that wit is accompanied by a rudimentary sense, potentially excellent, which requires development by experience. However great the gifts of heaven, wit, without that development, falls short of its perfection: natural wit needs training for its proper expression in art. But such training does not propose to foster an alien power, at odds with wit. Pope tries to make himself clear in the following passage (lines 88–140). The training designed to perfect the rudimentary sense is an experience of the great wit of the past, first through a study of the rules, in which the principles underlying the mighty achievements of past art are set forth in simple abstraction; and second by a detailed study of "each Ancient's proper character" in every page of his work. Out of such experience should come *literary* judgment, *literary* taste, which is the accomplished phase of wit; or, to put it in another way, wit in the writer is not merely the power to conceive of objects and endow them with "Life, force, and beauty," but also the ability to find an appropriate style and form in which to express them; the latter ability, developed by knowledge of the rules and of masterpieces of literature, serves as taste and judgment. In the writer it is also art, invisibly guiding the energy of the conception so that it permeates the form and language, and achieves its desired end. Thus, if this sense (call it taste, judgment, or art) guides the creative energy and, in a way, contains it, nature is still the test of art, for this judgment must be constructed on the foundation of a natural artistic gift. And because this gift comes originally from Heaven, or nature, it may at times conduct the creative impulse to its objective by a route not recognized by the rules and untried by past masterpieces—so snatching a grace beyond the reach of art.

The important point is that Pope believed there was a special way of thinking peculiar to literature, a way called *wit*, which possessed unique values; he saw that wit (in the narrower sense) and judgment in the artist are but two aspects of a single way of thinking, and that judgment (or art) is not a churlish, rational

censor but a natural literary sense cultivated by a wide acquaintance with literary masterpieces. Literature therefore is good, not
because it charms eye or ear with sparkle and melody nor because
it borrows wisdom from philosophy or science, but because wit,
the unique mode of the literary artist, provides an insight into
nature, endows it with "Life, force, and beauty," and conveys
it directly to our hearts, charming us as it makes us wiser.

The *Essay on Criticism*, then, had something to say. There is
much more in it than we have either time or space to examine.
But if we can follow what Pope says of wit, we can grasp his
primary purpose. He had difficulty in expressing his ideas concerning wit because there existed no adequate critical vocabulary
for him to draw upon. There did, however, exist a body of
thought concerning wit, some expressions of which Pope was
certainly acquainted with, and some part of which could serve
to strengthen and clarify his own views. To the consideration
of that body of thought it is reasonable that we proceed.

The first fact about wit that struck observers was that it made
for a lively mind. Hobbes himself defined it as celerity of
imagining, and thought of it as a tenuity and agility of spirits,
which, as it distinguished its possessors from the dull and sluggish of soul, must to that extent have seemed to him as a virtue.[31]
If wit meant nothing more than liveliness, it would have its value.
Welsted, who liked to take an extreme position, remarked years
later, partly out of admiration for sheer life and animation, that
even the sprightly *nonsense* of wit is preferable to the dull sense
of plodding, earth-bound creatures.[32]

A number of writers, however, refused to confine the liveliness of wit to sprightly nonsense. Liveliness, indeed, was the
first quality that impressed the author of *Remarques on the
Humours and Conversations of the Town* (1673), who described
wit as "properly the vivacity, and the agreeableness of the
fancy"; nevertheless he adds immediately, "yet there ought to
belong something more to that high quality, than a little flash
and quibble."[33] "Something more," as he explains in the follow-

---

[31] *Leviathan*, I, viii.
[32] *Epistles, Odes, &c* (1724), Dedication, p. xli.
[33] P. 93.

ing pages, meant to him an intelligent subject, delivered "sweet and pleasantly, in the native beauties of our Language." In that high quality, true wit, we see, sense, liveliness, and worthy expression might coalesce. So likewise it appeared in the opinion of the great Robert Boyle, who remarked that wit, "that nimble and acceptable Faculty of the Mind," involves both a readiness and subtlety in conceiving things, and a quickness and neatness in rendering them[34]—a way of putting the idea that neatly anticipates Pope's phrasing in a letter to Wycherley dated December 26, 1704: true wit is "a perfect conception, with an easy delivery."[35]

The vivacity of wit could be valuable for one of two reasons: either because it naturally operated to charm other minds, or because it was the mark of a soul capable of unusual powers, beyond the reach of ordinary men. There is a point at which vivacity and subtlety melt into swiftness and acuity. To the soon-to-be-duncified Fleckno, wit appeared to have an extraordinary force; it was, he said, a spiritual fire that rarefies and renders everything spiritual like itself.[36] To Margaret, Duchess of Newcastle, it seemed unearthly, mysterious, "the purest Element, and swiftest Motion of the Brain: it is the Essence of Thoughts; it incircles all things: and a true Wit is like the Elixir, that keeps Nature always fresh and young."[37] And, lest we smile at this, let us remind ourselves that the mysterious power of wit to penetrate to the heart of darkness is attested by the greatly influential La Rochefoucauld, whose Augustan translator (perhaps Stanhope) rendered him thus:[38]

The making a Difference between Wit and Judgment, is a Vulgar Error. Judgment is nothing else but the exceeding Brightness of Wit, which, like Light, pierces into the very Bottom of Things, observes all that ought to be observed there, and discovers what seemed to be past any bodies finding out: From when we must conclude, that the Energy and Extension

[34] *Occasional Reflections* (1665), p. 37.

[35] Elwin-Courthope, VI, 16.

[36] "Of Wit," in *A Farrago* (1666), pp. 58–59.

[37] *The Worlds Olio* (2d ed., 1671), p. 11.

[38] Maxim 98, in La Rochefoucauld, *The Moral Maxims and Reflections* (2d ed., 1706), as reprinted in the edition of George Powell (New York: F. A. Stokes Company, n.d.).

of this Light of the Wit, is the very Thing that produces all those Effects, usually ascribed to the Judgment.

The comparison between wit and light appealed strongly to a few writers of the age, who reveal something of the mystic's fervor when they address themselves to it. Thus an unknown author wrote at the turn of the century:[39]

> Wit is a Radiant Spark of Heav'nly Fire,
> Full of Delight, and worthy of Desire;
> Bright as the Ruler of the Realms of Day,
> Sun of the Soul, with in-born Beauties gay. . . .

And at the time when the ideas of the *Essay on Criticism* were beginning to take form in Pope's mind, another author, rejecting the notion that wit consists of merely exotic language, satire, floridity, quibbles or trifles, banter, or smart repartee, insisted:[40]

> No, 'tis a Thought sprung from a Ray Divine,
> Which will through Clouds of Low'ring Criticks shine:
> When in a Clear, Innubilous Serene,
> The Soul's Abstracted, Purg'd from Dross and Spleen. . . .

These mystic utterances are interesting but rather less important than the remarks of men like La Rochefoucauld, who looked upon wit as a natural instrument for probing the secrets of nature, and apparently as a mode of thinking unlike the rational method operating in mathematics. As representative of this group we may take Joseph Glanvill, who instructed his readers that true wit might be useful even in sermons:[41]

. . . For true Wit is a perfection in our Faculties, chiefly in the Understanding, and Imagination; Wit in the Understanding is a Sagacity to find out the Nature, Relations, and Consequences of things; Wit in the Imagination, is a quickness in the phancy to give things proper Images. . . .

And in another work he castigates those who debase wit, which is truly fitted for "great and noble Exercises of the Mind." It is in reality, he remarks, "a Faculty to dive into the depth of

[39] *A Satyr upon a Late Pamphlet Entitled, A Satyr Against Wit* (1700).
[40] *The British Apollo*, September 1–3, 1708.
[41] *Essay Concerning Preaching* (2d ed., 1703), pp. 71–72.

things, to find out their Causes and Relatives, Consonancies and Disagreements, and to make fit, useful, and unobvious Applications of their respective Relations and Dependencies."[42] The simile and metaphor of literature, therefore, *may* become, not the trifling ornaments laid upon the truth, but instruments of the profoundest thinking, the natural way of revealing the discovery of hidden relationships. A second representative of this group is Francis Atterbury, later a friend of Pope's, who discussed the subject in a sermon printed in 1708, while Pope was establishing his defenses against Wycherley. Atterbury wrote, "Wit, indeed, as it implies a certain uncommon Reach and Vivacity of Thought, is an Excellent Talent; very fit to be employ'd in the Search of Truth, and very capable of assisting us to discern and embrace it . . ."[43] His subsequent remarks show clearly that wit was not to be employed, as Shaftesbury proposed, in banter and raillery, to strip the mask from falsehood and thus arrive, indirectly, at truth; rather, it plunged straight to its object by virtue of its own range, acuity, and vivacity.

Even though Addison accepted Locke's definition of wit, thereby splitting off wit from judgment and demoting wit to the role of a mild spice serviceable in making morality pleasing to the palate, there were enough others who refused to be so misled. They persisted in thinking of wit as "a high quality," fitted for "great and noble Exercises of the Mind," as a special and valuable mode of apprehending nature and truth—not the plain and obvious, but the depth of things, where the complex relationships, the consonancies and disagreements, among the parts of nature lay open to wit alone. Some thought of judgment as a phase of wit; some thought of fancy as that part of wit which provided appropriate images and expression to deliver wit's discoveries. Wit and art are eternally wedded, and true wit is "a perfection in our Faculties."

This lofty conception of wit, making it possible to claim for literature a noble rank among human activities and a value far greater than can be granted that which merely entertains and pleases, was overshadowed in the early eighteenth century by the

[42] *A Whip for the Droll* (1700), pp. 4–5.
[43] "A Scorner Incapable of True Wisdom" (preached, 1694), in *Fourteen Sermons* (1708), pp. 158–59.

ideas of Locke and of men like him. And yet, sanctioned as it was by such formidable names as Robert Boyle, La Rochefoucauld, and Atterbury (some of whom were known to Pope), it offered an easily tenable position from which to defend literature from the assaults of those intent on debasing it.

There was one other type of answer to those engaged in depreciating wit, and it is worth examining because Pope was evidently attracted by it. At least from the Renaissance, men had been familiar with the idea that strangeness is an essential element in all excellent beauty. So Bacon had said. Wit and strangeness seemed inextricably connected in Davenant's mind, for he explained the wit of *Gondibert* to lie "in bringing Truth, too often absent, home to mens bosoms, to lead her through unfrequented and new ways, and from the most remote Shades . . . "[44] Likewise Leonard Welsted defined wit as "some uncommon Thought or just Observation, couch'd in Images or Allusions, which create a sudden Surprize"—a definition which admits the just Observation but stresses the uncommon and surprising.[45] In actual practice, wit became increasingly associated after 1690 with the strange, novel, and surprising.

But because novelty was so often connected with the ephemeral, with whim or fashion, and because subtle, uncommon ideas were often suspected of heresy, or the kind of enthusiasm which had led to the logic-chopping and violence of the Civil War, the charge was constantly made that wit depended on a love of quaintness and paradox, of novelty rather than truth, and was therefore offensive to the wise and good.[46] To meet this charge

[44] Preface to *Gondibert*, in Spingarn, II, 23.
[45] *Epistles, Odes, &c* (1724), Dedication, p. lx.
[46] Thus Atterbury, in *Fourteen Sermons* (1708), pp. 158–59, describing the forms most commonly taken by wit in his day, wrote: "Men of Quick and Lively Parts are apt to give themselves a loose beyond plain Reason and Common Sense; and to say many things not exactly Right and True, in order to say somewhat New and Surprizing." For this reason Wycherley himself remarked that wit is generally false reasoning—a remark that was pounced upon gleefully by Warburton in the *Divine Legation* (2d ed., 1738), I, xiv. The excellent author of the *Whole Duty of Man*, in *Works* (1726), Part II, pp. 47, 82, 85, 248, anticipates one of Swift's most brilliant essays in irony by observing that a great deal of wit depended on reversing universally accepted judgments on the most serious and sacred subjects and that if the Bible were taken away, the wit of many men would forthwith dry up.

certain writers began to stress the sound content of the product rather than the swiftness and acuity of mind that wit signified. Thus David Abercromby in 1685 defined wit as "either a senceful discourse, word, or Sentence, or a skilful Action."[47] Not "dead, and downright flat Sence" would do, but good sense properly animated. Something similar appears to have been in Boileau's mind when he remarked that "Wit is not Wit, but as it says something every Body thought of, and that in a lively, delicate, and New Manner"[48]—an observation that probably lays more stress on style and manner than the author intended; even as Pope's

> True wit is Nature to advantage dressed,
> What oft was thought, but ne'er so well expressed . . .

is easily misinterpreted to mean that any old saw will do as wit so long as it is well groomed and elegantly turned out. Actually Pope was far from desiring to confine wit to expression. His thinking at the time was close to that of William Walsh, who observed to him in a letter dated September 9, 1706, that nature alone is to be followed, and that we must carefully eschew similes, conceits, and all kinds of "fine things." And as for what you remark concerning expression, said Walsh, it is truly in the same relation to wit as dress is to beauty.[49]

Certainly Pope intended to oppose any idea of wit that separated subject matter from style. It is significant that in a letter dated November 29, 1707, he defined wit, in "the better notion of it," as propriety.[50] This, of course, was Dryden's definition, stated as early as 1677, and rephrased as "thoughts and words elegantly adapted to the subject."[51] It was Dryden's idea of wit to the end of his career, a definition which, as he says, "I imagin'd I had first found out; but since am pleasingly convinc'd, that Aristotle has made the same Definition in other Terms."[52] That Dryden's conception of wit interested other men than Pope at

[47] *Discourse of Wit* (1685), p. 7.
[48] *Works*, trans. Ozell (2d ed., 1736), I, iii.
[49] Elwin-Courthope, VI, 55.
[50] *Ibid.*, VI, 34–35.
[51] *Essays of Dryden*, ed. W. P. Ker, I, 190; cf. also I, 270, and II, 9.
[52] "Life of Lucian," in *Works of Lucian* (1711), I, 42.

this time is strongly suggested by the *Tatler's* article from Will's Coffee-house which begins, "This evening was spent at our table in discourse of <u>propriety of words and thoughts</u>, which is Mr. Dryden's definition of wit . . ."[53]

The term *propriety* conveys no very clear idea to us when it is applied to literary criticism, and for that reason Dryden's definition has been taken much less seriously by modern scholars than it was by the Augustans. It deserves to be understood. The *Tatler* supposed, incorrectly, that it involved a relationship between thoughts and words only. In reality Dryden was urging a threefold relationship, between thoughts, words, *and* subject, effected in such a way that the three elements appear to belong to one another (*propriety* conveyed the sense of *ownership*); and the words "elegantly adapted" point to the need of an active literary intelligence to produce the work of wit.

This account of wit as propriety bears a resemblance to an Augustan theory concerning the artistic process which may help to explain it. The theory, in brief, supposed that objects produce in genius (the artistic mind raised to a high degree of emotion and sensibility) certain thoughts which, in the very instant of their generation, take on forms and expression adequate to convey them and completely appropriate to them. A form of the theory can be found in the works of Dryden's young friend, John Dennis. In the genius, says Dennis, "as Thoughts produce the Spirit, the Spirit produces and makes the Expression; which is known by Experience to all who are Poets . . ."[54] The expression (which includes style, harmony, rhythm, etc.), then, is not the result of a separate act but exists in the most intimate and necessary relationship with the ideas, emotions, and attitudes of the artist, being engendered along with them. The thoughts do not become wit until they are animated and transfused by the shaping spirit which gives them expression—and all elements take form in perfect propriety.

To define wit, therefore, as "What oft was thought, but ne'er so well expressed," does not say or imply that wit is a stale

---

[53] *Tatler*, No. 62 (September 1, 1709).

[54] *Advancement and Reformation of Modern Poetry* (1701), in *Critical Works*, I (Baltimore, 1939), 222.

or commonplace thought nicely tricked out. The definition rather supposes that the writer, starting with a common and universal experience, sees it in a new light; and his sensitive spirit, endowing it with life and fresh meaning, provides it with form, image, language, and harmony appropriate to it. It presupposes the liveliness and insight of the creative mind; and it demands propriety, the perfect agreement of words, thoughts (as reshaped by the artist), and subject. The result is nature, and it is wit.[55]

When Pope composed the *Essay on Criticism*, there was need for a defense of wit—and that is to say, of literature as well. His own circumstances, involved as he was in a controversy with the most famous writer surviving from the court of Charles II and what was understood to have been the golden age of wit, demanded that he should justify his bold and rash treatment of Wycherley. Locke's conception of wit was of no use to him; in fact, it served the enemy better. But there were other ideas available which were consistent with a conviction of the high dignity and noble function of literature. Through this maze Pope attempted to thread his way. If he was not entirely successful in conveying his meaning with utter clarity, the fault lay partly in the lack of a critical vocabulary. But he had something important to say, and there are good clues to his intention. Pope saw, thought, felt, and wrote as the complete artist. Those who would like to understand his views of the literary art (and of criticism, its complement) must read the *Essay on Criticism* with a fuller awareness of its historical setting.

[55] The tendency to define wit in terms of the thoughts produced, or to emphasize the necessary presence in wit of common sense, is well illustrated by Bouhours, who in *Les Entretiens d'Ariste et d'Eugene* (Paris, 1737), p. 258, defined wit as: "*C'est un corps solide qui brille . . .*" It is no accident that Bouhours, after a neglect of three decades, was becoming influential in England by 1710. Garth had recommended him to Oldmixon, as he probably had to Pope; and Addison in the *Spectator* was to proclaim him the greatest of the French critics. Although Bouhours in *La Maniere de Bien Penser* seemed to lay heavy stress on common sense and the logical element in wit, he made it clear that he was really concerned not with thought but with the turn given the thought by the ingenious mind and with the appropriateness of the style and language to that turn or attitude. Common sense did not strike him as wit until it was vivified and illuminated by the author. This much Pope and Bouhours had in common; in what remains, Pope's superior artistic sense is obvious.

# MILTON'S TREATMENT
## OF REFORMATION HISTORY IN
### *THE TENURE OF KINGS AND MAGISTRATES*

MERRITT Y. HUGHES

W HEN Milton wrote *The Tenure of Kings and Magistrates*, he saw the history of the Reformation brightening down from precedent to precedent to its political fulfillment in the condemnation of Charles I to a traitor's death. When he was at work on the tract in January 1649, his job, as he saw it, was less to prove that the pioneers of the Reformation, from Luther to Pareus, had believed in constitutional government with tyrannicide by legal process as its corollary than it was to justify that principle by "Scripture and Reason." The result was an essay on tyrannicide which—like Tom Paine's *Common Sense*—spoke both to reason and passion. Milton wrote violently because he was angry at the refusal of the Presbyterians—who had "hunted and pursued [Charles] round about the Kingdom with sword and fire"—to support the Rump Parliament in his legal prosecution. He wrote in a temper which Sir Herbert Grierson has called "prophetic," but which others may prefer to think religious, superstitious, or fanatical, when they find Milton convinced that the righteousness of his cause has been providentially marked by the mere fact of the King's being brought to "justice, which is the sword of God, superior to all mortal things, *into whose hands soever by apparent signs his testified will is to put it.*"[1] It is a miracle that *The Tenure* moves

---

[1] The words are quoted from *The Tenure* (p. 3) by Sir Herbert Grierson in *Milton and Wordsworth* (New York, 1937), p. 63.

at all in the cool realm of reason, yet, says W. E. Gilman in *Milton's Rhetoric: Studies in Defense of Liberty*, it does move in that realm and channels all its passion into the skillful orator's appeals to indignation, shame, and fear.

Our interest, however, is not in Milton's candor and insight in stating his case for calling kings to account; it is rather in the handling of the historical evidence for his view of the political meaning of the Reformation. In the first edition of *The Tenure*, which was published on February 13, 1649, only two weeks after Charles' execution, he had very little to say on the topic. It is treated briefly at the climax of a passage reviewing medieval and recent European constitutional precedents for challenging wicked kings, which mentions only the familiar instances of the organization of the League of Smalkald to resist Charles V, the defiances of the Queen Regent, Mary of Guise, and Mary Queen of Scots by the Scottish Calvinists, and the classic challenge to Philip II of Spain by the States of Holland in 1581. In conclusion, Milton remarked that such examples were needless to convince Presbyterians of "the lawfulness of raising War against a Tyrant in defence of Religion, or civil libertie; for no Protestant Church from the first *Waldenses* of *Lyons*, and *Languedoc* to this day but have don it round, and maintain'd it lawful."[2] Aside from this passage Milton had little to say about the Reformation in the first edition of *The Tenure* except to make a promise to fortify his argument with a host of authorities, many of which were to be "Christian, Orthodoxal, and which must needs be more convincing to our Adversaries, Presbyterial."[3] Why he should have kept this promise only a full year later in his second edition is a double question, the answers to which may throw some light on his roll call of Reformers in the Appendix which he added to his second edition in February 1650.

Behind Milton's survey of the Protestant record for organized resistance to "tyrants" in the first edition of *The Tenure* was a challenge that was being commonly proclaimed in Presbyterian pulpits during the trial of Charles and that was officially formulated in "A SERIOUS AND FAITHFUL REPRESENTATION

[2] Milton, *Works*, V, 31. All references are to the Columbia Edition.
[3] *Works*, V, 8

OF . . . MINISTERS OF THE GOSPEL within the Province of London contained in a LETTER from them to the General and his Council of War . . . 18 Ja. 1648/9." On the twelfth of the eighteen pages of this manifesto, which its modern editor[4] regards as marking the tactical superiority of the Presbyterians to the prosecutors of the King, the forty-seven clergymen signing the letter boldly asserted that Scripture gave absolutely no warrant for tyrannicide, and added that

. . . consonant to the tenor of the Scriptures herein, hath alway been the constant judgement and doctrine of Protestant Divines both at home and abroad, with whose Judgements we do fully concurre; disclaiming, detesting and abhorring the wicked and bloody Tenents and Practices of Jesuites, (the worst of Papists,) concerning the opposing of lawfull Magistrates by private Persons, and the murthering of Kings by any, though under the most specious and colourable pretences . . .[5]

In reply to this attempt to give the deepest possible royalist tinge to the folklore of Protestantism, Milton wrote his survey of Protestant resistance to tyranny from the earliest Waldensians in Italy to the revolt of the States of Holland. If his brief excursus into modern history had seemed to him to dispose of his adversaries, his complacence was pardonable. The most distinguished of Parliament's literary champions, the Reverend John Goodwin, in the most influential of the tracts that were written to justify Charles' trial and execution, *The Obstructours of Justice*,[6] writing in May 1649, had quoted Milton's summary

[4] R. W. K. Hinton, in his Introduction. His edition is reprinted in the *School of Art of the University of Reading*, 1949.

[5] The effect of the "REPRESENTATION" can be measured by the numerous replies which it provoked. Without by any means exhausting the list, Hinton mentions six of them in the Introduction to his edition, pp. iv-v. In the very influential *Elenchus Motuum Nuperorum in Anglia* of Charles' personal physician, George Bate, we have (pp. 184–85) a picture of the clergy of all England uniting to protest the proceedings of the High Court of Justice as *contra Sacrae Scripturae & Religionis dictamina*. (The imprint of the first edition, "Lutetiae Parisiorum . . . 1649," has been shown by F. F. Madan in "Milton, Salmasius, and Dugard," in *Transactions of the Bibliographical Society*, N.S., Vol. IV, No. 2 [September 1923], pp. 141–43, to disguise the fact that the book was printed in London.)

[6] Υβριστοδίκαι. *The Obstructours of Justice. Or, a Defence of the Honourable Sentence Passed upon the Late* KING, *by the High* COURT *of* JUSTICE. Opposed Chiefly to *The Serious and Faithfull Representation and*

of the Protestant attitude toward kings "from the first Waldenses . . . to this day" as demolishing the position of the Presbyterians. In Goodwin's eyes, of course, their case could hardly seem anything but indefensible. He declared that they must have said what they did about the passive obedience of the pioneer Reformers, "not only with secret regret, but even with the loud reclamations of their consciences." When a man like Goodwin felt that Milton had done the job so well, we should not be surprised to find that the first edition of *The Tenure* went to press without the Appendix which was added in the second to refute the position of the Presbyterians. Why then, a year later, should he have felt it necessary to bring the second edition to a climax by adding a seven-page annex of quotations from Luther, Calvin, Pareus, and four lesser Reformers, committing them all to the doctrine of the accountability of kings?

The answer may be found in the fact that in spite of Milton and Goodwin the summer and autumn of 1649 found more and more pulpits asserting that the regicide Parliament had been guilty of the first betrayal of the principle of passive obedience to kings in the entire history of the Reformation. The doctrine had also received a kind of international Protestant sanction from the protest of the Ambassadors of the States General on the eve of Charles' execution and from the official condolence of the Dutch clergy as well as of the States General with Charles II on his father's death. Abroad and at home the regicides were being made to look like traitors to the heritage of the Reformation. It was to halt the spread of that belief that Milton supplemented the second edition of *The Tenure* with the Appendix of quotations from the Reformers that we must now examine as an example of his honesty and skill in handling historical evidence.

---

*Vindication of Some of The Ministers of* LONDON. . . . (London, 1649). Thomason Index, E 557 [2]). The passages quoted in the present study occur on pp. 70–71. Goodwin's position as vicar of St. Stephen's, Coleman Street, and one of London's most popular Independent preachers, has been indicated by William Haller in *Tracts on Liberty in the Puritan Revolution* (New York, 1934), I, 19–20 and *passim*. The relation of *The Obstructours* to *The Tenure* has been indicated by William R. Parker in *Milton's Contemporary Reputation* (Columbus, Ohio, 1940), pp. 80–82.

## II

The first of the seven Reformers to be quoted in Milton's Appendix is Luther. Like the others, he is quoted in fragments —mere drops of water out of the ocean of his works—and at once we rightly suspect that he is being quoted at second or at n'th hand from sources perhaps less authentic than the best popular editions of his *Table Talk*. Indeed, Milton tells us himself what his sources were, for the first of them was the best Protestant account of the German Reformation, and he could inspire confidence by quoting from *A Famous Cronicle of Oure Time, Called Sleidanes Commentaries, Concerning the State of Religion and Commonwealth, During the Raigne of the Emperor Charles the Fift*.[7] When the modern reader finds Milton corroborating his quotations from Sleidan from the Catholic humanist, Johannes Cochlaeus, as honest a writer as Sleidan though a frankly bitter enemy of Luther, uncertainty of Milton's motives arises. His modern editor, William T. Allison, holds that the impression that one gets from reading Luther's original statements in his addresses to the rebels and to the nobles in the Peasants' War in 1525 is "quite the contrary of the doctrine supported by Milton."[8] And Allison goes on to accuse him of "committing the sin for which he reproaches his opponents, wresting authorities to his own purpose in a most unscrupulous manner." Even in the full and careful account of the Peasants' War in Sleidan's fifth book Allison sees the historian's view of Luther as very different from Milton's. He ignores Milton's appeal to Cochlaeus. Nor is Cochlaeus likely to carry weight

[7] This title is that of the translation by John Daus that was published in London in 1560. Passages from Sleidan that are quoted in English are from this work. It was first published in Latin at Strasbourg in 1555 under the title *Io. Sleidani, de Statu Religionis et Reipublicae, Carolo V Caesare, Commentarii XXV libris comprehensi*. The British Museum copy has been used. Milton's page references (as J. H. Hanford pointed out in *PMLA* XXXVI [1921], 271) do not agree with "any of the Latin editions in the British Museum or the Harvard College library," but Ruth Mohl has recently discovered that they do agree with an edition in one of the New York libraries.

[8] *The Tenure of Kings and Magistrates*, edited by W. T. Allison, was published in 1911 as No. 51 in the "Yale Studies in English." The quoted words are taken from pp. 139–40.

with modern readers who have learned from Troeltsch to think of both Luther and Calvin as standing essentially together "in a very strict demand for respect for authority, even in cases where those who wield authority are not particularly estimable."[9] The reader must judge in the light of the passages that Milton chose to quote from Luther, and in that of their previous history of quotation.

Omitting only a digressive conclusion of Milton's, the passages which he quoted from Luther and his remarks on them are these:

## LUTHER.
### *Lib. contra Rusticos apud Sleidan. 1. 5.*

Is est hodie rerum status, &c. *Such is the state of things at this day, that men neither can, nor will, nor indeed ought to endure longer the domination of you Princes.*

Neque vero Caesarem, &c. *Neither is Caesar to make Warr as head of Christ'ndom, Protector of the Church, Defender of the Faith; these Titles being fals and Windie, and most Kings being the greatest Enemies to Religion. Lib: De bello contra Turcas. apud Sleid. 1. 14.* What hinders then, but that we may depose or punish them?

These also are recited by *Cochlaeus* in his *Miscellanies* to be the words of *Luther*, or some other eminent Divine, then in *Germany*, when the Protestants there entred into solemn Covnant at *Smalcaldia*. Ut ora ijs obturem &c. *That I may stop thir mouthes, the Pope and the Emperor are not born but elected, and may also be depos'd as hath bin oft'n don.* If *Luther*, or whoever els thought so, he could not stay there; for the right of birth or succession can be no privilege in nature to let a Tyrant sit irremoveable over a Nation free born, without transforming that Nation from the nature and condition of men born free, into natural, hereditary, and successive slaves. Therfore he saith furder; *To displace and throw down this Exactor, this Phalaris, this Nero, is a work well pleasing to God;* Namely, for being such a one: which is a moral reason.[10]

In commenting on this passage an editor should, if possible, consult Cochlaeus to see how his *Miscellanies* bear upon Sleidan's treatment of him as well as upon Milton's. Allison mentions the work only to regret that it was not available to him. If he

---

[9] Ernst Troeltsch, *The Social Teaching of the Christian Churches*, translated by Olive Wyon (London, 1931), p. 613.
[10] Milton, *Works*, V, 46–47.

had seen it, he would have found two of Milton's quotations presented as positively by Luther and in the first case twice introduced in what the Catholic writer regarded as damning catalogues of Luther's animadversions against princes.[11] Cochlaeus' own animus against Luther—as Carl Otto pointed out—was the reluctant but finally deep hatred of the humanist who, like Erasmus, had much initial sympathy with the Reformer but was later frightened away by his defiance of authority in Church and State. It would be interesting to learn whether Milton knew the witty verses in Cochlaeus' satire of "the hooded Minotaur of Wittenberg" and Luther's heavy-handed reply in his book, *Against the Armed Man Cochlaeus*.[12] In the *Miscellanies* Cochlaeus was using all the violence to which controversialists then felt themselves entitled, but he was not overstating the case as he understood it. He honestly saw the Reformer's character as ready to rebel against all human authority in the name of the will of God. He would have approved Jacques Maritain's summing up: *"Chez Luther . . . c'est la conception de la vie qui est atteinte, on peut dire qu'il est le premier grand romantique."*[13]

The farthest-reaching justification of Milton's interpretation of Sleidan's account of Luther is to be found in the last of the passages for which he appealed for confirmation to Cochlaeus —*"Ut ijs ora obturem &c."* The passage in the *Miscellanies* cites Luther's *"libellus Teuthonicus cum rota fortunae, absque nomine Authoris & impressoris, usque adeo seditiosus ac san-*

[11] *"In Causa Religionis Miscellaneorum libri tres in diversos Tractatos antea non aeditos, ac diversis temporibus, locisque scriptos digesti.* Per Iohannem Cochlaeum. Ingolstadii excudebat Alexander Vveissenborn. . . . MDXLV."
Milton's first quotation from Luther—*"Is est hodie etc."*—is found on pp. 59v and 61v; his last, on p. 49v. The explanation of his inclusion of the second, which I have not found in Cochlaeus, may have been the overemphasis laid in the anonymous tract, *Of Resisting the Lawfull Magistrates upon Colour of Religion* (1643; Thomason, E 102 [19], p. 25), on Sleidan's account of Luther's opposition to the Turkish wars of Charles V as amounting to an absolute declaration that "the cause of Religion, although it were of Christianity against Mohametisme, was not for him (Luther) sufficient warrant for a defensive war." Since *Of Resisting* went into later editions in 1644, 1646, and 1647, Milton may have wished to correct its appeal to Luther's authority against Parliament in the civil war.

[12] *Adversus Armatum Virum Cokleum* (Wittenbergae, 1523).

[13] *Trois Reformateurs* (Paris, 1925), p. 42.

*guinarius, ut nihil possit in Principes crudelius aut periculosius excogitari.*" The charge is that Luther accused all rulers of pillaging their realms by taxation and so deserving to be treated like Phalaris and Nero. And the passage concludes, reversing the order of the sentences that Milton quotes, by observing that "*Papa & Caesar non nati sed electi sunt Principes, qui possunt deponi, Id quod propter eorum malefacta saepe factum est. Et tamen hi sunt summi Principatus, Et eorum delegati, ut sunt Principes & alij domini, non deberent deponi de mala potestate sua?*" From this passage it would seem that Milton was fully entitled to read Cochlaeus as regarding Luther as a dangerously revolutionary advocate even in his younger days of the accountability of kings to their earthly creators. That seems to be his interpretation of Luther's behavior during the Peasants' War, both when he seemed to be the rebels' advocate and later when he urged the princes to suppress their violence. On this point Cochlaeus is unambiguous. Sleidan may seem in some passages to take an opposite view of Luther's behavior in the course of the year 1525, and Allison may be entitled to think that Milton deliberately distorted the evidence of his fifth book; but it is at least equally possible to read Sleidan as no more eager to clear Luther of complicity with the peasants in their violent revolt than he was determined all the way along to show him as missing no opportunity to adjure "the Princes, Noblemen and Gentlemen of the Empire . . . for God's sake and their own peace and safety, to use their subjects like men, not like beasts for the yoke and the slaughter."[14] This is not the place either to discuss Sleidan's view of Luther's political opinions or to balance the charge of a modern Luther-baiter like P. F. Wiener, for whom he was "the creator and leader of the whole peasant movement"[15] as well as its destroyer in the end, with the insistence of an historian like Preserved Smith that there is no basis whatever for the belief that Luther "sided with the insurgents while they

[14] It would be interesting if we could confirm the probability that Milton knew that these words of Luther—in just the English which is quoted above—figured on the first page of an anonymous *History of the Anabaptists* which was published in London in 1642.

[15] Peter F. Wiener in *Martin Luther, Hitler's Spiritual Ancestor* (London, n.d.), p. 45.

were likely to win and then turned to curry favor with the princes when *they* triumphed."[16] There can be no reasonable doubt that, throughout the Peasants' War, Luther was independent enough of both sides to excoriate both. Milton was too much of an idealist not to approve his plague of both their houses.

It may be added that Milton was too much of an historian not to look beyond Luther's part in the Peasants' War for an estimate of his place as a political thinker. His quotations show that in summing up Luther's political thought he was looking beyond the Peasants' War to the time when the German princes won the Reformer's reluctant consent to their decision to fight if necessary against their Emperor in defense of their faith. When a modern historian can write that from the *Appeal to the German Nobility* in 1520 to the very end of Luther's life he always "clearly recognized a right of reform in accordance with the constitutional principles of a government,"[17] Milton can hardly be accused of straining the evidence in entertaining the same idea.

A final word in defense of Milton's tactical use of Cochlaeus' *Miscellanies* may be said in the light of the abuse of *Eikonoklastes* and perhaps (in the passage which interests us) of *The Tenure* by an obscure Burgundian who wrote a reply to the former in 1652 under the title *Carolus I Brittaniarum Rex.* Though the little volume pretended to have been issued in Dublin, it seems to have been printed in Dijon and to have been the work of a certain Claude Barthelemy Morisot, who took many of his facts from Bates's *Elenchus.*[18] Writing as a Catholic Frenchman, eager simply to show that Milton was apologizing

---

[16] Preserved Smith in *The Life and Letters of Martin Luther* (Boston and New York, 1911), p. 164.

[17] Luther Hess Waring in *The Political Theories of Martin Luther* (New York and London, 1910), p. 138.

[18] According to Didot's *Biographie Nouvelle Universelle,* as quoted in *A Catalogue of the Bradshaw Collection of Irish Books in the University Library Cambridge* [Cambridge, 1916], II, 1121), *Carolus I* "is by Claude Barthelemy Morisot, and is in answer to Milton's *Eikonoklastes.* Query—printed in Dijon." Although the Cambridge bibliographer does not mention them, there are clear implications in the text that the book was a Frenchman's work, and they are confirmed by the identity of an ornament on A2v with the ornament on a3r (in both cases at the end of a preface) of "*Claudii Bartholomaei Morisoti Perwiana.* Divione . . . M DC XLV." *Carolus I* is mentioned in Mason's *Life of Milton,* IV, 436–37.

for his country in the black guilt of its murder of its king, and writing with no desire to whitewash the traditional Protestant attitude toward tyrannicide, Morisot looked at the Reformation as a consistently subversive political movement. From John Huss to John Calvin he regarded the Reformers as rebels against their lawful rulers. Luther and Thomas Münzer, the peasants' leader in 1525, seemed to him equally guilty of that crime against society. Fairfax and Cromwell, he said, had learned from the continental Reformers how to betray their king. Morisot quoted the very passage from Calvin's "Commentary on Daniel" which Milton quoted to prove that Calvin was a foe of kings if not of the institution of kingship itself. If Milton had issued a third edition of *The Tenure* in 1652, he might have capped his appeal to Cochlaeus by observing that his own Burgundian critic fully confirmed the view of Luther's old adversary about the real drift of Luther's political thought.

## III

With the passages that Milton chose to quote from his six remaining Reformers the modern reader is unlikely to quarrel, though he may think that those from Calvin and Pareus represent their authors in suspiciously minor works. He cannot think that of the Swiss Reformer, Ulrich Zwingli, who is represented by six theses from his *Opus Articulorum sive Conclusionum*[19] which everyone knew and valued as a kind of Magna Charta of Protestant political action against kings who "reign perfidiously." Zwingli's lifelong pursuit of personal influence within the democratic framework of Zurich's municipal government was known to have squared with the theses that he had been prepared to defend in public debate. His motives and judgment might be questioned, but not the consistency of his writings with his public record. With Martin Bucer the case was very different, but Milton was on equally safe ground. As he knew from his study of the Alsatian Reformer's works when he wrote *Martin Bucer*

[19] All of Milton's passages are taken from pp. 84–86 of the *Opera D. Huldrychi Zuinglii, vigilantissimi Tiguranae ecclesiae Antistes, partim quidem ab ipso Latine conscripta, partim vero a vernaculo sermone in Latinum translata* (Zurich, 1545).

*on Divorce* in 1644, their concern with politics was comparatively slight. In the treatise that he wrote for Edward VI during the two years of exile that ended his career in England in 1551, the *De Regno Christi*, Bucer had no reason to urge his political doctrines upon the friendly boy king. He had stated them explicitly in his Commentaries on the Four Gospels (*Sacra Quattuor Evangelia*) in his discussion of Matthew 39:5—"Resist not evil"—by which Milton knew that his writings were best represented to the English public. As a foundation for the doctrine of lawful resistance to tyrants or "ungodly" kings, Christ's doctrine of nonresistance to evil was familiar to Milton's readers from passages like the one that we shall see him quoting from Pareus. Bucer's statement of it fell just a little short of drawing the clear conclusion that the abuse of power justifies rebellion or even passive resistance, and Milton betrayed his dissatisfaction with his excerpt from Bucer by adding his own note to the effect that "the less tolerable" a supreme power makes itself, "the more unpardonably to be punish'd."[20]

The first Reformer to extract the fully sanctioned principle of resistance to unworthy kings from the Biblical doctrine of nonresistance of evil was Calvin, writing in the famous final chapter of the *Institutes of the Christian Religion*. From a passionate opening assertion of St. Paul's principle in Romans 13:1 —"Let every soul be subject to the higher powers"—Calvin moved on through thirty-one utterly logical paragraphs to a closing defense of the constitutional subjection of rulers to control by officers like the Tribunes of the People in ancient Rome or the Ephors in ancient Sparta. His final position was that, if such officers "winke at kinges wilfully raging over and treading downe the poore communaltie, their dissembling is not without wicked breache of faith, because they deceitfully betray the libertie of the people, whereof they know themselves to bee appointed protectors by the ordinaunce of God."[21] Milton ignored this passage and chose to represent Calvin in his sampling

[20] *Works*, V, 49.

[21] *The Institute of the Christian Religion, written in Latine by M. John Calvine, and translated into English . . . by Thomas Norton* (London, 1587), p. 507r.

of the political teaching of the Reformers simply by a single passage from his Commentary on Daniel. To modern eyes the fragment about Daniel is far less dangerous political dynamite than the conclusion to the *Institutes*. In preferring it Milton incurs no suspicion of misrepresenting Calvin by quoting him in an unguarded moment. Readers of *The Tenure* could be expected to know the last chapter of the *Institutes* as American college students are supposed to know the Constitution of the United States. And they could be expected to know that Calvin closed by illustrating his revolutionary doctrine with the case of Nebuchadnezzar in the Prophecy of Daniel as a classical example of an ungodly monarch who was brought to punishment for his pride. The picture of Nebuchadnezzar as a proud emperor who

> wende that God, that sit in magestee,
> Ne myghte hym nat bireve of his estaat,

was an old one, but Calvin gave it new meaning. In his Commentary on Daniel as well as in the *Institutes* Nebuchadnezzar became a symbol of royal ungodliness ripe for punishment by the godly. The core of Calvin's political thought was generally recognized as having been put into the second of the two passages that Milton quoted from the Commentary: "Abdicant se terreni principes, &c. *Earthly Princes depose themselves while they rise against God, yet they are unworthy to be numberd among men: rather it behooves us to spitt upon thir heads then to obey them. On Dan: c. 6. v. 22.*"[22]

In *Carolus I*, Morisot pounced upon Milton for quoting this passage—not because it misrepresented Calvin, but because, in Milton's defense of the judgment of the High Court upon King Charles, Morisot found a fresh instance to confirm his conviction that Calvin's principles had always been a weapon to be used against legitimate kings who were so ill-advised as to refuse to bow to Calvinism.[23] In the following paragraph in *Carolus I*, John Knox and George Buchanan are assailed for using Calvin's

---

[22] *Works*, V, 48.

[23] After quoting the passage from Calvin on Daniel which Milton quoted, Morisot wrote: "Contra Deum autem Principes insurgunt qui Calvinistis non favent, solis, ut ipsi aiunt, verè Catholicis, & Gens Dei. Cui illud datum, ut legitimè periuret, & in legitimos suos Principes rebellet." *Carolus I*, p. 8.

doctrine against Mary Queen of Scots and the young James VI of Scotland. It almost seems as if Morisot wrote with *The Tenure* in mind and was attacking Milton both for echoing Calvin and for repeating—earlier in the pamphlet—Knox's account of his famous debate with Maitland of Lethington in June 1564, when he quoted Calvin, Bucer, and Luther to establish the right of the people and the Kirk to "execute jugementis aganis thair King, being an offendar."

From the Scottish Calvinists Milton turned to their English contemporaries, men like Dudley Fenner, Thomas Cartwright, Anthony Gilby, and Christopher Goodman, all of whom had suffered exile under Mary or Elizabeth. He may not have known them well, for he quoted only Gilby and Goodman, the former fragmentarily. But Goodman's book, *How Superior Powers Ought to Be Obeyed*, which was published in the last year of Mary's reign, must have been beside him as he wrote. Though his quotations vary insignificantly from the text as we have it in the modern facsimile edition, his page references are all accurate. He saw the work in just the light that its modern editor[24] does, as marking "the first definite shift of opinion under the pressure of religion, away from the doctrines of almost unlimited obedience which characterize the political thought of the first half of the [sixteenth] century." At greater length than he quoted from any of the other early Reformers, Milton gave his readers Goodman's versions of the Calvinist doctrine that subjects are absolved from obedience to unworthy kings, that guilt should disqualify every ruler, and that "No person is exempt by any law of God from this punishment, be he King, Queene, or Emperor, he myst dy the death."[25] The words, it seemed, might have been written to apply to King Charles as well as to Queen Mary a century earlier. No Royalist, of course, would brook such an application of them; but no Royalist would have denied that the words meant just what Milton took them to mean.

For the modern reader the strangest passage that Milton

[24] Charles H. McIlwain, writing on the first page of his Bibliographical Note to the edition of the Facsimile Text Society in 1931.

[25] *Works*, V, 51.

put into his very international Appendix to *The Tenure* was the paragraph from the German Calvinist Pareus on Romans 13, giving the final extension to Calvin's political interpretation of it in the last chapter of the *Institutes*. Milton quoted Pareus very briefly as simply saying:

> Quorum est constituere Magistratus, &c. *They whose part it is to set up Magistrates, may restrain them also from outragious deeds, or pull them down; but all Magistrates are set up either by Parlament, or by Electors, or by other Magistrates; They therfore who exalted them, may lawfully degrade and punish them.*[26]

The interpretation here put upon St. Paul's admonition that every soul should be subject to the higher powers is even more ingenious than Calvin's. None of the ingenuity was due to Milton. His translation is faithful to the Latin original as he found it in Pareus' *Theological Works*. The straining of St. Paul's text in the passage as Milton rendered it was entirely Pareus' doing. Beginning with a distinction between the higher powers and the men to whom in the course of human events they are entrusted, Pareus went on to assert that obedience was due only to the abstract, divine ordained power itself and never directly to any magistrate or ruler who might temporarily be clothed with it. His argument expanded into a philosophical account of all the powers, physical and moral, upon which life itself depends. All human well-being emerges in his discussion as consisting in obedience to a hierarchy of powers that in their essence are divinely otherworldly though they must be vested in various creatures upon whose claim to individual respect we cannot depend. Not undeservedly, since Pareus wrote with imagination and sincerity as well as with acumen, his treatment of Calvin's interpretation of Romans 13 became famous. In John Goodman's *Right and Might Well Met*,[27] for example, it is mentioned as justifying resistance to tyrants as if they were no

---

[26] *Works*, V, 49. Milton found the passage in *D. Davidis Parei Operum Theologicorum Exegeticorum* Tome I (Frankfurt, 1647), Pars Tertia, p. 262 (misnumbered 266). It occurs in a section "De Potestate Civili" in the work entitled "D. Parei Explicatio Dubiorum in Cap. xiii ad Romanos." Again on p. 281 he found it repeated between a résumé of David Owen's attack on it and a reply to Owen by Pareus' editor, who was his son, Philip Pareus.

[27] London, 1643. Pp. 41–42. (Thomason Index E 536 [28].)

better than highwaymen, and Pareus' entire case is summarized from the initial distinction between abstract and concrete power to the final denial of the obligation to obey an evil ruler. At least at second hand, Milton could expect his readers to know something about Pareus' revolutionary interpretation of the Biblical injunction of the duty of obedience to the higher powers.

At second hand also Milton could count upon general familiarity with Pareus through a controversy that began at Cambridge three years before his death in 1622 and ended his long and honorable career as a professor of theology at Heidelberg. It was begun by a Cambridge don, David Owen, whose gifts and principles as a political philosopher and theologian are suggested by the title of one of his later works, *Puritano-Jesuitismus, the Puritan Turn'd Jesuite; or Rather Out-vying Him in Those Diabolicall and Dangerous Positions, of the Deposition of Kings.* In 1619 Owen saw fit to challenge Pareus in a Latin disputation that was translated and published in 1642 under the title, *Anti-Pareus, or, A Treatise in Defence of the Royall Right of Kings: Against Paraeus and the Rest of the Anti-Monarchians, Whether Presbyterians or Jesuits. Wherein Is Maintained the Unlawfulnesse of Opposing and Taking Up Arms Against the Prince, Either by Any Private Subject, Inferior Magistrate, the States of the Kingdom, or the Pope of Rome* . . . On the second page, after acknowledging that in 1612 Pareus had "writ very elegantly concerning the Lawfull Right of Kings . . . against *Bellarmine, Becanus,* and other Popish Parasites," Owen proceeded to inveigh against him for brandishing "the inferior Magistrates Sword against Kings and greatest Emperours." To his castigation for that crime Owen devoted the *Anti-Pareus* and perhaps thereby provoked Milton to give him immortality in England by quoting him in *The Tenure.*

Milton may have found Owen's strictures on Pareus' interpretation of Romans 13 in the magnificent edition of the Reformer's *Theological Works* which his son Philip issued at Frankfurt in 1647 with a full résumé of all the criticism that had been leveled at his father. We may read Owen in the English of the *Anti-Paraeus,*[28] where he has this remark to make

[28] Pp. 37–38.

about the passage which Milton quoted from the commentary of Pareus on Romans 13: "This Assertion is Capitall, which the Emperour will not admit, the King will not suffer; which *Bellarmine* himselfe doth affirme to be rejected by the consent of all Divines, that it is not necessary for me to refute it." Can it be that in quoting what Owen had declared to be unworthy of refutation Milton hoped that some of his readers would be well enough acquainted with the history of the controversy to smile? One of them at least was struck by his quotation. In *Respublica Anglicana*,[29] George Wither thanked him for quoting what Pareus had said "upon that place in the Epistle to the Romans, be subject to the higher powers, &c," and added that it was "confirmed by a multitude of Protestant Divines, and reasons, as you may see at large in a late treatise, entituled, *The tenor of Kings and Magistrates*."

Wither's remark about Milton's use of a famous passage from Pareus suggests that it seemed to him to have been put into a correct historical perspective as well as brought tellingly to bear upon the question which the High Court of Justice had just determined. Modern criticism has been inclined to minimize the influence of *The Tenure* upon contemporary thought and to question the ingenuousness of Milton's use of his historical authorities. Did Wither see more clearly on both points than we can? Or are we right to question the faith of the nineteenth century in Milton's candor and competence as an historian? Our conclusion in the light of his treatment of Reformation history in *The Tenure*, though it may not be to recognize him as the essentially critical student of sources that Sir Charles Firth and Professor J. Milton French have seen in the author of *The History of Britain*, must yet be to clear him of having distorted the record that ran from Luther to Paraeus. The distorters of that record—as he later recalled in *The Second Defence*[30]—were the

[29] George Wither, *Respublica Anglicana* (Thomason Index, E 780 [25], 1650), p. 41.

[30] "Tum vero tandem, cum Presbyteriani quidem Ministri, Carolo prius infestissimi, nunc Independentium partes suis anteferri, & in Senatu plus posse indignantes, Parlamenti sententiae de Rege latae (non facto irati, sed quod ipsorum factio non fecisset) reclamitarent, & quantum in ipsis erat, tumultuarentur, ausi affirmare Protestantium doctrinam, omnesque ecclesias reformatas

"magnificently ignorant or impudent clergy" who, as much as in them lay, were vociferating that Protestant doctrine by its essence was at war with the regicide sentence on King Charles. It was in reply to that pious distortion of history that Milton added his Appendix to *The Tenure.* In doing so he was anything but the deliberate betrayer of Truth to a specious perversion of justice that Professor S. B. Liljegren would have us believe him because in the last chapter of *Eikonoklastes* he declared Justice stronger than Truth.[31] By insisting in *The Tenure* and again in *The Second Defence* that the Presbyterians were deliberately wrenching fact in favor of faction, Milton did a service to historical truth as well as to a partisan cause to which his unfriendliest modern critics must acknowledge that both Britain and the United States of America owe much that is characteristic in their respective constitutions.

ab ejusmodi in reges atroci sententiâ abhorrere, ratus falsitati tam apertae palàm eundum obviàm esse, ne tum quidem de Carolo quicquam scripsi aut suasi, sed quid in genere contra tyrannos liceret, adductis haud paucis summorum Theologorum testiminiis, ostendi; & insignem hominum meliora profitentium, sive ignorantiam sive impudentiam propè concionabundus incessi." *Works,* VIII, 134, 136.

[31] S. B. Liljegren, *Studies in Milton* (Lund, 1918), pp. 141–43.

# TRAVEL AS EDUCATION

## George B. Parks

S
URELY you have traveled enough, and the manners and cities of foreign peoples are an open book to you." So the government of Florence wrote to Petrarch in inviting him to return home to lecture in the new university.[1] The sentence sums up the dual aim of travel as understood throughout the Renaissance and long afterward. The traveler was to study countries and men, and, like Ulysses in a favorite illustration of the theory, was to become wise:

Felix qui mundi mores cognovit et urbes.

"Humble and plebeian souls stay at home, bound to their own piece of earth," wrote the humanist Lipsius, following Plato; "that soul is nearer the divine which rejoices in movement, as do the heavens themselves. Therefore almost all great men from earliest times to our own time were travelers."[2]

The flood of treatises on travel which expanded and varied these sentiments during the late and post-Renaissance makes an interesting part of the literature of education.[3] From 1570 to

[1] "Satis nempe pervagatus es, et mores urbesque tibi exterarum gentium clare sunt": the Priors and Gonfalonier of Florence to Petrarch, probably in 1351, ut cit. Alessandro Gherardi, *Statuti della Università e Studio Fiorentino* (*R. Deputazione Toscana sugli Studi di Storia Patria, Documenti*, Vol. VII, 1881), p. 284.

[2] Justus Lipsius, "Epistola ad Philippum Lanoyum . . . iter in Italiam cogitantem" (1578), in *Epistolarum selectarum centuria prima* (Leyden, 1586), Ep. 22. The letter was frequently reprinted; it was translated, much expanded, into English by John Stradling (1592).

[3] It is the subject of the excellent pioneer study by Professor Clare Howard, *English Travellers of the Renaissance* (London, 1914). I venture a somewhat different view of the course of the literature in the seventeenth century.

1630 is roughly the period of writing of the treatises, both Continental and English. By the later date, at least the English writers on the subject might seem to have lost the high earlier enthusiasm, and so recommended travel for arts and manners rather than for serious understanding of the world. Later, indeed, Milton, Gilbert Burnet, and Locke leave little place in their educational theory for travel as currently undertaken, and we might suppose that the idea was already an anachronism, an abandoned hope of the Renaissance.

Actually it was not so. A survey of the treatises reveals at the same time greater strength of idea and greater variety than might have been supposed. Moreover, and what may prove more important than the treatises, the literature describing the actual travel demonstrates its effectiveness. Far from destroying the Renaissance ideal of a Ulysses grown wise by travel, the seventeenth century, in England at least, in fact multiplied the educational possibilities. Travel makes not merely a Ulysses, it might then have been written; it may make also an Aristotle or a perceptive Maecenas.

I perceive three phases of English thought and action with respect to educational travel. In the first, from 1570 to 1620, English theorists and travelers alike expect the view of men and cities to produce a full political knowledge of foreign countries; travel thus becomes training for public life. This idea was never abandoned; it continued to make one, though not the only one, of the aims of travel, and can be discovered guiding the travels of various later persons.

In the second phase, the traveler is expected to take account of the new aesthetic interest in works of art, which came to supplement the early scholarly interest in ancient works of art as merely antiquities. This tendency begins to appear about 1620.

In the third phase, the traveler is expected to show interest in scientific and technological matters. First unmistakably seen in the educational travel of John Evelyn, the interest naturally finds strong support in the world-wide research program of the Royal Society. It seldom became, however, the sole aim of even the most determined "philosophical" traveler, and except in the *Transactions* of the Society it remains but one theme among the several we have noted.

## II

Francis Bacon is the author of a classic statement of the humanist aims of travel. The obvious purpose of travel, he wrote to the young Lord Rutland in 1596,[4] is

to see the beauty of many cities, know the manners of many countries, and learn the language of many nations. Some of these may serve for ornaments, and all of them for delights; but your Lordship must look further than these; for the greatest ornament is the inward beauty of the mind, and when you have known as great variety of delight as the world will afford, you will confess that the greatest delight is . . . to feel that you do every day become more worthy; therefore your Lordship's end and scope should be that which in moral philosophy we call *cultum animi*, the tilling and manuring of your own mind.

That mind here means soul is evident from what follows. Beauty of mind, the advice continues, is evidenced by sweetness of behavior; health by freedom from passions; strength by the power to do great and good things. Travel promotes beauty of mind by revealing an infinite variety of behavior and manners to imitate. It promotes health by revealing one's own passions in the presence of the new delights which stir new passions. It promotes strength if it afford opportunity to go to the wars, and otherwise at least it promotes knowledge.

So the end of education is moral. The means is intellectual, the subject matter civil (that is, political) knowledge. From the liberal arts and from history, studied with a tutor or in a university, and by comparison of expert opinions, one learns judgment. From observation one becomes aware of the effect of both ability and chance in the affairs of men. In modern terms, one would learn to know the dynamics of the rise and fall of individuals.

Travel has receded from view in the course of the letter, and in any case Bacon can hardly have spoken his whole mind

[4] The letter was first published, signed "E" and ascribed to the Earl of Essex, in *Profitable Instructions* (1633), pp. 27–73. It was edited from several MSS by James Spedding, *Letters and Life of Francis Bacon*, II (1862), 6–15, who assigned it to Bacon on the strength of close parallels to the language and ideas of the *Advancement of Learning*. The two other letters of advice to the same youth which Spedding also prints (pp. 16–20) are merely routine, and there is no evidence for assigning them to Bacon.

to a youth. His essay "Of Travel," first published in the 1625 volume of the *Essays*, is more precise, saying little about theory and much about the sharply practical matters of travel. Perhaps the main activity of the traveler is to see all that can be seen: as scholar, all that universities have to offer, and the view of antiquities and ruins as evidences of history; as political inquirer, all possible light on the structure and functioning of states, princes, armies and navies, courts of justice, and church hierarchies; as observer of manners, all varieties of ceremonies of courts and upper classes. Manners and governments would be his study.

In these essays, each incompletely developed, Bacon both sounds and evades the specifically English theme of travel as political education. Continental humanists sometimes set political study as one goal among several for the travel of youthful nobles or princes; but English theory and apparent English practice imposed on the traveler a singly political form of education. The tradition begins with Lord Burghley in 1570, writing down a veritable course in political intelligence for an earlier Lord Rutland, who was to bring back a full knowledge of the political, military, and financial organization of France and other countries.[5] The youth made some notes in this direction when he crossed the French frontier,[6] but we do not know if he continued to do so. Nor do we know the results of the travel of his son, for whom Bacon and Essex wrote advice.

The political interest continues after Burghley (I sum up rapidly) in the instructions for travel of two other secretaries of state, Sir Francis Walsingham[7] and William Davison;[8] in the practice of Philip Sidney in the early 1570's,[9] and in his and his father's instructions to Robert Sidney after 1577;[10] in the

[5] State Papers Domestic, Elizabeth, Vol. LXXVII, Art. 6.

[6] Historical Manuscripts Commission, *Report 12, Appendix*, Part IV, p. 91.

[7] Conyers Read (ed.) in *Mr. Secretary Walsingham* (1925), I, 18–20.

[8] Printed in *Profitable Instructions: Describing what speciall Observations are to be taken by Travellers* (1633), pp. 1–24.

[9] Described in his *Correspondence* with Languet, collected and translated by Steuart A. Peers (1845).

[10] Philip Sidney's most important letter was printed in *Profitable Instructions*, pp. 74–103; re-edited from MS by Albert Feuillerat, *The Complete*

practice of Thomas Bodley, turning from academic life in 1576 to four years of travel in preparation for diplomatic service; perhaps in the three years in France, from 1576 to 1579, of Francis Bacon, of which we are ill-informed, and certainly in the practice of his brother Anthony, whose twelve years abroad laid the basis for his intelligence network built up for the service of Essex; in the theoretical support given to the idea of travel as preparation for diplomacy by the influential Alberico Gentili, professor of civil law at Oxford, in his work, *De legationibus*, of 1585;[11] certainly in the practice of his students Henry Wotton and Fynes Moryson, both of whom traveled abroad for several years of active study; in the political studies produced by them and also by John Eliot, Robert Dallington, and Edwin Sandys as a result of their *ad hoc* travel in the 1590's; in the actual practice of Francis Davison, following his father's advice in 1596 and 1597 by collecting numerous political "relations" of foreign countries and by compiling one or more himself;[12] in the instructions on political travel published by Thomas Palmer in 1606,[13] who advised that the student sum up his political study abroad by intelligence reports to English envoys abroad and to the Privy Council at home; in the instructions of Fulke Greville in 1609[14] to a young cousin, the elderly Greville no doubt remembering Philip Sidney's devoted study abroad as a kind of model; in the instructions about 1620 of the ninth Earl of Northumberland[15] to his heir in the ways of acquiring political knowledge useful to both legislator and landowner; and finally in Bacon's essay "Of Travel."

Then the fashion changed: or at least we find conscious exception taken to it. Edward Lord Herbert of Cherbury re-

---

*Works*, III, 124–27. Other letters by Philip, Sir Henry, and Robert were edited by Arthur Collins, *Letters and Memorials of State* (1746), I, 246–47, 271–72, 283–86.

[11] Lib. III, chap. xiv.

[12] His letters were edited by Sir Harris Nicolas in his edition of the *Poetical Rhapsody* (1820), I, v–li.

[13] *An Essay of the Meanes how to make Our Travailes, into forraine Countries, the more profitable and honorable.*

[14] "A Letter of Travel," in *Certain . . . Works* (1633), pp. 295–98; reprinted in A. B. Grosart, *The Works of Fulke Greville* (1870), IV, 302–6.

[15] "Instructions for the Lord Percy in his Trauells," ed. Francis Grose in *Antiquarian Repertory*, IV (1809), 374–80.

membered of his travel year in France in 1608 only the idle
life of a courtier. The young Owen Felltham's essay on travel
in the *Resolves* (about 1620) scorned the idea of book-learning
abroad, such as was naturally needed by students of government,
preferring persons "well versed in the World, languaged and
well read in men: which for Policy and Negotiation is much
better." The ideal of knowledge of men and cities seems to have
shrunk to knowledge merely of men. The same dilettante air
is conveyed by the educator Henry Peacham's *The Compleat
Gentleman* (1622), in which the chapter "Of Trauaile" advises
only training in manners; while his later essay "Of Travaile"[16]
is devoted mostly to merely practical advice for the road.

The political note was not, however, lost. In 1633, for some
reason which I have not guessed, a body of earlier instructions
on travel was brought together and published: a letter of Sidney,
the letter of Essex which was largely written by Bacon, the
letter of Davison. These *Profitable Instructions*, as the little
book was called, quite clearly meant to keep alive the political
survey; and the same year also saw published a translation from
the Italian of Cardinal Sermonetta, actually Enrico Caetani, as
*Instructions for Young Gentlemen*, a similar document written
fifty years before as advice to a youth on his travel to the court
and army of the Duke of Parma in the Low Countries.

Here ends the formal promulgation of the theory of travel
as political education. Yet the lesson was not forgotten. The
theory found a strange echo in Milton's essay *On Education*
(1644), which prescribed that youths in their later 'teens should
travel through their own country to observe "places of strength,
all commodities of building and of soil, for towns and tillage,
harbors and ports for trade,"[17] exactly in the manner formerly
prescribed for travelers abroad. The theory also found a place
in the practice of John Evelyn, who, though he did not mention
political observation when he was writing up his travel diary,
nonetheless dutifully wrote a political study of *The State of
France* (1652) when he had completed his formal travels. The

---

[16] Included in *The Truth of our Times* (1638); in Facsimile Text Society ed. (1942), pp. 127–44.

[17] Oliver M. Ainsworth (ed.), *Cornell Studies in English*, XII (1928), 63.

theory was still the essence of one treatise on travel contained in the *Institution of a Gentleman,* written before 1657 by William Higford for his grandson, and perhaps harking back to an earlier time when "Your observations in travel must be versed in the polity and ordering of states," that is, in the political information which was fashionable in Higford's youth.[18] It was still one of the three major aims of travel as suggested to a friend by the young Isaac Newton in 1669.[19] It was still *de rigueur* even for scientists like Dr. Edward Browne and John Ray to devote much space in their travel writings to political matters. Perhaps we should not count here Sir William Temple's *Observations on the United Provinces* (1673) or the largely political *Some Letters* (1687) of the mature Gilbert Burnet, traveling in exile to observe political forces at work in Switzerland and Italy, since both statesmen were adult travelers and therefore, if we follow Bacon's distinction between younger and older travelers, in search rather of "experience" than of "education." The same remark will not apply to the young Joseph Addison, whose clearly political observation was strongly mingled with the mainly literary aims of the travel reported in his *Remarks on Several Parts of Italy* (1705).

So the political theme, which had been the special English contribution to the theory and practice of travel for education, continued to sound, though it was no longer dominant. One might suppose it had lost interest because it was too difficult to keep up. Even a modest list of topics called for a deal of inquiry: whether the six items listed by Erpenius[20]—language, region, government, history, manners, eminent men—or the more than two hundred listed by Albert Meier in a list to end all lists.[21] We know that some travelers were indeed zealous students, collecting books and especially printed or manuscript "relations," and compiling their own from them: so, e.g., Sidney, Wotton,

[18] The pamphlet, published in 1660, was reprinted in *Harleian Miscellany,* Park ed., Vol. IX: the section on travel at p. 598.

[19] Sir David Brewster (ed.) in *Memoirs of the Life of Newton* (1855), I, 387–89.

[20] *De Peregrinatione Gallica* (Leyden, 1631).

[21] *Methodus Describendi regiones, urbes & arces* . . . (Helmstadt, 1587; English translation by Philip Jones, 1589[–90]).

and Francis Davison. Doubtless enthusiasm died down after these devoted Elizabethans, if only because the works published by them and their contemporaries left little to do. From about 1592, indeed, the description of country after country was published, more or less according to the prescribed pattern, usually by youthful travelers. France was described by John Eliot (1592) for topography and by Robert Dallington (1604) for political organization. The Low Countries were described in translations of foreign texts, to be sure, beginning with the *Epitome* of Ludovico Guicciardini (1593); but the young Sir Thomas Overbury made his own political survey (written 1609, published 1626). Italy was not described in one volume. Robert Dallington's pungent *Tuscany* was printed, and suppressed, in 1605; Thomas Coryat's journey to Venice was recorded in print in 1611, a sober and conscientious work far removed from the buffoonery which surrounded its author, and the first English narrative of travel to Italy to be published in a century; and Fynes Moryson's gigantic *Itinerary* (1617) provided both travel narrative and political survey for both Italy and Germany. In addition, Contarini's standard work on the government of Venice was translated in 1600, and a French history of Venice was translated in 1612. Russia had meantime been surveyed by an ambassador, Giles Fletcher, in 1591. The Near East was covered by the travels of Fynes Moryson and George Sandys (the latter's *Relation* was 1615), though neither achieved a political survey.

Even more ambitious works were written as studies of international foreign policy: by Philip Sidney, of which we know only the idea, not the text, as reported by Fulke Greville's *Life*; by Henry Wotton, whose *The State of Christendom* was written in 1594, though not published until 1657; and notably by Edwin Sandys, whose *Relation of the State of Religion* (1605), later entitled *Europae speculum*, was a large survey of the papacy and its power in Europe. These were the work of young men, and doubtless there were more young men whose treatises are omitted and should be added here.

At any rate, a notable body of political studies was put together in England within twenty-five years. It is indeed not the least sign of that expansive reckoning with the outside world which was a special phase of the Elizabethan mind, and parallels the like publishing by Hakluyt and Purchas of the record of English contacts with the farther world overseas. These studies of Europe are, to be sure, uneven and perhaps often impression-istic: neither sound geography, on the one hand, nor sound so-ciology on the other. Nonetheless, they make an achievement, and it was accomplished largely by young men on their travels.

Much was left to be done, notably on Spain and Scandinavia; but after this outburst, the later studies straggle into view in the casual fashion which is normal to travel literature. Perhaps the first enthusiasm for political study was gone. Perhaps the pub-lishing in the Netherlands of the Elzevir "Respublica" series, which contained just such studies of individual countries, often by several authors, as these English forerunners, may have re-strained English travelers from doing any more themselves. Perhaps it was easier to stay at home and compile at least certain political studies from books: Edward Brerewood was not a trav-eler when he compiled the *Enquiries Touching the Diversity of Languages and Religion* (1615), nor was Samuel Purchas when he wrote his *Pilgrimage* (1613), a survey of religion out-side of Europe. At all events the flood was over, and the tide that began to flow in Elizabethan days had changed.

### III

We cannot know whether travelers were more frivolous in Lord Herbert's time than in Sidney's. Certainly the Earl of Oxford, who was Sidney's contemporary, was thought frivolous enough, and Burghley's own son had been a model of idleness on his travel abroad as a boy. Satire of idle travelers is more-over distributed over many decades, and will not serve us. We do better to generalize from the treatises and the actual recorded travel.

Following Felltham and Peacham in the rejection of travel as political education, we note a continuing trend of lesser serious-ness than the Elizabethans showed. James Howell, veteran traveler and tutor of traveling youth, prescribed the study only of language and manners, with some inquiry into political matters, in one year each in France, Spain, and Italy, which would not have allowed much time for real inquiry.[22] Thomas Neale, writing for an apparently heedless younger brother, was concerned mainly with morals and somewhat with manners.[23] Milton objected to the transforming of youth by foreign travel "into mimics, apes, and kickshaws," and would have only mature persons of twenty-three or twenty-four travel "to enlarge experience and make wise observation."[24] Evelyn in principle approved only the "Ethicall and Morall part of Travel, which embellisheth a Gentleman," when he had finished his own travels by 1652;[25] but the very writing of his political survey belied his theory, and his *Diary* in turn reveals still other aims for travel, as will appear.

The most categorical denials of educational value in travel are still to come. Francis Osborne of Oxford thought travel a mere sham and debaucher, most improperly praised.[26] The young Thomas Browne, son of Sir Thomas the physician, was exhorted merely to learn the foreign language, and to mind his manners, when he went to France at fourteen;[27] his brother Edward, traveling to France and later to eastern Europe after he had obtained his medical degree, was a quite different and more serious traveler, as will be shown. Gilbert Burnet, at twenty-five, saw no excuse for travel during the period of serious education, which for him lasted until the age of twenty-five; he admitted, however, that a nobleman who might become a courtier or an ambassador might travel when mature, "to know more of the world and of mankind."[28] Lord Clarendon distrusted the effect on both manners and morals of foreign travel and of foreign study (since universities abroad exerted no control over students); he was, however, willing to admit a three-year so-

[22] *Instructions for Forreine Travell* (1642).

[23] *A Treatise of Direction, how To travell safely* (1643).

[24] *On Education* (1644), ed. cit., p. 63.

[25] *The State of France*, "Prefatory Letter" (1652), Sig. B 3.

[26] *Advice to a Son* (1656).

[27] The letters to Thomas Browne (1660–61) are printed in Simon Wilkin's edition of Sir Thomas Browne's *Works* (1836), I, 1–16.

[28] "Thoughts on Education" (1668), in edition of John Clarke, *Aberdeen University Studies*, LXVII (1914), 77–80.

journ abroad for youths of twenty who had been at the University and the Inns of Court, and who might then go abroad to learn manners.[29] John Locke finally may be thought to have given the coup de grâce to the theory of travel for education. Writing when he was past fifty, after experience as traveler and as tutor of traveling youth, Locke saw virtually no value in such travel. Writing incidentally on the subject in *Some Thoughts Concerning Education*,[30] he noted that language should be learned between seven and sixteen, at too early an age for travel; manners after twenty-one, when youth would be mature enough to learn for himself: whereas sixteen to twenty-one, the usual age for travel, was an age interested only in play and pleasure abroad when it should be at serious study at home.

It is clear from these statements that the arguments and the diatribes turned on the age of traveling youth. When one sifts out the positive remarks from the denunciations, it is apparent that travel was still admitted to have educational value: preferably for mature individuals, past their formal education, who might go abroad for maturing and for improving their knowledge of the world. Men and manners, but hardly explicitly cities, would be the nuclear minimum. This is not very much to travel for, however, and something must have been found to replace the political element in education which was once thought essential. One substitution might be the training in the gentlemanly arts which the French academies had made important: fencing, dancing, music, drawing, riding the great horse, some of which were the special object of Milton's contempt. These arts were not new. They had been recommended by Philip Sidney (music, horsemanship, sword and dagger), Robert Dallington (dancing, riding, fencing), and Thomas Palmer (arms, music, poetry, dancing, portraying, vaulting, running, dexterity) of the old school. They continued to be recommended by James Howell (horsemanship, dancing), Richard Lassels (music, painting, fencing, dancing, riding, vaulting, arms), and John Gailhard (fencing, dancing, horsemanship, drawing landscapes,

[29] "A Dialogue concerning Education," in *A Collection of Several Tracts* (1727), pp. 313–48.

[30] Written 1684, published 1693: in the edition of J. W. Adamson (Cambridge, 1922), pp. 175–78.

playing the guitar), who were all traveling tutors; and they were not overlooked in the practice of John Evelyn and John Reresby, among others. But these accomplishments are still auxiliary rather than primary with these writers and travelers. Manners and fashions and gentlemanly arts might be the actual aim of what Lassels was the first to call (in 1670) the Grand Tour, but neither theorist nor traveler was likely to admit as much, or as little. Further aims must be found to justify the long foreign sojourn.

## IV

Two such additional aims reveal themselves in the *Diary* of the thoughtful traveler John Evelyn. His travel for education took him to France and Italy in the years 1643 to 1646, beginning when he was twenty-three and had been to the University and the Inns of Court. Abroad, he devoted himself, in addition to languages and gentlemanly accomplishments, to an assiduous visiting of art collections and of notable buildings and gardens; he himself made pencil drawings of landscapes, and had copies made of Italian paintings. He attended concerts and operas, and himself studied instruments. He cultivated in sum the fine arts; and on his eventual return home, he continued his interest by publishing a number of books, original and translated, on painting, architecture, engraving, and numismatics; moreover, he worked himself, and he advised his friends, on the art of the garden, here meaning landscape architecture as well as botany.

Evelyn's other interest abroad was scientific. He not only visited collections of scientific instruments and curiosities, and met scientists like the geographer and orientalist Father Kircher, but he enrolled as a student at Padua to study both anatomy and botany. This interest again continued on his return home, and the Royal Society encouraged his publications in gardening and forestry.

It is my thesis that these interests in the fine arts or the sciences now came to be woven into the complex of travel motives, thus like political study giving substance and discipline to the energy of the traveler. It is unusual, to be sure, to find as strong and equal an interest in both disciplines as Evelyn attests. The interest in the fine arts normally bulks larger.

We should speak here only in passing of the professional artist going to foreign parts for training or inspiration. The first we know is John Shute, painter, who was sent to Italy in 1550 by his patron, the Duke of Northumberland, to study architecture, and who published the first English book on the classical orders.[31] Inigo Jones went on at least two Italian journeys, one soon after 1600 and one with the Earl of Arundel from 1613 to 1615. William Smithe, painter and sculptor, traveled in France, the Low Countries, Germany, and Italy for at least seven years, from 1609 to 1616, "having seene the best workemanshippe" in those countries.[32] Nicholas Stone, architect and sculptor, married into a Dutch family of artists; one of his sons, Henry, was apprenticed in 1635 to his uncle in Amsterdam, and then added to his training by joining his brother Nicholas, Jr., in a four-year student journey to Italy.[33]

This travel for the sake of professional education is, of course, of the same sort as that of students of medicine or law to a foreign university. What interests us instead is the travel for a somewhat more liberal education, or cultivation. We cannot be sure when the fine arts first began to attract the amateur or dilettante traveler from England. We guess that one of the first was Henry Fitzallan, Earl of Arundel, who brought back some pictures, and probably much marble furniture, from Italy, where he traveled in the 1560's.[34] Presumably he did not himself collect, in further personal travel, the most part of his collection, but his agents must have traveled for him in the Netherlands and in France.

Henry Wotton might be thought the first active connoisseur among travelers if we could believe Isaak Walton's *Life* of him

[31] *The First and Chief Groundes of Architecture* (1563).

[32] His letter of 1616 to the Earl of Arundel is printed by Mary F. S. Hervey, *The Life . . . of Thomas Howard* (1921), p. 501.

[33] *The Joyrnall of N.S.*: Harleian MS 4049, ed. Walter Lewis Spiers in 7 *Walpole Society* (1919), pp. 158–200.

[34] *The Lumley Inventories*, ed. Lionel Cust in 6 *Walpole Society* (1917–18), pp. 17, 26.

(1651). In his five years of study in Italy, which were in the early 1590's, Wotton was acquainted, says Walton, "with the most eminent men for Learning, and all manner of Arts; as Picture, Sculpture, Chymistry, Architecture, and other manual Arts, even Arts of inferiour nature; of all which, he was a most dear Lover, and a most excellent Judge."[35] The statement sounds like anachronism. The evidence of Wotton's letters, and other of his activities in Italy, points to so much political study, including the collecting of "relations" and the writing of a long book, that it is doubtful that Wotton could have gone in for either art or science then. It was probably later, during some of his several ambassadorships, that these interests developed as tastes changed. We know that Wotton did arrange for the purchase of pictures for the Earl of Arundel and others; moreover, on his final return to England in 1623, he composed a handbook, *The Elements of Architecture*, which, though derived largely from the treatises of Vitruvius, Alberti, and Vasari, drew upon much personal observation, especially in the state of Venice. There is no question of his interest in the arts; there is question of his interest as early as the 1590's; and the interest in chemistry certainly belongs to a later period.

In the absence of other undoubted names, we may with a clear conscience put at the head of the list of connoisseur travelers the second Earl of Arundel (Thomas Howard). In 1612, at the age of twenty-seven, he traveled to Padua for his health, and may then have acquired his new enthusiasm. In 1613 he made a long stay in Italy, together with Inigo Jones and his physician, William Harvey, and there seems to have laid the foundation for his collecting. It was then, according to Peacham's *The Compleat Gentleman*, that he brought "the first sight of Greeke and Romane Statues" to England;[36] his agents were thereafter busy buying in several countries; and during the Civil War, the Earl retired to Padua with much of his collection, and died there.

Arundel differs from most other collectors in that he traveled abroad himself to see art and artists, though his purchasing

[35] World's Classics ed., p. 107.
[36] 1906 ed., p. 107.

was in the main actually done by agents. Of the several collectors of whom we begin to hear in King James's time, Prince
Henry, Prince Charles, Somerset, Buckingham, the Earls of
Pembroke and Montgomery, and Endymion Porter did not
travel to collect. Burghley's great-grandson, Lord Roos,
brought statues back from Italy, whither he traveled, and was
converted to the Roman church, in 1606; his statues were presented to the Earl of Arundel in 1616.[37] In 1619, Sir Thomas
Roe brought back a collection of art objects on his way home
from his embassy to India. Sir Kenelm Digby brought back
statues from his own travels in Greece in the 1620's. In all these
activities of collecting in the formative years of the new English
art collections, travel played some part; it is difficult, nonetheless, to say how large a part it played in forming the artistic
taste of the collectors and the amateurs. For Arundel, Wotton,
Roos, Digby at least, as for Evelyn, travel may have been an
inspiration to aesthetic and therefore educational ends.

It will still take some time before the usual traveler will
add pictures and statues to his educational materials. For
Thomas Palmer in 1606, Italy's attractions in the form of "the
speciall gallerie of monuments and olde aged memorials" was
merely fantastical and "glutton-feeder."[38] Henry Peacham was
perhaps the first to record an interest in works of art per se and
not merely as antiquities. To be sure, his chapter "Of Trauaile"
in *The Compleat Gentleman* makes no mention of the traveler
with aesthetic interests; but in his references elsewhere in the
book to his own travels (which seem to have occurred between
1612 and 1614) he refers to collections in Florence, Paris, and
Rome, and passes judgment on some of their statues; moreover,
he has read Vasari, and draws from him a brief history of Italian
painters from Cimabue to Raphael; and he is well acquainted
with music and musicians in Italy and the Low Countries.[39] All
this is only what we should expect from the author of the first
English book on drawing, who now becomes our first art-critic
traveler.

[37] Mary F. S. Hervey, *op. cit.*, p. 103, note 3.
[38] *An Essay of the Meanes* . . . , p. 44.
[39] Pp. 99–102, 105, 137–54.

Whether *The Compleat Gentleman* (1622), or, for that matter, Wotton's *Elements of Architecture* (1624), influenced the
aims of travelers I do not know. There is no evidence in the
travel record of Robert Boyle, who devoted himself to languages
and mathematics; but he was only fourteen when he went to
Italy for a year with a tutor. In Rome in 1641 he saw the "principal rarities," but to what end is not clear.[40] Meantime, Milton
had made his tour of Italy as poet among poets and scholars, not
presumably "to learn principles but to enlarge experience and
make wise observation," as he wrote himself.[41] For his interest
in the fine arts, we know that he bought music,[42] and that he
was presumably impressed by classical architecture.[43] Otherwise
we cannot be sure of his aesthetic interests.

We have returned to Evelyn, whom for the moment we may
take as the first articulate amateur traveler of aesthetic interests. After him, the travelers, especially of course to Italy, give
increasing attention to the arts. John Raymond in 1646 and
Francis Mortoft in 1658 pass from antiquities to modern works
of art. The two records left by Sir John Reresby, who traveled
from 1654 to 1658 in France and Italy, are both revealing. The
*Travels*, presumably written not long after the journey, is very
full on the sights observed, including objects of art especially
in Florence; it mentions also some mechanical curiosities seen
in collections, such as Evelyn also noted; it contains some brief
political descriptions in the older manner, and also the nuclear
impressions of places and people. Here are the several normal
kinds of travel observation. Later in life, Sir John composed
his *Memoirs*. In these we are surprised to find a complete shift
of interest in the travel record. Now he gives the impression of
spending a rather frivolous stay abroad. Though with a gov-
ernor, and aged twenty-two at the start, he indicates that he
learned languages, music, dancing, and fencing; and though he
enrolled at the University of Padua, he actually studied only

[40] *An Account of Philaretus*, ed. Thomas Birch in *The Works of Robert Boyle* (1744), I, 14.
[41] *On Education*, ed. cit., p. 63.
[42] Masson, *Life of Milton*, I, 651.
[43] B. Sprague Allen, *Tides in English Taste* (1937), I, 49.

Italian and the art of fortification.[44] I do not know how to explain this change from serious study to frivolity. At least it is clear that, about 1660, it was the fashion to study pictures abroad as well as follow the other aims of the traveler; later the north-country justice apparently wanted to pass off his youth as frivolous.

It was by 1660 fashionable for a prince to know about pictures. When Sir Balthazar Gerbier wrote his *Subsidium Peregrinantibus* in 1665 for the guidance of the Duke of Monmouth, he included a number of princely studies, in manners, in the recognition of noble families and orders of knighthood, together with the appropriate coats of arms. For Italy he was careful to specify at length the statues and pictures which should be seen in Rome. Three years later, we learn from Gilbert Burnet's *Thoughts on Education* that, though travel was unnecessary to most education, a nobleman should "know as his fingers" both architecture and statues. He practiced as he preached. When Burnet went on his own travels twenty years later, he was alert to record in his travel letters to Boyle not only the political features of the countries but also the memorabilia of art, nature, architecture, pictures, and so on, and to report on collections of "vertu." Meantime, Richard Lassels, tutor to traveling youth, assumed in his *Voyage of Italy* (1670) that his charges studied music, painting, architecture, and mathematics.

After 1670, I infer, a certain prejudice sprang up, as natural reaction, against a too easy attention to works of art as an excuse for travel. One tutor, for example, John Gailhard, proposing to benefit the mind rather than the fancy in his *Compleat Gentleman* (1678), declared himself not interested in writing a relation of Italy which merely listed titles of paintings, dimensions of buildings, notable things to see as a mere guide might show them, or religious curiosities. He proposed a serious study for traveling youth, to include government, geography, history, the natural sciences, as well as polite manners; but he also included in his curriculum "skill in ancient and modern Curiosities, whether Pictures, Statues of Brass, Marble, Alabaster, &c.,

[44] The *Travels* were edited, from an MS not now extant, in *The Travels and Memoirs* (1813). The *Memoirs* were first adequately edited by Andrew Browning (Glasgow, 1936).

Medals, and other fair and curious things."[45] The aesthetic was
not to be ignored, but I infer that it was to be justified by its historical interest primarily, as one might expect of persons given a
classical education.

But another justification is also stated by the enthusiasts for
the new science. Edward Leigh's "Diatribe of Travel" (1671)
was dedicated to the scientific traveler Francis Willughby, but
it is not for all that limited in its scope. An educated traveler
is now expected to be skillful in architecture; able to limn or
paint, in order to represent castles or cities or fortifications; and
also, by implication, to be well read in the fine arts, a requirement which Leigh justifies by a statement from the *Transactions*
of the new Royal Society: "Painting and Sculpture are the
Politest and Noblest of antient Arts; what Art can be more help-
ful or pleasing, to a Philosophical [i.e., scientific] Traveller."[46]

We shall return to speak of the full implication of Leigh's
treatise. I think we may safely assume that from this time travelers will normally include in their aims the study of the fine arts.
One traveler in the 1670's tried to draw up a catalogue of Italian
paintings in order to show the value of travel; he was unable to
complete it, but finding a like catalogue published by a Vene-
tian painter, he translated and enlarged it for the use of Englishmen.[47] His book goes far to proving our point, which is
further strengthened by William Acton, whose *New Journal
of Italy* (1691) dealt with "Antiquities; with strength, beauty,
and scituation [of cities]; with Painting, Carving, Limning, and
Curiosities." We find further proof in Maximilian Misson,
another tutor of youth, whose *New Voyage to Italy* (1695) proposes to describe "the Chief Towns, Churches, Tombs, Libraries,
Palaces, Statues, and Antiquities." His Preface complains that
travelers to Italy are too likely to be inadequate: some study
only antiquities, some only painting and architecture, some only
libraries and cabinets of curiosities, some only churches and
relics. He proposes therefore a more varied and not merely
partial account—though the terms are new, his complaint is

[45] Pp. 58–59.
[46] *Three Diatribes or Discourses*, p. 5.
[47] *The Painters Voyage of Italy* (1679): translated by W[illiam] L[odge]
from Giacomo Barri, *Viaggio Pittoresco* (Venetia, 1671).

familiar. The danger once was that travel would be frivolous; now the danger is that it might be dilettante. At all events, the fine arts are clearly taken for granted.

Misson's own travel narrative in letters, which makes up the book, is in fact broad in scope. Covering somewhat critically people and places and travel, with some minimum observation of the temper of a given government, the letters also take account of curiosities, the arts, literature, and antiquities. This array of interests provides the just balance sought after at the end of the century. It will not be far in fact from the actual interests of another traveler, Joseph Addison, whose *Remarks* will be concerned with the political, with manners when significant, with classical antiquities (as befits a student and author of Latin verse), and with objects of art.

Altogether the interest in the arts was prepared in the first half of the seventeenth century by the importing of ancient and modern art into England; by the careful interest of pioneer artists and connoisseurs like Inigo Jones, the Earl of Arundel, Henry Wotton, Henry Peacham, and John Evelyn; and came in the end to require of all educated travelers an interest in the aesthetic heritage. I do not find evidence that the interest was ever as engrossing as had formerly been that in politics. Peacham, Wotton, Evelyn carried on at home their aesthetic studies begun abroad; but they made no studies of the arts to compare with the earlier political studies. At the same time, it is clear that a new dimension of thought and feeling has been added to the mind of the educated man.

## V

Travel for the sake of still another aim, the study of the natural sciences, might seem as an idea to begin to be held in the formative days of the Royal Society, making its anticipatory appearance for us in John Evelyn's studies in the 1640's at Padua and Paris. To say so is, however, to ignore a long educational tradition. For centuries, students had gone abroad to Padua or elsewhere to take a degree in medicine, in which faculty were included the natural sciences. Thomas Linacre, John Caius,

William Harvey were among the more recent well-known graduates of Padua, and students continued to go there throughout the seventeenth century, as they did to Montpellier and to Leyden and elsewhere.

For what concerns less professional study, we observe the fixation in one late treatise on travel of the scientific interest. This is "A Diatribe of Travel" by Edward Leigh (1671), mentioned before. The "Diatribe" is first of all a kind of disjointed bibliography of treatises on travel. Furthermore, it sums up after a fashion much of the current thought on travel which was not due on the one hand to a special interest in political study or another or on the other to the special preoccupations of the tutors of traveling youth (Lassels, Gailhard, Misson). Leigh would require the traveler to be above eighteen or twenty years of age, possessed of Latin and of some knowledge of the liberal sciences (once called the liberal arts), skilled in architecture and so on as we have said, well grounded in his religion, well acquainted with the government and geography of his own country. So equipped and matured, the youth was to study in advance the country of his travel; arrived, he was to follow Erpenius' scheme of study of government and manners, to frequent the court and the upper classes, as Bacon had prescribed, to make the acquaintance of learned men and books, and to study plants, animals, and minerals in addition to all the topics of geography and intellectual history long since laid down by Albert Meier and still being reprinted.

The study of nature takes up little room in Leigh's massive program, which adds up to one impossible whole all the travel aims of a century of speculation. For our purposes it is enough to note the aim, however obscured, of scientific study. It is of course no accident that this program should be stated in the early years of the Royal Society, nor that travelers should already be making observations of the kind which the Society demanded. Leigh is very vague about the sort of study required, and we suppose that he was merely paying tribute to a current fashion.

The scientific traveler, the traveler intent on observations of scientific interest, is naturally no new phenomenon, though the later seventeenth century gave him the new label of "philosophical." Earlier, the historian Purchas clearly linked Ulysses and Aristotle as travelers in search of learning, the former "in the Schooles of divers Nations and Navigations," the latter as one who "travelled with Alexanders Purse and Experience to furnish himselfe, and succeeding Ages with Naturall Science and Wisdom"; while a third ancient, King Solomon, had sponsored sea voyages to study "Minerals, Gems, Beasts, Fowles, Fishes, Serpents, Wormes, Trees, Fruits, Gums, Plants, Men; Climates, Winds, Seasons, Seas, Lands, Soyles, Rivers, Fountaynes, Heavens, and Stars."[48] From these beginnings, numerous travelers had made their observations, which Purchas now collected, not "professing Methodically to deliver the Historie of Nature according to rules of Art, nor Philosophically to discusse and dispute; but as in way of Discourse by each Traveller," who provided "individuall and sensible materials . . . to those universall Speculators for their Theoricall structures."[49]

This is the Baconian explanation of the work of Hakluyt and Purchas, which has preserved the records of many English scientific travelers overseas of their time. The records would be for the most part mathematical and physical, we should think, the observations of navigators; but they would also include such observations as the description of the natives of Virginia written by Thomas Hariot, mathematician, sent out by Ralegh as scientific observer with the colony. Presumably Hariot was no better skilled in anthropology than most travelers, and we might make some difficulty about calling him a scientific observer. There is no such difficulty over some later travelers bent on professionally scientific travel. John Tradescant, the botanist, was one, who collected plants at Archangel in 1618 while accompanying an embassy to Russia; likewise his son John, who was in Virginia in 1637 collecting plants for his father's physic garden. John Greaves the orientalist was another, whose Mediterranean voyage, 1637–40, achieved several scientific ends, such as the measurement of the pyramids, the purchase of a Greek manuscript of Ptolemy, and some geographical observations which later found publication in the Royal Society *Transactions*.

[48] Samuel Purchas, *Purchas His Pilgrimes* (Glasgow ed., 1905), I, 51–52.
[49] *Ibid.*, "To the Reader," I, xl.

Presumably the seventeenth century could yet make little difference between the professional tasks and the certainly less qualified observations of Hariot in Virginia. At all events, when the Royal Society came to its deliberate program of supplementing Hakluyt and Purchas among others, it did so by demanding not a new kind but rather an additional body of observations, which could be supplied for the most part by any educated person. Specifically, in the first two years of its monthly publication, the *Philosophical Transactions* published some twelve programs of research for travelers.[50] One of these programs, which was extended, discussed, and restated, was addressed to seamen, and asked for the setting down in ship journals or logs an extended set of nautical observations, with the ultimate aim of a more accurate charting of the world. This purely professional program, which originated with the mathematician Lawrence Rooke of Gresham College, is rather beyond the scope of our study of the liberal (as we may call him) traveler. The further programs were more nearly within his range. Robert Boyle launched them with his "General Heads for a Natural History of a Countrey." The observations required could be divided under two heads: first, the sciences appropriate to the heavens, air, water, and earth (meteorology, oceanography, geography): the second, the study of the inhabitants. In the latter section, any observant traveler could presumably note the stature, shape, features, and diet, and could have a try at describing the strength, ingenuity, and inclination of the people. With medical help he could learn something of the fruitfulness of the women and the relative ease of childbirth, and could note their diet and exercise; he could also learn something of the characteristic diseases of the inhabitants. Passing to the natural products of the country, the traveler would note its trees and fruits and best soil, its animals and insects with their uses, and its metals, clays, and salts, with the methods of procuring them. And he might finally inquire into "Traditions."

The other programs are specific applications of this larger

[50] In the monthly numbers 8, 9, 11, 13, 18, 19, 20, 23, 24, 25, 29, 33, between January 1665–6 and March 1667–8: for the most part reprinted together in a book of 1692 entitled *General Heads for the Natural History of a Country*.

one. Mines, their nature and the methods of working them, made one subject of inquiry; the others were directed to individual countries, and were suggested by gaps left in the reports of earlier travelers. In other words, Boyle and others had read through Purchas and others to test their adequacy. Now questions left unanswered were presented to travelers to Turkey, Egypt, Poland (especially on the nature and effects of a cold climate), Hungary (especially on mines and metallurgy), Surat in India, Persia, Virginia and the Bermudas, Guiana and Brazil, the Caribbean Islands, and Greenland (Spitsbergen). Most of the queries related to natural products and their authenticity or use. Altogether the programs would contribute appreciably to the history of nature which was a major aim of the research of the Society; and in their endeavor to enlist the aid of as many persons as possible, they form part of the Society's plan for a world-wide network of scientific correspondents.

The efficacy of the plan may be judged in two ways: first by the response made by travelers as judged at least by the reports printed in the *Philosophical Transactions*; second by the extent to which travelers adopted on their own account the Society scheme of observation.

For the first, it is clear that the Society obtained an immediate response. In the first three volumes (forty-four monthly numbers) of the *Transactions*, some fifty pages were taken up with travelers' reports (out of nine hundred pages); in the second three volumes (thirty-six numbers) about the same amount (but out of twenty-two hundred pages). The response continued. In each volume of the *Transactions* down to the end of the century, at least one long report appeared from a traveler or resident abroad on his scientific observations, or perhaps a long review of a travel work of scientific interest, in addition to a number of smaller items. One whole number indeed was filled with a report from William Byrd in Virginia on the dissection of an opossum. The travel material in the *Transactions* might even fill as much as one-fifth of the annual volume, as it did in 1684 and again in 1695–97.

The reports have an obvious importance for the history of science as a social process. For our study of the history of travel in its social meaning, the reports testify to the adoption by a number of Englishmen, traveling or residing abroad, of the new task of observation in foreign parts. Most of the reports came from the more distant and less familiar parts of the world, where there was more knowledge to collect; but it was still possible to report on the mines of Hungary or the cold in Poland or on medical researches in Paris or Rome. Many of the persons reporting were, of course, scientists, but some were merchants, seamen, soldiers, landowners. There were few who could be called travelers for educational reasons, at least in the strict sense of the word educational; most were like Ulysses, traveling and incidentally being educated thereby, rather than like Aristotle, supposed a traveler purely for scientific investigation.

We should note some of the scientific travelers of the various kinds, necessarily omitting the numerous travelers to Asia and America. Turning back, we find first Robert Boyle, who studied mathematics to the point of reading the *Dialogues* of Galileo during his travel years abroad, when, however, he was only in his early 'teens. His fragment of autobiography gives only this sign of an early passion for the sciences, hardly enough to make him then a scientific traveler. Evelyn we have seen at the age of twenty-six taking up anatomy and botany. Dr. Edward Browne, son of the physician Sir Thomas, after taking his first medical degree in England, traveled in France and Italy; he noted in his letters various medical matters, as well, it should be noticed, as observations of works of art.[51] On taking his second degree in England, he traveled to Austria and beyond. His observations, published in the *Philosophical Transactions* from time to time, and brought together in his *Brief Account of Some Travels in Hungaria* . . . (1673), do not differ too greatly from the usual travel narratives. They include a discussion of the military uses of the Hungarian plains, together with lists of bridges and fortifications. They are engrossed by the usual interest in matters important to the traveler (money, safety, treatment by the natives, lodgings, language) and by a usual human interest in clothes and manners. The shadow of the

[51] Printed in *The Works of Sir Thomas Browne*, ed. Simon Wilkin (1836), I, 60–114.

Royal Society program might perhaps be found in the "observation of natural Remarkables, in Hilly and Mountainous Countryes"; in the drawings, mentioned but not shown, of "Habits, Postures, Hills, Castles, Forts, Monasteries, Sepulchres, Fountains, Ruines, Medals, Coyns, Bridges, Columnes, Statuas, &c"; but most of all in some observations on the nature and working of mines of silver and mercury, information specifically sought in the Royal Society program.

The scientific traveler is still only in part specialized, as may further appear, amusingly enough, from a letter of advice to a young traveler written by Isaac Newton in 1669.[52] Then twenty-six, Newton wrote from Cambridge to advise Francis Aston first on discreet behavior in travel, this advice being lifted complete, without acknowledgment, from Francis Osborne's *Advice to a Son* (1656), which we have mentioned; second, on inquiry into the government and also the economics of foreign countries, the new economic items to be sought including the state of trades and arts, the products of nature, the prices of food, and the mode of guiding ships; third, inquiry into certain matters of technology: the mode of "transforming" iron into copper in Hungary and Italy, of precipitating gold from gold-bearing sands, of "grinding" glass, of protecting ships against marine worms, of the value of pendulum clocks in figuring longitude. These queries have been called perfunctory.[53] They are rather unorganized, but at least one, on iron and copper, repeats the Royal Society inquiry, and altogether the questions reveal that mingling of natural and social science which is characteristic of the time and is incidentally bewildering to us.

Several more sample travelers of scientific interest may reveal more clearly the superimposing of the new on the old. The botanist John Ray, F.R.S., published in 1673 his *Observations Topographical, Moral, and Physiological: Made in a Journey Through part of the Low-Countries, Germany, Italy, and France: with A Catalogue of Plants not Native of England . . . Whereunto is added A brief Account of Francis Wil-*

[52] Sir David Brewster (ed.), *Memoirs of the Life of Newton* (1855), I, 387–89.
[53] By Professor G. N. Clark, *Science and Social Welfare in the Age of Newton* (1937), p. 67.

*lughby, Esq., his Voyage through a great part of Spain.* The title does not quite reveal the full extent of the mixture of old and new. The long five hundred pages of the travel narrative are devoted to a full itinerary and description of places, manners, and political organization; incidentally if prominently, much interest is shown in natural phenomena, in plants and food, in machinery such as that of canal locks; and as a special piece of information, the schedule of lectures in all subjects is copied down for each of the universities visited.

Ray's *Catalogus Stirpium,* occupying a separate one hundred fifteen pages, is the scientific fruit of the travel. Looking back on this double work, it is easy enough for us to draw the line between the discursive and varied observations of the traveler on the one hand, and the careful collections (whether or not we can yet call them scientific) of the botanist on the other. Both parts were in fact equally welcome to seventeenth-century thought, which was still bound to be engrossed by the collection of data; in this light the *Catalogus,* however authoritative, might well be read as an index to one part only of the observations. Certainly the review of Ray's book in the *Philosophical Transactions* professes to find in it a completely orthodox inquiry of the kind required, moral and political equally with natural.[54] It is true that a year later the review of Edward Browne's book refuses to consider the political portions of it, "as not properly belonging to our task";[55] it is also true that a large part of the travel material in the first thirty years of the *Transactions* is devoted to natural rather than social science. Men were doubtless of two minds, moved by a humanist education as well as by good Baconian precept to breadth of view, moved by a new enthusiasm to depth of knowledge.

I think we may conclude that travelers at least still felt obliged to seek breadth. Browne and Ray both did so. John Locke wrote back to Boyle from Montpellier about gardening and vineyards and olive-growing and scientific instruments; he also wrote of visits to antiquities and to meetings of legislatures. The veteran naturalist Dr. Martin Lister wrote in *A Journey to*

[54] *Philosophical Transactions,* VII (1673), 5170–72.
[55] *Ibid.,* VIII (1674), 6049.

*Paris* (1699) "first of the Streets and publick Places, and what may be seen in them: Next of the Houses of Note: and what Curiosities of Nature or Art, also of Men and Libraries I met: Next, of their Diet and Recreations: Next of the Gardens, and their Furniture and Ornaments: of the Air and Health. We shall conclude the whole with the present state of Physic and Pharmacy here." The traveler is "philosophical," but not scientific.

The upshot of our story is simple. Travel, and the travel literature which reported it, has in the main had serious educational purposes. These purposes have not changed like fashions; they have rather grown, from simple becoming complex. To the "men and cities" of the Ulysses tradition, and to the obvious interest in history which derives from humanist training, have been added the statesman's education in government, the connoisseur's education in the fine arts, and the natural philosopher's study of the world. The story is characteristic of the Renaissance and post-Renaissance expansiveness of the spirit of man.

# MILTON AND THE ATTEMPTED
# WHIG REVOLUTION

GEORGE F. SENSABAUGH

JOHN MILTON, together with other opponents of Anglican-
ism and of absolute government, appeared in the famous
Oxford University decree of July 21, 1683, as a contributor
to events leading up to the Rye House Plot. This Plot—a pur-
ported attempt on the life of Charles II—never matured. It
focused attention, however, upon the previous activities of powerful Whigs, implicated and sent to the block Algernon Sidney
and William Lord Russell,[1] and brought to a close the attempted
Whig revolution which had begun with Shaftesbury's thrust for
power during the conflict over the succession of James, Duke of
York. The Plot thus conveniently placed in the hands of the
Crown an instrument to deliver a crushing defeat to the Whig
party and to assure, at the same time, the succession of York,
whose adherence to Rome had been the main reason for Whig
opposition. With the defeat of a party which many people now,
because of the Rye House Plot, associated with the heinous policy
of king-killing, a wave of relief swept over the nation, accompanied by a momentary if illusory confidence in the policies of
Charles II. Anglican clergymen, eloquent over what they considered a wonderful deliverance, reiterated in sermons and pam-
phlets the doctrine of passive obedience and stressed the divine
right of kings; and Oxford University officials, interested, as
scholars should be, in cause and effect, solemnly searched into
and laid open "those impious Doctrines, which having of late

[1] For a recent discussion of William Lord Russell and the Rye House Plot,
see Harold Armitage, *Russell and Rye House* (Letchworth, 1948).

been studiously disseminated, gave rise and growth to those nefarious attemts."[2] This search resulted in a list of twenty-seven subversive propositions, to which were subjoined the authors and books from which they were drawn—all of them, according to Oxford officials, "fitted to deprave good manners; corrupt the minds of unwary men, stir up seditions and tumults, overthrow States and Kingdoms, and lead to Rebellion, murther of Princes, and Atheism it self."[3]

On this list Milton appeared twice, once as the joint author of the multiple proposition that "All Civil Autority is derived originally from the People," that "there is a mutual compact, tacit or express, between a Prince and his Subjects," "that if he perform not his duty, they are discharg'd from theirs," and "That if lawful Governors become Tyrants, or govern otherwise then by the laws of God and man they ought to do, they forfeit the right they had unto their Government";[4] and once as an asserter that "King Charles the first was lawfully put to death, and his murtherers were the blessed instruments of Gods glory in their Generation."[5] By all rights Milton's name should have appeared under two more propositions: (1) that "The doctrine of the Gospel concerning patient suffering of injuries, is not inconsistent with violent resisting of the higher powers in case of persecution for religion,"[6] and (2) that "There lies no obligation upon Christians to passive obedience, when the Prince commands any thing against the laws of our country; and the primitive Christians chose rather to die then resist, because Christianity was not yet setled by the laws of the Empire."[7] The first proposition, to be sure, was attributed to Samuel Rutherford's *Lex Rex*, John Brown's *Apologetical Relation*, and Samuel Johnson's *Julian the Apostate*,[8] and the second to *Julian*

---

[2] *The Judgment and Decree Of The University of Oxford Past in Their Convocation July 21. 1683, Against Certain Pernicious Books and Damnable Doctrines Destructive to the Sacred Persons of Princes, Their State and Government, and of All Humane Society* (1683), pp. 1–2.

[3] *Ibid.*, p. 7.

[4] *Ibid.*, pp. 2–3, Proposition 1.      [5] *Ibid.*, p. 7, Proposition 26.

[6] *Ibid.*, p. 3, Proposition 8.      [7] *Ibid.*, p. 4, Proposition 9.

[8] *Julian the Apostate: Being a Short Account of His Life; The Sense of the Primitive Christians About His Succession; And Their Behaviour Towards Him* (London, 1682).

*the Apostate* alone; but the form they took in this latter volume shows them to be only refinements of the same propositions which Milton had presented earlier in his *Defensio Prima*. Indeed, Thomas Long, who answered Johnson in *A Vindication of the Primitive Christians*, claimed that *Julian the Apostate* was nothing other than a *"Notorious Plagiary,"* that Johnson took his *"whole design"* from "an *Argument* of that *profligate Villain, John Milton"*;[9] and detailed analysis shows this claim to be substantially sound, that Johnson simply tailored Milton's arguments concerning resistance to kings and passive obedience to fit specific issues which arose over the succession of York.[10] Oxford officials were thus quite right in placing Milton on their list of authors who had corrupted, or at least affected, men's minds. How far did Milton's influence go beyond the realm of pamphleteer warfare and reach into the arena of actual political combat? An examination of the opinions of William Lord Russell, together with an inquiry into the sources whence they sprang, will reveal that this high-ranking and active member of the Whig party trod to the measure of Milton's thought, that, through his chaplain, Samuel Johnson, he absorbed the very principles which implicated him in the Rye House Plot and thus made him a martyr to the Whig cause.

The task of examining the opinions of Lord Russell presents genuine difficulties in that he left no organized body of political doctrine. On the day of his death, however, which coincided with the Oxford proclamation, he delivered to the sheriffs a paper containing, among other things, some indication of his political thought. The importance of this paper as a political document is attested by its reception in town and court. Within an hour after Lord Russell had walked to the scaffold, put his neck on the block, and received the axe of the headsman for "Conspiring the Death of the King and the subversion of the Government," it issued fresh from the press to become the center of royal concern and public debate. According to Gilbert Burnet, it "highly

---

[9] *A Vindication of the Primitive Christians, in Point of Obedience to Their Prince, Against the Calumnies of a Book Intituled The Life of Julian, Written by Ecebolius the Sophist* (London, 1683), p. 293.

[10] See "Milton and the Doctrine of Passive Obedience," *The Huntington Library Quarterly*, XIII (1949), 19–54.

enflamed" the Court.[11] So concerned were the King and the Duke of York that both Burnet and John Tillotson, who had been with Lord Russell during the last days of his life, were called in for questioning before the Cabinet Council. Tillotson had little to say, except that Lord Russell had shown him the paper before the execution and that proper remarks had been made. Gilbert Burnet was questioned in greater detail and even accused of having written some of the sentiments, an accusation which, in his *History*, he quickly denied, though he admitted that he had helped Lord Russell in matters of organization and form.[12] Both King Charles and the Duke of York thus apparently believed that the paper spoke cogently to political issues of the day. Moreover, it aroused among pamphleteers violent emotions. It was soon taken up, its contents dissected, and its sentiments cursed or praised in accordance with the individual author's political bias.[13] The paper could have hardly aroused more interest if it had been a complete statement of Lord Russell's political doctrines.

Unfortunately, the paper Lord Russell delivered to the sheriffs is not a complete statement. Quite to the contrary, it is somewhat cryptic, aside from the conventional statements of a man on the scaffold, and therefore needs to be read for full understanding in the light of Lord Russell's trial and of events immediately preceding the execution. Lord Russell had been convicted chiefly on the Twenty-fifth Statute of Edward Third,

[11] *Bishop Burnet's History of His Own Time* (London, 1724), I, 561.

[12] *Ibid.*, pp. 558–62. For further information on this matter, see *A Supplement to Burnet's History of My Own Time*, ed. H. C. Foxcroft (Oxford, 1902), p. 131. See also T. E. S. Clarke and H. C. Foxcroft, *A Life of Gilbert Burnet: Bishop of Salisbury* (Cambridge, 1907), p. 195. Here it is stated that, at the suggestion of Burnet, Lord Russell cleared in his paper the Country leaders from the charge of suborning Titus Oates and deleted some lines "on the dangers of *slavery.*" It thus appears that Burnet did more than help Lord Russell in matters of organization and form.

[13] See, for example, *Animadversions upon a Paper, Entituled, The Speech of the Late Lord Russell, &c.* (London, 1683); *Animadversions on the Last Speech and Confession of the Late William Lord Russell* (London, 1683); *Some Succinct Remarks on the Speech of the Late Lord Russell . . .* (London, 1683); *An Antidote Against Poison* (London, 1683); and *A Vindication of the Lord Russell's Speech and Paper, &c. from the Foul Imputations of Falshood* (London, 1683).

which, as read by the Clerk of the Court, declared, in part, that to "COMPASS OR IMAGINE THE DEATH OF OUR LORD THE KING" was high treason.[14] Witnesses testified that Lord Russell, at the house of a Mr. Sheppard, had talked with other conspirators about plans for a rebellion and this talk in turn was connected with the Rye House Plot. "This," as Gilbert Burnet observed, "gave the greatest advantage to the duke and his party that was possible, for now they twisted the design of murdering the king with the other consultations that were among the lords, and made it all appear as one complicated thing, and so the matter went over England and over all Europe."[15] But as the trial proceeded, in spite of confused and uncertain testimony, it became evident that Lord Russell had no connections with the Rye House conspirators. The Lord Chief Justice himself, in his summary of the case, made this clear:

You have not evidence in this Case as there was in the other matter that was tried in the morning or yesterday, against the Conspirators to kill the King at the *Rye.* There was a direct evidence of a Consult to kill the King, that is not given you in this Case; this is an act of contriving Rebellion and an Insurrection within the Kingdom, and to seize his Guards, which is urged as an evidence, and surely is in it self an evidence to seize and destroy the King.[16]

Lord Russell, then, was convicted not for taking a direct part in the Rye House Plot but for contriving rebellion and insurrection, for, in short, consulting with other members of the Whig party on the advisability of resisting the King in the struggle over the succession of York. On the right to resist kingly authority in this matter Lord Russell held strong convictions.

These convictions emerge from his conversations with Gilbert Burnet and John Tillotson during the week preceding his execution. Both these divines, bent on saving Lord Russell's life, visited the condemned man and attempted to persuade him that resistance to kings under any circumstances was unlawful.

[14] *The Tryals of Thomas Walcot, William Hone, William Lord Russell, John Rous & William Blagg. For High-Treason, for Conspiring the Death of the King, and Raising a Rebellion in This Kingdom* (London, 1683), p. 50.

[15] *A Supplement to Burnet's History of My Own Time,* p. 111.

[16] *The Tryals of Thomas Walcot . . . ,* p. 61.

On one of these visits, Burnet found Lord Russell so moderate in his views that he thought Lord Russell had come to a "willingness" to be convinced of the "absolute illegality of resistance." Upon leaving Lord Russell, Burnet met Tillotson, in whom he confided this willingness on Lord Russell's part, along with the request that Tillotson convey it to Lord Halifax, who in turn might relate it to the king in such a manner "as to be the means of saving Lord Russell's life."[17] Lord Halifax did so, and reported to Tillotson that the King seemed more moved by this news than by anything he had heard before, whereupon Tillotson reported back to Lord Russell the King's feelings but found him not as convinced as Tillotson had supposed. Indeed, Lord Russell was far from convinced, in witness of which he showed Tillotson a passage from the paper he expected to deliver to the sheriffs on the day of his death:

For my part, I cannot deny, but I have been of opinion, that a free nation like this might defend their religion and liberties, when invaded, and taken from them, though under pretence, and colour of law. But some eminent and worthy divines, who have had the charity to be often with me, and whom I value and esteem to a very great degree, have offered me weighty reasons to persuade me, that faith and patience are the proper ways for the preservation of religion; and the method of the Gospel is to suffer persecution, rather than to use resistance. But if I have sinned in this, I hope God will not lay it to my charge, since he knows it was only a sin of ignorance.[18]

Tillotson was naturally much disturbed by this passage, since its sentiments ran directly athwart the impression which had been conveyed to the King. Consequently, in order to clarify his part in the negotiations which had so signally failed, he composed a long letter stating the position of the Church on obedience to kings, in which he declared

First, That the Christian Religion doth plainly forbid the Resistance of Authority.

Secondly, That though our Religion be Established by law, (which your Lordship urges as a difference between our Case, and that of the Primitive Christians) yet in the same Law which Establishes our Reli-

---

[17] Lord John Russell, *The Life of William Lord Russell* (London, 1819), p. 212. See also Clarke and Foxcroft, *op. cit.*, pp. 194–96.

[18] Lord John Russell, *op. cit.*, p. 213.

gion it is declared, That it is not Lawful upon any pretence whatsoever to take up Arms, &c. . . .

Thirdly, Your Lordships opinion is contrary to the declared Doctrin of all Protestant Churches; and though some particular Persons have taught otherwise, yet they have been contradicted herein and condemned for it by the Generality of Protestants. And I beg your Lordship to consider how it will agree with an avowed asserting of the Protestant Religion, to go contrary to the General Doctrine of Protestants. My end in this is to convince your Lordship that you are in a very Great and Dangerous Mistake, and being so convinced, that which before was a Sin of Ignorance, will appear of much more heinous Nature, as in Truth it is, and call for a very particular and deep Repentance; . . .[19]

Lord Russell received this letter on the day before his death; but, rather than changing his opinions, it apparently confirmed them. For, though at Burnet's request, as suggested by Tillotson, Lord Russell struck out the offending passage from his paper to the sheriffs, he remained unconvinced, declaring that his notions of law and of English government were simply different from those belonging to Burnet and Tillotson.[20] He went to the block firm in his original convictions.

The account of Lord Russell's trial and the record of his conversations with Burnet and Tillotson during the last days of his life both clarify and supplement the much-discussed paper delivered to the sheriffs. Lord Russell was quite right, as the trial disclosed and as the paper declared, in denying his complicity in any plot to kill the king, let alone the Rye House Plot, from which the Lord Chief Justice had virtually exonerated him. He made it clear that nothing had been sworn against him except some "consulting and discoursing," except "some Discourses about making some Stirs"; and this was not, he claimed, "levying War against the King, which is Treason by the Statute of *Edward* the Third."[21] He implied that the Court had con-

[19] *A Letter Written to My Lord Russell in NewGate, the Twentieth of July, 1683* (London, 1683), p. 2.
[20] Lord John Russell, *op. cit.*, p. 215, and Clarke and Foxcroft, *op. cit.*, pp. 195–96.
[21] *The Last Speech & Behaviour of William Late Lord Russell, upon the Scaffold in Lincolns-Inne-Fields, A Little Before His Execution, on Saturday, July 21. 1683* (London, 1683). All references to this paper are from this edition.

siderably stretched this Statute to cover his case, that he had been convicted not for any overt act but for holding illegal opinions in opposition to men powerful in both church and state. He stressed, for instance, that he had lived and would die in the "Reformed Religion, a true and sincere Protestant, and in the Communion of the Church of *England*"; but he admitted that he "could never yet comply with, or rise up to the heights of some People," which was to say, in view of his conversations with Burnet and Tillotson, that he had held firm in his convictions concerning resistance to kings in cases of religion and had rejected the doctrine of passive obedience. Moreover, he presented his plight as one growing out of his active role in the Whig party. He had been fearful of Popery and had sided with Shaftesbury in the turmoils which had attended the Popish Plot. He had supported the Bill of Exclusion because he thought a Popish successor would be a threat to the Anglican faith. "Earnestness in that matter," he declared, had "no small Influence" on his "present Sufferings." Furthermore, from the time of the turmoils over the election of sheriffs Lord Russell had feared "that the Heat in that Matter would produce something of this kind"; hence he was not now surprised to find the axe falling on him. The implication of a good part of the paper was that his opposition to the Crown could no longer be tolerated, that he had been tried and convicted for not complying with opinions of men high in church and state, that he was important enough to be dangerous and hence his head had to roll, not for a direct attempt to waylay and kill Charles II but for his possessing strong convictions and being willing to act upon them.

Lord Russell, then, was removed from the political scene because he had, prior to the Rye House Plot, acted upon his political principles and had clung, during the excitement the Plot had engendered, to his conviction in the lawfulness of resisting kings in cases of religion; or, to phrase it another way, because he had not conformed to and could not comply even in the face of powerful opposition with the details of what churchmen of the time believed was the singular article of the Anglican faith, the doctrine of passive obedience. From the evidence in John Tillotson's letter, he argued against this doctrine with considerable precision. The specific argument he employed will be analyzed later; perhaps at this juncture it should be noted that Tories had, during their conflict with the Whig party over the succession of York, invoked the theory of divine right and the doctrine of passive obedience, saying flatly that it was unlawful to oppose Charles II on any occasion, even though he might be (God perish the thought) a tyrant. In support of their claim, they triumphantly pointed to the story of the Primitive Christians, who, they said, were obedient even to Julian, the Apostate, one of the bitterest enemies of the Christian faith. By the same token, Englishmen should be obedient to their kings, even though the future might bring a Popish successor. This doctrine appeared in many a sermon and pamphlet during the years preceding the Rye House Plot, but no one expressed it any better than Francis Turner, later the Bishop of Ely, in a sermon commemorating the martyrdom of Charles I:

But then suppose a King of another Character, instead of one *under whose shadow we should live*, suppose a Tyrant had sate on the Throne, had it been lawful to Dethrone him? Is the greatest Misgovernment a sufficient pretence for any *Pope* or *Consistory* upon Earth to Depose a Sovereign Prince? To Legitimate Treason, Rebellion, the Parricide of a King by his Subjects? I will only put one Case, as hard a case as ever was, or perhaps as can be supposed, that is, the Case of *Julian the Apostate* Emperor. After so clear Conviction, after so full Instruction as he had in the Christian Religion, having, as some *Historians* report, taken one of the lower *Orders* in the Clergy before he came to the Throne, after all this he renounc't his Baptism, he turn'd a very Plague to the Church, he prov'd the most formidable Persecutor, that is, a Tempter of his Christian Subjects to Apostasie. He offended with that *malicious Wickedness*, that the Church, not any *Pope* or *Consistory*, or *Assembly*, but (which is a great deal more) the Catholic Church and all her Guides justly suppos'd he had committed that unpardonable *Sin against the Holy Ghost*; they lookt upon him as one that had cut himself off from their Body with the greatest Excommunication, even to *Anathema Marantha*, that is, *till the Lord come to Judgment.* Now in this case was it lawful for Christians to cast off Him that had so openly and maliciously cast off his Christianity? We have the Judgment of the whole Church to the contrary: They thought themselves oblig'd, by S. *Pauls* Apostolical Canon, *to make Supplications and Prayers* even for Him, that whatsoever he was, and howsoever he behav'd himself toward them, *they might still lead a quiet and peaceable life in all godliness and honesty.* And they had the Grace they pray'd for, they did live peaceably under him, they never took upon them to *Unking* him, they drew out no Forces against him, but onely their *thundring Legion* of Prayers and Tears. *He was restrain'd,* said Nazianzen, *by the mercy of God, and by the Tears of Good Christians, which they shed in great abundance, the only remedy* (saith he) *that they us'd against their Persecutor.* Such was the Practice of the Church conformable to the Doctrine of all her Ancient Fathers, none excepted.[22]

Now Tillotson, apparently, in his efforts to save Lord Russell from the block, had employed this very argument, and Lord Russell presumably had countered it with a statement questioning the accuracy of the Anglican story about the Primitive Christians, particularly as it applied to the struggle over the succession. It will be recalled that Tillotson had stated in his letter that Lord Russell had drawn a distinction between the case of the Primitive Christians and that of Christians under Charles II, the similarities of which Anglicans had been so fond of presenting. The distinction Lord Russell made, Tillotson explained, was that Christians under Charles II possessed their religion by law, whereas Primitive Christians did not. Such a distinction, of course, was highly significant, for it meant that the example of the Primitive Christians, upon which defenders of the doctrine of passive obedience had built most of their case, could not be accurately applied to the issues of the day. In short, it may be inferred from Tillotson's letter, as well as from the passage expunged from the paper Lord Russell was to deliver to the sheriffs, that Lord Russell attributed the obedience of Primitive Christians to their tyrannical princes not to the injunctions of Scripture but to the weight of the law, and believed that only when Christianity became established by law could Christians resist the encroachments of tyrannical kings. It followed from this that Christians under Charles II possessed the right to rise up in defense of their liberties whenever royal power invaded their religion, which was established by law. Lord Russell, then, held clearly defined beliefs on resistance to kings and on passive

[22] *A Sermon Preached Before the King on the 30 | 1 of January 1680 | 1. Being the Fast for the Martyrdom of Charles I. of Blessed Memory* (London, 1681), pp. 22–24.

obedience and knew how to defend them with precision and care. Moreover, his positions were exactly the same as those in the Oxford decree attributed mainly to Samuel Johnson's *Julian the Apostate*. Did Lord Russell's opinions stem from this source? An examination of *Julian the Apostate*, together with a glance at several contemporary witnesses, will make it clear that Lord Russell found the principles which sent him to his doom in his vigorous chaplain.[23]

*Julian the Apostate* was the most complete answer to the Anglican doctrine of passive obedience to be published during the debates over the succession. In the first eight chapters, Johnson sketched "*A Short Account of* Julian'*s Life*," showing that the Anglican interpretation of the Primitive Christians under Julian not only was historically inaccurate but also had been irresponsibly applied to the present. Rather than submitting to Julian and sending up only a thundering legion of prayers and tears, the Primitive Christians, Johnson explained, actually called him names, derided the shape of his body, and even prayed against him. Moreover, he went on, when news came of his death, Christians fell to dancing and rejoicing; and rumor reported that he died not by enemy action but by his own troops.[24] From this account, Johnson turned next to his *Reflections on the Behaviour of These Christians.* He recalled how Christians had not been moved by Julian's injunction that they submit to his will, even when he invoked the divine right of kings and the laws of Nature and of God. Julian might as well have fallen among barbarians. And Christians had a right to treat Julian thus, for by this time Christianity had been established by law. With the Primitive Christians just before Julian's time, however, matters were different; they suffered under a tyrannical yoke because Christianity had not yet been established by law, and therefore could not lawfully resist kingly authority:

The plain truth of the Matter is this; Their Case differed very much, and they were in quite other Circumstances than the first Christians were. When *Julian* came to the Crown, he found them in full and quiet

[23] See *DNB*, under "Samuel Johnson," for a statement of the influence Johnson had on his patron.

[24] *Julian the Apostate* . . . , pp. 1–65.

possession of their Religion, which they had enjoyed without interruption for almost fifty Years, and which was so inestimable a Blessing, that they had plainly undervalued it, if they had not done their utmost to keep it. And then to have this Treasure wrested out of their hands, by one that had been bred up in the Bosom of the Church, who profes'd himself a Christian, and never pull'd off his Masque, till it was too late for them to help themselves; this was enough to raise, not only all their Zeal, but all their indignation too. Whereas the poor Primitive Christians of all, were born to Persecution, they neither knew better, nor expected it. They professed their new Religion, as in some places they propounded new Laws, with an Halter about their Necks. The Laws of the Empire were always in force against them, though not always put in execution; and the edge of the Ax stood always towards them, though it were not at all times stained with their Blood.[25]

With this distinction made, Johnson went ahead to explain that Christians under Charles II enjoyed their religion "setled by such Laws as cannot be altered without" their own "consent"; and in view of this difference between them and the Primitive Christians, he wondered

at those Men, who trouble the Nation at this time of the day, with the unseasonable prescriptions of Prayers and Tears, and the Passive Obedience of the *Thebæan* Legion, and such-like last Remedies, which are proper, only at such a Time, as the Laws of our Country are armed against our Religion. What have we to do with the *Thebæan* Legion? Blessed be God, who has made the difference. . . . What have we to do with their Example?[26]

These are exactly the sentiments, of course, which Lord Russell expressed. And the close relation which existed between Samuel Johnson and his patron, as well as the identity of their thought, can lead only to the conclusion that Lord Russell derived his positions on resistance and obedience to kings from his sharp-minded chaplain.

Contemporary witnesses confirm this conclusion. Tillotson spoke in his letter of "particular persons" who had "taught otherwise" than the Church; and Thomas Sprat, two years after the Rye House Plot, specifically mentioned that Lord Russell had

[25] *Julian the Apostate* . . . , pp. 68–69.
[26] *Ibid.*, pp. 73–74.

been "seduced by the wicked Teachers of that most Unchristian Doctrine, which has been the cause of so many Rebellions, and was so comformable to his Presbyterian Education, That *it is lawful to Resist and Rise against Soveraign Princes for preserving Religion.*"[27] Neither Tillotson nor Sprat named the culprit, but others did. He was none other than Samuel Johnson, who made Lord Russell pursue his course to the very last, "because this might become any Heroick Christian drawn in Armour by the Pensil of the author of *Julian*; and is not unlike to the practices of the Ancient Christians, so shamefully disguised by the same Author."[28] Roger L'Estrange developed this accusation in some detail. In his *Considerations upon a Printed Sheet*, published under royal authority, he questioned whether Lord Russell could have been the author of the paper delivered to the sheriffs. The speech which preceded the paper was undoubtedly his, yes; but as for the paper itself—this was the work of an *"Evil Genius,"* of *"Julian"* himself, that is, of Samuel Johnson:

A Man shall not need to Guess twice, who was the Author of this Sentence; for 'tis written with the very Spirit of a *Carguelite* that makes *Treason*, a *Virtue*, and *Repentence* a *Mortal Sin*: And my *Poor Lord*, in the *Anguish* of his *Thought*, is left here to Answer for the *Lewdness* of *Another man*, who, (Notwithstanding the *Justness* of my Lords *Sentence*,) is *Incomparably the Greater Criminal*. If he ever *was*, or *Pretended* to be a *Minister* of the *Gospel*, (For there are *Julians* in BLACKCOATS, and *more Julians* then *One* too) what could be more *Luciferian*; then to turn *Penitence* into a *Scandal*; And to *Preach* it for a Point of *Religious Honour*, in a *Christian*, not to *Discover* his *Complices* in a *Rebellion*. Surely the Author of this Paper was afraid of being Discovered himself; And therefore *Inculcates* the *Principle*, and *Recommends* it.[29]

As L'Estrange developed his theme further, commenting on particular passages, he recalled how Lord Russell had been

[27] *A True Account and Declaration of the Horrid Conspiracy Against the Late King, His Present Majesty, and the Government: As It Was Order'd to be Published by His Late Majesty* (In the Savoy, 1685), p. 21.

[28] *An Antidote Against Poison* (London, 1683), p. 3.

[29] *Considerations upon a Printed Sheet Entituled the Speech of the Late Lord Russell to the Sheriffs: Together, with the Paper Delivered by Him to Them, at the Place of Execution, on July 21, 1683* (London, 1683), p. 37.

"somewhat *deeper Dyed* then *ordinary*"; but he found this hardly surprising, since he had all too frequently "most desperate *Seducers* at his *Elbow*." L'Estrange even made Samuel Johnson responsible for Lord Russell's implication in the Rye House Plot, claiming that *Julian the Apostate* was "the very *Scheme* of this *Conspiracy*, and *Calculated* for the *Murder* of the *King*, and the *Dissolution* of the *State*," and that "it was *the same Poysonous Position* that brought this *Unhappy Lord* to his *Ruine*."[30] L'Estrange next recalled how Tillotson had made friendly and pious visits to Lord Russell with the hope of dissuading him from his dangerous position, and how this godly man was troubled to find Lord Russell "*Possess'd* with the *Principle* of his Chaplains [*Julian the Apostate*] that *Resistance was Lawful in the Case of Religion, Liberties* and *Properties being Invaded*."[31] Then, with a final flourish, L'Estrange virtually exonerated Lord Russell and placed the blame for the tragedy on Samuel Johnson himself:

> There is more then enough said in Reflection upon this *Scandalous Paper*; that takes so much pains to possess the World that this Unhappy *Execution* was a *Murder*. There WAS, Effectually, a *Murder* in the *Case*. It was in the *Law* an Act of *Justice*: But it was in *Him* that *Poysoned this Unfortunate Gentleman* with that *Seditious Maxim* that brought him to the *Block*, and that afterwards Encouraged him to persist in't: It was in HIM, I say, the *Basest*, and the most *Treacherous* of *Murders*: *A*nd I look upon *Julian*, with a Respect to *this Conspiracy* only as the RULE to the EXAMPLE, *the* ONE DIRECTS *the Rebellion; and the* OTHER PROVES *it*.[32]

In this statement, L'Estrange succinctly summarized the case. Lord Russell had gone to the block for holding and persisting in a "Seditious Maxim," a maxim he derived from Samuel Johnson's *Julian the Apostate*; Samuel Johnson had supplied the principles for the conspiracy and Lord Russell had carried them out. Though Roger L'Estrange, in assuming that Lord Russell had actually taken part in the Rye House Plot, perhaps pushed his analysis beyond the realm of actual fact, no doubt should

---

[30] *Considerations upon a Printed Sheet* . . . , p. 46.
[31] *Ibid.*, p. 47.
[32] *Ibid.*, p. 52.

remain that Lord Russell derived from his chaplain the principles which sent him to his doom. Since *Julian the Apostate* is in great measure a plagiary of parts of the *Defensio Prima*, since Samuel Johnson refined Milton's arguments concerning resistance to kings and passive obedience and shaped them to fit issues which arose during the attempted Whig revolution, it is no exaggeration to say that Milton himself must share some of the blame for Lord Russell's fate.

Lord Russell, then, may in a very real sense be called one of Milton's disciples. He did not, to be sure, leave written evidence of his discipleship, like Samuel Johnson in his *Julian the Apostate*, or Thomas Hunt in his *Postscript*,[33] or Charles Blount and William Denton in their adaptations of *Areopagitica*.[34] But in the arena of deadly political combat he confronted his enemies with weapons upon which Milton had placed an original stamp. He used them well; and, though he lost his life in the attempted Whig revolution, the principles he adhered to, not those proposed by John Tillotson, triumphed in the Revolutionary Settlement. Indeed, by the time of the Settlement, Lord Russell had been vindicated, Samuel Johnson had achieved a wide recognition, and John Milton had been designated as one of the main proponents of resistance to kings and the chief early enemy of passive obedience.[35] Oxford University officials, in their inquiry into the causes of the Rye House Plot, thus made no mistake in placing Milton on their list of subversive authors. Had they looked more sharply at the *Defensio Prima* and had they been blessed with prophetic vision, perhaps they would have not only listed Milton more frequently in their decree but also deemed him, among their numerous enemies, one of the most dangerous and influential.

[33] "Milton and the Doctrine of Passive Obedience," *op. cit.*, XIII (1949), pp. 32–38.

[34] "Adaptations of *Aeropagitica*," *The Huntington Library Quarterly*, XIII (1950), 201–5.

[35] "Milton and the Doctrine of Passive Obedience," *op. cit.*, XIII (1949), pp. 42–54.

# POPE AND "THE GREAT SHEW
# OF NATURE"

### George Sherburn

In the romantic tradition of poetry, nature was like beauty —chiefly an end in itself but also a source of agreeable sensations. To poets of the school of Pope nature was rather an ordered universe, into which the individual would ideally fit as a small part, harmonious to the whole. The categorical imperative of such a poet is, "Know thy own point," and the function of the poet is to interpret the "point," the status quo, by a study of the origin and the destiny of the grand system of which the individual is a part. Hence when Wordsworth gave modified approbation to "a passage or two" in *Windsor Forest*—presumably the lines about the pheasant (ll. 111–18)—he was praising the plumage but forgetting the bird. For Pope's objective with regard to external nature is practically never primarily descriptive: nature is to be interpreted and understood especially in its relations to humanity. It is not primarily a source of agreeable sensation. To Pope, Nature, Reason, Light, are among the best words he knows, and to him "Nature and Nature's Laws" were the second most important field of study man could consider. The foremost field was man himself: "Know then theyself!" But to know one's self, one's "own point," implied knowing the Whole System of things, which is Nature.

At least two aspects of Pope's attitude toward nature should be recognized. The first (and here the less important) is the Platonic, abstractionist tendency in his poetic art; the second is the shaping influence of the science of his day. The abstractionist tendency neglects particularity in detail and tries to seize upon essential traits of objects. Its aim is not to present either the streaks of the tulip or the blackness of ash buds in March or other minutely observable details. The "images" are not specific or particular (except at times in satire): they are, however, interpretative: they express the essence of the object. Neglecting "minuter discriminations" the poet "is to exhibit," as Dr. Johnson tells us in a famous passage, "in his portraits of nature such prominent and striking features, as recall the original tó every mind." A more detailed account of this procedure can be found in the first notable commendation of Pope by a critic, in Joseph Spence's *Essay on Pope's Odyssey* (1727). In a passage dealing with "epithets" as a poetic device Spence emphasizes various points:

Epithets [he writes] . . . like Pictures in Miniature, are often entire descriptions in one Word. This may be either from their own significance, or by their immediate connexion with some known object. We see the thing, when the Poet only mentions the *Nodding Crest* of an Hero; and form a larger Idea of *Jove* from the single Epithet of *Cloud-compelling*, than we might find in a description more diffuse. It was chiefly from *two Poetical Epithets*, that *Phidias* design'd the countenance of his *Olympian Jupiter*; as, in Reverse, we often see the Person in his Epithet, from our being acquainted with some Statue, or Picture, to which it refers: Thus when *Apollo* is call'd the *Archer-God*, it recalls to our memory the representations we have so often seen of that Deity: the compleat Figure is rais'd up in the Mind, by touching upon that single circumstance.

'Tis by the same means, that one single Epithet gives us the Idea of any Object, which has been common and familiar to us. Meadows, Fields, Woods, Rivers, and the Sea itself, are often imag'd by one well-chosen word. Thus in that beautiful Description of *Calypso's* Bower, you see the Groves *of living green*; the Alders *ever quivering*; the *nodding* Cypress, and its high Branches, *waving* with the Storm: 'Tis by Epithets that the ancient Poets paint their *Elysian Groves*: and the Modern, their *Windsor-Forests*.[1]

Spence goes on to admit more diffuse methods of description, and to commend epithets that add strength and emphasis or those that heap concentrated abuse (e.g., Polypheme's con-

[1] *Essay on Pope's Odyssey* (1727), II, 17–18.

temptuous line: "Those *air-bred people* and their *goat-nurs'd Jove*") as all concisely stimulating. When they combine boldness with naturalness, they are supremely effective.

But, at the moment, this aesthetic tradition in which Pope lived concerns us less than the shaping influence that physical science of his day had upon his art. It may surprise some that such an influence should be asserted, but in an age when Nature was being studied as never before it would be strange if Pope underwent no influence of such study. The influence obviously operates paradoxically; for Pope is clearly aware of both the largeness and the smallness of science. It may involve study of the universal system (the age was celebrated for its astronomers), or it may involve—to use a favorite Popean bit of denigration—the study of flies. Dulness, one recalls, exclaims

> O! would the Sons of Men once think their Eyes
> And Reason giv'n them but to study *Flies*![2]

and the poet echoes the idea more than once; for example, when he objects to those whose study is "T'inspect a Mite, not comprehend the heav'n."[3] Such students "See Nature in some partial narrow shape,"[4] and are lacking in the larger view.

The adverse criticism of science set down by Swift and Pope has more than once been summarized by those writing about *Gulliver's Travels* or *The Memoirs of Martinus Scriblerus*. The narrowness of such study is said to warp and impair personality; the results of experiments are useless or (as in the case of flies) supposedly frivolous. Experimentation often stems allegedly from a mere thirst for novelty, highly offensive to the complacent; and the larger views of science are condemned as completely conjectural—a fact that might seem to take them out of the scientific field altogether. The complete intellectual might naturally react to the cosmogonies of Pope's day much as did Gulliver's Houyhnhnm master: "When I used to explain to him our several systems of natural philosophy, he would laugh that a creature pretending to reason should value itself upon the knowledge of other people's conjectures, and in things where that knowledge, if it were certain, could be of no use."[5] Swift

---

[2] *Dunciad*, Book IV, ll. 453–54.	[3] *Essay on Man*, Ep. I, l. 196.
[4] *Dunciad*, Book IV, l. 455.	[5] *Gulliver's Travels*, Part IV, chap. viii.

may have been strong-minded enough to maintain this position, but for Pope precisely these larger, conjectural aspects that deal with the origin and destiny of the Universe and of Man are what fascinate. The only soundly scientific aspect of this cosmological preoccupation would of course be astronomy, and like other men of his day Pope was much stimulated by the recent developments in the study of the heavens. While frequently commending empirical methods, Pope was not quite content to stop with them. Newton and others among the ablest scientists had tactfully avoided the discussion of final causes, but Pope is caustic concerning failure to study "The source of Newton's light, of Bacon's sense."[6] He did of course admire Newton's work greatly, as his famous epitaph shows. He always mentioned Newton with reverence, and even helped John Conduitt, the editor, write a proper dedication to the posthumous *Chronology of Ancient Kingdoms Amended* (1728). Pope is altogether a humanist rather than a scientist, and any ideas, right or wrong, that he may have acquired concerning science are negligible except in so far as they influence his poetic expression. One might indeed have expected more in the way of technical knowledge from a man who almost from childhood was in the hands of doctors trying to make supportable "this long disease, my life"; or from the reviser and editor of *The Memoirs of Martinus Scriblerus.* Pope's diverse if superficial reading was doubtless greater in amount than critics have sometimes thought, but it tended to lie in the field of literature or of "polemic divinity" rather than in science—though divinity and science were in his day striving for an alliance or at least a reconciliation.

An example of this last fact may be seen in the work of the man who seems first to have interested Pope in the one field of science that really attracted him. William Whiston had in 1703 succeeded Newton as Lucasian professor at Cambridge, where he lectured on mathematics and natural philosophy—which he tried to combine with theology. In 1707 he delivered the Boyle lectures, and published them as *Eight Sermons.* They were speedily attacked, and it is interesting that in the year 1707 Pope in his rhyming epistle to Henry Cromwell speaks of the "wicked

[6] *Dunciad*, Book III, l. 218.

works of Whiston." Later, Whiston's heresies became notorious, and in 1710 he was deprived of his professorship and banished from the University. At this point that supposed model of orthodoxy, Joseph Addison, stepped in and arranged to have Whiston give popular lectures on astronomy and other subjects in the coffeehouses of London. In his *Memoirs* (1749, 1753) Whiston himself tells of this patronage:

> Mr. Addison . . . was my particular friend; and . . . with his friend Sir *Richard Steel*, brought me, upon my banishment from *Cambridge*, to have many astronomical lectures at Mr. Button's coffee-house, near *Covent-Garden*, to the agreeable entertainment of a good number of curious persons, and procuring me and my family some comfortable support upon my banishment."[7]

These lectures, or some of them, in the summer of 1713 Pope evidently heard, and they at least dazzled his mind, if they did not altogether illuminate it. On August 14, 1713, Pope wrote to his friend John Caryll a letter which in 1735 he printed as if sent to Addison. In the original letter he writes concerning the society at Button's:

> You cannot wonder my thoughts are scarce consistent, when I tell you how they are distracted. Every hour of my life my mind is strangely divided. This minute, perhaps, I am above the stars, with a thousand systems round about me, looking forward into the vast abyss of eternity, and losing my whole comprehension in the boundless spaces of the extended creation, in dialogues with Whiston and the astronomers; the next moment I am below all trifles, even grovelling with Tidcombe in the very centre of nonsense. . . . Good God! what an incongruous animal is man![8]

In another letter written to Caryll jointly by Gay and Pope and possibly dating 1715, Pope is spoken of as discussing astronomy with General Tidcombe.[9] The interest in this science, so much cultivated in Pope's day, was for him permanent. Possibly the fact that Whiston in conversation had a keen, witty manner of speaking may have aided the influence.

[7] I, 257.
[8] *Works*, ed. Elwin and Courthope, VI, 190–91.
[9] *Ibid.*, VI, 226.

Whiston was one of the group of "world-makers,"[10] who, following Thomas Burnet, the author of *Telluris Theoria Sacra*, passed on to the eighteenth century the torch of millennial myth. These people would agree with Fontenelle, who remarked that "Nature is but a great shew, resembling that of an opera."[11] Such thinkers did not "see Nature in some partial narrow shape"; they sat as in a theater contemplating the whole universal spectacle—and to their own satisfaction curiously reconciling it with the revelation in the Holy Scriptures. The "opera" naturally began with the Creation, and hexameral traditions or theories colored much of their thinking. The Fall was less scientific in coloration, but the Deluge gave room for no end of speculation in days when fossils were major problems in the awakening science of geology. One recalls that the Scriblerians satirized the geologist Woodward as "Fossile" in *Three Hours After Marriage* (1717). From the dark backward and abysm that was the Deluge the "opera" hastily by-passed the present, and strained its eyes forward to the Millennium. The sweep, obviously, was more than epic in scope: it obsessed an age learning new theories of history and eager to look either before or after, and thus avoid the depressing present.

This large view entranced Pope. In more than one of his letters there is evidence of his interest in millennial thinking. Writing to his friend Robert Digby (October 10, 1723—or, better dated, 1725) he mingles scientific phrases with allusions to primitive Christianity (one of Whiston's chief topics) and to Berkeley's Utopian project for a college in the Bermudas—all in a facetious but somewhat dazzled tone:

You [Digbys] are all of one heart and one soul, as was said of the primitive Christians: it is like the kingdom of the just upon earth; not a wicked wretch to interrupt you. . . . Why will you ever of your own accord, end such a millenary year in London? transmigrate (if I may so call it) into other creatures, in that scene of folly militant, when you may reign forever at Holm Lacy in sense and reason triumphant?

---

[10] See Ernest Tuveson, "Swift and the World-Makers," *JHI*, XI (1950), 54–74. This present paper is obviously indebted to Professor Tuveson's article as well as to his book, *Millennium and Utopia* (Berkeley and Los Angeles, 1949).

[11] *A Discourse of the Plurality of Worlds*, tr. Knight (Dublin, 1687), p. 5.

. . . I am not without hopes . . . that I may come upon you with such irresistible arguments another year, as may carry you all with me to the Bermudas, the seat of all earthly happiness, and the New Jerusalem of the righteous.[12]

And, possibly a few days later (October 15, 1725), Pope writes his long-banished friend Swift in much the same tone:

I have fancied, I say, that we should meet like the righteous in the millennium, quite in peace, divested of all our former passions, smiling at all our own designs, and content to enjoy the kingdom of the just in tranquillity. But I find you would rather be employed as an avenging angel of wrath . . .[13]

Pope had at this moment caught at least temporarily the high enthusiasm of his friend Berkeley. And when Berkeley in a letter to his friend Lord Percival (February 10, 1725/6) enclosed his famous quatrains,[14] there entitled "America or the Muses Refuge, a Prophecy," he was thinking in terms of the millennium rather than merely in terms of Rhode Island. His last three quatrains—published later without change—read as follows:

There shall be sung another golden age
    The Rise of Empire and of Arts
The Good and great inspiring Epic Rage
    The Wisest heads and noblest hearts

Not such as Europe breeds in her decay
    Such as She bred when fresh and young
When heavenly flame did animate her Clay
    By future Poets shall be sung.

Westward the Course of Empire takes its way
    The four first Acts already past
A Fifth shall close the Drama with the Day
    The Worlds great Effort is the last.

This, the most enthusiastic moment in Berkeley's career, was also a rare mood of his time. The drama was unfolding, and

[12] *Works*, ed. cit., IX, 88–89.
[13] *Ibid.*, VII, 58–59.
[14] Found in Percival's letter books, BM Add. MS 47031, pp. 213–15.

was pointing toward a divine, far-off state of bliss. Even Pope was affected; and though he was a satirist, the half-playful passages in his letters concerning the millennium reflect shaping influences on his poetry. The *Essay on Man* should have ended with some epic view of a blissful condition; but it does not—perhaps because that would have involved Pope in Scriptural imagery, and the Scriptures were, for one reason or another, being left out of his *Essay on Man*. But in his account in Epistle III of the poem, where the great drama of human development is unfolded from the Golden Age to the desperate moment when, for political salvation, the

> Poet or Patriot rose but to restore
> The Faith and Moral Nature gave before—[15]

we might expect a climactic conclusion with the millennium at least glimpsed. We do not get it. One may suggest, however, that the whole of Epistle IV is a substitute for the conclusion that might have ended the social evolution depicted in Epistle III. Happiness (its subject) and the millennium are surely allied if not identical.

Naturally perhaps, Pope's most significant application of his millennial thinking to poetry is negative—is the millennium transversed. Throughout his *Dunciad* the cosmic background is the warfare between God and Nature, on the one side, and Chaos and Old Night on the other. Nature is Order, and Dulness is the queen of Chaos. This idea, emphatic in Book IV of the poem, is not first found there. Pope had expressed it earlier in the *Dunciad* of 1728, where at the very start Dulness is "Daughter of Chaos and eternal Night." This parentage (I, 12) is echoed in the second line of Book IV (thus tying together the poem?) and in various other lines of Book IV, until the final passage (ll. 627–56) presents the awful triumph "Of Night primaeval and of Chaos old!" Here instead of the millennium that had so comforted Pope we find the scientific decay of nature blackening out the stars one by one; neglect of the Final Cause debasing philosophy, and, in general, conjectural theory leading to chaotic

[15] *Essay on Man*, Ep. III, ll. 285–86.

confusion. Nature had begun with the fiat, Let there be Light! Here the opposite takes place:

> Lo! thy dread Empire, CHAOS! is restor'd;
> Light dies before thy uncreating word;
> Thy hand, great Anarch! lets the curtain fall,
> And universal Darkness buries all.[16]

The great shew of Nature is over, and it proved a tragedy.

In Pope's day the universe (Nature) could be conceived as drama. It more commonly, of course, was conceived as divine revelation, as God's handiwork. Witness Addison's well-known lines beginning "The spacious firmament on high," or indeed the whole of Thomson's *Seasons*, but particularly his "Hymn" to the Seasons. In the *Essay on Man* Pope presented Nature as a magnificent mechanism, held together by the principle of "attraction"; but he had ennobled that poem notably by use of symbols from the scientific teachings of Newton, Whiston, and others, about the heavenly bodies. These symbolic images convey the largeness of view that Pope associated with the sort of science that he both loved for its largeness and satirized for its conjectural lack of evidence. In general, he makes most frequent use of symbols of order as opposed to lawlessness. The lawless man may

> meteor-like, flame lawless through the void,
> Destroying others, by himself destroy'd.[17]

Pope shudders at the thought of cosmic confusion:

> Let Earth unbalanc'd from her orbit fly,
> Planets and Suns run lawless through the sky . . .[18]

Divine reason apparently has no such qualms. It sees

> with equal eye, as God of all,
> A hero perish, or a sparrow fall,
> Atoms or systems into ruin hurl'd,
> And now a bubble burst, and now a world . . .[19]

The presumptuous man is pictured as claiming "My footstool

---

[16] *Dunciad*, Book IV, ll. 653–56.
[17] *Essay on Man*, Ep. II, ll. 65–66.
[18] *Ibid.*, Ep. I, ll. 251–52.        [19] *Ibid.*, ll. 87–90.

earth, my canopy the skies";[20] but the total scheme of things implies subordination and, above all, harmony. Man must submit to his lot, and contribute his small office to the good of the whole. Pope is speaking of more than a political system of checks and balances—he is speaking of the Universe, when he exclaims:

> Such is the World's great harmony, that springs
> From Order, Union, full Consent of things . . .[21]

At times, Pope was highly irreverent with regard to things sacred in the eyes of others and even in his own eyes; but the irreverence was superficial, the result of a too quick wit that led him to say not what he really thought but what on the instant he thought of saying. In the passages just quoted, however, Pope shows a reverence for Universal Nature that is both inspiring and noble. The "scarlet-circled eyes"[22] of the pheasant and other particular details appear in his verse largely by accident, and not much would be lost if they did not appear at all. One cannot, however, make that remark concerning his glimpses of the millennium and his symbolic use of astronomical images, which open wide visions in a spirit of lofty cosmic reverence.

[20] *Ibid.,* l. 140.
[21] *Ibid.,* Ep. III, ll. 295–96.
[22] *Windsor Forest,* l. 116.

# ADDISON'S CONTRIBUTION
# TO CRITICISM

Clarence D. Thorpe

ONE of the favorite clichés of literary historians is that Addison was peculiarly representative of his age. But like most clichés this one may be misleading. For though Addison did belong to his age, he did not belong to it, at least as a critic, in the way that Pope did. Pope's *Essay on Criticism* belongs to the age and to the past; Addison's "Essay on the Imagination" belongs to the age and to the future. Pope is performing the office in his essay of a near-perfect synthesizer, giving us in precept and example an epitome of English neo-classicism. But the Augustan age was not a static age; it was a period not only of neat summation and integration, but also of transition and forward movement; it helped to initiate and to transform and transmit the new as well as to take on to itself and make use of the old. Unlike Pope, Addison's peculiar service to aesthetics and criticism was not to utilize the old—though he did some of that, too—but to accept and adapt and transmit the new, and in such a way and to such a degree that he became thereby one of the chief constructive forces in the literary theory of the century that followed. There was a new as well as an old criticism in the Augustan period, just as there is a new and an old criticism today—and of the new critics Addison was the outstanding and distinctive figure.

By the "new criticism" I have in mind that movement in English aesthetic theory, extending roughly from Hobbes to Alison and preparing the way for Wordsworth and Coleridge, which sought means of explaining and evaluating literature on psychological and pragmatic rather than on traditional, formal-istic grounds. The key terms of this criticism were Imagination, Taste, Original Genius, Beauty, Sublimity, Novelty, Associa-tion of Ideas, Nature. The questions that most concerned it, especially after about 1730, were not those having to do with conformity to the theory and practice of the ancients, with ad-herence to certain formal patterns or particular stylistic modes, or with evidence of learning and judgment; they were more likely to be, "Does this work please?" "If so, why and how does it please?" "What are the special sources, what are the particular qualities of the pleasure it gives?" "Is it the work of a man of native genius and imagination?"

Most of the new critics still believed in rules or principles; but the principles in which they were interested were those rooted in natural law—the great law of nature. And by nature they came to mean more and more not universal cosmic nature and universal human nature formed in the image of "natural law"— that is, idealized human nature reflecting the inner order and harmony of the universal frame of things—but common human nature as it manifests itself in the passions, motives, and actions of individual men and women. They, therefore, put their main trust not in reason and learning but in natural response, in in-stinct, emotion, imagination, and original genius.

The theoretical critics of the period were, almost to a man, devotees of the new sensational psychology. The laws they had in mind were psychological laws; and their methods of ascer-taining these laws were the empirical ones of appeal to common experience and of observation of the ways of the mind, especially as related to imaginative creation and to response to nature and art. Introspection became increasingly the chief instrument of aesthetic speculation of the time.

Corollary to intensified interest in the ways of the mind was a shift in emphasis in practical criticism from action to character. Likewise, corollary was a shift of attention from mechanical structure to design and to the successive events of a narrative as evidence of the skill with which the author had introduced event and speech to lead to climactic moments and to produce desired effects upon the mind of the observer. Convincing por-

trayal of individualized characters moved by dominant passions
became more important than adherence to decorum in the creation of rigid types. Appeal to the imagination by way of the
softer emotions of beauty and novelty and of the great and
stirring passion of sublimity, the satisfaction of taste rather than
of the reason, rapidly gained ground as the primary aim of the
creative artist—though the satisfaction of a "rational" taste was
usually considered most desirable.

Addison's role in getting the new criticism going has been
described in enthusiastic terms. J. G. Robertson, for example,
sees Addison as an originator, who "laid the foundation of the
whole romantic aesthetics in England," and who became a significant factor in the "building up of a new aesthetic doctrine in
both France and Germany."[1] W. Basil Worsfold makes similar
claims.[2] Professor E. F. Carritt regards Addison as a primary
influence on Kant, whose aesthetic theory, he asserts, was little
more than a redaction of "distinctions and oppositions current in
English for the preceding eighty years." Of Kant's ideas of
sublimity and related theories Carritt goes so far as to say, "All
is Addison's except the style."[3] Through his followers and Kant,
Carritt also argues, Addison not only foreshadowed Wordsworth and Coleridge in their most distinctive theories—those of
imagination and sublimity—but did much to prepare the way
for their practice. Carritt is himself so convinced of the validity
of these conclusions and of the general importance of Addison
as a critic that he is ready to lay down the proposition that "Addison may justly be thought the father of modern critical theory."
Addison, he asserts, owed little to his English predecessors, "but
to him the succeeding critics of his century owed almost everything."[4]

Other scholars have recognized Addison's importance in
more limited departments. Samuel Monk has shown how large

[1] *The Genesis of the Romantic Theory in England* (Cambridge, 1923),
p. 241.

[2] *The Principles of Criticism* (London, 1923), pp. 82 ff.

[3] "Effects in England of Kant's Philosophy," *The Monist*, XXXV (1925),
322, 323.

[4] "Addison, Kant and Coleridge," *Essays and Studies of the English Association*, XXII (1936), 27, 32, 35.

a part he played in giving impetus to the idea of sublimity in the eighteenth century; Edward Niles Hooker has described his role in the development of taste; and Martin Kallich, in his thesis and articles, has accorded him the honor of writing the first systematic treatise on aesthetics in England and of doing much to relate the association of ideas to the imagination.

There is truth in these evaluations, and yet some of them stand in need of qualification. Accuracy requires that we think of the "new criticism" not as having sprung full-blown from the head of one man but rather as having evolved over a long period of time and through the efforts of many important thinkers. In considering this evolution we must not forget such predecessors of Addison as Hobbes, with his seminal speculations on the fancy (imagination), on aesthetic effects, and on the association of ideas, or Dryden, who contributed so much in the way of lively, forward-looking discussion of basic critical problems that it might be argued to some purpose that there was little in Addison's theory that had not been at least intimated in his great essays. We cannot then accept without question Carritt's view that Addison owed little or nothing to his predecessors or the implications of Robertson and Worsfold to the effect that he was the one begetter of a new aesthetics in England.

Nor can Carritt's assertion that succeeding critics of the century owed "almost everything" to Addison quite be taken without reservation. Eighteenth-century criticism is a "mingled skein." Addison contributed much to the final dominant pattern, but others contributed, too, and in ways that went beyond, though rarely if ever entirely outside of Addison's formulation. It will not do, therefore, to minimize the work of the long line of English writers who, after Addison, made notable additions to the new psychological aesthetics: of Burke, who materially broadened and modified concepts of sublimity and taste; of Hume, who developed, most importantly, the principle of association of ideas in relation to the imagination; of Akenside, Young, Tucker, and Duff, of Gerard, Kames, and Blair, Hartley, Beattie, and Alison, who supplied, if not always new ideas, at least ever new variations on the themes of taste, original genius, beauty, sublimity, novelty, association of ideas, and imagination. All of these, neither neoclassic nor yet Romantic critics, but new critics of the transition between the two, were clearing the ground, though sometimes indirectly, for Coleridge and Wordsworth, and were moving, in one way or another, in their general direction.

Addison's place in this evolutionary development need not be overrated to give him ample credit. For, though he was not the sole originator of the new criticism, since most of the separate ingredients of idea and method had already been known and employed by others, it was he who put them together in the first effective atomiclike bombshell of systematic formulation. Faced with a situation where, in constant attempts to find ways to square a native relish of the great English poets with a formalistic aesthetic which had no place for them, compromise had become the rule in English critical practice, Addison cut the Gordian knot by boldly proposing a theory based on psychological rather than on formalistic, rhetorical principle, of such nature and scope as to account for Shakespeare and Spenser as well as for Homer and Sophocles—to account in a general way, indeed, for all great art.

The characteristic fact about Addison as a critic was his zeal for excellence. This was the motivating force in his main critical ventures from the early comment on the *Georgics* to the end. He was interested in what was fine. He thought that the duty of the critic was to discover and explain the specific "distinguishing perfections" of a writer. When he found excellence he was courageous enough to say so and fair enough to offer his reasons. His defense of the old ballads and his championship of true versus false wit are illustrative; also, most importantly, are his papers on *Paradise Lost*. The last twelve of these papers represent a deliberate attempt to isolate for inspection and admiration the "beauties of the several books of this great poem." And Addison clearly shows in his fifth and sixth essays that in doing this he was consciously defying the current fashion of satiric and fault-finding criticism. Addison's quest was for excellence; all that fault-finding could do was to obscure excellence. So his last twelve papers stood as a superb example of the positive method in criticism, for any to follow who would; and as the century went on there were many who chose to follow.

The papers on the imagination likewise represent a quest for excellence, this time especially for its causes and effects. Interestingly enough, the last paragraph of *Spectator* 409, which is, in effect, a prospectus of the theory that is to follow—laying down the issues at stake, announcing the principle of Taste as intrinsic in judgments of literary value, and stating with fair precision Addison's intentions in the forthcoming essay—would suggest that this is to be a part of a long-range, carefully considered campaign, perhaps the final climactic move in this campaign, to give England a better aesthetic and criticism. As a corrective to the English taste for artificial style, Addison tells us, he has written an "Essay on Wit" pointing out those false kinds which have been too much admired and showing "wherein the Nature of true Wit consists." Later he has given, in his criticism of the ballads, "an Instance of the great Force which lyes in a natural Simplicity of Thought to affect the Mind of the Reader"; and he has also "examined the Works of the greatest Poet which our Nation or perhaps any other has produced and particularized most of those rational and manly Beauties which give a Value to that Divine Work." Now he is about to enter "upon an Essay *on the Pleasures of the Imagination,* which . . . will perhaps suggest to the Reader what it is that gives a Beauty to many passages of the finest Writers both in Prose and Verse."

Whether they were in fact a part of such a long-range plan as Addison's words imply, it is certain that the papers on the Imagination were not written on the spur of the moment. In their original form they were not written as papers at all, but as a continuous essay, some scholars believe as early as Addison's Oxford days. In *The Spectator* this essay is to appear in much revised, greatly enlarged form, as a professedly deliberate attempt to formulate a new and improved method of dealing with the basic literary problem of excellence versus nonexcellence.

The Sheldonian Latin Oration of 1693 reveals not only that Addison had the right temper of mind but that he was, as early as his college days, in possession of essential equipment for revised thought on aesthetic questions: namely, a spirit receptive to change and a knowledge of and belief in the basic modes and principles of the psychological philosophy of Descartes, Hobbes, and Locke.

This oration exalts the new philosophy at the expense of ancient and scholastic thought. Descartes is played up and Aristotle is played down. The moderns have brought on the stage a new method of philosophizing through which the whole mass of the universe has been so clearly traced "as to leave no occult matter untouched." The net result is emancipation from outworn shibboleths and the gift of improved modes of discovering truth:

> We no longer pay a blind veneration to that barbarous Peripatetic jingle, those obscure scholastic terms of art, once held as oracles; but consult the dictates of our own senses, and by late invented engines force Nature herself to discover plainly her most hidden recesses.[5]

This, of course, smacks of sophomoric bravado, but it suggests, none the less, the extent to which Cartesian and Lockian ideas had fired a youthful receptive mind. The mature writings of Addison show continued interest in the new philosophy. He is intrigued with the wonders of minute life as revealed by the microscope and with the marvels of the heavens disclosed by the telescope. He reflects on the habits of the shellfish, on the multiplicity of living animals, on the remarkably designed chain of being with no gaps below man, with probably no gaps between man and God; on the phenomenon of pleasure and pain, on pride and ambition, on the ways of the mind in general; on the goodness of Providence in having added to the drab "real qualities" of matter those "imaginary qualities" of colors, sounds, tastes, and smells which brighten the world and cheer the soul of man. Some of these speculations carry a flavor of pseudo science, others suggestions of seventeenth-century divinity, but most of them bear strongly the marks of the new philosophy.

It is not strange, therefore, that when, partly under the cogent influence of Longinus, partly through his own insights and dissatisfactions, Addison had come to feel the inadequacies of the old criticism and the urgent need for some new system which would enable critics to "enter into the very spirit and Soul of fine Writing, and shew us the several sources of that Pleasure which rises in the Mind upon the Perusal of a Noble Work" he

[5] Translation by Richard Rawlinson. *The Works of Addison* (Bohn Library), IV, 602–9.

turned to the new philosophy for his model. In spirit, method, and substance, the "Papers on the Imagination" reveal the fountainhead of Addison's inspiration. Mindful of the fact that in other departments of knowledge new light had come from consulting the "dictates of our own senses," he begins in his search for a fuller understanding of his special subject where Descartes, Hobbes, and Locke had begun: with the ways of human nature and the relation of the external world of sense to the perceiving responsive self. And throughout the essay he follows more or less closely the lead of the new philosophy, with its groundwork of sensational psychology, its reliance on experience, its powerful instrument of empirical inductive investigation.

Isolate the main ideas of this essay for a moment and we may see something of their distinctive character. Instead of the rules, taste is to be the final arbiter of excellence; in decisions of taste the appeal is to the imagination, not to the reason or judgment; to know the ways of the imagination we must know the ways of the mind, especially in its relation to external nature; observation proves that there are three main sources and types of aesthetic appeal—the beautiful, the novel, and the sublime; beauty, novelty, and sublimity are really things of the mind— products of a sort of creative act in a pleasurable response to objects in nature or to literature and art; one factor in the explanation of aesthetic pleasure is the principle of the association of ideas, another is the Lockian theory of the primary and secondary qualities of matter; the power of imagery on the mind is such that even historians, scientists, and philosophers would do well to embellish their writings with allusion and metaphor; aesthetic pleasures are divorced from practical interests, but they have unique values in that they "open a Man's thoughts," raise and "enlarge his Imagination," and in general exert a stimulating, healthful influence on both mind and body.

All these have to do with imaginative response. The list for imaginative creation is shorter—Addison was not too productive on the creative problem. The mind of the poet has the power of selection and combination in representing that which is better and more pleasing than nature (Bacon's version of ideal imitation); the poet may also create worlds and persons that have no

existence except in his fancy (Dryden's "Fairy Way of Writing"); success in this way of writing can be achieved only by a
writer endowed with great original genius, such as Shakespeare;
the poet should be born with a vigorous faculty of imagination,
but he should also educate this faculty with as much pains as a
philosopher takes in forming his understanding.

The importance of Addison's theory lies not so much in its
overt enunciation of ideas as in its method and spirit, its primary
assumptions, the fabrics from which it was created. And it lies
less in its actual worth as a completed synthesis than in its implications and its potentialities. Viewed as a systematic presentation
of final theory, the essay is as imperfect as can be and is suscep-
tible to all manner of captious or strictly logical criticism. But
viewed as a set of tentative pronouncements charged with dy-
namic suggestion and exemplifying a method of almost illimit-
able possibilities of development, it is worthy to be classed as
one of the great critical documents of all time.

Whatever its imperfections, Addison's treatise carried
weight, enough apparently to furnish decisive impetus to a
movement that was completely to discredit the merely formal-
istic parts of neoclassicism and was to eventuate in a new aesthetic
for England and to aid in establishing a similar one for Germany
and France as well. It is no small thing surely that looking back
now we are able to see that virtually all of the outstanding characteristics of the new empirical pragmatic criticism as it evolved
in the eighteenth century were in one way or another anticipated
by Addison.

Wherever we go in eighteenth-century criticism, whatever
the specific subject of speculation, we almost invariably find that
Addison had been there. If it is Hutcheson on beauty and aesthetic response, we find parallels to or echoes of Addison's
"Pleasures of the Imagination"; if it is Burke on taste and
sublimity and beauty, Young and Tucker on original genius,
Hume and Gerard, and Kames, Blair, and Alison on taste, imagination, sublimity and novelty, the association of ideas, and original genius, we are again in the presence of theory partially
developed or at least adumbrated in the *Spectator* papers.

The influence of Addison on subsequent literary thought is

nowhere more impressively exemplified than in utterances of such more conservative critics as Hugh Blair and Samuel Johnson. Blair, though rather tightly bound even in his judgments of Shakespeare by the conventions of the older criticism, pays due attention to genius, taste, imagination, and sublimity and gives Addison credit for priority in exploring these fields. It was Addison, he says, who first attempted a regular inquiry into the principles of taste, "and he has the merit of having opened a track, which was before unbeaten." Johnson, rebuking those who feel superior to Addison, invites them to consider Addison's remarks on Ovid as an example of refined criticism. "Let them peruse likewise," he continues, "his essays on wit, and on the pleasure of the imagination in which he founds art on the base of nature, and draws the principles of invention from dispositions inherent in the mind of man, with skill and elegance, such as his contemners will not easily attain."

In practical criticism, too, over and over in the eighteenth century, we see Addison at work. The anonymous essay on *Hamlet* (1736) illustrates the double-barreled effects of his theory and example. Anonymous not only extols Addison but, candidly taking the papers on *Paradise Lost* as his model, proposes to examine a great tragedy "according to the Rules of Reason and Nature, without having any regard to those Rules established by arbitrary Dogmatizing Critics . . ." More specifically, he proposes to show the why of our pleasure in this tragedy: "And as to those things which charm by a certain secret Force and strike us we know not how or why; I believe it will not be disagreeable if I shew to everyone the Reason why they are pleas'd." The spirit and method of Anonymous in fulfilling his promise, his general appeal to common human nature, his analysis of character, his emphasis on psychological preparation, on illusion, on the principle of design, his attention to detailed beauties in a scene-by-scene study of the play, in general disregard of the traditional rules: these are all, often separately it is true, to be repeated again and again in subsequent Shakespearian criticism, in the writings of Kames, Morgann, Richardson, Walter Whiter, even of Warton and Johnson—and they are all Addisonian.

Commenting, in *The Life of Reason*, on the broader influence of Locke, D. G. James has recently said that of early eighteenth-century men, "it was Addison and Butler who had most of Locke's temper and fairness of mind"; and in another passage he remarks that in contrast to Swift and Bolingbroke, Addison had a mind "eminently fair and open to intellectual inquiry." In assessing Addison's contribution to English criticism such a judgment has special pertinence, for it may be truthfully said of Addison that he introduced into aesthetic discussion, more effectively than anyone before him, a spirit of full and free investigation.

Whatever else in the way of specific detail in theory and practice he gave us may be traced for its origin and development to this spirit. One may almost say that Addison was most himself where he questioned the accepted and worked toward something off the main path of current theory and practice. He faced problems squarely and set an example of reaching solutions through the empirical mode of testing fact and experience. Through his adaptation of the new psychology to aesthetic speculation he gave to the theory of judging by taste something of the philosophical foundation that any aesthetic must have before it can gain acceptance by men of thought, and he established a pattern that, broadly speaking, became the norm for his century. It is one thing to assert that "I like what I like, rules or no rules" or to talk about a "I know not what" that gives a work its grace and charm. It is quite another to argue for the integrity of taste on the grounds of "dispositions inherent in the mind of man"—to borrow Johnson's words descriptive of the "Essay on the Imagination." Therein, no doubt, is an explanation of why Addison's methods and ideas took hold.

Later critics were to attempt to solve more definitely than Addison what these dispositions were and what laws might be deduced from their operation. But Addison probably did more than any other one man to start his century afresh down the long road of exploration of the mysteries of artistic creation and aesthetic response.

Addison's approach to aesthetic problems was basically sensational, but he was not, therefore, a materialist. Though he follows the method of the new philosophy, he holds to the God and the Soul of the Scholastics, and like the Scholastics he sees the soul and body getting on in harmonious relationship. Here as elsewhere Addison's views were essentially moderate. Descartes had set the soul off on its own little island of the pineal gland, restricting the imagination to the sensory and physical, with an essentially mechanical function of supplying the rational soul with materials but otherwise having small traffic with it. Hume, Hartley, and other associationists promoted a tendency to regard the imagination as largely an instrument of mechanical process in a mechanical mind. Their mode was empirical and their chief subject of study the human mind, so that in method and subject they were in the tradition of the new criticism; but in their theory the law of the rules was merely supplanted by the even more mechanical law of association. Addison avoided these extremes. His imagination was an intermediate power lying between the senses and the understanding, owing something to both, and in a rather specific way serving the needs of the whole soul, which in turn had close relations with God. Altogether Addison's ideas were such as to render them more readily assimilable in Romantic theory than were those of the more mechanically minded theorists among his predecessors and successors, with which in the end Coleridge, especially, would have no traffic whatever.

There are, it is true, wide gaps between Addison and the Romantics, differences that may be roughly indicated under four heads: (1) incompatibilities in specific philosophical outlook; (2) inequalities in intellectual last; (3) such divergencies as ordinarily prevail between the incipient and the more fully developed, Addison's best ideas often standing as partial conceptions or hints, sometimes naïvely expressed, which in the Romantic period are to emerge in relatively full-bodied theory; (4) the appearance of concepts in Romantic aesthetics virtually foreign to Addison's view: as, for example, Coleridge's idea of organic form and his theory of the secondary imagination as an esemplastic power operating on the materials of experience subsequent to reflective and subconscious processes. Addison's idea of the function of the creative imagination was the relatively elementary one of enlarging, compounding, and varying materials of experiences or of inventing new forms beyond the realm of experience.

Such differences are, however, relatively unimportant in consideration of the numerous points at which Addison's thought touches that of the Romantics. Basically, the larger concerns of Wordsworth and Coleridge were much the same as Addison's: the aesthetic experience and the imagination as the central facts in matters of art, the ways of the imagination in creation and in aesthetic response, beauty and sublimity, and to a less extent novelty, the problem of excellence in art, the nature of the mind and its relations to its universe, final causes. Their approach, too, was, like Addison's, psychological, and their chief method, also like his, was reasoning from the data of introspection.

Among more particular issues is Addison's idea of the creative perceptive quality of imaginative response, which neighbors closely, it seems to me, the Romantic theory of a modifying, creative imaginative perception. Another is Addison's belief in immediate spontaneous response: "It is but the opening of the Eye and the Scene enters . . . We are struck we know not how, with the symmetry of any thing we see, and immediately assent to the Beauty of an Object . . ." Anticipatory of Wordsworth certainly, as Carritt has pointed out, is Addison's discovery that objects at first sight pleasant "appear more so upon Reflection . . . Memory heightens the Delightfulness of the Original." Addison is once more near Wordsworth, and Keats, too, when he urges that the poet should cultivate his natural imagination and designates as the first step in his education a close acquaintance with and a due relish of "the Works of Nature." A further instance of anticipation occurs in Addison's suggestion, quite in contrast to prevailing neoclassic views, that the aesthetic experience is nonutilitarian and disinterested, which in turn relates closely to his emphasis on pleasure as the primary function of poetry and his belief in the ameliorating effects of the imaginative activity on both soul and body—a good born of and inseparable from pleasure as it were. Addison and Wordsworth would, in fact, have got along very agreeably on the subject of the general beneficent effects of external nature and of good poetry, just as Addison and Shelley would have understood each other quite clearly, up to a point, on the ways in which the imagination can be a blessing to the spirit of man—though, no doubt, Addison would have been a little puzzled by Shelley's more mystical utterances and Shelley would have balked at some of Addison's physiological implications.

These similarities do not necessarily imply influence, either direct or indirect by way of Kant or others. It is perhaps more accurate to describe them in terms of inheritance, a process which in a way is of more honor to the progenitor as an indication of deeply engrained viable qualities than is influence, which may be only a temporary and surface affair. Coleridge and Wordsworth brought into the integration which was their main achievement many and diverse ingredients. The Platonic element was there, accommodated to and supplemented by current transcendental thought; so also were some of the best parts of the psychological modes and discoveries of the past hundred fifty years, as, stripped of their mechanical intentions, they were related to the perceptive and creative functions of mind. But the most fundamental components of this integration bear marks of unmistakable relationship to the ideas of Addison. Modified by a century of intervening Addison-like aesthetic speculation and transformed as they were by the capacious minds of Coleridge and Wordsworth, they still show the certain signs of their ancestry. So that though we may be reluctant to name Addison as father of Romantic criticism, we can safely speak of him as one of its most important grandfathers, through whom were transmitted some of its characteristic dominant traits.

# A NOTE ON DRYDEN'S CRITICISM

### E. M. W. TILLYARD

LITERARY criticism, when it rises to excellence, is, usually, either scrappy or elusive. The scrappy kind consists of aphorisms or of brilliant brief perceptions of great literature; and Longinus and Coleridge are two of its practitioners. The elusive kind owes its greatness less to the separate perceptions than to a spirit or a disposition that arises from the sum of the parts. And that spirit is apt to elude definition. Horace and Boileau, so little interesting from their separate perceptions, are great in this way. And of course one kind does not exclude the other.

It is generally agreed that Dryden is among the greatest literary critics. But when we ask in what his greatness consists, the answer is not easy. And the reason is not so much that we lack the materials for an answer as that we cannot easily see the shape of them; the very abundance of excellence embarrasses. Of course if we confined Dryden's critical greatness as a critic to the first of the two kinds I have mentioned, to his power of throwing out, amidst much that is conventional, an abundance of fine critical perceptions, we should not find him hard to place. But his greatness is so much more than that, for it is of that second kind also; a scent as it were, pervading and distinguishing nearly all his work. It is indeed right to seek to enumerate his critical perceptions; and doubtless some general truths would emerge from such an enumeration. But, unlike some critics, he does not really thrive by anthologising; and nothing but the whole does justice to his inmost critical disposition.

Attempts to define that disposition are not lacking. Saintsbury[1] ranges Dryden's critical excellence under three headings:

[1] *A History of Criticism* (3d ed.; Edinburgh, 1914), II, 373-74.

in the last resort Dryden, unshackled by the rules, judged literature as he found it; he took technical questions seriously; and he
believed that poetry *must* delight. Now Saintsbury may be correct in all these contentions, but they apply to Edith Sitwell, for
instance, equally with Dryden. And though Edith Sitwell is
a very good critic in her way, she is not at all like Dryden.
So Saintsbury has not characterised Dryden very sharply.
W. P. Ker wrote more precisely:

Dryden's power as a writer of criticism does not depend upon his definite judgments . . . His virtue is that in a time when literature was
pestered and cramped with formulas he found it impossible to write
otherwise than freely. He is sceptical, tentative, disengaged, where most
of his contemporaries, and most of his successors for a hundred years,
are pledged to certain dogmas and principles.[2]

Ker's words about Dryden's scepticism and freedom are excellent as far as they go. But they are on the negative side; and
surely his first sentence is mistaken, unless by "definite judgments" he means no more than Dryden's fairly frequent itera-
tion of certain commonplaces of critical theory generally accepted in his day. Anyhow the attempt to carry an assessment
of Dryden's general critical powers beyond Ker is worth making.

First, let me correct Ker's first sentence by saying that
Dryden made definite judgments on certain authors and that
some of those judgments are admirable, constituting considerable
power in Dryden as a writer of criticism. As it is fairly long, one
instance will suffice. It is his judgment on Lucretius from the
Preface to *Sylvae*:

The distinguishing character of Lucretius (I mean of his soul and
genius) is a certain kind of noble pride, and positive assertion of his
opinions. He is everywhere confident of his own reason, and assuming
an absolute command, not only over his vulgar reader, but even his patron
Memmius. For he is always bidding him attend, as if he had the rod
over him; and using a magisterial authority, while he instructs him. . . .
Lucretius . . . seems to disdain all manner of replies and is so confident of his cause, that he is beforehand with his antagonists; urging for
them whatever he imagined they could say, and leaving them, as he

[2] *Essays of John Dryden* (Oxford, 1900), I, xv.

supposes, without an objection for the future. All this too with so much scorn and indignation, as if he were assured of the triumph, before he entered into the lists. From this sublime and daring genius of his, it must of necessity come to pass, that his thoughts must be masculine, full of argumentation, and that sufficiently warm. From the same fiery temper proceeds the loftiness of his expressions, and the perpetual torrent of his verse, where the barrenness of his subject does not too much constrain the quickness of his fancy. For there is no doubt to be made, but that he could have been everywhere as poetical, as he is in his descriptions, and in the moral part of his philosophy, if he had not aimed more to instruct, in his system of Nature, than to delight. But he was bent upon making Memmius a materialist, and teaching him to defy an invisible power; in short, he was so much an atheist, that he forgot sometimes to be a poet.[3]

Casting my mind back on a now distant classical education and trying to recollect the kind of thing that was said about Lucretius, I register the faint impression of an old-fashioned poet superb (and better than Virgil) in some purple patches, but to be read in between those patches not because you would want to read him but because, as a classic, you must read him. No one ever told me that Dryden had written of Lucretius, but what an inspiration that writing would have been and what a contrast Dryden's majestic seizing of the vital generalities would have made to the feeble picking on the surface I have described! Dryden goes straight to the animating principle; he sees that the plastic stress of Lucretius' passionate imagination could torture some but not all of the dross in his system of nature into the form he desired, but he sees that Lucretius leaves the intractable part interesting, that it is no mere series of dreary flats in between the exciting elevations and that it is livingly if imperfectly related to the centre of his genius. Now such success in grasping the general properties of a work of art and expressing them clearly and emphatically argues the highest critical power. And the passages where Dryden thus succeeds could be multiplied. He qualifies for critical greatness through being a writer from whose works could be compiled a critical scrap-book of the highest distinction.

Omitting other grounds for his critical excellence I revert

[3] Ker, *op. cit.*, I, 259–60.

to the question whether out of Dryden's critical writing there emerges any one positive principle that projects above any other emergent principles and constitutes his proper critical genius. I believe there is and I will try to describe it.

Brunetière considered that Boileau was a great critic because he substituted Reason for the Ancients as the authority for literary judgments. In other words, Boileau did for literature what Descartes did for philosophy: he grounded his belief not on ancient received opinion but on the dictates of the human mind. And just as Descartes reached the same conclusion on the existence of God that authority had demanded, so Boileau accepted, by however different a route, the main tenets of neoclassicism. The point, however, is that Boileau had achieved a new freedom and, if he had found Reason and the Ancients at odds, he could have rejected the Ancients. Dryden, highly sensitive to the happenings of his age, was open to this new Cartesian freedom. He probably derived most of his knowledge of Descartes from talk with his learned acquaintance, in the manner described so masterly by Johnson in his *Life of Dryden*. That he knew the most famous detail of Cartesianism and that he knew his audience to be familiar with it appears from the way he adapted an episode in *Paradise Lost* to his own uses in the *State of Innocence*. In *Paradise Lost* Adam's first conscious act after creation was to "turn his wondering eyes toward heaven." He then scanned the landscape, found he could name the things he saw, asked the natural objects around him if they could tell "how came I thus, how here," and, answering his own question, concluded:

> Not of my self; by some great Maker then,
> In goodness and in power prae-eminent.

At the beginning of the second act of the *State of Innocence* Adam is discovered "as newly created, laid on a bed of moss and flowers, by a rock." His first words are:

> What am I? or from whence? for that I am
> I know, because I think;

*after* which he concludes that there is a divine power, of which he is. Unlike Milton's, Dryden's Adam begins from within himself, from the doctrine that thought proves existence, according to the then novel philosophy of Descartes.

Dryden, then, knew Descartes and was free to profit by Descartes' initial scepticism.[4] And profit he did, in a way very different from Boileau. Whereas Boileau was mainly concerned with rebuilding the old principles on new and better foundations, Dryden used his new option to turn a highly inquisitive and absorbed, but perfectly impartial, eye on all the literature (and it was extensive) that interested him. Freed from a superstitious regard for the Ancients, he used his skill not to test their products by new assumptions but to look at them quite coolly and with no more initial respect than he accorded to the writers of his own day. The result is a perfection of *tone* in matters of comparative literature that was not equalled before or since. And this is his paramount critical achievement.

In speaking of Descartes I do not wish to exclude or depreciate the effect of the English scientific movement of the Restoration on Dryden, for it certainly contributed to his freedom. As the scholar to whom the present volume is dedicated has written:

Not that science did not exert influence on critical ideas. It was the chief liberalizing force playing upon neo-classical dogma. Dryden's vacillation may in part be explained by the influence, on the one hand, of classical and neo-classical critics, and, on the other, of the new science, in which he was interested. It is true that other poets of the time were members of the Royal Society, but for the most part they were little influenced by it.[5]

This passage at once sets Dryden apart from the other poets and suggests the width of the bounds within which his criticism was free to range.

Dryden did not reach perfection of tone at once. There is something rather set and formal about the way he treats Ancients, French, and English in the *Essay of Dramatic Poesy*, as if he were arguing for freedom and impartiality, not taking them

---

[4] Dryden knew his own freedom. See his *Defence of the Epilogue* (Ker, *op. cit*, I, 163): "For we live in an age so sceptical, that as it determines little, so it takes nothing from antiquity on trust."

[5] Richard Foster Jones, *Ancients and Moderns* (St. Louis, 1936), pp. 282–83.

serenely for granted. But from the *Author's Apology for Heroic Poetry* (1677) onwards the tone is perfect. Take this from the Preface to *Troilus and Cressida* on the different dramatists' skill in giving a king his true character:

Sophocles gives to Oedipus the true qualities of a king, in both those plays which bear his name; but in the latter, which is the Oedipus Colonaeus, he lets fall on purpose his tragic style; his hero speaks not in the arbitrary tone; but remembers in the softness of his complaints that he is an unfortunate blind old man; that he is banished from his country, and persecuted by his next relations. The present French poets are generally accused, that wheresoever they lay the scene, or in whatsoever age, the manners of their heroes are wholly French. Racine's Bajazet is bred at Constantinople; but his civilities are conveyed to him, by some secret passage, from Versailles into the Seraglio. But our Shakespeare, having ascribed to Henry the Fourth the character of a king and of a father, gives him the perfect manners of each relation, when either he transacts with his son or with his subjects.[6]

Dryden may be unfair here to Racine, but, if so, it is not the critical tone that is wrong but the criticism itself.

There was another reason than Descartes why Dryden should have been able to speak in one and the same tone of Sophocles and Shakespeare, of Virgil and Milton. By living when he did he escaped the idolatry with which the classics were invested both before and after his age. At its outset the Renaissance enthusiasm for the classics was too lively and noble to be called idolatry but it could easily degenerate into a dead and uncritical acceptance. Against such an acceptance Dryden did not need to fight; its day was over. Nor had there yet arisen the much more selective and pedantic idolatry that reached its climax in the public schools and ancient universities of nineteenth-century England and Ireland. To speak more specifically, scholars and teachers had not then agreed to call a selection of Greek and Latin authors correct, on account of the supposed purity of the language they used, and to make the writing of pastiche of these authors one of the absolute values of life. Dryden could think of Statius as just Statius and not as a Silver Latin poet; while at Westminster School and at Cambridge he

[6] Ker, *op. cit.*, I, 217–18.

wrote original, if not correctly Augustan, Latin, and did not have to translate small passages of English prose laboriously into the closest possible imitation of one of the authorised classical prosaists. This later idolatry may have served an educational purpose, but it did not promote a true critical tone. Nineteenth-century criticism of the classics cannot touch the quality of Dryden's.

Lastly, Dryden not only achieved a perfect critical tone, he made a full use of the freedom on which that tone was based. He did in fact criticise in a number of different ways, as the spirit moved him. I shall not attempt to enumerate those ways, but shall confine myself to citing one which was original in his day and to which I have not come across any tribute. It is the longish passage in the *Dedication of the Aeneis* where he explains on historical grounds why Virgil was justified in writing so political a poem as the *Aeneid*. In order to make quite clear how Virgil stood to Augustus, Dryden rapidly reviews the main political events in which Marius, Sulla, and the two Triumvirates were the actors. And this is the conclusion he reaches:

Virgil having maturely weighed the condition of the times in which he lived, that an entire liberty was not to be retrieved; that the present settlement had the prospect of a long continuance in the same family, or those adopted into it; that he held his paternal estate from the bounty of the conqueror, by whom he was likewise enriched, esteemed and cherished; that his conqueror, though of a bad kind, was the very best of it; that the arts of peace flourished under him; that all men might be happy, if they would be quiet; that, now he was in possession of the whole, yet he shared a great part of his authortiy with the Senate; that he would be chosen into the ancient offices of the Commonwealth, and ruled by the power which he derived from them; and prorogued his government from time to time, still, as it were, threatening to dismiss himself from public cares, which he exercised more for the common good than for any delight he took in greatness; these things, I say, being considered by the poet, he concluded it to be the interest of his country to be so governed; to infuse an awful respect into the people towards such a prince; by that respect to confirm their obedience to him, and by that obedience to make them happy. This was the moral of his divine poem; honest in the poet; honourable to the Emperor, whom he derives from a divine extraction; and reflecting part of that honour on the

Roman people, whom he derives also from the Trojans; and not only profitable, but necessary, to the present age, and likely to be such to their posterity.[7]

This is surely a most remarkable exercise of the historical imagination in the interests of critical truth and quite surprising in the age where it occurs: the fruit at once of the freedom Dryden enjoyed and of his own incomparably fresh and inquiring critical spirit.

But, the reader may ask, was Dryden really being original here? Have not Saintsbury and Ker told us that Dryden's three long essays, on satire, painting and poetry, and the *Aeneid*, are inferior works, rather laboured and clogged with borrowed learning, though enlivened by many original touches of detail? In particular, the *Dedication of the Aeneis* is said to derive largely from Segrais. Now it is perilous to assert that any passage in seventeenth-century criticism is not stolen from another. But at least I can assert that the passage under discussion reads uncommonly fresh, as if it issued straight from the deep knowledge Dryden had acquired of the *Aeneid* in translating it and the passionate interest that knowledge bred. And as for Segrais, Dryden mostly acknowledged his debts (modest enough) as they occur, and for a source of Dryden's long discourse on history the following is the only possible passage that could come into question:

Virgile se trouva sujet d'Auguste, il vescut pendant la splendeur de l'Empire Romain dans le siecle le plus poly, le plus delicat, et le plus juste qui ait jamais esté dans toute la durée de la langue Latine: Il passa sa vie sous le regne d'un Prince qui le combla de richesses, et qui a esté l'un des plus grands hommes qu'on puisse proposer aux autres pour example. . . . Aprés avoir achevé ses Eglogues et son Poëme de la vie rustique. . . . il crût que pour monter à la plus haute reputation ou puisse aspirer un Poëte, il falloit exceller dans le genre sublime, comme il avoit fait dans les deux autres; et concevoir en mesme temps un ouvrage qui fust honorable à son Auteur et à sa Patrie; et qui témoignast sa reconnaissance envers son Prince.[8]

[7] Ker, *op. cit.*, II, 171–72.

[8] M. de Segrais, *Traduction de L'Eneïde de Virgile* (Paris, 1668), I, 7–8.

And Segrais goes on to say that the reader must put himself into the changed position of the age in which a poet writes. But even if this was the hint Dryden took up in writing of the historical background of the *Aeneid*, his treatment is so ample and so far transcends anything in Segrais that it is virtually original.

It would be possible greatly to enlarge on the theme of Dryden's positive achievements in criticism, but I hope I have said enough to show that not only was Dryden "sceptical, tentative, disengaged" but that out of this scepticism and disengaged, experimental criticism there emerged a free critical disposition which was not only admirable in itself but which achieved positive results of a very high quality.

# PHILOSOPHY AND ROMANCE IN
# SHAKESPEARE'S "PROBLEM" COMEDIES

## Virgil K. Whitaker

T HE following discussion of "Philosophy and Romance
in the 'Problem' Comedies" is in no sense an attempt to
explain away the puzzling contrast between the unsatisfactory impression produced by *Troilus and Cressida* and *Measure for Measure*, especially, and the great poetry and character
drawing which show them to be Shakespeare's work at the height
of his powers. It offers, instead, the hypothesis that Shakespeare
wrote them because he was interested in applying to comedy the
same fund of ideas and the same philosophic analysis of human
action that he employed in writing the mature tragedies; but
the kind of romance material that had proved adequate for
building the romantic comedies was quite unable to support close
intellectual analysis, especially when worked into a plot by techniques developed for the earlier comedies, and it required a more
thorough reshaping than he gave it in either *Troilus and Cressida*
or *Measure for Measure*. These plays therefore seem confused
in purpose and, at times, pedantic in expression.

It is obvious that *Troilus and Cressida* states explicitly the
philosophic ideas fundamental to the great tragedies. However
misshapen it may be, the play is actually the keystone in the arch
of Shakespeare's mature thought. Ulysses' famous speech on
degree (I, iii, 78–136), describing the social order as part of
universal order, to which the alternative is chaos, is too well
known to need quotation.[1] Shakespeare apparently derived it

[1] Cf. the discussions in E. M. W. Tillyard, *The Elizabethan World
Picture* (New York: Macmillan, 1944), pp. 7–8; Tillyard, *Shakespeare's*

from three sources: the opening paragraphs of Sir Thomas
Elyot's *The Gouernour*;[2] the beginning of the tenth of the first
series of official homilies, "An Exhortation Concerning Good
Order and Obedience to Rulers and Magistrates";[3] and Book I,
chapter iii, of Richard Hooker's *Laws of Ecclesiastical Polity*,
which was published in 1594.[4] Ulysses' striking reference to
"appetite, an universal wolf" which must at last "eat up himself," does not occur in any of the three contexts cited, although
it is a clear implication of Hooker's teaching in Book I.[5]

The reference to appetite leads us to a passage of equal importance, the full implications of which have apparently escaped
notice,[6] an exposition of the nature of human sin and of laws
which is the equivalent in the Trojan council of what Ulysses
says to the Greeks and is attributed to a man of equal standing,
namely Hector. It is given an even more important position at
the climax of its scene:

> Nature craves
> All dues be rend'red to their owners: now,
> What nearer debt in all humanity
> Than wife is to the husband? If this law

---

*History Plays* (New York: Macmillan, 1946), pp. 14–17; Theodore Spencer,
*Shakespeare and the Nature of Man* (New York: Macmillan, 1945), pp. 21 ff.

  [2] Ed. Henry Herbert Croft (London: Kegan Paul, Trench, 1883), I, 3–4.
For discussion of the sources cf. Paul Deutschberger, "Shakespeare on Degree:
A Study in Backgrounds," *Sh. Assoc. Bull.* XVII (1942), 205–6.

  [3] *Certain Sermons or Homilies Appointed to be Read in Churches in the
Time of Queen Elizabeth* (London: S.P.C.K., 1914), pp. 109–10. Cf. Alfred
Hart, *Shakespeare and the Homilies* (Melbourne: Melbourne University Press,
1934), pp. 22–23.

  [4] Richard Hooker, *The Works*, ed. John Keble (7th ed.; Oxford: Clarendon Press, 1888), I, iii, 2 (Vol. I, pp. 207–8).

  [5] Cf. I, vii, 7 (Vol. I, p. 224) and I, ix, (Vol. I, p. 237).

  [6] Deutschberger cites the allusion to "laws of nature and of nations" to
prove Shakespeare's knowledge of Hooker (*op. cit.*, p. 206); Spencer quotes
it without noting its implications (*op. cit.*, pp. 112–13; O. J. Campbell, *Shakespeare's Satire* (London: Oxford University Press, 1943), pp. 100, 225, and
*Comical Satire and Shakespeare's Troilus and Cressida* (San Marino, Calif.:
Huntington Library Publications, 1938), p. 192, regards the phrase as reflecting the thought of "Alberico Gentili (since 1587 Regius Professor of
Civil Law at Oxford)." [Hiram Haydn's *The Counter-Renaissance* (New York:
Charles Scribner's Sons, 1950), which discusses the passage at some length
(p. 608), appeared after this paper was read to the Modern Language Association in September 1949 and later sent to press; and only this acknowledgment
can be added in proof.]

> Of nature be corrupted through affection,
> And that great minds, of partial indulgence
> To their benumbed wil, resist the same,
> There is a law in each well-ord'red nation
> To curb those raging appetites that are
> Most disobedient and refractory.
> If Helen then be wife to Sparta's king,
> As it is known she is, these moral laws
> Of nature and of nations speak aloud
> To have her back return'd. Thus to persist
> In doing wrong extenuates not wrong,
> But makes it much more heavy. (II, ii, 173–88)

The passage may perhaps be paraphrased as follows in terms of the ideas upon which it rests. The law of nature demands that Helen be returned to her husband. But men sometimes sin against the law of nature. Since man's reason naturally chooses what is good, "there was never sin committed wherein a less good was not preferred before a greater, and that wilfully."[7] This false choice may be made (1) because of ignorance (which is not involved in this passage), (2) because the affections or passions have solicited the will and prevailed against reason, or (3) because a habit of indulging the appetites had corrupted the will and made reason ineffective. Since wills so benumbed by habit are insensitive to the law of nature, each well-ordered nation[8] has established laws to control men whose raging appetites (of which the affections or passions are manifestations) lead them to sin. Both the laws of nature and of nations demand that Helen be returned.

There was, of course, only one work readily available to Shakespeare in which he could find these ideas combined— namely, Hooker's *Laws of Ecclesiastical Polity*. From it the speech on degree was in part derived; upon it is based the pre-

[7] Hooker, *op. cit.*, I, vii, 7 (Vol. I, p. 224).

[8] Shakespeare's use of the singular here, as well as the parallelism between the entire passage and Hooker, seems to me to make Hooker a more likely source than Gentili, since it implies that the laws of nations mentioned below are merely the laws of individual states rather than international law or even universally accepted law in the Roman meaning of *ius gentium*. But cf. James E. Phillips, *The State in Shakespeare's Greek and Roman Plays* (New York: Columbia University Press, 1940), pp. 16–17.

ceding summary of the causes of sin;[9] and it explains that the laws of nations, "ordained for external order and regiment amongst men, are never framed as they should be, unless presuming the will of man to be inwardly obstinate, rebellious, and adverse from all obedience unto the sacred laws of his nature."[10] Many of the ideas just summarized—especially the importance of order and the conflict between reason and man's will "benumbed" by affections—were commonplaces of Christian tradition and of the Elizabethan age. Shakespeare had used several of these same ideas repeatedly in his earlier plays. But the systematic philosophical exposition given by Ulysses and Hector is new to him, and it seems very likely indeed that he owed to Hooker the organization of these ideas into the logical system outlined in *Troilus and Cressida,* and that it was Hooker who showed him the exciting implications of the system and led him to use it as the basis of his tragedies, where it is exemplified both in their content and in their structure.[11]

Except for *Hamlet,* all of the tragedies from *Julius Caesar* on show the hero's fall as resulting from a failure of reason which leads him to unnatural and therefore sinful conduct. Macbeth, as Professor Curry has pointed out,[12] chose the illusory glory of the kingship in preference to his immortal soul, a false choice of a lesser instead of a greater good as Macbeth himself recognizes in his soliloquies. In the crucial argument between him and Lady Macbeth, Shakespeare seems to have stressed false reasoning itself rather than the prompting of ambition.[13] The other

[9] Cf. Hooker, *op. cit.,* I, vii (Vol. I, pp. 220–24).

[10] *Ibid.,* I, x, 1 (Vol. I, pp. 239–40). In this same context Hooker states the principle which Angelo urges upon Isabella in *Measure for Measure* that "our compell'd sins stand more for number than for accompt" (II, iv, 57–8), but the same point occurs in the source in Whetstone; cf. Hooker, *op. cit.,* I, ix, 1 (Vol. I, pp. 237–38).

[11] A. C. Bradley does not mention *Troilus and Cressida* in elaborating Shakespeare's notion of tragedy (*Shakespearean Tragedy* [2d ed.; London: Macmillan, 1937], pp. 31–39), nor does he mention Hooker. But his interpretation is virtually that outlined in *Troilus and Cressida.* Elsewhere (p. 268) he cites Ulysses' speech for its notion that evil is self-destructive. For his interpretation of nature and a reference to Hector's speech see pp. 301–2.

[12] Walter Clyde Curry, *Shakespeare's Philosophical Patterns* (Baton Rouge: Louisiana State University Press, 1937), pp. 103–19.

[13] With the structure of *Macbeth* I, vii, and especially with Macbeth's "If we shall fail," cf. Hooker: "The Will notwithstanding doth not incline to have

heroes fall because "through affection" they "corrupt"—that is, break—the laws of nature and therefore of right reason. The part played by the affections or passions in Shakespeare's depiction of his tragic heroes has been studied, of course, by Professor Ruth L. Anderson and Professor L. B. Campbell.[14]

Shakespeare's great example of a will "benumbed" by "indulgence" is Macbeth as he sinks from crime to crime after the murder of Duncan. But the sisters in *Lear* would serve almost as well. *King Lear* and *Macbeth* are, in fact, simply full-scale studies of all the ideas in the two key speeches in *Troilus and Cressida*, in that both exemplify the disturbing effects of human sin upon universal order. But *Lear* might be described as primarily a development of Ulysses' words, *Macbeth* of Hector's, in that the former is centered in the distintegration of social and then universal order because Lear's own irrationality is abetted by the sins of many people, while the latter is worked out in terms of the causes of a single sin and its consequences for the individual and only incidentally for the social order.

To present this concept of sin as resulting from a failure of reason, Shakespeare furthermore developed a characteristic formula which determined the structure of the tragedies mentioned. First the choice facing the hero is explained, and one or more characters are developed who for their own reasons wish the hero to make a false moral choice—Cassius, Iago, Lady Macbeth, and so on. Then, in violation of all probability the actual choice is made in a single scene, the most improbable of all being that in which Othello enters speaking of his devotion to Desdemona and exits resolved to murder her. The false moral choice then leads to a decisive act, and from that act follows the hero's downfall. One or more minor characters are made to point out the irrationality of the hero's acts repeatedly. Cassius, Iago, Lady Macbeth, Goneril and Regan, Menenius Agrippa, and

or do that which the Reason teacheth to be good, unless the same do also teach it to be possible" (cf. *op. cit.*, I, vii, 5 [Vol. I, p. 222]). My attention was first called to this parallel between Hooker and *Macbeth* by Professor J. V. Cunningham. See his unpublished Stanford dissertation, "Tragic Effect and Tragic Process in Some Plays of Shakespeare," p. 345.

[14] Anderson, *Elizabethan Psychology and Shakespeare's Plays* (Iowa City: University of Iowa Press, 1927). Campbell, *Shakespeare's Tragic Heroes: Slaves of Passion* (Cambridge: University Press, 1930).

Enobarbus all explain the weaknesses which predispose the hero to irrational action, Iago and Enobarbus at length in technical language in terms of the passions of jealousy and love respectively. Antony, Emilia, Banquo, Kent and the Fool, and Volumnia are also used to point out the hero's folly, at the time of his false choice or later. It is also interesting that, as we move from concern with the individual in *Othello* to *Macbeth*, which emphasizes the individual but presents the social order, to *Lear*, which considers both social and universal order, the scene of moral choice moves forward from Act III, scene iii, in *Othello* (the climax of the play); to Act I, scene vii, in *Macbeth*; to the opening scene in *Lear*, which telescopes exposition, false choice, decisive act, and explanation of character weaknesses into the opening scene, so that the entire play may be devoted to consequences.[15]

It is clear, therefore, that Shakespeare tried to work into *Troilus and Cressida*, for whatever reason, the whole system of ideas that was fundamental to his tragedies and was presumably occupying his mind at the time. But what developed into plot and characterization as well as great poetry in the tragedies became in the comedy half-irrelevant and overlengthy talk that only confused the outline of the play, for the philosophic discussions are out of all proportion to the actions to which they lead. Let us now examine the possibility that this same preoccupation with philosophic ideas led Shakespeare to an altogether different attitude toward his material than he had shown in writing the romantic comedies.

The philosophical system just outlined logically implied a theory of causation based upon the operation of laws of nature, a theory to which Shakespeare first gave explicit statement in *2 Henry IV*:

> There is a history in all men's lives,
> Figuring the nature of the times deceas'd;

[15] For scenes of moral choice cf. *Julius Caesar*, II, i; *Othello*, III, iii; *Lear*, I, i; *Macbeth*, I, vii; *Antony and Cleopatra*, III, vii (here the choice of a course of action determined by passion rather than a moral choice is involved); *Coriolanus*, III, ii, iii (another interesting variation: right choice in preparation; wrong choice in practice, III, iii, being the scene of false choice). On the soundness of Antony's judgment of Brutus cf. Phillips, *op. cit.*, pp. 184–85.

The which observ'd, a man may prophesy,
With a near aim, of the main chance of things
As yet not come to life, which in their seeds
And weak beginnings lie intreasured.  (III, i, 80–85)

The "seeds" are, of course, the "seeds of time" of which Banquo speaks in *Macbeth* (I, iii, 58). As Professor Curry has shown, they are the *rationes seminales*, the material essences in things which lead to the working out in nature of the archetypal pattern in the mind of God the creator.[16] The mature tragedies and crucial episodes in *Troilus and Cressida* and *Measure for Measure* show a careful attempt to motivate action either in terms of antecedent action or as an outcome of human character, and the human motives leading to deeds are explained either in soliloquies and asides or by comment of the minor characters such as has been noted. This kind of motivation is almost completely absent from the romantic comedies, where Shakespeare's technique was, in fact, to conceal weakness of motivation by telling a crowded, fast-moving story and creating vivid characters to give the action life rather than probability or plausibility.

Motivation of events is actually far weaker in the romantic comedies than in their sources. *Il Pecorone*, the source of *The Merchant of Venice*, explains the bond as a last desperate effort to set up his foster-son as a trader made by a bankrupt merchant who literally has nothing to offer as security but his own flesh. He, and not the moneylender, proposes the bond. The process by which the lady of Belmont gets herself into the court has some resemblance to a plausible line of procedure even if it is much too involved for a crowded play. At all crucial points, and in minor matters as well, *Il Pecorone* at least makes an attempt to give probability to actions that Shakespeare simply presents as happening or makes depend upon an extreme coincidence, such as Portia's going to her cousin, the learned Bellario, whom, it turns out, the Duke has already summoned to give advice. Examples have been chosen from *The Merchant of Venice*, because its details are well known; but, in view of the possibility that Shakespeare based it upon an earlier play, it is well to emphasize that similar examples could be cited from the

[16] *Shakespeare's Philosophical Patterns*, pp. 29–49.

other comedies. Shakespeare's handling of Don John's plot and of Margaret in *Much Ado about Nothing* is far more implausible than either of the two versions in his sources, and so is Viola's role in *Twelfth Night*. *As You Like It*, however, is about on a par with Lodge's *Rosalynde*, except for the usurping duke's conversion at the end.

"Who ever lov'd that lov'd not at first sight?" wrote Marlowe, and this simple axiom Shakespeare found sufficient for motivating his characters. A little reflection will show that, for the most part, we have no more idea why they do things than they seem to have themselves. The individuality of the women rests upon the rich wit of their speech and the spirit with which they act, not upon analysis of their mental processes. Shakespeare's method is artistically sound, for we infer motives and character from what these women do and say, just as we habitually make the same inferences about our friends. But the technique of the tragedies is fundamentally different. In them such inference is unnecessary and, in fact, will lead us astray, for Shakespeare tells us what his heroes think as well as what they do. In general, soliloquies and asides, the means by which the tragic heroes reveal their motives and their character, are not used in the romantic comedies. Nor do "chorus" characters like Enobarbus appear.

To the generalization just made, Shylock and Don John are, to some extent at least, an exception, perhaps because Shakespeare drew upon the tradition of the villain hero who explained himself in soliloquies and formulated his motives for the audience. It is perhaps significant that the only other exceptions occur in the elaborate soliloquies of Benedick and Beatrice in *Much Ado* and in the motivation of the comic subplot of *Twelfth Night*. These plots do not come from the sources and are Shakespeare's own invention. In them he showed what he was, in effect, already doing in the tragedies, for it must not be forgotten that *Twelfth Night* probably belongs to the same year as *Hamlet*.

In addition to a notion of causation, the philosophic system outlined in *Troilus and Cressida* also involved a judgment of actions in terms of an ethical doctrine. This, too, does not occur in the romantic comedies, where Shakespeare was content if he made enough changes to bring the usually "unmoral" source action superficially into line with conventional morality[17] and ignored resulting improbabilities or inconsistencies.

As told in *Il Pecorone*, the wooing of the lady of Belmont outraged not only morality but also consistency of character. After drugging and despoiling her suitors by an immoral ruse, she became the brilliant defender of the merchant, as in the play; Bassanio possessed her and then married her, and in his selfish happiness he forgot all about the bond. The whole episode could not be presented on the stage; furthermore, it would have left both Portia and Bassanio without a shred of character or sympathy. So Shakespeare fell back upon the casket story and, with the assistance of Morocco and Aragon, established Portia as both a spirited young woman and a great lady. His failure to account for the lapsing of the bond can only be regarded as capitulation to a difficulty in plotting his play. The simple forgetfulness of the source was consistent enough with the selfishness always displayed by Bassanio's original, but it was impossible to call attention to Bassanio's failure to act if his character was to be salvaged. How to reconcile the few days' action at Belmont with the three months provided by the bond Shakespeare was unable to puzzle out. He was, furthermore, extremely careless of details of time, and he doubtless expected the audience to be like himself.

Bandello's cynical atmosphere, in which Don Timbreo (Claudio) decided to marry Fenicia (Hero) only after he was unable to seduce her, is completely absent from *Much Ado*; but again morality was achieved by sacrificing convincing motivation, especially in Don John's subplot. Margaret is the villain's lover in Ariosto and Spenser, and she dresses in her lady's clothes to make herself more attractive to him. She is immoral but convincing, and she has every reason to remain silent in the face of Hero's disgrace. All this is left quite unexplained in Shakespeare, where Margaret is moral but incomprehensible.

[17] Shakespeare's acceptance of conventional morality is, of course, the theme of Alfred Harbage's *As They Liked It* (New York: Macmillan, 1947). Cf. Virgil K. Whitaker, "Shakespeare's Use of his Sources," *Philological Quarterly*, XX (1941), 385–88.

When Shakespeare came to write *Troilus and Cressida* and *Measure for Measure*, he was using similar romance source material, even if the ultimate source of the former was Greek and the immediate source of the latter a play; and he might have glided over difficulties of motive and moral conduct as blithely as in the earlier plays. But he did not do so. Instead he kept his technique of following the source action with minor variations, but he subjected that action to the thorough ethical analysis that he was using in the tragedies. The result was a confusion of effect of which critics have complained. Space does not permit a full examination of what happened. So, merely noticing that the immoral atmosphere of *Troilus and Cressida* and in *Measure for Measure* is parallel in the comic world to the breakdown of the moral order in Lear, let us pass on to two points: the handling of love in *Troilus and Cressida* and of sin and forgiveness in *Measure for Measure*.

Professor O. J. Campbell has argued convincingly that *Troilus and Cressida* was intended as a learned but bawdy satire upon current thought for some festive occasion at one of the Inns of Court.[18] If so, the idea of writing such a play must have come to Shakespeare as he reflected upon the well-known story, not looking for ways to apply the techniques of the romantic comedies, but subjecting it to ethical analysis of the sort that he had just written into the closet scene in *Hamlet*. That scene, incidentally, must have been suggested by the old play, for much of what Hamlet says to Gertrude in the closet scene is to be found in Belleforest.[19] And Chaucer may also have stimulated ethical scrutiny of his story both by his failure to make convincing Cressida's yielding to Diomedes and by two stanzas defending Cressida from the charge of falling in love with Troilus at first sight (II, 666–79):

> Now myghte som envious jangle thus:
> "This was a sodeyn love; how myght it be
> That she so lightly loved Troilus,

[18] *Shakespeare's Satire*, pp. 99–100.

[19] *The Sources of Hamlet: With Essay on the Legend by Sir Israel Gollancz* ("The Shakespeare Classics") [London: Oxford University Press, 1926], pp. 206–29.

Right for the firste syghte, ye, parde?"
Now whoso seith so, mote he nevere ythe!
For every thyng, a gynnyng hath it nede
Er al be wrought, withowten any drede.

For I sey nought that she so sodeynly
Yaf hym hire love, but that she gan enclyne
To like hym first, and I have told yow whi;
And after that, his manhod and his pyne
Made love withinne hire herte for to myne,
For which, by proces and by good servyse,
He gat hire love, and in no sodeyn wyse.

The questions implied by these stanzas Shakespeare in effect answers by subjecting love itself to scrutiny in terms of the conflict between appetite and reason in a way that deprives the war of any meaning and the love of any idealism. As Thersites inelegantly but graphically says of the war: "All the argument is a cuckold and a whore; a good quarrel to draw emulous factions and bleed to death upon" (II, iii, 78–79). And the Trojans can do no better at justifying themselves. After proving that the laws of nature and of nations demand that Helen be returned, Hector, as Professor O. J. Campbell remarks,[20] abjures reason and follows will, advising that Helen be kept (II, ii, 188–93). The war is no defense of true lovers but an irrational protection of lust; the foundation of the love between Troilus and Cressida is equally rotten.

In confessing that she loved at first sight (III, ii, 125–26), Cressida is, of course, like the heroines of the romantic comedies. But at that point the parallel ceases, for the swift falling into love on the basis of appearance that is characteristic of romance could be justified in terms of the court of love or even of Renaissance Platonism but was contrary to Christian ethics and psychology. Worthy love presumably would result from a choice by the reason of a real good, but the reason would require time and knowledge to evaluate. Love at sight must rest upon sense and therefore appetite; and it must be a triumph of passion in

[20] *Shakespeare's Satire*, pp. 109–10.

defiance of reason, a sin. And such it is throughout this play, where each mood is elaborately dissected. Cressida says:

> for to be wise and love
> Exceeds man's might; that dwells with gods above.
>
> (III, ii, 163–4)

Or, at the end of the play

> Ah, poor our sex! this fault in us I find,
> The error of our eye directs our mind.
> What error leads must err; O, then conclude
> Minds sway'd by eyes are full of turpitude.
>
> (V, ii, 109–12)

For Troilus, love is an exhilaration of the flesh (III, ii, 19–21), subject to the monstrous limitation that "the will is infinite and the execution confin'd, that the desire is boundless and the act a slave to limit" (III, ii, 87–90).

Whatever Shakespeare's intentions in *Troilus and Cressida*, this skeptical view of love at first sight was no passing mood of cynicism or satiric *jeu d'esprit*. When next he portrayed genuine and worthy love, he made absolutely clear that it had not come at first sight and that it did not rest merely upon appearances. In *All's Well* Helena has grown up with Bertram, and, however implausible we find her enduring love, it is rooted in long and intimate acquaintance. The love between Othello and Desdemona, noble and rational if ever love was, grew slowly as he visited her father and she listened to his experiences; in fact, Desdemona instances this slow development and Othello's unattractive "visage" as proof that their love is rational and pure (I, iii, 249–55). Imogen and Posthumous have grown together. How Perdita and Florizel fell in love we are not told precisely. Only Miranda, under stress of unity of time, falls in love at sight; and she is protected by an omniscient magician father, who subjects Ferdinand to ordeal by woodpile to try his love. Antony, in contrast, succumbs to his first ravishing sight of Cleopatra in her barge. In other words, worthy love at first sight very nearly disappeared from Shakespeare with *Twelfth Night*.

What would have happened if the standards of *Troilus and Cressida* had been applied to Rosalind, who was infatuated by a handsome face and a superior display of muscles at a wrestling match? Or to Portia or Olivia? We need not speculate what would happen to whole plots, for, in the Preface to the New Cambridge *Merchant of Venice*, Sir Arthur Quiller-Couch has analyzed the play in terms of realistic moral standards, with results as devastating as they are false to Shakespeare's manifest intentions. In *Troilus and Cressida* Shakespeare himself achieved similar results.

In *Measure for Measure* Shakespeare again subjected romance material to searching scrutiny, this time in terms of fundamental Christian doctrines. His source was George Whetstone's *Promos and Cassandra* of 1578, which was in turn based upon Geraldi Cintio's *Ecatommiti*, the source of *Othello* also. What Shakespeare was trying to do is unclear. Recent critics have regarded the play as to be read "on the analogy of Jesus' parables"[21] or formed "after the pattern of the Christian doctrine of the Atonement."[22] The soundest interpretation seems to me to be that of R. W. Chambers' "The Jacobean Shakespeare and *Measure for Measure*,"[23] which sees the action as turning upon fundamental Christian doctrines rather than as being itself a kind of allegory of Christianity. It should be noted, perhaps, that only a year separated *Measure for Measure* from *Macbeth*, an elaborate study of sin in all its aspects and the most thoroughly Christian among all Shakespearean plays in its intellectual basis.

Much of the dismay with which modern readers view *Measure for Measure* is certainly due to its uncompromising adherence to Christian principles that we like to forget. First of all, like Christ himself, it insists: "What shall it profit a man if he gain the whole world and lose his own soul?" Isabel says of her own life:

> O, were it but my life,
> I'd throw it down for your deliverance
> As frankly as a pin. (III, i, 104–6)[24]

[21] G. Wilson Knight, *The Wheel of Fire* (Oxford: University Press, 1930), pp. 80, 91. Cf. S. L. Bethell, *Shakespeare and the Popular Dramatic Tradition* (Westminster: P. G. King and Staples, Ltd., 1944), pp. 106–7.

[22] Roy W. Battenhouse, "*Measure for Measure* and the Christian Doctrine of Atonement," *PMLA*, LXI (1946), 1058–59.

[23] Annual Shakespeare Lecture of the British Academy, 1937.

[24] *Ibid.*, pp. 37–40.

But of her soul she has said to Angelo:

> Better it were a brother died at once,
> Than that a sister, by redeeming him,
> Should die for ever.  (II, iv, 106–8)

And her terrible dialogue with Claudio must be read against a full realization, perfectly obvious to any Elizabethan, that in demanding the life of his body at such a price Claudio is condemning his own soul to death, if not hers as well. Claudio himself subsequently realizes that his demand that she submit to Angelo is outrageous, and, as he prepares for death, he says to the disguised Duke: "Let me ask my sister pardon" (III, i, 173). This is a stern code, the code of the martyrs in the Roman arena, but it is undoubtedly Christianity.

But why, after her eloquent plea to Angelo for mercy, with its reference to the Atonement, does Isabella tell Claudio:

> Mercy to thee would prove itself a bawd;
> 'Tis best that thou diest quickly.  (III, i, 150–51)

The answer involves not only the point just made but also a second Christian principle—the reality of sin and of absolute standards of right and wrong. "Sure, it is no sin," says Claudio; "Or of the deadly seven it is the least" (III, i, 110–11). "Which is the least?" replies Isabella, and, if sin is an absolute, her argument is unanswerable. Shakespeare sharpened the issue further by making her a votaress of St. Clare and writing a scene (I, iv) to make sure that the audience understood clearly that she was on probation—that is, on trial before God and man, a "thing ensky'd and sainted" (I, iv, 34). It is in this realm of absolute and final standards—final and absolute because they have been established by God and not by fallible man—that Angelo's logic, specious as applied to his judgment of Claudio, is sound, and justice is the highest mercy. Angelo's mistake lies in confusing this justice with God's, but Isabella makes no such error in telling Claudio, as he stands in the presence of the law of God and in danger of losing his immortal soul as well as hers: "Mercy to thee would prove itself a bawd."

But if the justice of God is absolute, so, for those who "do truly and earnestly repent," is his mercy. This is the fundamental paradox of the Atonement, to which Isabella alludes (II, ii, 73–79). Shakespeare prayed: "Forgive us our trespasses, as we forgive them that trespass against us." He therefore pushed the mercy granted by man to the same extreme that man must demand of God. That Angelo has repented he tries to leave us in no doubt:

> I am sorry that such sorrow I procure;
> And so deep sticks it in my penitent heart
> That I crave death more willingly than mercy.
>                                    (V, i, 479–81)

So Angelo escapes being judged with the judgment that he meted out, and he receives not the "mercy of the law" for which he argued but the mercy of Christianity. When he says:

> When I perceive your Grace, like power divine,
> Hath look'd upon my passes, (V, i, 374–75)

his words seem to point a parallel between the Duke's "Grace" and God's, for "power divine" is about as close to God as Shakespeare could come under the law of 1605 against stage profanity.

If we find these elements in the play unacceptable, Shakespeare might argue, as R. W. Chambers argues for him, that the fault is not in the play but in our unwillingness to face the implications of Christianity. To a degree that is true, and we are repelled by the rigorous application of Christian doctrine in *Measure for Measure* just as by the elaborate philosophical exposition in *Troilus and Cressida*. But something else is wrong. My own first reaction to Professor Battenhouse's study of *Measure for Measure* and the Christian Doctrine of the Atonement" was, I confess, that, if Shakespeare intended to mirror the process of the Atonement, he had involuntarily produced a parody upon which a skeptic might pounce as revealing all the weaknesses of that central Christian doctrine. Why, for example, did the Duke make a mess of his administration and then turn it over to Angelo to straighten out while he spied from concealment? Why did the Duke appoint Angelo at all, knowing of his faithlessness to his betrothed? One thinks of the *Rubaiyat's* famous, if sophomoric, stanza:

O Thou, who man of baser earth didst make,
And ev'n with Paradise devise the snake:
For all the sin wherewith the face of man
Is blacken'd—man's forgiveness give—and take!

Similarly, no device can make acceptable Mariana's substitution for Isabella.[25] Nor is the trouble centered in these folk situations which Shakespeare himself added to the source plot.[26] In trying to preserve Isabella's chastity, as he reformed Portia and many another unchaste character in his sources, Shakespeare introduced the "bed trick" and made the Duke a kind of continuous *deus ex machina* to settle difficulties in the plot. But both of these were familiar devices which he had used in *All's Well* and *Romeo and Juliet* respectively, and Friar Lawrence, at least, bothers no one by his stratagems and white lies. One difficulty consists, as in *Troilus and Cressida*, in the incongruity between the romance materials of the plot and the Christian standards of the characters. A woman who is confronted with a choice between her brother's life and soul and who is working out her conduct in terms of fundamental Christian principles is not a fairy-tale character even for the most skeptical of us; and she sheds upon her surroundings the cold light of our own standards of conduct.

In short, in *Measure for Measure* as in *Troilus and Cressida*, Shakespeare tried to make a philosophical (or theological) play by loading philosophical analysis upon a simple source plot which he patched up in the easygoing fashion of the romantic comedies. The result was simply confusion. What was needed was drastic reshaping of his source material to bring it into line with a controlling purpose, whether that purpose was philosophic satire or philosophic romance. Just such a thoroughgoing revision of his sources in terms of a philosophic theme Shakespeare attempted and achieved successfully in *Lear* and *Macbeth*. The plot of his final and successful philosophic comedy, *The Tempest*, he fashioned for himself.

[25] Cf. Chambers, *op. cit.*, pp. 31–32; also W. W. Lawrence, *Shakespeare's Problem Comedies* (New York: Macmillan, 1931), pp. 94–102.

[26] Lawrence points out that the "bed trick" and the Duke's role are Shakespeare's additions (*op. cit.*, pp. 79–80).

# JOHN DONNE AND THE PSYCHOLOGY
## OF SPIRITUAL EFFORT

### Helen C. White

THE problem of John Donne's adjustment to his age is such an interesting one, especially to a reader of the mid-twentieth century, that it is all too easy to overlook the fact that his greatest struggle was with himself. It is true that the character of his time, like the very special circumstances of his family background, made his personal problem more difficult than it might otherwise have been. But in any age or in any circumstances John Donne would have had a real job of spiritual integration on his hands.

It was more than adolescent perversity and extravagance that made Donne so avid of paradox in his youth. It was the need of a safety valve for intolerable pressure within himself. For Donne had at the heart of his being a whirlwind of incompatibilities that would have made living with himself difficult at any time. He was fascinated with himself, and yet he had an alert and ranging curiosity about the rest of the world. He had to take his own way, bristling at every interference, and yet he needed beyond most men "to belong." Concentration was impossible for him, and so was superficiality. He was intensely preoccupied with the appetites and passions of John Donne, and yet he knew that he must look beyond himself for their satisfaction. Even in his youth he makes one think of St. Augustine's great verdict on the heart's yearning which he was later to quote in one of his sermons and translate pithily enough: "Lord thou has made us for they selfe, and our heart cannot rest, till it get to thee."[1]

The inevitable comparison with St. Augustine helps us to define what we may call the spiritual complexion of Donne. Like the great African Church Father whom he so much admired, Donne always stands out as very much himself, and quite unlike anybody else. But his originality is very different from St. Augustine's, as becomes apparent when we compare the two men in the realm of ideas, which meant so much to both of them.

Donne is forever rushing out beyond the edges of his and his time's acceptances. He has ever an ear cocked for news from alien regions; yet one misses in him what is so characteristic of St. Augustine, and that is the drive to reach a conclusion, to push beyond the paradox to the reasoned and sustained solution, and reconciliation. Donne's relation to the new science is as good an example as any; he was quite aware of the explosive potentialities of the new philosophy, but he was never really tempted to throw away the intellectual world he had and cast himself upon the tide of the unknown. It was not timidity; it was rather a failure of that intellectual compulsion so characteristic of St. Augustine. Here Donne could stop short.

The fact is that Donne's originality did not lie in any capacity for fresh discovery or invention. His originality consisted rather in the fullness and intensity of his realization of the data given by conviction. It is another way of saying that Donne's basic genius was not philosophical but literary.

And yet I suspect that the difference was not by any means entirely intellectual. Donne's mind was a very fine one, quite adequate for any undertaking to which he really wished to give it. The real secret is in motivation. Donne could and did stop short in his brooding on new and old philosophy. For that was, for all his intellectual eclecticism, not the main theater of his interests. Like most Renaissance men he was far more interested in the moral realm, far more profoundly preoccupied with man's relation to himself and his God than with the structure of the physical or metaphysical universe. And this was no mere theo-

[1] John Donne, *Fifty Sermons* (London: J. Flesher for M. F., J. Marriot, and R. Royston, 1649), Sermon XLIV, p. 420.

retic or speculative interest. It was practical and specific and immediate in the highest degree, and here Donne showed no disposition to stop short or draw back. Here the whole force and energy of his personality drove him on. This was his realm. In other words, it was not the definition of the intellectual position that interested him; it was the realization of its implications, and the realization not by his hearers but by himself. Even when the passion of youthful ambition had been dampened, Donne had ever a clear sense of his own scope and his own nature's necessities, a kind of integrity that persisted through all his compromises. And yet he was not content to remain complacently within the defenses of his own limitations as so many middle-aged men are. He was always yearning for the perfection that would not so much complete his imperfection as transform it. After his first youthful defiances, he spent little time rationalizing or defending his shortcomings. Quite aware of his own changefulness and instability, he yet yearned for the enduring and the immovable and looked wistfully to eternity. And though he shared the activist suspicion of his time and place of the self-surrender of contemplation, he yearned to tear away the partitions of self-will and move into the larger vision of God. And though he held firmly to the cosmic distinctions which the Protestantism of his day had in its terror of blasphemy felt obliged to re-enforce between the Creator and the creature, Donne was always leaping over them. He wished not only to know about God but to know God.

There is no need, however, of laboring further the complexity and tension in the spiritual life of John Donne. That has from the time of the first of Mr. Eliot's essays received due attention. What has not received anything like its proper share of consideration is Donne's own attitude toward that complexity. That was very different from what some of the current descriptions would suggest. Donne was a very subtle and searching self-analyst, and everything he ever wrote exhibits to a striking degree the self-exploitation and the self-validation of the lyric poet. But there was nothing supine or complacent in his attitude toward himself, once he was past the period of his youthful love poems. For he saw human life as a struggle, and he plunged into that struggle with characteristic vigor and energy. "How *ruinous* a farme hath *man* taken, in taking *himselfe*!" so begins the twenty-second meditation of the famous *Devotions upon Emergent Occasions.*[2]

Donne accepted the orthodox positions of his time on justification by faith, and faith and works, but his basic orientation was fundamentally antipredestinarian. On the crucial issue of the relations between knowledge and action, Donne instinctively adhered to the common medieval position, holding that "wisdome is not so much in knowing, in understanding, as in electing, in choosing, in assenting. No man needs goe out of himselfe, nor beyond his owne legend, and the history of his owne actions for examples of that, that many times we know better, and choose ill wayes."[3]

In other respects, too, faith was not so simple a matter for Donne as it was for some of his contemporaries. There is a petition in *The Litanie* that suggests the all too common view of reason as a threat to faith:

> Let not my minde be blinder by more light
> Nor Faith, by Reason added, lose her sight.[4]

But more commonly Donne regarded faith not as something given once for all and static but as something growing and deepening, at least so far as the believer's relation to it is concerned. That more habitual way of thinking is represented by the following distinctly reassuring sentence from the sixty-first of the *LXXX Sermons*: "Waite thou therefore upon God, his way: present unto him an humble and a diligent understanding; conclude not too desperately against thy selfe, if thou have not yet attained to all degrees of faith, but admit that preparation, which God offers to thine understanding, by an assiduous and a sedulous hearing; for a narrower faith that proceeds out of a true understanding, shall carry thee farther then a faith that seems

[2] John Donne, *Devotions upon Emergent Occasions,* ed. John Sparrow, with a Biographical Note by Geoffrey Keynes (Cambridge, 1923), p. 133.

[3] *Fifty Sermons,* Sermon XXIX, p. 258.

[4] *The Poems of John Donne,* ed. H. J. C. Grierson (Oxford, 1912), I, 340.

larger, but is wrapped up in an implicite ignorance; no man beleeves profitably, that knows not why he beleeves."[5]

And yet though Donne firmly vindicated reason's dignity in this realm, he gave to faith a larger competence: "But as by the use of the Compass, men safely dispatch *Ulysses* dangerous ten years travell in so many dayes, and have found out a new world richer than the old; so doth Faith, as soon as our hearts are touched with it, direct and inform it in that great search of the discovery of Gods Essence, and the new *Hierusalem*, which Reason durst not attempt."[6]

And always in Donne, whether it be faith or reason that he is discussing, there is the appeal to experience. In view of what he has to say quite candidly of his own record, he is of course far from a disinterested witness on the theme of the mercy of God (as indeed, who is?), but the fact that he launches his protest against the severity of the extreme position on predestination not in a private meditation or a poem but in the public form of the sermon redresses the balance. Certainly, what he has to say on this subject in the sixty-ninth of the *LXXX Sermons* is revealing of his whole position on this most central dogma of his time: "And therefore hee that conceives a God, that hath made man of flesh and blood, and yet exacts that purity of an Angel in that flesh, A God that would provide himselfe no better glory, then to damme man, A God who lest hee should love man, and be reconciled to man, hath enwrapped him in an inevitable necessity of sinning, A God who hath received enough, and enough for the satisfaction of all men, and yet, (not in consideration of their future sinnes, but meerely because he hated them before they were sinners, or before they were anything) hath made it impossible, for the greatest part of men, to have any benefit of that large satisfaction. This is not such a Terriblenesse as arises out of his Works, (his Actions, or his Scripture) for God hath never said, never done any such thing, as should make us lodge such conceptions of God in ourselves, or lay such imputa-

[5] John Donne, *LXXX Sermons* (London: for R. Royston and R. Marriot, 1640), Sermon LXI, p. 611.

[6] John Donne, *Essayes in Divinity* (London: T. M. for R. Marriot, 1651), p. 38.

tions upon him."[7] Calvin, needless to say, would make short work of that passage, but the attitude and its psychological foundations are clear and firm and eminently characteristic of Donne.

Donne has a good deal to say of faith and works and justification in his sermons from first to last. Sometimes, as in the passage above, he is wrestling with his own and other men's temptations to despair, common temptations in that age as the religious biographies and devotional books of all schools eloquently attest. More rarely, he is trying to deflate self-righteousness, as in the twenty-fourth of the *LXXX Sermons*: "He hath opened heaven for us all; let no man shut out himself, by diffidence in Gods mercy, nor shut out any other man, by overvaluing his own purity, in respect of others."[8] But more commonly, he is rebuking complacency: "Deceive not yourselves then, with that new charme and flattery of the soule, That if once you can say to your selves you have faith, you need no more, or that you shall alwaies keep that alive,"[9] or on the positive side, "*Ecce scalam*, Behold the life of a christian is a Jacob's Ladder, and till we come up to God, still there are more steps to be made, more way to bee gone."[10]

For "God hath not accomplished his worke upon us, in one Act, though an Election; but he works in our Vocation, and he works in our Justification, and in our Sanctification he works still."[11] Another time Donne distinguishes four links in justification: efficient justification in God's purpose, material justification in Christ's death, instrumental justification in faith, and fourth and last, declaratory justification in good works.[12] But although Donne can always do a pretty piece of seventeenth-century definition and analysis in working out the theory of the thing, here as always, it is the personal realization that most engages his interest. For he was always of the mind expressed in the seventy-second of the *LXXX Sermons*: "The Scriptures

[7] *LXXX Sermons*, Sermon LXIX, p. 702.
[8] *Ibid.*, Sermon XXIV, p. 241.
[9] *Ibid.*, Sermon LXXX, p. 819.
[10] *Ibid.*, Sermon XLIII, p. 427.
[11] *Ibid.*, Sermon XXIV, p. 240.
[12] *Ibid.*, Sermon XXXVII, p. 368.

will be out of thy reach, and out of they use, if thou cast and scatter them upon Reason, upon Philosophy, upon Morality, to try how the Scriptures will fit all them, and beleeve them but so far as they agree with thy reason; But draw the Scripture to thine own heart, and to thine own actions, and thou shalt finde it made for that; all the promises of the old Testament made, and all accomplished in the new Testament, for the salvation of thy soule hereafter, and for their consolation in the present application of them."[13]

The necessity of continuous spiritual effort is one of the classic themes of the preacher in any dispensation and in any age. Too often the listener thinks of the giver of such counsel as commending something which he in his superior spiritual state finds not too difficult to the ordinary man who is bound to find it very difficult indeed; or, when the preacher is known to have been a noted sinner in his day, as urging something of which the difficulty is only a memory on the peaceful height from which he now speaks. The literature of conversion is full of such serene reminiscences of past effort, even when the struggle is remembered only to pay homage to the goodness of God who gave the victory. Indeed, there are not wanting examples, particularly in the seventeenth century, of converts who colored their wicked past with a good deal of gusto out of the best of motives. Even Bunyan's *Grace Abounding* is not always free of this disposition to blacken the background of the more radiant present.

But Donne's conversion is of a different kind. To begin with, it is a conversion in process, not a conversion consummated. True, certain sins are behind him, those more spectacular sins of the flesh that made him soon after he had taken orders write to a friend, "I have the honor of a letter from your Lordship: and a testimony that though better then any other you know my infirmity yet you are not scandalized with my chang of habitt."[14] But Donne never made the mistake so often made in his day and since, of limiting sin to the sins of the flesh. "The

---

[13] *Ibid.*, Sermon LXXII, p. 736.

[14] Evelyn M. Simpson, *A Study of the Prose Works of John Donne* (Oxford, 1924), p. 318.

nature, the definition of sin, is disorder."[15] And that disorder was quite as likely to be pride as lust, as in the third petition of *The Litanie*:

> O Holy Ghost, whose temple I
> Am, but of mudde walls, and condensed dust,
>     And being sacrilegiously
> Halfe wasted with youths fires, of pride and lust,
>     Must with new stormes be weatherbeat."[16]

But Donne never thought of his sins as something safely past, something to be surveyed with the disengaged condescension or complacency of a surer present. His definition of repentance in the sixty-fourth of the *LXXX Sermons* makes that quite clear: "Repentance of sins past is nothing but an Audit, a casting up of our accounts, a consideration, a survey, how it stands between God and our soule."[17]

That audit the penitent and converted Donne continued to make. It is of present sins that he speaks in the prayer that follows the fifteenth meditation in the *Devotions*. It is present and daily sins that might be professionally embarrassing to acknowledge that the famous Dean of Saint Paul's confesses in his sickbed audit: "It is a heavy and indelible sinne, that I brought into the world with me; It is a heavy and innumerable multitude of sins, which I have heaped up since; I have sinned *behind thy backe* (if that can be done) by wilful absteining from thy *Congregations*, and omitting thy *service*, and I have sinned *before thy face*, in my hypocrisies in Prayer, in my *ostentation*, and the mingling a respect of *my selfe* in preaching thy Word; I have sinned in my *fasting*, by repining, when a penurious fortune hath kept mee low; and I have sinned even in that fulnesse, when I have been at thy table, by a negligent examination, by a wilfull prevarication, in receiving that heavenly *food* and *Physicke*."[18]

Donne could and did free himself of various specific forms of lust and pride, but he never lost the sense of the continuing struggle. It is from the inside that he speaks always of the nature and psychology of sin. Sometimes it is in general terms, as in one

[15] *LXXX Sermons*, Sermon XXXVII, pp. 368–69.     [16] *Poems*, I, 338.
[17] *LXXX Sermons*, Sermon LXIV, p. 639.
[18] *Devotions upon Emergent Occasions*, p. 91.

of the prayers from the *Essayes in Divinity*, where he observes that "we have found by many lamentable experiences, that we never perform our promises to thee, never perfect our purposes in ourselves, but relapse again and again into those sins which again and again we have repented."[19] Sometimes there is a very practical, even pragmatic approach, as in the forty-sixth of the *Fifty Sermons*: "Our idlenes, our high diet, our wanton discours, our exposing our selves to occasion of sin, provoke and call in the Devill, when he seeks not us."[20] And sometimes the preacher lays his own (and every other sinner's) heart bare in a delicate but remorseless searching out of the hidden springs of the interior life, as in a long sentence of the seventh of the *XXVI Sermons*: "There is a sin before these; a speechless sin, a whispering sin, which no body hears, but our own conscience; which is, when a sinful thought or purpose is born in our hearts, first we rock it, by tossing, and tumbling it in our fancies, and imaginations, and by entertaining it with delight and consent, and with remembering, with how much pleasure we did the like sin before, and how much we should have, if we could bring this to pass; And as we rock it, so we swathe it, we cover it, with some pretenses, some excuses, some hopes of coveraling [*sic*] it; and this is that, which we call *Morosam delectationem*, a delight to stand in the air and prospect of a sin, and a loathness to let it go out of our sight."[21]

There is in all Donne has to say of sin and the sinner this shrewd appraisal of the complicated web of weakness and distraction and self-bewilderment and self-betrayal that weaves the net of temptation. In an age when men did not scruple to paint their past darkly, Donne is often curiously temperate and exact in his tracing of the lineaments of spiritual failure. Even in his profoundest spiritual wrestlings he never wholly loses sight of a truth put very casually in one of his verse letters:

> For though to us it seeme,' and be light and thinne,
> Yet in those faithfull scales, where God throwes in
> Mens workes, vanity weighs as much as sinne.[22]

[19] *Essayes in Divinity*, p. 221.   [20] *Fifty Sermons*, Sermon XLVI, p. 437.
[21] John Donne, *XXVI Sermons* (London: Thomas Newcomb, 1661), Sermon VII, p. 90.
[22] "To Mr. Rowland Woodward," *Poems*, I, 185.

Vanity as Donne used that often abused term involved not only the pettier manifestations of personal arrogance and egotism, but the shallowness of perspective that made them possible. In his Preface to the *Pseudo-Martyr*, the younger Donne has some very harsh things to say of himself in this regard, things which might well be said with even more justice of a good many other members of the intellectual set in his London. He is especially forthright on the subject of what he terms, "My natural impatience not to digge painefully in deepe, and stony, and sullen learnings: My Indulgence to my freedome and libertie, as in all other indifferent things, so in my studies also, not to betroth or enthral my selfe, to any one science, which should possesse or denominate me."[23] That is the intellectual counterpart of the lover who would not be bound, and it should not be forgotten that in the event just as marriage was to transform one, so the devotion to his professional studies was to transform the other. But it was a long time before that happened, and though we may rejoice in the literary result, the limitations of this habit of mind were to contribute greatly to the re-enforcement of that moral confusion which the older Donne was to describe as "a vertiginous giddiness, and irresolution," in which "[I] almost spent all my time in consulting how I should spend it."[24]

And yet here, as in other items of the continuing audit of his repentance, Donne was never content to take refuge in the memory of the past. Not even St. Augustine was more resolute in bringing the account up to date, and on the score of professional dignity Donne was perhaps a little more ruthless. For the fourteenth of the *Fifty Sermons* contains the preacher's own confession, not of the weakness now happily overcome and left behind but of the wavering in the present moment's unremitting battle: "I am not all here, I am here now preaching upon this text, and I am at home in my Library considering whether *S. Gregory*, or *S. Hierome*, have said best of this text, before. I am here speaking to you, and yet I consider by the way, in the same instant, what it is likely you will say to one another, when I have done."[25]

[23] John Donne, *Pseudo-Martyr* (London: W. Stansby for W. Burre, 1610), sig. B2.
[24] *Devotions upon Emergent Occasions*, p. 46.
[25] *Fifty Sermons*, Sermon XIV, p. 116.

Donne then proceeds to a more normal preacher's reminder of the congregation's imperfect attention, an admonition one suspects more effective than usual because of the preacher's admission of the common infirmity.

There is the same contemporaneity but with a certain almost savage self-contempt in one of the "Holy Sonnets":

> As humorous is my contritione
> As my prophane Love, and as soone forgott:
> As ridlingly distemper'd, cold and hott,
> As praying, as mute; as infinite, as none.
>
> . . . . . . . . . .
>
> So my devout fitts come and go away
> Like a fantastique Ague.[26]

That is a devastatingly thorough arraignment of himself, and yet even in its self-contempt there is a certain strength, the strength of a resolute if not always consistent spirit, able to face itself.

What was the secret of Donne's strength in so facing his own weakness? What was the remedy which he could invoke for his own and for others' sore need? So much has been said already of Donne's fear of hell and damnation that it would be easy to find in that terror the motive for his lifelong battle with himself, and in the lively invocation of that horror to his own and others' imaginations the necessary energy for the galvanizing and integration of the faltering and distracted will. But there is no need of underscoring again an element in John Donne's religious psychology that has received at least its due share of attention, except to remind the armchair moral strategist that there is nothing cowardly in fearing the fearful, nor morbid in weighing all too logical possibilities. Rather it is the positive side of Donne's thinking on the subject of sin and redemption that should be stressed.

In more recent times there has been a tendency to water down both the concepts of God's justice and sin's terror. Such an attenuation was quite as foreign to Donne's thinking as to the thinking of his age. In any case, it would not have been in Donne's nature to rationalize or to sentimentalize in matters of

[26] *Poems*, I, 331.

such vital moral moment. What Donne needed to meet such realities as sin and God's judgment was something even more real, more powerful, and that greater reality and power he found in the love and mercy of God as expressed in the Redemption.

One will not find in Donne's handling of the Redemption much of the human element that one so often finds in medieval treatments of that central Christian theme; that was not the fashion of his day or of the tradition which he had made his own. Indeed, one will often find in his work considerable traces of the arid and forbidding legalism of definition that had so largely taken its place. But what is to be found in Donne and what make his treatment of these themes so distinctive is the remarkable energy and immediacy and vitality of his conception of those too often then as now theological commonplaces. That power is to be seen in its fullness in some of the *Divine Poems*, for instance in the great invocation of "The Ascension:"

> O strong Ramme, which hast batter'd heaven for mee,
> Mild Lambe, which with thy blood, hast mark'd the path;
> Bright Torch, which shin'st, that I the way may see,
> Oh, with thy owne blood quench thy owne just wrath.[27]

And the glowing energy of that more general invocation takes on an even keener edge of personal urgency in the fourteenth of the "Holy Sonnets":

> Batter my heart, three person'd God; for, you
> As yet but knocke, breathe, shine, and seeke to mend;
> That I may rise, and stand, o'erthrowmee,' and bend
> Your force, to breake, blowe, burn and make me new.[28]

For with all his instability, and his wandering, and his distraction there was nothing halfhearted or timid about John Donne. As he said in one of the most revealing sentences of the *Devotions upon Emergent Occasions*, "I have not the *righteousnesse* of *Job*, but I have the desire of *Job*,: I *would speake to the Almightie* and I *would reason with God*."[29] And for all the vanity he deplored and the arrogance which such a sentence undeniably suggests, Donne did not make the mistake of thinking that he was unique in this. He might not put it as pithily as

[27] *Poems*, I, 321.    [28] *Ibid.*, I, 328.
[29] *Devotions upon Emergent Occasions*, p. 18.

St. Augustine, but the Augustinian sentiment is to be discerned in a sentence of the very beautiful sermon which he preached in commemoration of his friend, the Lady Danvers: "As God has provided us an *Endlessnesse*, in the world to come, so, to give us an Inchoation, a Representation of the next world, in this, God hath instituted an *endlessnesse* in this world too; God hath imprinted in every *naturall man*, and doth exalt in the *supernaturall*, and *regenerate* man, an endlesse, and undeterminable desire of more, then this life can minister unto him."[30]

It was not in the nature of Donne to leave that next world to the future. Already his imagination was busy with it, and spiritual hunger gave poignancy to the vision in the most completely contemplative of all his sermons, the twenty-third of the *LXXX Sermons*:

God made light first, and three dayes after, that light became a Sun, a more glorious Light: God gave me the light of Nature, when I quickned in my mothers wombe by receiving a reasonable soule; And God gave me the light of faith, when I quickned in my second mothers womb, the Church, by receiving my baptisme; but in my third day, when my mortality shall put on immortality, he shall give me the light of glory, by which I shall see himself. To this light of glory, the light of honour is but a glow-worm; and majesty it self but a twilight; The Cherubims and Seraphims are but Candles; and that Gospel it self, which the Apostle calls the glorious Gospel, but a Star of the least magnitude. And if I cannot tell, what to call this light, by which I shall see it, what shall I call that which I shall see by it, The Essence of God himself? and yet there is something else then this sight of God, intended in that which remaines, I shall not only *see God face to face*, but I shall *know* him, (which, as you have seen all the way, is above sight) and *know him, even as I* am knowne.[31]

That is perhaps the highest reach of Donne's speculation about the positive goal he sought across the barrier of his sins. But brilliant and awe-inspiring as that passage is, I do not think it comes as close to indicating the full measure of his achievement as a much more modest passage in the *Devotions*. To appreciate that passage, we must remember how hard it was for Donne

[30] John Donne, *A Sermon of Commemoration of the Lady Danvers* (London: I. H. for P. Stephens, and C. Meredith, 1627), pp. 145–47.
[31] *LXXX Sermons*, Sermon XXIII, p. 231.

even then, with what one might call his professional conversion accomplished and seasoned and matured in the grief and depriva- tion of his wife's death, to surrender himself completely in a full and patient waiting on the will of God. That difficulty was in all probability the chief remaining obstacle to the fullness of con- templation which he so passionately yearned for. It is certainly one of the main themes, if not the main theme of the anguished prayers and aspirations of the *Devotions upon Emergent Occa- sions,* which reach their climax in the prayer following the nine- teenth meditation and expostulation:

O Eternal and most gracious *God,* who though thou passedst over infinite millions of generations, before thou camest to a *Creation* of this *world,* yet when thou beganst, didst never intermit that *worke,* but con- tinuedst *day* to *day,* till thou hadst perfected all the *worke,* and deposed it in the hands and rest of a *Sabbath,* though thou have been pleased to *glorifie* thy selfe in a long exercise of my *patience,* with an *expectation* of thy *declaration* of thy selfe in this my *sicknesse,* yet since thou hast now of thy goodnesse afforded that, which affords us some hope, if that be still the *way* of thy *glory,* proceed in *that way* and perfect *that worke,* and establish me in a *Sabbath,* and *rest* in *thee,* by this thy *seale* of *bodily restitution.* Thy *Priests* came up to thee, by *steps* in the *Temple*; Thy *Angels* came *downe* to *Iaacob,* by *steps* upon the *ladder*; we find no *staire* by which *thou thyselfe* camest to *Adam* in *Paradise,* nor to *Sodome* in thine *anger*; for *thou,* and *thou onely* art able to doe all at once. But, *O Lord,* I am not *wearie* of thy *pace,* nor *wearie* of mine owne *patience.* I provoke thee not with a *praier,* not with a *wish,* not with a *hope,* to more haste than consists with thy *purpose,* nor looke that any other thing should have entered into thy *purpose,* but thy *glory.* To *heare* thy steps coming *towards* me is the same comfort, as to see thy face present with mee; whether thou doe the worke of a *thousand yeeres* in a *day,* or extend the *worke of a day* to a *thousand yeeres,* as long as *thou workest,* it is *light* and *comfort.* Heaven it selfe is but an *extention* of the same *joy*; and an *extention* of this *mercie,* to proceed at thy *leisure,* in the way of *restitution,* is a *manifestation* of *heaven* to me here upon *earth.*[32]

When he wrote that passage, Donne might very well have said in the words of his most famous pun, "Thou haste done."[33] Certainly, he had won within the limits of this life his hardest battle with himself.

[32] *Devotions upon Emergent Occasions,* pp. 118–19.
[33] "Hymne to God the Father," *Poems,* I, 369.

# THE TOUCH OF COLD PHILOSOPHY

## Basil Willey

In order to get a bird's-eye view of any century it is quite useful to imagine it as a stretch of country, or a landscape, which we are looking at from a great height, let us say from an aeroplane. If we view the seventeenth century in this way we shall be struck immediately by the great contrast between the scenery and even the climate of its earlier and that of its later years. At first we get mountain-ranges, torrents, and all the picturesque interplay of alternating storm and brightness; then, farther on, the land slopes down to a richly cultivated plain, broken for a while by outlying heights and spurs, but finally becoming level country, watered by broad rivers, adorned with parks and mansions, and lit up by steady sunshine. The mountains connect backwards with the central mediaeval Alps, and the plain leads forwards with little break into our own times. To drop the metaphor before it begins to be misleading, we may say that the seventeenth century was an age of transition, and although every century can be so described, the seventeenth deserves this label better than most, because it lies between the Middle Ages and the modern world. It witnessed one of the greatest changes which have ever taken place in men's ways of thinking about the world they live in.

I happen to be interested in literature, amongst other things, and when I turn to this century I cannot help noticing that it begins with Shakespeare and Donne, leads on to Milton, and ends with Dryden and Swift: that is to say, it begins with a literature full of passion, paradox, imagination, curiosity, and complexity, and ends with one distinguished rather by clarity, precision, good sense, and definiteness of statement. The end of the century is the beginning of what has been called the Age of Prose and Reason, and we may say that by then the qualities necessary for good prose had got the upper hand over those which produce the greatest kinds of poetry. But that is not all: we find the same sort of thing going on elsewhere. Take architecture, for example: the Elizabethan or Jacobean style is quaint and fanciful, sometimes rugged in outline, and richly ornamented with carving and decoration in which Gothic and classical ingredients are often mixed up together. By the end of the century this has given place to the style of Christopher Wren and the so-called Queen Anne architects, which is plain, well proportioned, severe, and purely classical without Gothic trimmings. And here there is an important point to notice: it is true that the seventeenth century begins with a blend of mediaeval and modern elements, and ends with the triumph of the modern; but in those days to be "modern" often meant to be "classical," that is, to imitate the Greeks and Romans. We call the age of Dryden, Pope, and Addison the "Augustan" age, and the men of that time really felt that they were living in an epoch like that of the Emperor Augustus—an age of enlightenment, learning, and true civilisation—and congratulated themselves on having escaped from the errors and superstitions of the dark and monkish Middle Ages. To write and build and think like the ancients meant that you were reasonable beings, cultivated and urbane—that you had abandoned the shadow of the cloister for the cheerful light of the market-place or the coffee-house. If you were a scientist (or "natural philosopher") you had to begin, it is true, by rejecting many ancient theories, particularly those of Aristotle, but you knew all the while that by thinking independently and taking nothing on trust you were following the ancients in spirit though not in letter.

Or let us glance briefly at two other spheres of interest: politics and religion. The century begins with Cavalier and Roundhead and ends with Tory and Whig—that is to say, it begins with a division arousing the deepest passions and prejudices, not to be settled without bloodshed, and ends with the mere opposition of two political parties, differing in principle, of course, but socially at one, and more ready to alternate peaceably with each other. The Hanoverians succeed the Stuarts, and what more need be said? The divine rights of kings is little more heard of, and the scene is set for prosaic but peaceful development. Similarly in religion, the period opens with the long and bitter struggle between Puritan and Anglican, continuing through Civil War, and accompanied by fanaticism, persecution, and exile, and by the multiplication of hostile sects; it ends with the Toleration Act, and with the comparatively mild dispute between the Deists and their opponents as to whether Nature was not after all a clearer evidence of God than Scripture, and the conscience a safer guide than the creeds. In short, wherever we turn we find the same tale repeated in varying forms: the ghosts of history are being laid; darkness and tempest are yielding to the light of common day. Major issues have been settled or shelved, and men begin to think more about how to live together in concord and prosperity.

Merely to glance at this historical landscape is enough to make one seek some explanation of these changes. If the developments had conflicted with each other we might have put them down to a number of different causes, but since they all seem to be setting in one direction it is natural to suppose that they were all due to one common underlying cause. There are various ways of accounting for historical changes: some people believe, for instance, that economic causes are at the bottom of everything, and that the way men earn their living, and the way in which wealth is produced and distributed, determine how men think and write and worship. Others believe that ideas, rather than material conditions, are what control history, and that the important question to ask about any period is what men then believed to be true, what their philosophy and religion were like. There is something to be said on both sides, but we are concerned with a simpler question. We know that the greatest intellectual change in modern history was completed during the seventeenth century: was that change of such a kind as to explain all those parallel movements we have mentioned? Would it have helped that drift towards prose and reason, towards classicism, enlightenment, and toleration? The great intellectual change was that known as the Scientific Revolution, and I think the answer to these questions is, Yes. It is not my present purpose to describe that Revolution, or to discuss any of the great discoveries which produced it. My intention is only to consider some of the effects it had upon men's thoughts, imaginations, and feelings, and consequently upon their ways of expressing themselves. The discoveries—I am thinking mainly of the Copernican astronomy and the laws of motion as explored by Galileo and fully formulated by Newton—shocked men into realizing that things were not as they had always seemed, and that the world they were living in was really quite different from what they had been taught to suppose. When the crystal spheres of the old world-picture were shattered, and the earth was shown to be one of many planets rolling through space, it was not everyone who greeted this revelation with enthusiasm as Giordano Bruno did. Many felt lost and confused, because the old picture had not only seemed obviously true to common sense, but was confirmed by Scripture and by Aristotle, and hallowed by the age-long approval of the Church. What Matthew Arnold said about the situation in the nineteenth century applies also to the seventeenth: religion had attached its emotion to certain supposed facts, and now the facts were failing it. This note of loss can be heard in Donne's well-known lines:

> And new philosophy calls all in doubt;
> The element of fire is quite put out;
> The sun is lost, and th'earth, and no man's wit
> Can well direct him where to look for it.

Not only "the element of fire," but the very distinction between heaven and earth had vanished—the distinction, I mean, between the perfect and incorruptible celestial bodies from the moon upwards, and the imperfect and corruptible terrestrial bodies below it. New stars had appeared, which showed that the heavens could change, and the telescope revealed irregularities in the moon's surface—that is, the moon was not a perfect sphere, as a celestial body should be. So Sir Thomas Browne could write:

> While we look for incorruption in the heavens, we find they are but like the earth;—durable in their main bodies, alterable in their parts; whereof, besides comets and new stars, perspectives begin to tell tales,

and the spots that wander about the sun, with Phaeton's favour, would make clear conviction.

Naturally it took a long time for these new ideas to sink in, and Milton still treats the old and the new astronomies as equally acceptable alternatives. The Copernican scheme, however, was generally accepted by the second half of the century. By that time the laws governing the motion of bodies on earth had also been discovered, and finally it was revealed by Newton that the law whereby an apple falls to the ground is the very same as that which keeps the planets in their courses. The realization of this vast unifying idea meant a complete re-focussing of men's ideas about God, Nature, and Man, and the relationships between them. The whole cosmic movement, in the heavens and on earth, must now be ascribed, no longer to a divine pressure acting through the *primum mobile*, and to angelic intelligences controlling the spheres, but to a gravitational pull which could be mathematically calculated. The universe turned out to be a Great Machine, made up of material parts which all moved through space and time according to the strictest rules of mechanical causation. That is to say, since every effect in nature had a physical cause, no room or need was left for supernatural agencies, whether divine or diabolical; every phenomenon was explicable in terms of matter and motion, and could be mathematically accounted for or predicted. As Sir James Jeans has said: "Only after much study did the great principle of causation emerge. In time it was found to dominate the whole of inanimate nature . . . The final establishment of this law . . . was the triumph of the seventeenth century, the great century of Galileo and Newton." It is true that mathematical physics had not yet conquered every field: even chemistry was not yet reduced to exactitude, and still less biology and psychology. But Newton said, "Would that the rest of the phenomena of nature could be deduced by a like kind of reasoning from mechanical principles" —and he believed that they could and would.

I referred just now to some of the immediate effects of the "New Philosophy"; let me conclude by hinting at a few of its ultimate effects. First, it produced a distrust of all tradition, a determination to accept nothing as true merely on authority, but only after experiment and verification. You find Bacon rejecting the philosophy of the mediaeval Schoolmen, Browne writing a long exposure of popular errors and superstitions (such as the belief that a toad had a jewel in its head, or that an elephant had no joints in its legs), Descartes resolving to doubt everything —even his own senses—until he can come upon something clear and certain, which he finally finds in the fact of his own existence as a thinking being. Thus the chief intellectual task of the seventeenth century became the winnowing of truth from error, fact from fiction or fable. Gradually a sense of confidence, and even exhilaration, set in; the universe seemed no longer mysterious or frightening; everything in it was explicable and comprehensible. Comets and eclipses were no longer dreaded as portents of disaster; witchcraft was dismissed as an old wives' tale. This new feeling of security is expressed in Pope's epitaph on Newton:

> Nature and Nature's laws lay hid in night;
> God said, *Let Newton be!* and all was light!

How did all this affect men's religious beliefs? The effect was very different from that of Darwinism on nineteenth-century religion. In the seventeenth century it was felt that science had produced a conclusive demonstration of God, by showing the evidence of His wisdom and power in the Creation. True, God came to be thought of rather as an abstract First Cause than as the personal, ever-present God of religion; the Great Machine implied the Great Mechanic, but after making the machine and setting it in motion God had, as it were, retired from active superintendence, and left it to run by its own laws without interference. But at a time when inherited religious sentiment was still very powerful, the idea that you could look up through Nature to Nature's God seemed to offer an escape from one of the worst legacies of the past—religious controversy and sectarian intolerance. Religion had been endangered by inner conflict; what could one believe, when the Churches were all at daggers drawn? Besides, the secular and rational temper brought in by the new science soon began to undermine the traditional foundations of belief. If nothing had ever happened which could not be explained by natural, physical causes, what of the supernatural and miraculous events recorded in the Bible? This was a disturbing thought, and even in the seventeenth century there were a few who began to doubt the literal truth of some of the Biblical narratives. But it was reserved for the eighteenth century to make an open attack upon the miraculous elements in Christianity, and to compare the Old Testament Jehovah disparagingly with the "Supreme Being" or "First Cause" of philosophy. For the time it was possible to feel that science was pious, because it was simply engaged in studying God's own handiwork, and because whatever it disclosed seemed a further proof of His almighty skill as designer of the universe. Science also gave direct access to God, whereas Church and creed involved you in endless uncertainties and difficulties.

However, some problems and doubts arose to disturb the prevailing optimism. If the universe was a material mechanism, how could Man be fitted into it—Man, who had always been supposed to have a free will and an immortal soul? Could it be that these were illusions after all? Not many faced up to this, though Hobbes did say that the soul was only a function of the body, and denied the freedom of the will. What was more immediately serious, especially for poetry and religion, was the new tendency to discount all the products of the imagination, and all spiritual insight, as false or fictitious. Everything that was real could be described by mathematical physics as matter in motion, and whatever could not be so described was either unreal or else had not yet been truly explained. Poets and priests had deceived us long enough with vain imaginings; it was now time for the scientists and philosophers to take over, and speak to us, as Sprat says the Royal Society required its members to do, in a "naked, natural" style, bringing all things as close as possible to the "mathematical plainness." Poets might rave, and priests might try to mystify us, but sensible men would ignore them, preferring good sense, and sober, prosaic demonstration. It was said at the time that philosophy (which then included what we call science) had cut the throat of poetry. This does not mean that no more good poetry could then be produced: after all, Dryden and Pope were both excellent poets. But, when all has been said, they do lack visionary power: their merits are those of their age

—sense, wit, brilliance, incisiveness, and point. It is worth noticing that when the Romantic Movement began a hundred years later, several of the leading poets attacked science for having killed the universe and turned man into a reasoning machine. But no such thoughts worried the men of the Augustan age; their prevailing feeling was satisfaction at living in a world that was rational through and through, a world that had been explained favourably, explained piously, and explained by an Englishman. The modern belief in progress takes its rise at this time; formerly it had been thought that perfection lay in antiquity, and that subsequent history was one long decline. But now that Bacon, Boyle, Newton, and Locke had arisen, who could deny that the ancients had been far surpassed? Man could now hope to control his environment as never before, and who could say what triumphs might not lie ahead? Even if we feel that the victory of science was then won at the expense of some of man's finer faculties, we can freely admit that it brought with it many good gifts as well—tolerance, reasonableness, release from fear and superstition—and we can pardon, and even envy, that age for its temporary self-satisfaction.

# INDEX

(Only names and subjects discussed at some length are listed)